Siting Culture

The notion of culture has been subject to critical debate in anthropology during the past decade. This is related to a shift in emphasis from the bounded local culture to transnational cultural flows. At the same time that cultural mobility and flux are being emphasized by anthropologists, the very people that they study are recasting culture as a place of belonging as they construct local identities within global fields of relations.

So far, much of the critical analysis of the role of place in culture has been carried out at a more general level of theoretical debate. *Siting Culture* argues that it is only through rich ethnographic studies that anthropologists may explore the significance of place in the global space of relations which mold the everyday lives of people throughout the world. It does this by examining the concept of culture through a number of case studies from Europe, Africa, Oceania, Latin America, and the Caribbean in order to probe the methodological and theoretical implications of the divergent scholarly and popular concepts of culture.

Siting Culture focuses on new sites of cultural construction which embody the interrelationship between local, supposedly "permanent" frameworks of life, and global, supposedly "transitory" flows of relations. This involves the foregrounding of the methodological and political implications of identifying people with particular places, and the critical analysis of the significance of topical metaphors in anthropological research.

Karen Fog Olwig is Senior Lecturer and **Kirsten Hastrup** is Professor of Anthropology, both at the University of Copenhagen.

Siting Culture

The shifting anthropological object

Edited by Karen Fog Olwig and
Kirsten Hastrup

London and New York

First published 1997
by Routledge
11 New Fetter Lane, London EC4P 4EE

Simultaneously published in the USA and Canada
by Routledge
29 West 35th Street, New York, NY 10001

Typeset in Times by Keystroke, Jacaranda Lodge, Wolverhampton
Printed and bound in Great Britain by Redwood Books, Trowbridge, Wiltshire

British Library Cataloguing in Publication Data
A catalogue record for this book is available from the British Library

Library of Congress Cataloging in Publication Data
A catalogue record for this book has been requested

ISBN 0-415-15001-9 (hbk)
ISBN 0-415-15002-7 (pbk)

Contents

Contributors

Thomas Hylland Eriksen, University of Oslo
James Ferguson, University of California, Irvine
Jonathan Friedman, University of Lund
Ulla Hasager, University of Hawaii
Kirsten Hastrup, University of Copenhagen
Liisa H. Malkki, University of California, Irvine
Judith Okely, University of Hull
Karen Fog Olwig, University of Copenhagen
Karsten Pærregaard, Center for Development Research, Copenhagen
Ann-Belinda Steen Preis, University of Copenhagen
Marc Schade-Poulsen, Center for Development Research, Copenhagen
Jonathan Schwartz, University of Copenhagen
Birgitte Refslund Sørensen, United Nations Research Institute for Social Development, Geneva
Ninna Nyberg Sørensen, Center for Development Research, Copenhagen

Introduction

Kirsten Hastrup and Karen Fog Olwig

The idea that cultures and, consequently, people are naturally rooted in particular places has long been questioned in theoretical anthropology. Yet the methodological and analytical implications of this insight are still being worked out. This book seeks to contribute to this critical process by examining the role of place in the conceptualization and practice of culture. The idea that cultures can be conceptualized as separate and unique entities corresponding to particular localities has not just been a means of bringing order into an otherwise disorderly world, it has also been a means of erecting frameworks within which anthropologists might perceive and understand cultural difference. The erection of cultural distinctions and borders is thus closely related to the anthropological practice of understanding culture from an internal, local point of view, followed by a more external, generalized analysis. This approach to culture has been basic at all levels of anthropological thinking. The anthropologist conducting field work endeavours to understand the way in which local people themselves experience and interpret their lives by participating in and thus becoming part of local life. At the same time, anthropologists also remove themselves, at least intellectually, from the local context of life in order to subject the data gathered in this way to more external, social scientific considerations. The field data that are obtained through participant observation are similarly analyzed with a view to both the inner workings of a culture, and a more general, transcendent, interpretation within the larger theoretical context of the discipline. The ethnographer will often highlight conclusions concerning certain cultural phenomena among the people under study through cross-cultural comparison, which will allow for even more general conclusions to be drawn than is possible on the basis of the study of a single culture.

If anthropologists (and their social science) and the people under study (and their cultural knowledge) do not belong to two distinct socio-cultural wholes, but are part of one global ecumene of interconnections as Hannerz (1992) has termed it, how is it possible for anthropologists to maintain the external–internal distinction? Is it largely the creation of European ideology and the need to make sense of, and to control, an otherwise messy world of interrelations? If so, the whole anthropological project is called into question. Instead of cultures located in a particular landscape we face a transnational culture of sounds and images, such as the raï music discussed here by Marc Schade-Poulsen, or the videos made by Tamils across the distance of their flight examined by Ann-Belinda Steen Preis.

A companion concept to that of culture is that of the culture area. Culture areas are aggregates of cultures which are believed to display some similarity despite their individual unique character, and they usually coincide with geographical regions. Much cross-cultural comparison has taken place within culture areas where it is believed to be possible to do "controlled comparisons" between somewhat similar cultures (Eggan 1954). Through such comparative studies a general consensus seems to have been reached concerning certain cultural themes which are thought to be of particular salience in specific culture areas, and this in turn has influenced further research in the area. India, as Appadurai (1988) has argued, has thus come to signify hierarchical societies. An inadvertent effect of this is that forms of social organization or thinking which are not hierarchical have tended to be ignored, or been regarded as uncharacteristic of the area. Again it seems as if the desire to establish clear-cut categories and to create an orderly field of study has led anthropologists to downplay cultural diversity or to brand it as abnormal. Furthermore, as was the case in the study of local cultures, the culture-area approach has had difficulty in dealing with relations that extend beyond the defined area. At this level, too, the localizing strategy of anthropology, and the accompanying regionalization of ethnographic accounts, to which Richard Fardon (1990) drew our attention, crumples under the weight of manifest global relationships.

Many anthropologists would probably agree with much of this criticism. Yet most would probably also be quick to point out that critics have offered few alternatives to the traditional anthropological methods which have, after all, succeeded in making anthropology a recognized and constructive field of study. The notion of separate and distinct cultures has enabled the carving of the world into smaller units, which could be studied in the "laboratories" of the anthropological field sites. It has offered the analytical perspective of cultural holism which has helped anthropologists to avoid imposing Western frameworks of analysis upon studies of other ways of life. And it has allowed for comparative analysis of different cultures and hence the establishment of a field devoted to human culture and society in general.

We suggest that a fruitful response to the critique of traditional approaches to culture in anthropology is a re-examining of key concepts in anthropology through careful ethnographic case studies. By maintaining an awareness of the problems inherent in anthropological theory and method, it may be possible to see them as productive foci for further ethnographic research. In this vein, the following chapters examine, explicitly or implicitly, the cultural importance of place and space in various ethnographic contexts. Through analyses of concrete cases, they point toward renewed understanding of the relation between place and culture.

Despite the fact that we are living in an era of apparent globalization, the concept of cultural wholes is still very much with us. It seems to be on the agenda, all over the world, as some kind of totalizing reference point (Strathern 1993). At the same moment that the anthropological profession experiences a loss of faith in this concept of culture, it has become embraced by a wide range of culture builders world wide. The paradoxical result is that anthropological works are increasingly being consulted by people desiring to construct cultural identities of a totalizing sort which the anthropologist finds deeply problematic. Even though anthropologists may fear that the desired cultural identity derives from an earlier anthropological discourse that has become naturalized in various local contexts, this identity cannot be discarded as irrelevant. It has become irrevocably part of ethnography. We suggest, therefore, that rather than discarding the notion of culture, it should be reinvented, as it were, through an exploration of the "place" of culture in both the experiential and discursive spaces that people inhabit or invent. Thus, instead of taking local cultural entities for granted, we want to explore the siting of culture as a dynamic process of self-understanding among the people we study (Olwig, Chapter 1 of this volume). We will do this through a number of empirical case studies which allow for an examination of the methodological and theoretical implications of such a repositioning of the anthropological object.

SPACE AND PLACE

Until recently, space or place operated as fixed coordinates of the ethnographic world map. Anthropologists went places, and their implicit claim to fame was related to the fact that these places were far away, exotic, and potentially perilous. In "the heart of darkness" everything was possible, including the return to the enlightened West. As discussed here by James Ferguson, the idea of the field as a place to which one went and from which one came back, cemented the idea of separate worlds; worlds, moreover, that were firmly placed on the world map. People, including anthropologists, moved in space. The idea of a solid spatial context is reflected also in the anthropological propensity towards spatial metaphors in the "theoretical landscape" (Salmond 1982).

Of late we have realized that space may in fact be contested. As Michel de Certeau has it: "space is a practiced place" (de Certeau 1986: 117). Practices overlap, intersect and blur the boundaries of place to the extent that we may speak of a continuous global place in the analysis of certain practices. Just as histories are intertwined so territories are overlapping, if not always on equal terms (cf. Said 1993). This represents an acceptance of the theoretical importance of the manifest and terrible conflicts over so-called national boundaries that we are witnessing today. It is a painful acknowledgement of the fact that realities are defined in practice, rather than by pre-established social structures or the fixed coordinates of a semantic space. This recognition that cultural places are constructed within an equally constructed spatial matrix does not abnegate their importance, quite the opposite. The role of space and place in social life has become a topic of renewed interest within anthropology.

The place-focused concept of culture has been seen by several anthropologists to be the consequence of a conceptual bias closely related to the strong influence of nationalist thinking in the Western countries where anthropology developed as a scholarly discipline. An aspect of the disciplining of the field's practitioners was an implicit internalization of the idea of culture, reflecting the romanticist idea of the nation, as a set of beliefs and customs shared by a people living in a well-defined area and speaking a particular language. Thus, in the anthropological rethinking of received wisdom, "culture" has been viewed as an outgrowth of nationalist ideas of nations as naturally rooted in the native soil of their people (Handler 1985; Kahn 1989; Malkki 1992; Gupta and Ferguson 1992). The fact that this remains not solely an analytical construct but also very much a popular image is vividly testified to by the Norwegian case discussed by Thomas Hylland Eriksen. Nationalism has led to a notion of culture as something which is possessed by all of humankind, but in separate, bounded and unique cultural wholes which correspond to distinct and localized social groups. This has given rise to the idea that each of these socio-cultural wholes should be described and analyzed on their own terms in order to document the cultural variety and particularities of humankind. One of the important projects within anthropology has therefore been that of mapping out the entire world in separate cultures which, with few exceptions, could be located in their own contiguous places, as discussed by Jonathan Schwartz for Macedonia. If it is true that the nation state is unraveling, this should not only fuel a critique of the nation, but also of the idea that cultures can be neatly localized. The classic monograph documenting unique and self-contained cultures must then give way to a new genre, taking its point of departure in those nodal points in the networks of interrelations where there is a mutual construction of identities through cultural encounters.

The basic research tool in the classical study of cultures has been the time-honoured method of field work. This has also been one of the main targets of criticism in the debate on the place-focused notion of culture within anthropology (Rosaldo 1988; Clifford 1992; Appadurai 1988). Prolonged field work among a group of people living in a particular area has allowed anthropologists to develop close relations with the people under study and a detailed knowledge about ways of life which in many ways *are* radically different from those of the anthropologist. Indeed, few would question the value of the many insightful ethnographic monographs which today constitute a major part of the anthropological literature. These monographs provide rich and unparalleled evidence of the variety of epistemologies and ways of communicating them within the shared range of humanity. It is also beyond question, however, that these works, and the field work upon which they are based, illustrate some of the limitations inherent in the approach to the study of culture that has been dominant until now.

One of these limitations is the tendency of anthropologists to study those "natives" who stay put in the particular area, where the anthropologists are doing their field work. Karsten Pærregaard began his field work in the Peruvian Andes in a remote rural region, supposedly authentic, and discarding the migrants as noise. Only later did he realize that they were part and parcel of local culture, and – indeed – vice versa. The general problem is that people who are mobile, and therefore not immediately present in the research site while the ethnographer is paying his or her fleeting visit, have often been ignored, even though they are in fact often of great importance to the more settled people. As abundantly testified to by Ninna Nyberg Sørensen's study of Dominicans "at home" and in New York, the fact of travel and migrancy may be a strong parameter in the self-definition of people in either place.

The difficulty of seeing movement as an aspect of social life in general is related to the fact that mobility, in so far as it involved settled people, has been regarded as a special and temporary phenomenon which has been examined under headings such as migration, refugee studies, and tourism. As Schwartz notes, migration has been viewed in terms of unilineal, and finite, movements between a point of origin and a point of destination. As his study of Macedonian migrants shows, however, migration often involves a long chain of movements which affect many people in different places over an extended period of time. Refugees, who remain in a state of exile for an extended period of time, have been more difficult to handle within this conceptual framework. They have often, as Liisa Malkki notes (1992, and Chapter 10 of this volume), been seen to represent an abnormal, or even pathological condition.

In anthropology, the image of people as being firmly settled in a home environment has been matched by an equally strong vision of displacement, uprooting, chaos and catastrophe as but temporary instances of unrest and disorder. Gypsies and nomads were the exceptions who proved this rule – nomads, nevertheless, moved within well-defined patterns within fixed territories. The "natural" state of the world was conceived of in terms of stability and social coherence; flight and suffering were out of order (Davis 1992; Hastrup 1993). As the end of our millennium comes closer we are forced to take cognizance of the fact that disorder and suffering are becoming the order of the day in many parts of the world. Malkki's rendition of recent refugee experience in Burundi and Rwanda poses a terrifying example of the matter-of-fact way in which massacres are carried out and repeated locally. The next-to-inevitability of such atrocities is thereafter discursively cemented in the reportage of the "international community" which emphasizes the general features of pain and flight rather than the actual historicity of the refugee camp and the concrete collective experience of the refugees. It is about time that anthropology recognized its duty to deal with de-stabilization and suffering – always an integral part of human experience, if largely ignored because it has an unsettling effect upon theory which is predicated upon a more settled way of life.

The anthropological place-fixation can also be seen to be related to a tendency in the West to view non-Western people as somehow closer to nature. Thus Appadurai (1988: 37) has argued that anthropologists have incarcerated natives ecologically and intellectually in places, outside the Western metropolises, where their culture is regarded as closely adapted to their particular environment. Implicitly, this casting of the relationship between us and them in terms of the opposition between culture and nature testifies to a dominant view of the relationship as inherently asymmetrical, not unlike the relationship between empire and culture, as investigated by Said (1993). This suggests that once these categories have been de-essentialized and reconstructed as categories of thought, we may demask this asymmetry as part of the exoticizing nature of any discourse on the constructed other.

Due to the tradition of carrying out field work in "distinct cultures" which can be studied and analyzed in their own right, earlier anthropologists paid little attention to the fact that even the seemingly most remote and exotic people do not exist in isolation from the rest of the world. The very presence of the anthropologist is evidence to the contrary. As James Clifford (1992: 9) has noted, there has been remarkably little discussion of the missionary airplane which brought the anthropologist to the field, and which has long brought the natives in close contact with the Western world. Today, this field of interrelationships could be a main point of departure in anthropological research; the field is, by definition, a contact zone (cf. Pratt 1992). Gupta and Ferguson (1992) have argued that the world should be viewed in terms of a global space, which is characterized by hierarchical relations and power constellations extending from particular metropoles. In this global space of relations, clearly defined places do not exist in and of themselves. Rather they are constructed culturally as communities of relations constitute and demarcate themselves within hierarchically organized space of unequal relationships. The cultural construction of distinct places in a world of interconnectedness is therefore, for them, an important subject of anthropological study. Appadurai (1991) goes even further and suggests that the world consists of deterritorialized ethnoscapes whose culturally constructed places of identification often will not coincide with their actual physical locations. A more relevant framework of study, for him, is the imagined worlds, constructed on the basis of the creative resources, which are generated by the experience of deterritorialization itself.

With the loss of place as a dominant metaphor for culture goes a methodological redirection from order to non-order, which not only allows us to capture mobility in the landscape, but also the processes of deterritorialization and reterritorialization which this mobility involves. It also, and more significantly, enables us to understand the fact that "people's actions alter the conditions of their existence, often in ways they never intend or foresee" (Rosaldo 1989: 102–3). Preis's analysis of Tamil refugees in Denmark who must cope with a lack of ritual experts in times of crises, thus shows how their very coping alters the conditions of their existence. People act relative to their intentions, intentions that are always culturally shaped and historically positioned. Yet, through their acts people make history themselves; change rather than structure is the condition of culture as testified by most contemporary ethnographies. Only as icon does local culture remain untouched by history, as in the case of Constable Country, analyzed by Judith Okely. On canvas, the English landscape remains untouched by trusts, tourists and tea-cups.

ETHNOGRAPHIC RESEARCH

Despite the fact that traditional ethnographic field research has been the subject of criticism, we believe that it is only through rich ethnographic studies that space and place – and what we make of them in human relations – can be examined. This explains the emphasis on empirical analysis in the chapters presented below. The chapters can be seen to represent several different methodological approaches to the study of such cultural constructions.

A field of relations

While the field work upon which these articles are based has – of course – taken place in particular localities, it has not necessarily been confined to studying those relations that are circumscribed by these localities. If space is practiced place, the relevant space will often cut across boundaries; in practice East and West, North and South may be one. Thus, in what follows, the field work sites have been defined by the human relations that were the subject of study, be they discussed in terms of migrancy, refuge, diffusion or imperialism.

Generally, we may define the field, not primarily in terms of a locality, but as the field of relations which are of significance to the people involved in the study (cf. Barth 1992). This makes it possible to examine both the nature of the non-local relations and the way in which they molded and in turn were molded by the different localities where they touched ground. The following studies reflect, to a great extent, a processual approach to field work, where new locations are incorporated into the research, as the researchers become aware of their relevance to the topic under study. Pærregaard, as noted, decided to extend his study of an Andean village to include migrants in Lima and other urban areas; Schwartz's research on Macedonians took place in Canada, Sweden and Denmark as well as Macedonia; Olwig's research on a West Indian community brought her to North America and Great Britain as well as the Caribbean.

Focusing on relations, rather than on locations, will not necessarily mean, however, that our studies must encompass an ever-widening circle of ties. Out of the seemingly infinite range of relations, which span the globe today, only a few are, in fact, activated and imbued with meaning by particular people. Furthermore, many relations, which are geographically and socially close at hand, are studiously ignored. This is brought out in the concept of *endosociality* discussed by Jonathan Friedman in his analysis of a Hawaiian fishing village.

A process through time

The ethnographic case studies have not just been processual in terms of the locations involved, but also with regard to the temporal dimension covered. If cultural constructions, rather than cultural entities, are our object of study, studying the historical context within which they have been generated will help us understand their significance today. Nyberg Sørensen's and Olwig's studies thus came to involve extensive historical research, as it became apparent that contemporary perceptions of place are very much a reflection of historical developments in the Caribbean area. Likewise, Hasager's study of homesteading in Hawaii entailed careful study of the historical development of ownership and usage of land in Hawaii.

Uneven encounters

As these case studies have extended the boundaries of their field sites to relevant geographically and historically removed contexts of life, it has become apparent how different places have become demarcated in space and defined through time. In most cases this has occurred in close relation to, in several cases even in opposition to, centers of power, particularly those of the Western metropoles. As Ferguson notes, that which we in ethnographic research have regarded as "local culture" is often constituted out of "uneven encounters." Such local culture may be creole national culture developed by Dominicans in the face of colonial and neocolonial forces (Nyberg Sørensen); it may be the fierce maintenance of village culture in a Hawaii long dominated by economic interests from the outside (Friedman), or the establishment of strong local identities among both villagers and settlers in a governmental resettlement scheme in Sri Lanka (Refslund Sørensen).

Not all "local culture" is defined primarily by the "locals", however, nor does it necessarily serve local interests. The village in East Anglia painted by Constable, argues Okely, has been "preserved" according to ideas of "Constable Country", which reflect educated white upper-class perceptions of the rural English countryside. This not only leaves little room for the rural workers who have created the village and its surrounding countryside through their labor, it also detracts attention from the destruction of that English countryside which has not been designated as being of particular local value. In his study of Lesotho, Ferguson shows how designating this part of Southern Africa as an independent nation-state has depoliticized the poverty and powerlessness which its citizens have suffered.

Reflexivity

By making interrelationships (as they unfold in time and space) a primary focus of research, it is possible to take a point of departure in the reflexivity of the people under study toward the social and economic processes resulting from these relations. We thereby, as Pærregaard argues, avoid operating with an absolute distinction between internal (implicit) and external (explicit) points of view. Instead we may take our point of departure in the various ways in which people represent what they perceive as their culture. These representations need not be in agreement, but will often reflect contested ideas of local culture. This is also apparent in Refslund Sørensen's study of oral testimony by villagers and settlers concerning a Sri Lankan resettlement scheme. She views it as representing two forms of narratives which reflect the different processes of displacement in which the two groups have been involved.

Today we need not confine ourselves to data that we generate ourselves in the field through participant observation and interviews. We can also draw on the many written and visual forms of expression created by the people we study. Preis, for example, has used video productions made by Tamils as an important window to understanding their perception of their position as refugees from Sri Lanka. Schade-Poulsen has studied Algerian raï music productions and press articles on this to supplement his field research of the transformation of a local music form into the global music genre of "world music". Malkki finds newspaper articles and UN documents as well as statements by officials involved in refugee work and by refugees themselves to be important sources of information in her study of the way in which refugees are represented – and misrepresented – in the West. By including and focusing upon the ways people perceive and define the cultural space within which they exist and their own place in it, these studies therefore view distinctions between external and internal points of view as processes of life that are contingent upon the particular contexts in which they are made.

By drawing upon a wider array of data than that which is produced through face-to-face field research it becomes possible to move beyond the smaller, inter-personal communities that anthropologists typically have studied through field work. The chapters by Ferguson and Eriksen thus focus on the geographically contiguous, but much larger unit of the nation-state. This has not been subject to a significant amount of anthropological research (exceptions include Handler 1988, and Kapferer 1988), probably because it does not lend itself to the localized field work in smaller communities based on face-to-face relations. By examining nations as places which are created within specific historic contexts it is possible, however, to view them as cultural constructions on a par with other places. As such they become part of the anthropological project.

SITING CULTURE

Several of the studies show that while anthropologists are preoccupied with de-essentializing the concept of culture and deconstructing the notion of bounded, localized cultural wholes, many of the very people we study are deeply involved in constructing cultural contexts which bear many resemblances to such cultural entities. Homelands and fishing villages are important points of cultural identification among the Kānaka Maoli in Hawaii (Hasager, Friedman); Macedonian people from all over the world find their "roots" in mountain villages with fruit orchards (Schwartz); family lands in the Caribbean constitute important cultural sites for an African-Caribbean population that has developed through a long diasporic history (Olwig). It is not our point to dismiss such places of cultural identification as a figment of the imagination. On the contrary, we wish to examine the historical and social significance of these "cultural sites" as focal points of identification for people who, in their daily lives, are involved in a complex of relations of global as well as local dimension.

Hasager's study of the way in which Kānaka Maoli homesteaders turned seemingly barren and inhospitable homestead lots into a *home*land imbued with cultural significance provides a poignant example of the way in which "culture" is established on "site." From a somewhat different perspective, Preis shows how Tamils "seek place" in the space they occupy as refugees, thereby creating cultural difference, and hence a Tamil identity, in exile. These examples demonstrate the central importance of place as a source of life and a reference point which people may identify with from their particular position in the more global network of human relations. By viewing place as a cultural construction that is part of the process of human life, and not as a fixed entity, we will be able to examine critically the historical context within which such constructions take place. This also means that it is possible to examine the hierarchies of power within which these cultural constructions occur and become recognized. This is important at a time, when, as Hasager points out, human rights based on cultural grounds constitute an important means whereby indigenous people are able to demand improvements in their condition of life.

Behind the anthropological world view of a mosaic of unique and distinct cultures ready to be studied and documented by diligent field workers, one can now see the contours of a more complex field of social and economic interrelations, cultural reflexivity and culturally constructed places. This does not mean, however, that people necessarily experience their lives as being entangled in complicated social, cultural and economic processes of global dimension. Many people can be seen to lead fairly simple everyday lives, as Friedman argues, despite the complexities of the larger world system. The study of the way in which people create meaningful and manageable contexts of life in the modern world is an important topic for anthropological investigation. The simplicity of such everyday life should not, however, lead anthropologists to construct simple models of the complex cultural processes involved in this life. The siting of culture is an important element in this complexity, which must be reflected in a new demarcation of the anthropological object.

In the present volume, the first part, "Finding a place for culture," explores new approaches to the study of culture outside the traditional localized field sites. Important cultural sites in such research are found in nodal points in the diffuse networks of global and local relations that constitute the context of life of many people today. Such nodal points are grounded in cultural constructions associated with particular localities, be they collective forms of land ownership, individual images of natal communities, or pictures and sounds celebrating local spheres of life.

The second part, "The culture and politics of place," critically examines the implications of viewing people as associated with particular places, whether nation-states, regions or homesteading areas. It is demonstrated that such places may be perceived as a means of liberation or as a means of oppression, depending on the conditions under which they were created and sustained and the particular vantage point of the persons involved. Close scrutiny of the historical context and the wider political and economic system of relations within which place is constructed therefore constitutes an important research agenda in anthropology.

The third part, "Topical metaphors in anthropological thinking," investigates some of the ways in which key concepts in anthropology, and other social sciences, are related to specific ways of thinking about localities and the people who are associated with them. It is demonstrated that such conceptualization may not only present an obstacle to in-depth ethnographic research and understanding, but may also pose ethical problems with serious consequences for the people involved.

AKNOWLEDGMENTS

This chapter has benefited from the discussion generated at the workshop "Finding a Place and Space for Culture," held outside Copenhagen on 3–5 December 1993, where the chapters in this volume were first presented.

REFERENCES

Appadurai, Arjun (1988) "Putting Hierarchy in its Place," *Cultural Anthropology* 3: 36–49.

—— (1991) "Global Ethnoscapes. Notes and Queries for a Transnational Anthropology," in Richard G. Fox (ed.) *Recapturing Anthropology. Working in the Present*, Santa Fe: School of American Research Press.

Barth, Fredrik (1992) "Towards Greater Naturalism in Conceptualizing Societies," in A. Kuper (ed.) *Conceptualizing Societies*, London: Routledge.

Clifford, James (1992) "Travelling Cultures," in Lawrence Grossberg et al. (eds) *Cultural Studies*, New York: Routledge.

Davis, John (1992) "The Anthropology of Suffering," *Journal of Refugee Studies* 5: 149–61.

de Certeau, Michel (1986) *The Practice of Everyday Life*, Berkeley: University of California Press.

Eggan, Fred (1954) "Social Anthropology and the Method of Controlled Comparison," *American Anthropologist* 56: 743–60.

Fardon, Richard (ed.) (1990) *Localizing Strategies. Regional Traditions*

of Ethnographic Writing, Edinburgh: Scottish Academic Press, and Washington: The Smithsonian Institution.
Gupta, Akhil and James Ferguson (1992) "Beyond 'Culture': Space, Identity, and the Politics of Difference," *Cultural Anthropology* 7: 6–23.
Handler, Richard (1985) "On Dialogue and Destructive Analysis: Problems in Narrating Nationalism and Ethnicity," *Journal of Anthropological Research* 41: 171–82.
—— (1988) *Nationalism and the Politics of Culture in Quebec*, Madison: University of Wisconsin Press.
Hannerz, Ulf (1992) *Cultural Complexity. Studies in the Social Organization of Meaning*, New York: Columbia University Press.
Hastrup, Kirsten (1993) "Hunger and the Hardness of Facts," *Man* 28: 727–39.
Kahn, Joel S. (1989) "Culture. Demise or Resurrection?" *Critique of Anthropology* 9, 2: 5–25.
Kapferer, Bruce (1988) *Legends of People, Myths of State*, Washington: Smithsonian Institution Press.
Malkki, Liisa (1992) "National Geographic: The Rooting of Peoples and the Territorialization of National Identity Among Scholars and Refugees," *Cultural Anthropology* 7: 24–44.
Pratt, Marie-Louise (1992) *Imperial Eyes. Travel Writing and Transculturation*, London: Routledge.
Rosaldo, Renato (1988) "Ideology, Place, and People without Culture," *Cultural Anthropology* 3: 77–87.
—— (1989) *Culture and Truth. The Remaking of Social Analysis*, Boston: Beacon Press.
Said, Edward (1993) *Culture and Imperialism*, London: Vintage.
Salmond, Anne (1982) "Theoretical Landscapes," in David Parkin (ed.) *Semantic Anthropology*, London: Academic Press.
Strathern, Marilyn (1993) Introduction to ASA Decentennial Conference.

Part 1

Finding a place for culture

1 Cultural sites

Sustaining a home in a deterritorialized world

Karen Fog Olwig

Anthropologists, in the past, have had a tendency to regard people as either settled in localized communities or as migrating and therefore involved in processes of moving and relocating in new places. Impressed by the growing importance of travel in the modern world, they are, however, beginning to critique the idea that settled life in particular places necessarily is a "normal" state of being. A great deal of attention is therefore now being directed at the cultural and social significance of moving in space and the transnational communities which may result from this. In the excitement about foregrounding movement and non-local relations we must be careful, however, not to overemphasize the global and transient character of human life on the loose. On the basis of a study of a West Indian community I shall argue that the strong propensity to migrate found among West Indians is counterbalanced by an equally strongly developed notion of attachment to place. In order to understand West Indian life it is therefore necessary to study the role of both fixed places and changeable and ever-expanding global networks of relations. I suggest that a useful concept in such studies may be found in the notion of "cultural sites," cultural institutions which have developed in the interrelationship between global and local ties. These cultural sites attain their significance because they are identified with particular places, at the same time as they accommodate the global conditions of life which have long characterized the West Indies. It is suggested that such cultural sites may be useful focal points in anthropological studies of the more general global and local condition of human existence.

CULTURAL SITINGS

> God created the earth for people to go to and fro,
> not to stay in one place.

This idea of movement as a religiously ordained foundation of human life was expressed by Mrs. Browne, an elderly woman from the West Indian island of Nevis whom I interviewed in the American Virgin Islands in 1980. She had lived on Nevis for most of her life, working as a market woman selling agricultural produce on the neighboring island of St. Kitts. Several of her brothers and sisters had moved to England during the 1950s and had helped support her seven children. When the oldest, a daughter, turned 17, Mrs. Browne purchased a ticket for her to go to St. Croix so that she might make a better living for herself – and for the rest of the family back on Nevis. The daughter soon began to send remittances to her mother, and some years later, when she had married a Virgin Islander, she obtained a permanent immigrant visa for her mother which would enable Mrs. Browne to obtain American immigrant visas for the younger children. When I met Mrs. Browne she had just succeeded in relocating all of her children to the Virgin Islands. Several of them were hoping to go on to mainland United States. Having accomplished her mission, Mrs. Browne was planning to return to Nevis to live there in her own house which was located next to her sister's. She expected, however, to go back and forth between Nevis and the Virgin Islands, explaining, "it is natural for people to move around."

This little case story presents a way of life and kind of folk wisdom which has not usually been associated with the sort of people who have been the traditional object of study by anthropologists. The image of the "native" prevalent in the anthropological literature has been one of settled persons whose lives can be conceptualized in terms of cultural wholes of shared values and meaning which unfold within a closely linked web of integrated social relations. In this line of thinking, to move, unless part of regular nomadic patterns, has implied uprootedness and hence the loss of a firm cultural foundation. This emphasis on rootedness has been criticized in recent writings which have argued that movement, far from being an interruption in ordinary, settled life, constitutes a normal condition of life for a great deal of people (Appadurai 1988, 1991; Rosaldo 1988; Clifford 1992; Malkki 1992). Thus Clifford has suggested that "travel" should be brought to the forefront in ethnographic analysis, and "cultures" be viewed as "sites of dwelling *and* travel" (1992: 103). He therefore proposes that "traveling-in-dwelling" and "dwelling-in-traveling" should constitute a central topic in cultural studies. In a similar vein, Appadurai sees the world as characterized by a state of deterritorialization "in which money, commodities, and persons unendingly chase each other around the world" (1991: 194). While this state generates a sense of displacement, the very experience of displacement is seen by him to fuel "the imaginative resources of lived, local experiences" (ibid.: 196). In his opinion, one of the most relevant subjects of ethnographic study today, therefore, is the imagined worlds which are constructed when "local historical trajectories flow into complicated transnational structures" (ibid.: 209).

If anthropology is not to turn into an imagined world itself, longing for a world of ordered and stable lives that we have lost, it seems that we must listen to Clifford, Appadurai, and Mrs. Browne from Nevis and begin to direct our attention to the interrelationship of moving and dwelling in a world of global interconnections. In this chapter I shall discuss such a global network of social relations and associated cultural values and some of the institutions which can be seen to ground this network in particular places. The study concerns people who are connected with Nevis, formerly a part of the British Leeward Islands, which today has become politically independent together with the island of St. Kitts.

The field work upon which this analysis is based has been carried out in four different locations: Nevis, the central reference point in the transnational network of Nevisians, as well as three migration destinations: New Haven (Connecticut) where Nevisians emigrated during the early part of this century; Leeds (England), which received a great number of Nevisians during the 1950s and 1960s, and the US Virgin Islands which have remained an important destination since the 1960s. Even though the field work of necessity was grounded in specific locations, it took place within a non-local cultural space related to the network of ties which connected individual Nevisians residing in these separate locations. Thus a great deal of the Nevisians' daily life was oriented toward activities and concerns of relevance to people and places in other points in the global network, giving me the feeling that Nevisian culture kept escaping me – it always seemed to be where I was not. This even applied to aspects of life related to institutions usually associated with a settled way of life, such as possession of land and a home. By viewing these institutions as sites, which have been molded by an interplay of perceptions of presence and absence, I believe it is possible to find a way of analyzing, and understanding, Nevisian culture. Before turning toward an analysis of the present-day Nevisian community, I shall examine the historical context in which it emerged. This will help provide a means of comprehending the particular form the community has taken and the role of place within it.

A HISTORY OF DETERRITORIALIZATION

The Caribbean has been seen to present one of the most extreme examples of deterritorialization in the contemporary world. The present population composition in the area is a result of massive importations of people from Europe, Africa and Asia occurring primarily from the early seventeenth to the late nineteenth century. This immigration, much of which was forced, was followed by extensive voluntary outmigration, during this century primarily to North America and Europe. On Nevis the current population of less than 10,000 is primarily of African ancestry. It is impossible to estimate the number of Nevisians who live outside the island, because there are no statistical records of the total number of Nevisians who have emigrated abroad. Furthermore, and perhaps more importantly, it is difficult to establish objective criteria by which to determine which of the emigrees and their descendants are to be defined as Nevisians and therefore included in the absent population. There is little doubt, however, that the global network of people of Nevisian ancestry who identify with Nevis involves a greater population than that which is present on the island itself.[1]

It would be a mistake to view deterritorialization primarily as a matter of physical removal from a territory. The most fundamental form of deterritorialization experienced by Caribbean people of African descent was that which took place within the Caribbean. The Africans were brought to Nevis, as well as the rest of the Caribbean, as a source of labor power to be used primarily on the sugar plantations. As I have shown elsewhere (Olwig 1993a, b, c, 1995a) the Africans were incorporated into the local societies through an institution of slavery which treated them as socially dead chattel labor with no identity apart from that of being their owner's private property. Being denied a place of their own in the social ranks of the colonial society, the Africans and their descendants developed social and economic ties among one another in the contexts of life that they were able to create outside the sphere of dominance of the colonial society proper. These ties came to form an important basis for the establishment of a social and cultural identity among the slaves.

One of the most important contexts within which a social identity could be established was that which emerged in connection with the subsistence farming that the slaves were able to perform in the forested mountain areas or ravines which were found on many plantations. Not being suitable for sugarcane cultivation these areas were left for the slaves to do kitchen gardening and rear small stock.

During slavery, slaves therefore can be seen to have lived a dual life. Within the plantation society, where they spent most of their time performing strenuous and menial labor for their masters, they remained chattel labor with no identity of their own. Within the context of the active social and economic life which they created in their spare time, however, they became persons with an identity in their own right. This was rooted in the places in the margins of the plantation society where they were free to carve out a life for themselves and generate a community of relations relatively undisturbed by their owners.

After the abolition of slavery in 1834, the freed attempted to acquire land where they could settle and thus realize in daily social practice the sort of life which had provided a source of identity and independence for them in the hostile plantation society. In many Caribbean societies, including Nevis, severe obstacles were placed in the way of this acquisition of land (Olwig 1995b), and the emancipated remained landless or acquired only small plots of land, many of them located in the same marginal areas where they had had their provision plots during slavery. On these plots small houses were built – usually simple two-room structures of wood or wattle – and the potentiality for cultivation was usually limited to a little subsistence cultivation. Most of these small landholders, therefore, had to supplement their farming with wage labor or sharecropping arrangements on the plantations. An increasingly attractive alternative for the emancipated became migration off the island. This was not intended as a permanent, once-and-for-all solution to the problems which the people of African descent had experienced on their island of birth. It was perceived as a temporary relocation which would enable them to return with the necessary resources to establish an economically independent life on land of their own. The migrants often left close relatives behind, including spouses, offspring and parents, to whom they expected to return having accumulated the necessary means. Many did not succeed in this and never moved back. They nevertheless usually maintained contact with their family on Nevis and sent remittances to them whenever possible.

The economic and social deterritorialization which the emancipated experienced on their native island was augmented, for many, by the cultural estrangement that took place as a result of British missionary activities which began during the 1780s. The sort of Christianity which was propagated by Methodist ministers, in particular, was closely related to an ideology of respectability which had developed among the rising middle classes in Great Britain. This respectability revolved around a frugal life of hard work, sexual restraint and family values centered on a nuclear family. The family, which was based on holy matrimony, was headed by the husband and father, who was regarded as the provider of the family, but nurtured by the wife and mother who was the moral guardian of the family. Important outward signs of respectability were possession of a modest, yet comfortable home on one's own property (the center of family life) and sufficient material means for the mother to devote herself to housewifely duties. It was also of great significance that the family was able to give the children proper religious and secular education (proof of the industriousness of the head of the family and the high moral virtues of the home). Those who were not able to become sufficiently economically secure to provide the proper home environment for the family were, by implication, not worthy of respect.

Most Nevisians did not find themselves among the respectable members of society. They experienced a great many problems just obtaining the basic means of subsistence, and the entire family was involved in economic activities, including the mother and the children who often labored in the plantation fields. Furthermore, many Nevisian families were not nuclear, nor were they necessarily based on marriage. It was very difficult for the young to acquire the economic means to build a house of their own, and they tended to stay with their parents and have children out of wedlock. It was also apparent, however, that the European concept of the independent father-headed nuclear family based on holy matrimony was quite different from the network of kin relations that had become the primary family form among the slaves. Kinsmen had provided a vital resource both in dealings with authorities on the plantations and in the development of the African-Caribbean communities which emerged in the margins of plantations. Thus the kin ties involved obligations to help and cooperate and were most intensive between close relatives, in particular mothers and children, who always lived on the same plantation. Ties between sexual partners, on the other hand, were of relatively less significance in the social and economic exigencies of daily life. The post-emancipation era therefore did not see the establishment of a "respectable" class of smallholders based on nuclear families. Rather it saw the further development of networks of kinsmen, some of them living on plantations, some in their own homes on small plots of land, and some outside the island.

A few years after emancipation, a pattern of deterritorialization had become firmly established among the emancipated on Nevis, along with many of the other Caribbean islands. Most Nevisians were either: (1) physically present on Nevis, but hoping to emigrate in order to help improve the social and economic situation of their family, and possibly acquire the wherewithal to build a home and establish a family of their own; or (2) physically absent from the island, but maintaining ties with their family on Nevis and investing a fair amount of their resources there, hoping eventually to return. Only the relatively few, who had in fact succeeded in returning from migratory work abroad with sufficient economic means to buy enough land to build a respectable house and lead a comfortable life, had become reterritorialized on their home island. The context within which African-Caribbean cultural values and social practices tended to become expressed was therefore not the local community. The continued domination of the colonial plantation society well into this century has meant that the places where this community was grounded remained too restricted for the development of such a territorialized community. The Nevisian community developed and grew during this time within a non-local space of networks of relations extending between Nevisians on and off the island. As this community constituted itself, it began to obtain a life of its own, and today it can be seen to be associated with cultural values of great import to Nevisians such as those values expressed by Mrs. Browne cited above. An important key to the success of this community, nevertheless, lies in the fact that despite its deterritorialized character it still has a territorial locus where it touches down. It thus attains its vitality and meaning by being grounded in places on Nevis, which are associated with the family of the migrants. These places have therefore become important cultural sites in the global Nevisian community. I shall here discuss two central institutions located in these places which have enabled Nevisians to exploit socio-economic resources outside the local society, while maintaining strong cultural ties with the home island. They are the institution of family land and the family house.

FAMILY LAND

Nevis is often described as one of the Caribbean islands where the plantocracy maintained its grip on the society long after emancipation (Pares 1950; Frucht 1966; Hall 1971). This is borne out by official statistics which leave an impression of an island entirely dominated by large plantations. In 1923, eighty-nine years after the abolition of slavery, the *Leeward Islands Blue Book* listed only eighty-two land holdings on Nevis. All of them were more than 10 acres in size, and fifty-eight (or 71 per cent) of them exceeded 100 acres (*Leeward*

Islands Blue Book 1923: n.p.). This official picture ignores, however, the many small lots which had been acquired by the African-Caribbean population since emancipation. *The Nevis Blue Book* of 1876 contains some information on these plots and the small acreage they involved. It reports that no less than 2,135 persons were "returned to the treasurer as Freeholders of Land in 1876, but only 129 were found to be in possession of Lots of two Acres and upwards" (1876: 126). These smallholders had disappeared entirely from the colonial reports in 1923, probably because no property tax was paid on lots below 2 acres. These landholders were therefore of no concern to the colonial authorities. The invisibility of the small landholders in the records may also be due to the fact that by the twentieth century much of their land had become family land, a form of ownership where land is not owned by individual legal persons. There were, therefore, no proper landowners, so to speak, to report to the colonial authorities.

The basic principle behind family land is the holding in common of a piece of land by a group of people who are descendants of the original purchaser of the property.[2] Family land has never been a legally recognized form of landownership on Nevis, and Nevisians seem to have operated with several different ideas about how people can lay claim to family land. This is reflected in the few wills made by people who decided to put in writing the principles by which they wished the land to be shared by their descendants (*Record of Nevis Wills*, 1880– , vol. 1–B). In the widest definition, all recognized descendants of the original owner have an equal right to the property. In some cases, however, certain restrictions can be seen to have been noted. Several wills stipulate, for example, that women are expected to move to their husband's land upon marriage, but are free to return should they become widows. One will states, however, that spouses (male or female) can be brought to the land only with the explicit consent of all, implying that both married sons and daughters have a right to stay if the others approve of the match. A third will emphasizes that only those who are willing to "work in harmony" and not become "unreasonable" retain their right in the land. A main purpose of family land therefore seems to be to provide a place for the family to live together in peace.

The most fundamental principle behind family land is its inalienability. This is inherent in this form of collective ownership, because as long as land is held in common by the family as such, there is no individual owner who has the authority to sell it. Many of the wills, however, explicitly state that the land cannot be sold, but must remain in the family. A will from 1893 stipulates that the land which will be inherited by a daughter must not be "sold or alienated but remain to her lawful issue. . . . "[3] A will from 1926 bequeaths a house spot to a son, his heirs or assigns for ever and directs that it cannot be disposed "to any person or persons outside of my family, by barter, sale, or gift." Another will from 1955 states that the heirs only have "life interest" in the land which is to "be handed down from generation to generation equally." The inalienability of family land therefore creates for the entire family a place on Nevis where they belong.

This place, however, has been for many quite intangible. One should not get the impression that several generations of descendants made up of large families crowd together on small family landholdings. As noted, a great many Nevisians choose to emigrate – at least temporarily – in order to improve their own economic situation and that of the relatives left behind. Since a claim in family land is acquired through descent and maintained through good relations with the relatives living on the land, a right in family land is not lost through migration, unless the migrant neglects the family on Nevis while away. Family land thus constitutes both a concrete place on Nevis to which migrants have a right to return and an incentive to remember the family on Nevis and to wish to be remembered by them. This can be accomplished by sending regular economic support. Family land therefore constitutes an important linchpin in the global family networks.

This role of family land is apparent in interviews that I carried out with older migrants. Knowledge of having family land on Nevis was important to them, even though they had been away from the island for many years and in all likelihood would never return there to live. One woman, who was born on Nevis in 1925, had left the island as a young woman first to go to St. Kitts, then Curaçao, and finally Leeds where she had lived for more than 30 years when I interviewed her in 1989. She had only been back to Nevis twice since leaving for England, yet she was quite aware of having family land on Nevis and her right to settle on it, should she wish to do so. Her sister had recently moved back to the land from England and was now paying the taxes on the land:

> The land that we have on Nevis is family land. . . . Anyone who wishes can go and build a house there, the land is not divided. . . . The land is from our grandfather, and he said that it was not to be sold, but was for the generations. My sister has all the receipts, and

legally she could sell, if she wanted to. But she will not do so, because the land belongs to the family.

This woman was only certain that she maintained her right in the land because she kept close contact with this sister. In contrast, another Nevisian interviewed in Leeds had had the unpleasant experience of learning that a more distant relative living on the land had actually sold some of it:

> When I grew up, the family just owned the land together, no rents were paid [i.e. no taxes], and different relatives worked it, like I had uncles who worked different pieces of the land, and they built their houses on it. Now taxes are paid on it, and the deed is very important. I heard from my sister, who just came back from a visit to the island, that a cousin of ours has sold some of the land, which rightly belongs to our forebearers. It is family land and owned by the family together, so he had no right to do this. . . .

This cousin might not have the moral right to sell the land, knowing that the land was regarded as family land to be held in common in perpetuity. Legally, however, there is nothing to prevent him from selling, once he has paid the taxes on the land. Furthermore, it is doubtful whether this Nevisian woman and her sister who live in England really have a moral right to complain about the sale of the land. Since they have failed to remain in contact with the member of the family who is living on and looking after the land, they have, in essence, lost contact with the land.

The inalienable right in family land can be seen to be, to a certain extent, counterbalanced by the duty inherent in this right to provide the necessary support and help to maintain the family land. Family land should therefore not be interpreted as an economic resource which people have in a piece of property that they might exploit whenever they wish to do so. It is rather a cultural site which offers a potential homeland and source of identification for those who honor and care for this site. This is apparent in a will from 1970, where a woman is taking the drastic step of disinheriting her son because he has abused his right to the land by ignoring it. She does this by giving him an inheritance of one shilling:[4]

> I also have a son . . . , who is now in San Domingo. He was in that island nearly thirty years (30 years) and he has never written me a line much more to send 1 d (one penny for me) I have the pleasure of leaving one shilling (1/-) in this my last will for him.
>
> (*Record of Nevis Wills*, 1880– , vol. 1–B)

Such wills, and the stories told about them, make it abundantly clear that those migrants who do not remain loyal to their family on Nevis run the severe risk of being disinherited and thereby, in effect, excommunicated from Nevis.

FAMILY HOUSE

The village where I concentrated my field work on Nevis during the 1980s had originally been located on small pieces of family land next to a ravine which extended from Mount Nevis through the plantation fields toward the coast. Beginning with the 1930s this land was gradually abandoned, as villagers moved to a more central inland location on an improved road where defunct estate land was being sold by the government in parcels of a few acres each. Much of the old family land is now covered with bush, and the exact location of the individual lots, which are typically quarter or half acre pieces, is somewhat uncertain to many villagers. A similar development has occurred elsewhere on the island, where the government has subdivided estate land and sold it off to the local population. Today many Nevisians are therefore living on plots of land that they have purchased themselves. It is quite apparent, however, that some of the ideas concerning family land are being transferred to these newer land possessions which are, strictly speaking, individually owned private property. This is particularly clear in attitudes and relations towards the family home which these landowners have established on the land.

The family home on Nevis, where the children have grown up, is an important focal point in the global family networks. Virtually all of the migrants that I interviewed send regular economic support to Nevis, if their parents are still alive and living there. It is believed to be a filial duty, beyond discussion, to look after the parents, who have struggled so much to rear all their children. Most of the Nevisians that I interviewed in England had just barely succeeded in sending a pound or two out of their first wages, when they arrived in England, being offered the lowest paid and most menial jobs. The Nevisians in the Virgin Islands experienced similar problems, not just because they were earning relatively low minimum wages, but also because they were living in a highly inflated tourist economy. Most of the migrants had left directly from their parents' house, having received the economic funds to travel from their parents, and a great number had even left small children behind in the care of grandmothers. This makes them greatly indebted to their parents for giving them the opportunity to improve their life abroad. Even after they have become more established and managed to "send for" their children, they take great pains to send support because of this indebtedness. As a woman on Nevis explained:

> My sister on St. Thomas sends two boxes to us, when *The Effort* [a boat] is going from the Virgin Islands to Nevis. She is really sending to my mother, because she took care of my sister's children, when she was on St. Thomas alone without them, and now she is showing her gratitude to her mother by sending things to her. She is thanking her.

It is also important for migrants to send money to the family home on Nevis, because this home offers a place with which they can identify and to which they can return at any time. Indeed, a great many of those who had emigrated to the Virgin Islands during the 1960s had lived for many years with the real possibility that they might need to go back to this family home. Having entered the American territory on temporary visas dependent upon the possession of full-time employment, they would be forced to leave should they fail to remain employed. When all of these visas were finally converted to permanent visas, some Nevisians had lived in the Virgin Islands for as many as twenty years. Even those who have experienced few legal problems, however, often experience difficulties adjusting to life in the Western migration destinations, and regard their place of residence as merely a location where they are working, not a place where they are living and creating a home for themselves.[5] For them the family home on Nevis remains of emotional, cultural, and social import.

In order further to secure the continued existence of the family home it is common for at least one of the children, often one of the youngest daughters, to stay behind with the parents to care for them in their old age and look out for the family property. This nurturing and caring for the family home is seen by many as entitling the siblings who stay behind to become the legal heirs to the parents' estate. One Nevisian explained, "there is the feeling that those who stay at home, while the others are out to glean, will think that they are entitled to the land." The feeling that it is only by caring for those in a family house that one can inherit is so strong on Nevis that many Nevisians are under the impression that there is, in fact, a law to that effect. One lawyer related, for example, that he had been contacted by a couple who wished to get legal title to property owned by a deceased person whom they had taken care of. They expected to get the property, even though the deceased had not left a will giving them the property and was no relative of theirs.

Since those who have devoted their life to caring for the parents usually have been dependent upon economic support from the other siblings, some Nevisians are of the opinion that the family home should instead go to the migrants who have provided the family on Nevis with the material means of living. One Nevisian explained that he received his parents' house and the plot of land on which it was built because he sent economic support to his parents when he was in England. In most cases, however, the providers of both the economic means of life and the actual care of the parents and their household are believed to have a stake, and hence a right, in the house. This was often expressed by Nevisians by saying that those who "buried the parents" would be entitled to the house. A Nevisian in the Virgin Islands explained:

> The place should have belonged to my sister, because she was the only one at home, when my mother died. But since she was too young to bury my mother, and didn't have the money, my brother and I did this, and so we should rightfully have the land. But we will leave it in our sister's name.

In many cases, a house is not deeded to one person, however, but given to all the children, in this way becoming family property to be held in common. This establishment of a family home is related to the desire to keep the home in the family, as is the case with the family land. One Nevisian who is involved in legal work in connection with the administering of property on Nevis claimed that the family home has today attained much of the significance which family land previously had as the source of family unity:

> Family property usually pertains mostly to the house in which the parents died. The will may state that the house in which they lived should not be sold but left for the children, including those abroad, so that they always have a home to return to. . . . Whereas I do not find strong ideas about family land being kept in the family, there are strong ideas about the parents' house being kept in the family.

The central role of the family home in the family networks is reflected in the prestige it confers on the migrants, if they are able to provide generous support for the family home. As migrants improve their economic situation abroad they tend to finance substantial and visible improvements on the house itself. These improvements have taken the form of expanding the building or even rebuilding the old wooden structure in blocks; equipping the house with running water, inside bathrooms, electricity and telephone, and furnishing it with a wide array of Western material goods such as radio and television, refrigerator, gas or electric stove and modern furniture. Many of the migrants working on Caribbean islands nearby, such as the Virgin Islands, also send boxes of food and clothing to the family home. If migrants are not thought to be providing adequately for the home this will be brought to their attention by other islanders living in the same migration destination. One woman living in Leeds learned, for example, from Nevisian friends there that neighbors in her village on Nevis were gossiping about her mother not owning a refrigerator. This was brought to their attention when her mother contracted diabetes and had to ask neighbors to store her medicine in their refrigerator. As a result of this gossip the woman immediately made sure that her mother received enough money to purchase a refrigerator, even though she really did not have any cash to spare. She explained,

> if we didn't send the money, we would have a bad name in the village, and I am happy that the villagers see that my parents have a 5 bedroom house with television, telephone and a fridge!

For the family home on Nevis, the migrants naturally have come to constitute an essential economic mainstay, and without their support life would be very difficult on the island. Small farming never has offered a sustainable income, and waged employment remains limited and poorly remunerated on Nevis. The absent relatives are an integral part of the family homes on Nevis, and they are often regarded as members of the households, even when they are located at a great distance from Nevis. For the children in the family home, absent relatives serve as important role models who are admired and perceived to be doing well abroad as long as they send generous support to the family home. This was reflected in a survey of Nevisian school children which I carried out in the early 1980s. It showed that the vast majority of children, impressed by the remittances sent by relatives abroad and the very limited economic possibilities on Nevis, were hoping to emigrate to areas of greater opportunity.[6]

To a certain extent, the abundance of Western material goods on Nevis has created an even greater awareness of the poverty of the local society as compared with the wealthy Western societies. Nevisians, however, are not necessarily alienated by Western material culture, because they appropriate it to their own cultural needs. By surrounding themselves with Western goods, Nevisians appear to be identifying strongly with Western consumer culture. I would argue, however, that this interpretation is only partially correct. The fact that Nevisians are concerned to be seen wearing industrially made clothing from the West and prefer eating imported canned or frozen foods to local produce, should also be seen in the light of the fact that these goods have derived, for the most part, from relatives abroad. They are, in other words, outward signs of a well-functioning family network where relatives abroad have been successful and remained supportive of their family on Nevis. Conspicuous consumption of Western material goods should therefore also be viewed as a way of asserting the cultural values of the deterritorialized Nevisian community.

For the migrants, providing economic support for the family home on Nevis is a crucial way of maintaining a place on Nevis with which they can identify and where they will always be welcome. As this home is modernized through the migrants' remittances and changes through time, it becomes more and more of an imagined place. Though the migrants, and the migrants' foreign-born children, may appreciate the modern amenities which their remittances have helped finance, they nevertheless wish to find some semblance of the island that they have left. This is the Nevis which the migrants associate with the family home of their childhood. For this reason some homes on Nevis, where imported foods from the West are the standard order of the day, maintain a small provision garden and stock of animals, in part so that the family can give absent relatives "a taste of home" when they visit. During the past twenty years, however, the role of preserving some of the old ways on Nevis which migrants can remember with nostalgia from their childhood has been taken over by a local festival called Culturama. At this festival, which is held every August, music, dance, cooking, handicrafts, and other expressive cultural forms of pre-1960s village life are displayed and celebrated at shows and competitions. Culturama has been extremely popular among migrants, and many will plan their visits to Nevis to coincide with it. At Culturama the entire island of Nevis is virtually being turned into one big nostalgic family home to be visited and celebrated by everybody.

This has been of particular significance to those whose families have left the island so many years ago that they no longer have personal ties to a particular family home on Nevis. Most of the migrants in New Haven, Connecticut, are in that situation. Due to a change in American immigration regulations, migration to New Haven ceased in about 1920, and most of those that I interviewed there were second or third generation Americans. While many of them regard themselves as Americans and have lost interest in Nevis, a significant number actively cultivate their family roots on Nevis. They have organized family clans, complete with family trees rooted in an ancestor on Nevis, and hold family reunions, both in various parts of the United States where members of the clan live and on Nevis. Reunions on Nevis are typically held in connection with Culturama, so that the clan members can feel at home on their ancestral island, even though they no longer have a family home there of their own.

Many Nevisians go to great pains to maintain a home on their island of birth, however. Thus some of those who have succeeded in earning a good income abroad and helping their children get established on their own there, have chosen to build their retirement home on Nevis. In this way, the family reclaims its roots on Nevis and becomes reterritorialized there. One elderly Nevisian couple whom I interviewed in Leeds was in the process of doing this. They had built a house on Nevis and were hoping to retire there within a few years. Showing me a picture of the house which they had finished building on Nevis three years previously the wife said:

> I have my mind on my little island, and I plan to go back to settle there. We have had a home built at Beach Road . . . which was completed about three years ago. A house with a split roof, built of concrete blocks. We have not used the house since it was built, and we will not rent it out, because people will mash it up. And then we also may rent it out to people who will not move when we want to use it, saying that they have nowhere to go. So we just leave it, and it is waiting for us to return. . . .

Even for many of the Nevisian migrants and their descendants who have been removed from the immediate concerns of life on the island, having succeeded in creating a new life for themselves abroad, Nevis continues to play an important role as a home to anchor. Like Mrs. Browne, who was quoted at the beginning of this chapter, they are reaffirming a home base on the island, not just for themselves, but also for any of their children who would like to go there.

TOWARD AN ANTHROPOLOGY OF CULTURAL SITES

The interrelationship between place and space has become an important topic within anthropology during the last few years. It has been argued that the time-worn anthropological tradition of viewing culture in terms of separate, spatially incontiguous entities, each placed in their own territories, bears little resemblance to the mobile and culturally complex lives that people can be seen to lead today. African-Caribbean culture is a striking example of some of the difficulties that arise when a territorially based concept of culture is employed. The name African-Caribbean itself points in two different directions: the African continent from whence the slaves came, some of them almost 500 years ago, and the Caribbean itself, where the African slaves were brought after the area had been emptied of its aboriginal population. While these referents point to two places that have been of great significance in the history of the African-Caribbean people, they in no way demarcate the primary context within which African-Caribbean culture has developed, particularly during the past 150 years. This context has been a diffuse one which cannot be identified with a particular, bounded territory. Rather its primary characteristic has been that it emerged in the margins of the territories corresponding to the Caribbean plantation societies, later to expand outside these territories to touch down in faraway destinations. While African-Caribbean people of necessity have lived in particular locations, some of their most important social relations have extended far beyond these locations, and they can be seen to have identified culturally with distant places.

Despite the fact that African-Caribbean life is fluid and diffuse in many ways, it would be a mistake, however, to view it as characterized by disjunction and transience. By focusing on the global relations which generations of people have developed and sustained at the same time as they have maintained a presence in their local island society, it is possible to detect the existence of institutions of some permanence. These institutions have accommodated the local and global conditions of life presented to African-Caribbean people and provided significant and stable points of cultural identification. I have here examined family land and the family home, which have been seen to reconcile the contradictory conditions of life presented by mobility in a deterritorialized world. These contradictions are those of being physically present in specific localities, while being part of translocal communities rooted in distant places; of staying put in the home, yet being dependent upon economic and social resources in remote destinations.

This West Indian case study would seem to have implications for ethnographic research in general even though it concerns a specific people with a history which is particularly betwixt and between the global and the local. Most anthropologists have operated with a notion of culture as something which is shared by people living in particular areas and which is therefore present in fieldwork sites corresponding to these areas. Accordingly, it has been possible for a thorough and sensitive field worker to experience the culture of a certain group of people by living with them, participating in, observing and discussing with them their lives. In a world where moving and dwelling are in constant interplay, sites are not experienced merely by being present in them, but also by leaving them behind. This, in fact, follows the etymological derivation of the word *site*, which derives from the past participle of *sinere*, meaning "to leave, place, lay" (*Webster's* 1965: 814). Being situated implies being left or placed, so that only that which has been left and placed can be sited.

If anthropologists traditionally have studied rooted peoples, the anthropologist has not been not rooted. Thus the insight that siting also implies displacement has been an integral part of the anthropological field work experience. The field work method of participant observation has involved a constant interplay between being part of life and stepping out of it, observing it and reflecting upon it. Displacement has also been seen as an important aspect of "native" culture in the concept of liminality, developed by Victor Turner (1989 [1967], 1977 [1969]). Here the act of temporarily stepping outside of one's normal socio-cultural context of life is regarded as an important part of the *rites-de-passage* which serve to sharpen the cultural competence of the participants.

The cultural sitings of anthropologists and liminals, however, are of quite a different order to those of the inhabitants of the fluid world of ethnoscapes and travelers depicted by Appadurai and Clifford. Anthropologists and ritual liminals return from their reflective absence, having sharpened their understanding of a culture as a well-ordered entity underlined by an integrated and structured system of values and meanings. The displaced do not experience temporary absences only to be confirmed in the well-ordered structure of normal life. Theirs is a more or less permanent experience of not being in situ, as they negotiate a diversity of experiences in a deterritorialized world. Their insights lead to the cultural construction of places, such as homelands, which are viewed from a local as well as a global perspective.

So far many of the empirical examples evoked to discuss theoretical approaches to deterritorialized culture have been found in literature and films. Few anthropologists have carried out research on the cultural constructions of such deterritorialized lives, and for good reasons – it is difficult for the anthropologists to get at the natives' point of view, when the natives' universe is made up of a wide variety of resources of worldwide dimension, and when it is not embedded in particular places where anthropological field work may be carried out. One way to solve this problem may be to study transient places, such as motels or airports which are designed to accommodate transient people, as discussed by Clifford (1992), or bar milieus, evoked by Appadurai (1991) in his analysis of the film "Bombay Bar." Such locales offer particular spots where the anthropologist can participate in and observe the ways in which people on the move create social and cultural contexts, or, in the words of Appadurai, imagined worlds which facilitate meaningful interaction.

Appadurai's approach has its limitations, however. If anthropologists merely remove their localized field work from the stable village to the transient environment of the hotel or bar, they will primarily focus on the more short-lived and flimsy contexts of modern life and therefore risk exaggerating its transient and "uprooted" character. I have argued that West Indians on the move are not primarily oriented toward their places of residence. They are also involved in less apparent, but more permanent non-local relations extending to people in different parts of the world with whom they have maintained social ties for longer periods of time. Furthermore, mobile people often can be seen to develop an attachment to a specific place which plays a central role as a common source of identity in their global network of relations, but which may not be their place of residence.

I would like to suggest that if we undertake the more laborious path of attempting to carry out field work within the translocal networks of relations existing between mobile people we may be able to detect socio-cultural contexts of greater permanence and sustenance. These contexts may be seen to be sustained by institutions which tie them to homelands in much more concrete ways than through the imagined worlds erected by the creative resources of fantasy. These institutions can be viewed as "cultural sites" in the sense that they are created through an interplay between dwelling and traveling, presence and absence, localizing and globalizing.

The Nevisian case study suggests that anthropologists should not expect to find localized, integrated and self-contained cultural units where they may carry out their field work. Nor, however, should they see disjunction, mobility, fluidity and imagined worlds as the only parameters of life in today's globalized world. Important frameworks of life and sources of identification should rather be sought in the cultural sites which have emerged in the interstices between local and global conditions of life. These sites encompass and embody the multiple and contradictory spheres of life in which people are involved today. This is reflected in the ways in which they allow for "traveling-in-dwelling" as well as "dwelling-in-traveling." Such cultural sites are hardly unique to Nevis or the West Indies, for that matter, and anthropologists therefore might do well to make such sites a focus of study in future research of the increasingly translocal world in which we live.

ACKNOWLEDGMENTS

This analysis is based on my book, *Global Culture, Island Identity. Continuity and Change in the Afro-Caribbean Community of Nevis* (Olwig 1993a). I would like to thank Kirsten Hastrup and Karsten Pærregaard for their useful comments.

NOTES

1 A fuller historical geographical treatment of Nevisian migration is found in Bonham Richardson's book, *Caribbean Migrants* (1983). Caribbean migration patterns in general are discussed by Thomas-Hope (1978, 1992).
2 The institution of family land in the Caribbean has been analyzed in detail in Besson (1987, 1995).
3 This case is unusual because it is apparently only the portion of land that the daughter received which could not be alienated. No such stipulation pertained to the land inherited by the three sons.
4 This study of Nevisian school children is analyzed in Olwig (1987).
5 The migration experience is discussed further in Olwig (1993d).
6 This study of Nevisian school children is analyzed in Olwig (1987).

REFERENCES

Printed sources

Appadurai, Arjun (1988) "Theory in Anthropology: Center and Periphery," *Comparative Studies in Society and History* 28, 1: 356–61.
—— (1991) "Global Ethnoscapes. Notes and Queries for a Transnational Anthropology," in R. G. Fox (ed.) *Recapturing Anthropology. Working in the Present*, Santa Fe: School of American Research Press.
Besson, Jean (1987) "A Paradox in Caribbean Attitudes to Land," in Jean Besson and Janet Momsen (eds) *Land and Development in the Caribbean*, London: Macmillan.
—— (1995) "Land, Kinship and Community in the Post-Emancipation Caribbean: A Regional View of the Leewards," in Karen Fog Olwig (ed.) *Society, Culture and Resistance in the Post-Emancipation Caribbean*, London: Frank Cass.
Clifford, James (1992) "Travelling Cultures," in Lawrence Grossberg, Cary Nelson and Paula Treichler (eds) *Cultural Studies*, New York: Routledge.

Frucht, Richard (1966) "Community and Context in a Colonial Society: Social and Economic Change in Nevis, British West Indies." Ph.D. Dissertation, Brandeis University.
Hall, Douglas (1971) *Five of the Leewards 1834–1870*, Barbados: Caribbean Universities Press.
Malkki, Liisa (1992) "National Geographic: The Rooting of Peoples and the Territorialization of National Identity Among Scholars and Refugees," *Cultural Anthropology* 7, 2: 24–44.
Olwig, Karen Fog (1987) "Children's Attitudes to the Island Community – The Aftermath of Out-Migration on Nevis," in Jean Besson and Janet Momsen (eds) *Land and Development in the Caribbean*, London: Macmillan.
—— (1993a) *Global Culture, Island Identity. Continuity and Change in the Afro-Caribbean Community of Nevis*, Reading: Harwood Academic Publishers.
—— (1993b) "Between Tradition and Modernity: National Development in the Caribbean," *Social Analysis* 33: 89–104.
—— (1993c) "Defining the National in the Transnational: Cultural Identity in the Afro-Caribbean Diaspora," *Ethnos* 58, 3–4: 361–76.
—— (1993d) "The Migration Experience: Nevisian Women at Home and Abroad," in Janet H. Momsen (ed.) *Women and Change in the Caribbean*, London: James Currey, pp. 150–66.
—— (1995a) "African Cultural Principles in Caribbean Slave Societies: A View from the Danish West Indies," in Stephan Palmié (ed.) *Slave Cultures and the Cultures of Slavery*, Knoxville: The University of Tennessee Press.
Olwig, Karen Fog (ed.) (1995b) *Small Islands, Large Questions: Society, Culture and Resistance in the Post-Emancipation Caribbean*, London: Frank Cass.
Pares, Richard (1950) *A West-India Fortune*, London: Longman.
Richardson, Bonham (1983) *Caribbean Migrants: Environment and Social Survival on St. Kitts and Nevis*, Knoxville: University of Tennessee Press.
Rosaldo, Renato (1988) "Ideology, Place and People without Culture," *Cultural Anthropology* 3, 1: 77–87.
Thomas-Hope, Elizabeth (1978) "The Establishment of a Migration Tradition: British West Indian Movements to the Hispanic Caribbean in the Century after Emancipation," in Colin G. Clarke (ed.) *Caribbean Social Relations*, Liverpool: Centre for Latin American Studies, Monograph Series no. 8.
—— (1992) *Explanation in Caribbean Migration*, Warwick University Caribbean Studies. London: Macmillan Press.
Turner, Victor (1989) [1967] *The Forest of Symbols*, Ithaca: Cornell University Press.
—— (1977) [1969] *The Ritual Process. Structure and Anti-Structure*, Ithaca: Cornell University Press.
Webster's Seventh New Collegiate Dictionary (1965) Springfield, Mass.: G. C. Merriam Company.

Archival records

Leeward Islands Blue Book (1923) Nevis Archives at Alexander Hamilton Museum, Charlestown, Nevis.
Nevis Blue Book (1876) Nevis Archives at Alexander Hamilton Museum, Charlestown, Nevis.
Record of Nevis Wills (1880–) vol. 1–B, Court House, Charlestown, Nevis, Registrar's Office.

2 Imagining a place in the Andes

In the borderland of lived, invented, and analyzed culture

Karsten Pærregaard

The growing body of studies concerning deterritorialized cultures and identities has had certain methodological implications for anthropological knowledge and research practice.[1] The aim of this chapter is to discuss some of these. Indeed, our notion of culture has shifted from that of a distinct lifestyle practiced by a territorially bounded group of people to a compound design of different forms of lives lived by people in separate worlds, which raises questions concerning not only our use of the concepts of place, community, and identity but also our understanding of people's own use of them (Sahlins 1993; Turner 1993). When studying migrants, exiles, refugees, and diasporic communities (Ferguson 1992; Safran 1991; Rouse 1991; Clifford 1994; Malkki 1992; Hall 1990) anthropologists must contemplate a variety of perspectives on culture and identity and examine not only how these interact with each other but also how they relate to the ethnographic representation. By applying a multiperspective approach, the anthropologist discovers that the view from afar is taken by many different actors, making it difficult to define precisely what anthropological knowledge is.[2] Accordingly, the rethinking of our notions of culture and space also implies a revision of what we perceive as the authority to practice ethnography, of who we consider to be the designers and the innovators of culture, and of how we define the difference between culture as a lived life, an invented construct, and an analyzed object.

The study of culture as a fabricated device has been addressed by anthropologists in different ways. Some examine cultural inventiveness within a historical and national context, while others address the theoretical and conceptual implications that the new view on culture has for anthropological knowledge. Hobsbawm and Ranger (1984) examine the invention of tradition as a social practice in societies undergoing change. They conclude that by establishing continuity with a suitable historic past, the invention of tradition structures parts of social life in the modern world as unchanging and invariant (Hobsbawm 1984).

Wagner (1981) discusses the inventive creativity embedded in culture and examines invention as a cultural practice on a par with the theoretical practice undertaken by the anthropologist. He argues that the anthropological project, itself an inventive practice, transforms indigenous creativity into "our opera-house Culture" by which he refers to the anthropologist´s own cultural creativity (Wagner 1981: 144) and concludes that "invention, then, *is* culture" (ibid.: 35) and that every human being is an "anthropologist" (ibid.: 36). While Wagner conceives of culture as an invention engineered by the anthropologist as well as the people being studied, Hastrup (1990: 47) defines culture as an analytical implication and suggests that the experiential counterpart of this implicational construct invented by the anthropologist is the lived space experienced by the people being studied. To Hastrup, this makes the anthropologist his own informant, and rather than following Wagner's invitation to include people's inventive creativity in anthropology's theoretical practice she calls for a differentiation between the native "implicit" knowledge and the anthropological "explicit" understanding of culture (Hastrup 1993: 175).

The distinction between an "implicit" and an "explicit" perspective, however, is blurred by the fact that the people we study increasingly act as "outsiders" as well as "insiders" (Clifford 1992: 99–100; Rodman 1992: 645–6). In the modern world, the crossing of national and cultural boundaries is no longer a privilege reserved for the anthropologist. As argued by Clifford recently, "the notion that certain classes of people are cosmopolitans (travelers) while the rest are local (natives) appears as the ideology of one (very powerful) traveling culture" (Clifford 1992: 108). We often share experiences and positions with the people we study, which sometimes make our perspectives converge (Maynard 1993; Lavie *et al.* 1993: 6). Yet our study of them and their awareness of their own culture are two different projects. Indigenous peoples and ethnic groups attempt to use culture as a device to change social identity and achieve political ends. Sahlins describes this development as: "a more or less self-conscious fabrication of culture in response to imperious outside 'pressure'" (Sahlins 1993: 16). He adds that rather than overthrowing the World System, "the local people's inventions and inversions of tradition can be understood as attempts to create a differentiated cultural space within it" (ibid.: 20). Thus, culture is more than just a theoretical construction forged by the anthropologist; it is the outcome of an inventional practice geared to accomplish purposes beyond the anthropological agenda (Turner 1993: 423–4).

In the following I shall discuss the relation between lived, invented, and analyzed culture through an examination of how migrants in Peru's major cities construct a sense of belonging by creating images of their native Andean village. Precisely how such forms of inventive practices affect those still living in the village is also analyzed; and likewise, how the attachment to a place of origin helps migrants to cope with problems of social and cultural adaptation to city life and to deal with the double life they lead as rural Indians and urban migrants. Yet another area of inquiry is how the images that migrants hold of their native village lead to different strategies for intervention in village life, and in some cases return migration. Finally, migrants' images are examined in terms of such concepts as the invention of tradition and cultural creativity, as are similarities and differences between migrants' and anthropologists' inventive and creative practices.

The discussion of cultural deterritorialization and the question of anthropology's implicit distinction between internal and external perspectives require that the category of migrant be addressed with caution. In contrast to the classical notion of migrants as acculturated individuals severed from their native village or homeland, and stripped of social identity, I shall refer to migration as a potential state of being which any subject in my study may pass through during his or her lifetime. This allows me to look at migrants as cultural innovators and designers of new identities, and to include their lifestyle and world view in my study of Andean culture. To avoid the insider/outsider dichotomy and to reach beyond the migrant/villager opposition I shall differentiate the subjects of my study according to the degree of attachment to the native village, rather than actual residence or current location. In his study of mine workers in Zambia, Ferguson suggests a similar approach to identify different types of urban migrants. He proposes a continuum,

> from one extreme (which I call localist) in which the rural home village is conceived as a primary home to which the worker returns at intervals, to the other (which I call cosmopolitan) in which the worker (often better off) regards the "home" village as a far-away place, rarely if ever actually seen or visited, to which one is connected more by nostalgia and sentimental attachment than by social and economic ties or life trajectory.
>
> (Ferguson 1992: 81)

Unlike Ferguson, I shall include the residents of the home village in my continuum, which allows me to operate with a wider range of migrant categories. By drop-out migrants, I am referring to individuals who have left the village for good and who have no contact with their fellow villagers. Visiting migrants, on the other hand, are migrants who reside outside their native village but travel and spend time there at intervals. Finally, I have defined returning migrants as villagers who have returned to settle in the village after a longer period of time outside, and non-migrants as villagers with no previous migration experience.

The material discussed deals with four images held by Tapeño migrants of Tapay, their native village. The first refers to the nostalgia many migrants invest in their childhood in Tapay. The second is concerned with a desire some migrants have to contribute to the economic and material development of their village. The third grows out of an attempt by a small group of migrants belonging to some of Peru's expanding Lutheran movements to convert their Catholic native village into a Protestant haven. The fourth emerges from a need felt by many migrants to maintain their ethnic and cultural roots in Tapay, and to affirm their links to and position in the village. Common to the four images is that they express a strong concern for Tapay and a desire among the migrants to participate and intervene in village life and, ultimately, to return and settle there.

My argument is that the invention of a Tapeño culture and the creation of a Tapeño identity is the result of a complex process of negotiation between different forms of representations, and that the actors in this process are made up of villagers, migrants, the rest of the Peruvian society as well as by the anthropologist. Moreover, migrants' inventional practice represents an implicational counterpart to the life of the people living in the village as much as the anthropological project does. Migrants not only possess an intimate knowledge of native life (along with their fellow villagers), they are also involved (along with the anthropologist) in a continuous process of understanding and interpreting it and, ultimately, changing it. Finally, the study of culture implies an analysis of the interplay between a variety of representations, and the drawing of borderlines between lived, invented, and analyzed life entails the recognition of all social and theoretical actors as potential designers of culture.

TAPAY: A LIVED SPACE

Located in the bottom of the Colca valley in the *departamento* (department) of Arequipa, Tapay appears cut off from the world and Western civilization. Apart from a few minor development projects financed by private development agencies and the Peruvian government, and the presence of seven school teachers sent by the Ministry of Education, the village receives no economic support or technical or professional assistance from the outside. The only product sold for money by Tapeños is cochineal, and the only items procured with money are alcohol, coca leaves, cigarettes, rice and sugar, and such manufactured goods as washing powder, candles, kerosene, and clothes. Rather than engaging in commercial trade, the villagers prefer to exchange their agricultural and pastoral produce – mainly fruit, meat, and wool – for potatoes, *ch'uño* (freeze-dried potatoes), maize, cereals, and salt in the regional bartering system.

Quechua is the native language, and not all Tapeños understand and speak Spanish. The village of Tapay is characterized by various forms of endogamy: only 20 per cent of the adult population have married outsiders, and marriage between villagers from different hamlets and subunits of the village is uncommon. Between agriculturalists and herders it is practically nonexistent (Pærregaard 1992). The strong tendency towards endogamy partly explains the corporative nature of Tapay and the strong tradition for cooperation and reciprocity between Tapeños. The vast majority benefit from a wide network of consanguineal and affinal relationships from which they recruit *ayni* assistance, i.e. a labor exchange.

One-third of Tapay's population lives in the two principal hamlets. One, the capital of the district, is called Tapay and lies in Hanansaya. The other, Cosnihua, is located in Urinsaya and has the greatest concentration of inhabitants in the district. This distribution of the population in hamlets rather than in one major village, as is common in other Colca districts, accounts for the decentralized nature of Tapay's social and political organization. The principal authority of the district is the *alcalde* (mayor), elected every three years. A judge and a police representative are appointed by the regional office of the Ministry of Justice and Internal Affairs. Irrigation water is distributed locally by the users, with no interference from central authority inside or outside Tapay. Two so-called peasant communities (*comunidades campesinas*, an officially recognized institution in Peru) also exist in Tapay. The authority of the community leaders is limited to such internal affairs as organizing *faena* (labor corvée), settling land disputes, and directing government allocations. Aside from the mayor, then, no central political authority exists in Tapay.

The chief event in Tapay's ritual and religious calendar is the celebration of the Virgin of Candelaria in February. Celebrated in the Hanansaya moiety and organized by three to four persons known as *altareros*, the Candelaria formerly involved ritual battles between young men from the two moieties. These battles no longer take place. Instead, music and drinking, financed by two *altareros*, now constitute the main elements of the Candelaria. It has become an event of great importance to Tapeño migrants who return in large numbers to participate in the fiesta and visit family and friends. They organize two separate fiestas, one in Hanansaya and one in Urinsaya, competing to be the *altarero* to hold the biggest and most extravagant fiesta of all. In other words, migrants have transformed an Andean ritual into a Catholic fiesta exploited by visiting Tapeños to compete for social prestige.

A few Tapeños who oppose the Andean-Catholic religious universe shun Tapay's ritual celebrations. They belong to three different Protestant movements introduced by Tapeño migrants who have either returned and settled in the village or travel back and forth between Tapay and Peru's major cities. The main objective of these Protestants is to induce the Tapeños to give up drinking, to abolish all Andean-Catholic rituals, and to convert their fellow villagers and fellow migrants to Protestantism.

In sum, Tapay is a Quechua community characterized by bartering, endogamy, and Andean rituals. Furthermore, a system of water distribution organized locally by the users, along with a politically decentralized power structure implies a high degree of economic and political autonomy and physical isolation from the outside world.

PERU: A WORLD OUTSIDE TAPAY

Half of all those born in Tapay, i.e. Tapeños, live in Lima, Arequipa, and other towns on Peru's coast. Most of them left their native village at the age of 10 to 12 after finishing the first five years of elementary school.[3] Brought to the city by their parents, older siblings or other family members and cared for by relatives or fellow villagers, these Tapeño children grew up with a dual background as Quechua Indians and urban migrants. To the Tapeños, spending their youth in Lima or Arequipa is a *rite de passage*; i.e. an indispensable experience in how to cope with urban life and survive in the city. Here they learn to speak proper Spanish, make money, deal with bureaucrats and government institutions, and, most importantly, act like *criollos*, i.e. Peru's coastal population of Spanish ancestry.

Because of a long history of cultural prejudices and racial discrimination against Andean culture, the Tapeños, like other highland migrants, attempt to conceal their rural background and alter their social status. In the city they are considered *cholos*, i.e. people trying to imitate a Western and urban way of life despite their roots in Andean culture. *Cholo* is a term loaded with negative connotations and traditionally coined by the *criollo* population to classify and discriminate against Andean migrants. Tapeños do not, however, identify themselves as *cholos*. When asked to identity themselves they refer to their regional or geographical origin: *arequipeños* (from the department of Arequipa) or *caillominos* (from the province of Cailloma). To Tapeño migrants, *arequipeño* implies a recognition of their efforts to improve their social and ethnic status in Peruvian society, whereas *cholo* is a reminder of their cultural past as Quechua Indians. By migrating to the city they want to make themselves visible on the economic and political scene of Peru, gain access to public resources, and enjoy the civil rights which they feel are denied them as Andean Indians in Tapay, eventually achieving recognition as Peruvians.

Thus, Tapeños do not migrate out of economic necessity, lack of land or political conflict. Migration is neither seasonal nor temporary; rather, it is permanent and motivated by the Tapeños' desire to become members of Peru's *criollo* society; to cast off their social status as Quechua-speaking rural Indians and become Spanish-speaking urban Peruvians. But cultural adaptation does not imply that Tapeño migrants pull up their roots in Tapay and forget all about the past. On the contrary, it reinforces their sense of belonging and gives them a perspective of Tapay different from that of Tapeños living there. To migrants, Tapay is more than just a territorially and politically defined unit; it is the central point of reference from which they set themselves apart from millions of other Andean migrants in Lima or Arequipa. In the city, Tapay becomes associated with a particular set of historical, geographical, economic, and cultural features, making it possible to distinguish the village from all other villages in the Colca valley and the rest of the Andes. To migrants, Tapay is more than just a physical location; it is a place which provides them with a feeling of being different from all other *cholos*. Identifying themselves as Tapeños is what makes them feel anything but *cholos*.

TAPAY: AN IMAGINED PLACE

But what does it imply to feel Tapeño and what does Tapay represent to the migrants? And what do the migrants associate with their native village and how do they imagine village life? In other words, how is Tapay constructed as a place? In the following I shall discuss four images of Tapay which all play a dominant role in the relationship between migrants in Lima and Arequipa and villagers in Tapay.

The nostalgic image

Many migrants conceive of Tapay as a picturesque rural setting, untouched by civilization and isolated from the world. They create an illusion of a place unspoiled by moral decadence, industrial pollution, Western greed, and economic interests; an island in history where time stands still. They imagine Tapay as a place where life is still whole and authentic, i.e. no one questions the meaning of culture, and people still live as did their ancestors. Here, everyone cares for each other; the villagers are happy and honest, they are physically strong and healthy with a life expectancy far beyond the average in the city. Food produced in the village is "natural" and free of chemical additives, the water which villagers drink is "clean," and the air they breathe is "pure." Tapay's inhabitants know nothing of economic exploitation, social injustice, racial discrimination, or stress. Here, all are equal and no one is snubbed because of his/her cultural background. In short, life in Tapay is worlds apart from city life.

However, by picturing Tapay as a paradise unspoiled by the modern world, migrants not only generate an antagonism toward urban life as they experience it; they also reconstruct a memory from the past. Thus, many migrants who left their native village before coming of age associate Tapay with their own childhood and imagine rural life as a world free of the frustrations and social problems they face in their struggle to survive in Lima and Arequipa. And since many migrants have no contact with fellow villagers in the city and few possibilities of communicating with relatives in Tapay, their primary source of information and knowledge about the village is their childhood memories. More than half of all migrants in Arequipa and Lima have visited their native village, but few spend more than a couple of weeks there at a time. And as the occasions for these visits in many cases are Tapay's ritual events, the knowledge migrants have of village life is limited. What migrants associate with the village are the intense moments of reunion, joy, and amusement when the monotonous and isolated life of Tapay's hard-working population gives way to music, dance, and drinking. A nostalgic image of a carefree childhood is evoked by the *huallacha* (music played by small groups with guitar and harps), the *wititi* (music played by big bands with trumpets and drums), and the reunion with fellow villagers (who are getting drunk and speaking Quechua) at the Candelaria fiesta.

The rational image

While Tapay to some evokes nostalgia, others think of it as a poor and ignorant rural population living in a stone-age economy. They portray their native village as a God-forsaken place, out of touch with the modern world and in desperate need of economic and technological support from the outside. To these migrants, Tapay represents more of an economic and social problem of today than a cultural reminder of a benevolent past. To them, Tapay suffers from just about every kind of shortage: no running water, no electricity, no roads, no sanitary installations, no doctors, no shops, widespread illiteracy, lack of modern technology, etc. They do, however, consider Tapay's agricultural and pastoral production, its geographical location, its archaeological ruins, and its folklore as important potentials for future economic development. Migrants make use of different strategies to exploit Tapay's natural and human resources, contributing capital, know-how and planning expertise, and thus stimulating development in the village. Some want to improve fruit production through grafting by introducing new varieties of fruit. They see Tapay as a future supplier of fruit to Arequipa and other nearby markets. Others plan to expand the production of cochineal and exploit the increasing demand for natural dye on the world market. Their dream is to replace Tapay's bartering economy with a cash-crop economy. Others, again, want to turn Tapay into a tourist attraction. To them, Tapay's major problem is its lack of shops, restaurants, and hotels.

Some migrants, however, are less concerned with their own possibilities of taking advantage of Tapay's economic potential. They want to help improve the living standard of their fellow villagers. To them, it is Tapay's cultural backwardness and geographical isolation that hinder the population in looking for the economic support and technological assistance required to stimulate progress in the village. As Spanish-speaking city-dwellers, these migrants believe they can help Tapeños become integrated in the money economy and expand their ties to the state bureaucracy and international development organizations operating in the area. Some of them make personal contributions to the village; one migrant gave the local authorities a public address system to communicate with the villagers while another donated money to buy concrete for the construction of irrigation canals. Others organize communal collections among fellow migrants in Lima and Arequipa to maintain and repair paths and bridges connecting Tapay with other Colca villages and the rest of Peru. Others, again, help Tapay's political leaders make official requests to regional authorities, government ministries, and the private development agencies.

The moral image

A small group of migrants are Lutherans. They have been recruited by the fast-growing number of Protestant denominations in Peru's capital and provincial cities. Some are members of the Pentecostal movement, some belong to the Assembly of God, others are Jehovah's Witnesses and yet others are Mormons or Methodists. Consequently, Protestant migrants make up a very heterogeneous group. While some are drop-out migrants with little contact with other Tapeños in the city and Tapay, others are visiting or returning migrants who show a great interest in introducing Protestantism in their native village and converting their fellow villagers. Unlike the nostalgic image, which focuses on Tapay's benevolent past, and the rational image, which stresses its miserable present, these Protestants are primarily concerned with the future salvation of their native village (Pærregaard 1994b). To them, the Catholic majority lives in sin and disgrace and can only expect salvation through conversion to Protestantism. What they find most disgraceful about moral life in Tapay is the worship of Catholic saints and Andean deities, and the villagers' considerable consumption of alcohol. They call for a new social order in Tapay and believe that if they set a good example of discipline, hard work, personal responsibility, initiative, sexual morality, and abstinence from alcohol, the Catholics will eventually convert. And although the Protestants share many of the views of other migrants in their critique of village life, their means and motives for introducing changes in Tapay differ radically from these. In their eyes, improving the living standard, stimulating economic development, and electing a new leadership in Tapay are merely the means to accomplish their goal: to compel the Catholics to convert and achieve moral salvation – an objective which, not surprisingly, causes much strife among Tapeños in Tapay as well as in Lima and Arequipa.

But Protestants are also at odds amongst themselves. They differ in their ideas about how to convert the Catholics. A small group of religious apostates a mere ten years ago, Tapay's Protestant movement is represented today by three competing denominations. The first, established by a young returning migrant who had converted to Protestantism while working in a coastal town in southern Peru, tries to influence the Catholic majority by gaining control of Tapay's political institutions and setting a good example by not partaking in fiestas and rituals. The second movement, led by another returned migrant who converted to Protestantism after returning to Tapay, believes that in order to gain the confidence of the Catholics and convert them, it is necessary to participate in their ceremonial activities and accept their drinking customs. The third denomination was introduced by a migrant who converted while living in Lima. He still lives there but frequently travels to Tapay to supervise his followers and recruit new members. This movement rejects the methods used by Tapay's two other Protestant denominations. It seeks confrontation with the Catholic majority at every opportunity and aims to abolish all traditions and institutions within the established order.

The division and strife between Tapay's Protestants is further deepened by the fact that the followers of the first two movements are largely made up of returning migrants while the third recruits its members among the non-migrant villagers who are in opposition to the returning migrant population. This explains why Tapay's Protestant movements fight each other as bitterly as they oppose the Catholic majority. Thus, Protestantism is not only an instrument whereby migrants construct images of their native village, it is also the cause of internal division and conflict among migrants living outside Tapay, returning migrants, and the non-migrant population.

The ethnic image

Migrants are increasingly taking over Tapay's political and religious institutions. For more than a decade returning and visiting migrants have been elected or appointed to the principal political and administrative positions in the village (mayor, president of the irrigation committee, police representative, the justice of the peace, etc.). And in the local elections in 1993, a visiting migrant who for the last thirty years has lived with his family in Arequipa while making frequent but short visits to Tapay was elected as mayor – the highest authority in the village. During the same period the positions of *mayordomo*, *devoto*, and *altarero*, i.e. the persons responsible for the organization and celebration of Tapay's fiestas, have mainly been occupied by visiting migrants who come to Tapay to participate in the village's ritual events. In many respects, the migrants' dedication to their native village is nourished by a nostalgic memory of a rural childhood and derives from a conceptualization of village life as backward and underdeveloped. Yet unlike the nostalgic and the rational image, the ethnic image is spurred by migrants' desire to affirm economic rights, accumulate social prestige, and achieve political influence in the village either to legitimize their current presence in Tapay or to provide them with the possibilities of returning in the future.[4]

These migrants conceive of themselves as absentee villagers with a special right as well as obligation to participate and intervene in village affairs. Making their impact on village life confirms their attachment to Tapay and gives them a sense of being a true Tapeño. More important, however, is that the taking over of the village's political and religious institutions allows the migrants to challenge the notion Peruvian society has of them as marginal and anonymous urban migrants. As village leaders or organizers of the village's fiestas, visiting and returning migrants not only affirm their rural roots but also question their own status as *cholos*. Holding the office of mayor, *mayordomo*, or *altarero* in their native village provides them with a sense of being different from other Andean migrants and helps them cope with social injustice and ethnic discrimination in the urban environments of Lima, Arequipa, and other Peruvian cities. Accordingly, by participating in village life, migrants evoke an image of themselves as absentee villagers, and at the same time they redefine their urban status as anonymous *cholos* who have no roots.

CULTURAL IMAGES AT WORK

It would be wrong to construe migrants' images of their native village as static or exclusive. Rather, the conceptions of Tapay tend to vary depending on the migrants' economic and social situation in the city and on the bonds that tie them to the village. The nostalgic image is particularly popular among potential returning migrants who are discontented with their economic situation in the city but who have no immediate plans of returning to Tapay. To them, the village represents an Andean haven far away from the city and the *criollo* world. The rational image, on the other hand, is generally held by drop-out migrants, particularly those who no longer have relatives in the village. They often think of their native village in terms of the physical efforts it requires to get there and associate Tapay with poverty and backwardness.[5] In turn, visiting migrants who are well-off and can afford to travel more often to the village tend to envision Tapay in terms of the rational or the ethnic image. They find it difficult to spend longer periods of time there because of commitments to family and work in the city, and are mostly concerned with the personal prestige they can achieve from volunteering for Tapay's religious cargo posts. In contrast to the visiting and the drop-out migrants, returning migrants or migrants who live in the city but search for a motive or a pretext to go back and settle in the village primarily think of Tapay in terms of the moral image or the ethnic image. Their major concern is to be elected as leaders of the village's political institutions and to introduce economic, social, and religious changes in the village.

Many migrants, however, do not envision their native village in terms of one but of several images, depending on their location and the social context. This becomes evident by observing visiting migrants traveling back and forth between the city and Tapay. Urban migrants who view the village as underdeveloped and primitive are often the most frequent visitors at Tapay's Candelaria fiesta. Although many cannot take the time to volunteer for the Candelaria fiesta, they enjoy assuming a nostalgic stance for a few days of dancing, drinking, and music. Although the fiesta is held in February, when the rains often create tremendous inconveniences for travelers, many visiting migrants bring along their whole family, including small children and babies. The trip takes the form of a pilgrimage during which the migrant often spends more time traveling between Tapay and the city than actually visiting the village.[6] An important aspect of this pilgrimage is the merging of the rational and the nostalgic image during the journey from Lima or Arequipa to Tapay. When the bus finally arrives at Cabanaconde, the neighboring village from which the traveler starts the strenuous trip on foot to the final destination, Tapay suddenly appears at a distance on the other side of the deep Colca canyon as an isolated and remote settlement recalling not only nostalgic memories of a past childhood but also the sufferings originating from primitive and archaic peasant life. Once back in Tapay, however, the migrants forget everything about the outside world and the troubles they have gone through. During the four days the Candelaria lasts, nostalgia takes over.

Concerned with the personal prestige and the economic expenditures involved in organizing the Candelaria, the *altareros*, however, rarely let themselves get carried away by nostalgia. Rather than evoking romantic sentiments about rural life, the Candelaria makes the fiesta organizers think of their self-image and social status. Since many *altareros* belong to the more affluent Tapeños in the city, they find the idea of returning to Tapay only somewhat appealing. Their vision of Tapay is primarily rational, and their interest in the village and the *altarero* office is driven by a desire to demonstrate the economic success they have had as migrants in the city. In 1993, a Tapeño woman living in Arequipa volunteered as *altarera*, spending almost US $8,000 on the fiesta. Her trip to Tapay that year was the first she had made for more than two decades. This woman, who makes her money running *contrabando*, i.e. smuggling goods from Bolivia or Chile into Peru, explained to me that volunteering as *altarera* had been a wish of hers for many years. That same year, a male migrant held another Candelaria fiesta in Lima.[7] The man, who sells fruit juice together with his wife at a local market in downtown Lima, spent more than US $3,000 celebrating the event. A band was hired from a Colca village and had come all the way to Lima for the sole purpose of playing at this fiesta, which proved that the *altarero* had made a great effort to create an authentic Tapeño atmosphere in the city. However, this man, who has not been back to his native village for over ten years, shows little interest in visiting Tapay himself. For him, as for his *altarera* counterpart in Tapay that year, the self-image and the ethnic image were of greater concern than the nostalgic image.

Other migrants who either live in Tapay or plan to go back in the near future negotiate and manipulate different images to achieve political or ideological ends. This is the case with the leaders of Tapay's Protestant denominations, who on several occasions have succeeded in being elected to important political or administrative offices in the village.[8] When promoting their candidature these religious crusaders are adept in combining and, if necessary, reconciling moral, rational, and nostalgic images. In the local elections in 1989, two Protestants were elected as mayor and vice-mayor respectively for the first time in the history of Tapay. In spite of religious differences, many Catholic voters supported the Protestants because their electoral campaign focused on economic development in the village rather than on spiritual salvation.

Once in office, however, the new mayor soon found himself constrained, on the one hand, by the vice-mayor and other Protestants who saw his election as an opportunity to promote an overall conversion of the village population and, on the other hand, by the Catholic majority who tried to pin him to his campaign pledges. As a result, one year before his term of office expired the mayor converted back to Catholicism, causing much frustration within the Protestant community. In 1993 the newly reconverted mayor ran for re-election. Now a Catholic, he promised to revive traditional Tapeño values and customs and to convert the remote and exotic village into a tourist site. The Protestant vice-mayor, on the other hand, who had been angered by what he considered the betrayal of his former religious *hermano* (brother) and political partner, joined the campaign of the mayor's main opponent, a former military officer currently living in Arequipa. In contrast to the incumbent mayor, they based their electoral campaign on the promise of constructing a new road to the village. This left the villagers with a choice between nostalgic tourism and a rational development. Eventually, they chose the latter.

Other images of Tapay are also at play among drop-out and visiting migrants in Lima and Arequipa. One female migrant explains that her native village has been invaded and is now controlled by the Protestants. As a faithful Catholic, she feels a strong commitment to go back, throw them out, and help re-establish what she considers traditional order. Unlike the four images discussed above, however, this counter-image has not compelled anyone to go back and settle or orchestrated an encounter between an imagined place and a lived space. In contrast, the nostalgic, the rational, the moral, and the ethnic images all result in visits and attempts to return to Tapay with the aim of accumulating personal prestige, introducing economic change, converting the Catholics, or running for political office. These images demonstrate the complexity of cultural invention in a situation of deterritorialization and migration, elucidating how migrants' sense of belonging stimulates innovation, encourages intervention, and leads to conflict.

My material suggests that life in Tapay is indeed influenced by the images that migrants hold of their native village.[9] Migrants have taken over the village's political and ritual institutions and used these to introduce economic, social, and religious change. And due to the migrants who return to Tapay to take part in the increasing cochineal trade, money has become a popular means of exchange at the cost of bartering. For Tapay's non-migrant population, however, these changes in the economic, political, and religious institutions have few implications for everyday life. Just as Tapeños in Lima and Arequipa have to cope with living a double life as rural Indians and urban migrants, Tapay's villagers experience a gap between the life they live as members of a community dominated by visiting and returning migrants and their lives as members of a household and of local networks of relatives and neighbors. Thus, when migrants return to Tapay in February to celebrate the Candelaria fiesta, city life as well as village life is temporarily interrupted. Nostalgia, drinking, and dancing provide both villagers and migrants with a sense of living in an imagined place and make them forget the life they live in lived space, i.e. as hard-working peasants in Tapay or persecuted *cholos* in the city.

CONCLUSION

If migrants' images of their native community generate a split in village life and leave rural Tapeños victimized by deterritorialization along with their fellow villagers in Lima and Arequipa, the imagining of Tapay as a place also provides Tapeños with a space to invent new cultural constructs and redefine their social and ethnic status. Thomas (1992) argues that the invention of tradition is often accompanied by a reactive process implying an inversion of tradition. He insists that "self-representation never takes place in isolation" and that it is "frequently oppositional and reactive: the idea of a community cannot exist in the absence of some externality or difference, and identities and traditions are often not simply different from but constituted in opposition to others" (Thomas 1992: 213). In other words, notions of place, culture, and identity are constructed in an oppositional process where acts of inversion accompany acts of invention.

I argue, along with Thomas, that migrants' images of Tapay are constituted in response to native conceptualizations of village life, and that migrants' searches for new identities emerge as a reaction to the racial and cultural prejudices they experience in the city. Similar forms of opposition exist between the nostalgic image of Tapay as an island out of touch with modern civilization and the rational image of the village as underdeveloped and backward; or between the image of rural life as healthy and happy and that of a corrupted and sinful existence. The Tapeño woman in Lima who plans to purge the Protestant rebellions and restore social order in her native village, and the migrants who associate Tapay with all the sufferings they have gone through since leaving the village, are other examples of just how the dynamic and oppositional relations between different forms of representation of culture really work. Non-migrant villagers, visiting migrants, returning migrants as well as the rest of Peruvian society are all actors in this process of inventing and inverting culture and creating new identities.

The objectification and reification of Tapeño culture and identity does not, however, emerge from oppositional processes of invention and inversion between an "outside" and "inside" perspective as suggested by Thomas. Rather, it grows out of an interplay between perspectives represented by different actors who may appear as "insiders" as well as "outsiders." No core of authenticity exists in this process of negotiation between visiting migrants, returning migrants, villagers, and other actors making claims of representing Tapeño culture. To the anthropologist, this means that rather than excavating layers of native interpretations in the way Geertz refers to, studying culture implies bringing together different forms of representation of experienced and lived life and explaining the dynamic and oppositional relationship between such constructions. More than just a construct invented to provide a feeling of continuity in a changing world, or an analytical design fashioned by the anthropologist, the imagining of Tapay as a place, and its identification with Tapeño culture is, in the words of Sahlins, "a more or less self-conscious fabrication of culture." Tapeño migrants develop their inventive practices in a context of deterritorialization and transcultural migration and in response to a racial and cultural discrimination urging Andean migrants to change their social and ethnic status.

By examining the encounter between imagined place and lived space I have tried to demonstrate how cultural creativity and invention come into play in a deterritorialized culture. In the urban environment, migrants create new individual livelihoods and establish different forms of communal life. A strong sense of attachment to the native village, however, persists among most migrants, evoking different notions and images of rural life. Accordingly, the distinction between the inside native vista and an outside anthropological vista is blurred. Like the anthropologist and other deterritorialized actors, migrants offer a perspective different from what anthropology traditionally has studied as the native or local point of view. In terms of the ethnographic report, this means that besides the lived life there is also an invented life to be considered. Such an account must deal with the different kinds of experience embodied in the lived, invented as well as analyzed perspectives. It must examine how these forms of experience are transformed into cultural imagination, inventional creativity, and, ultimately, anthropological knowledge. Only by exploring the wider context within which this knowledge is constituted, and by understanding the meaning attributed to it and the way it is used by social as well as theoretical actors, can we hope to know how culture works in a deterritorialized world.

Just as outside and inside perspectives intertwine, so too do the borderlines between analyzed, invented, and lived culture begin to fade. Yet a major difference still exists as to the strategical means and political ends of the anthropological project and the different "native" projects. Whereas migrants, refugees, diasporic communities, and other exiled people in different parts of the world are increasingly engaged in the imagining of native homelands, the invention or inversion of culture, the creation of new identities, and the revision of social and ethnic status, a growing body of anthropological studies of deterritorialization and transcultural migration is trying to deconstruct and deterritorialize the concepts of community and place, and attempting to account for the historical and political processes which constructed and empowered them. However, in this encounter between a constructing/territorializing perspective and a deconstructing/deterritorializing perspective, what eventually sets the anthropologist apart from the "native" is not our understanding of how cultural images and concepts are engendered and deployed in shifting social and cultural contexts. Rather, what produces anthropological knowledge is our understanding of how different forms of inventive and analytical practices mutually condition each other, and yet differ because of distinct commitments and devotions to those who not only invent and analyze culture but also live it.

ACKNOWLEDGMENTS

My field research was done in Tapay in 1986 and among Tapeño migrants in Lima and Arequipa in 1989–91 and in 1993 thanks to grants from the Danish Research Council for the Humanities and the Social Sciences, Danida (Danish International Development Agency), the University of Copenhagen, and the Carlsberg Foundation. While conducting field work I was associated with the Catholic University of Peru in Lima as a guest researcher. I'm indebted to Karen Fog Olwig for her encouraging comments.

NOTES

1 See Appadurai (1991), Basch, Schiller and Blanc (1994), Clifford (1992), Gupta and Ferguson (1992), Rodman (1992) and Rutherford (1990).

2 In her discussion of place as a social as well as an anthropological construct, Rodman (1992) suggests a similar approach. She introduces the concepts of multilocality and multivocality in order to study how a lived space is transformed into an imagined place.

3 The effect of such an extensive migration can be observed when examining the age distribution of Tapay's population. Thus, 67 percent of the village's 983 inhabitants are under 17 or over 50 years of age; see Pærregaard n.d.

4 Although the dream of retiring among relatives and fellow villagers in one's native village is strong among migrants in Lima as well as Arequipa only a few succeed in doing so.

5 Other drop-out migrants whose efforts to adapt to urban life have borne fruit turn their back on Tapay. They feel no need to recall or revive their cultural past as rural Indians and try to ignore their Andean roots.
6 Migrants often recall the physical efforts of traveling to Tapay and the sufferings they went through rather than the days they spent in the village. Paradoxically, the visits that migrants remember best were the trips which failed to bring them to Tapay because of rain, bad roads or buses which broke down.
7 For the last ten years, migrants in Lima have celebrated the Candelaria two weeks later than the village fiesta, which is held February 2–4. To many less affluent migrants who seldom travel to their native village, this represents an opportunity to experience a touch of Tapeño fiesta in a city. On the other hand, in Arequipa, only eight hours' bus ride from Cabanaconde, which is Tapay's neighboring village, no such celebration is organized.
8 For several years the Protestants have dominated the political arena in Tapay. One evangelista was elected mayor of Tapay, another appointed as police representative, and yet another as president of Tapay's peasant communinity; see Pærregaard 1994b.
9 Migrants are not the only actors to create images of an Andean world. For several decades anthropologists studying in the Andes have produced ethnographic accounts of a timeless society disassociated from the rest of the world (Mayer 1991; Silverblatt 1987: xxv; Starn 1991, 1994).

REFERENCES

Appadurai, Arjun (1991) "Global Ethnoscapes: Notes and Queries for a Transnational Anthropology," in Richard Fox (ed.) *Recapturing Anthropology: Working in the Present*, Santa Fe: School of American Research Press.

Clifford, James (1992) "Traveling Cultures," in Lawrence Grossberg, Cary Nelson and Paula Treichler (eds) *Cultural Studies*, New York: Routledge.

—— (1994) "Diasporas," *Cultural Anthropology* 9, 3: 302–38.

Basch, Linda, Nina Glick Schiller and Cristina Blanc-Szanton (1994) *Nations Unbound. Transnational Projects, Postcolonial Predicaments, and Deterritorialized Nation-States*, Langhorne, Pennsylvania: Gordon & Breach Drive.

Ferguson, James (1992) "The Country and the City in the Copperbelt," *Cultural Anthropology* 7, 1: 80–92.

Gupta, Akhil and James Ferguson (1992) "Beyond 'Culture': Space, Identity, and the Politics of Difference," *Cultural Anthropology* 7, 1: 6–23.

Hall, Stewart (1990) "Cultural Identity and Diaspora," in Jonathan Rutherford (ed.) *Identity. Community, Culture, Difference*, London: Lawrence & Wishart.

Hastrup, Kirsten (1990) "The Ethnographic Present: A Reinvention," *Cultural Anthropology* 5, 1: 45–61.

—— (1993) "The Native Voice – and the Anthropological Vision," *Social Anthropology* 1, 2: 173–86.

Hobsbawm, Eric (1984) "Introduction: Inventing Traditions," in Eric Hobsbawm and Terence Ranger (eds) *The Invention of Tradition*, Cambridge: Cambridge University Press.

Hobsbawm, Eric and Terence Ranger (eds) (1984) *The Invention of Tradition*, Cambridge: Cambridge University Press.

Lavie, Smadar, Kirin Narayan and Renato Rosaldo (eds) (1993) *Creativity/Anthropology*, Ithaca: Cornell University Press.

Malkki, Liisa (1992) "National Geographic: The Rooting of Peoples and the Territorialization of National Identity among Scholars and Refugees," *Cultural Anthropology* 7, 1: 24–44.

Mayer, Enrique (1991) "Peru in Deep Trouble: Mario Vargas Llosa's 'Inquest in the Andes' Reexamined," *Cultural Anthropology* 6, 4: 466–503.

Maynard, Kent (1993) "Protestant Theories and Anthropological Knowledge: Convergent Models in the Ecuadorian Sierra," *Cultural Anthropology* 8, 2: 246–67.

Pærregaard, Karsten (1992) "Complementarity and Duality: Oppositions between Agriculturalists and Herders in an Andean Village," *Ethnology* 31, 1: 15–26.

—— (1994a) "Why fight over Water? Conflict and Irrigation in an Andean Village," in William Mitchell and David Guillet (eds) *Irrigation at High Altitudes: The Social Organization of Water Control Systems in the Andes*, Washington: Society for Latin American Anthropology.

—— (1994b) "Migration, Conversion, and Social Identity: The Spread of Protestantism in Peruvian Andes," *Ethnos* 59, 3–4.

—— (n.d.) "The Dark Side of the Moon: Conceptual and Methodological Problems of Studying Urban Migrants and their Native Village," Unpublished ms. University of Copenhagen.

Rodman, Margaret (1992) "Empowering Place: Multilocality and Multivocality," *American Anthropologist* 94, 3: 640–56.

Rouse, Roger (1991) "Mexican Migration and the Social Space," *Diaspora* 1, 1: 8–23.

Rutherford, Jonathan (1990) "A Place called Home: Identity and the Cultural Politics of Difference," in Jonathan Rutherford (ed.) *Identity. Community, Culture, Difference*, London: Lawrence & Wishart.

Safran, William (1991) "Diasporas in Modern Societies: Myths of Homeland and Return," *Diaspora* 1, 1: 83–99.

Sahlins, Marshall (1993) "Goodbye to Tristes Tropes: Ethnography in the Context of Modern World History," *The Journal of Modern History* 65, 1: 1–25.

Silverblatt, Irene (1987) *Moon, Sun and Witches. Gender Ideologies and Class in Inca and Colonial Peru*, Princeton: Princeton University Press.

Starn, Orin (1991) "Missing the Revolution: Anthropologists and the War in Peru," *Cultural Anthropology* 6, 1: 63–91.

—— (1994) "Rethinking the Politics of Anthropology: The Case of the Andes," *Current Anthropology* 35, 1: 13–26.

Thomas, Nicholas (1992) "The Inversion of Tradition," *American Ethnologist* 19, 2: 213–32.

Turner, Terence (1993) "Anthropology and Multiculturalism: What is Anthropology that Multiculturalists should be mindful of It?" *Cultural Anthropology* 8, 4: 411–29.

Wagner, Roy (1981) *The Invention of Culture*, Chicago: The University of Chicago Press.

3 Which world?

On the diffusion of Algerian raï to the West

Marc Schade-Poulsen

> Music has no frontiers. It belongs to the world. It belongs to the universe.
>
> (Khaled in *The Daily*, Bombay, 27 September 1992)

> It seems that raï is well estimated in Europe because it represents all that is bad in the Algerian culture.
>
> (*El Moudjahid*, Algeria, 14 June 1989)

> Raï arrives in the US, in some ways, as the latest rage to hit the World Music record bins, the result of a new post-modern global marketing strategy.
>
> (*Middle East Report*, March–April 1991)

INTRODUCTION

This chapter deals with raï music from Algeria. Since its emergence in the late 1970s, raï has spread throughout the world and stands today as an exponent of "World Music." The chapter traces a transnational process that has taken place in the 1980s: the diffusion of raï from the cabarets of Oran (the second largest city of Algeria) to the stereo racks in the West. It evokes the existence of different places and spaces for the consumption of raï. Furthermore, it advances a critical view of the notion of *World Music* and, as such, the notion of global ecumenes with which it is closely associated.

The idea for this chapter comes from the simple observation that one of the first topics to be brought up in discussions, papers, and seminars on local–global processes and cultural complexity is commonly that of music (cf. Appadurai 1990; Hannerz 1989; Patterson 1994). It is seemingly one of the "things" in the world that most easily "flows," becomes "creolized," "syncretized," "heterogenized," etc.

But although studies of Third World music have established that there is no such thing as culturally "pure sound," and that *each* musical genre has its own internal musical structure, its particular musical technology, its own performative context, social environment, contexts of discourse and power, etc. (cf. Hebdige 1979; Malm and Wallis 1984, 1992; Manuel 1988; Nettl 1985; Waterman 1990), few studies have integrated more than a few of these elements in descriptions of "cut 'n' mixes" in musical flows.

The tendency to view music as being particularly flexible in terms of "flow" has an important parallel in spheres of music production. Many musicians seem to adhere to the idea that music flows freely in the world, and in that way sets an example for humanity to follow. The idea of the musical global ecumene has been promoted in the enormous Band Aid rock music charity concerts for Africa that took place in the mid-1980s, presenting "Chanteurs sans frontières" or pop stars proclaiming "We are the world!" (cf. Rijven and Straw 1989). Today it is alive among commentators on *World Music*, *World Beat*, *Musiques du Monde*, *Wereldmuziek*, and *Verdensmusik*. Iain Chambers's claim that the musics of the world "offer a space for musical and cultural differences to emerge in such a manner that any obvious identification with the hegemonic order, or assumed monolithic market logic, is weakened" (Chambers 1992: 141) is only one example of this trend.

The term World Music itself was created by the record industry in the latter part of the 1980s when it became clear that considerable quantities of records were being sold, often with names the public found impossible to pronounce, and moreover were often misfiled (Fairley 1989: 10; Malm and Wallis 1992: 215). This category encompasses popular music of the Third World, but also music of migrant communities, Eastern European music and the Third World fine art and folk art traditions. It operates on blurred boundaries bordering on musical products of such top names as Paul Simon, Peter Gabriel, Talking Heads, plus certain avant-garde jazz and New Age products that have integrated a number of elements from Third World music; however, it does not seem to include such musical styles as reggae, which has had enough commercial success in the West to earn a label of its own, and it certainly does not encompass the range of music products produced in the West for a Western mass audience. As such, the link between World Music and notions of a global, liberating musical ecumene is in itself problematic.

One method of situating the status of music in a world of increased interconnectedness is to begin with Hannerz's definition of cultural flows and Appadurai's notion of "the social life of things." The former understands flows as "the externalizations of meaning which individuals produce through arrangements of overt forms and the interpretations which individuals make of such displays" (Hannerz 1992: 4). The latter insists that "from a *theoretical* point of view, human actors encode things with significance; from a *methodological* point of view, it is the things-in-motion that illuminate their human and social context" (Appadurai 1988: 5). Both thus explain how the flows or things-in-motion cannot be accounted for without the contexts of production and consumption, and that it is precisely a focus on flows that illuminates the existence of specific sites in the global arena.

The idea of this chapter is thus to follow the flow of raï from its emergence to its apparent integration into the "World" category in the West, focusing on raï as a thing, a cultural commodity. And as such it will be borne in mind that musical commodities, once they become "objects of pure desire or immediate enjoyment" (Appadurai 1988: 3), i.e. once they are purchased, may indeed succeed in establishing a communicative relation to the consumer in which images, social scenes, and moods are produced.

Music can be seen as sounding forms in motion (Langer 1953: 107), structuring time by means of rhythm. As such, it not only involves the (e)motion of the body (Langer 1953: 126–9), it also enables the listener to move in time (evoking memories and sceneries). And in terms of songs, it enables the listener to be *in time* with the singer (sometimes dancing with the singer) and, by extension, with the images proposed by the performance embedded in the commodity. In this way, an imagined relationship between the listener and the singer can be created (cf. Hennion 1983, 1990). It is a relationship which can work through an identification with the "grain" of the singer's voice, i.e. the socio-cultural body of the voice as it sings a textual expression (Barthes 1987: 188; Frith 1983: 14).

In the description of the flow of raï, it will, moreover, be borne in mind that "music does not have selves, people do" (Waterman 1990: 6), and that "the surface bootlessness of talking about art seems matched by a deep necessity to talk about it endlessly" (Geertz 1983). When unfamiliar things appear, they must be talked about and given value. In the following I shall carefully trace how raï has been put into words in Algeria and the West, and how a narrative has been created, valorizing raï in a way that has been a prerequisite for its transfer to the West.

In sum, I shall follow the process by which raï was freed from its original place of performance in Algeria, and was subsequently materialized on mass-produced cassette tapes. From there, it was transferred into a space for written discourse, the press. Here, a biography of raï was established which, along with stage concerts, introduced raï to the Western media, the gatekeepers of popular music (cf. Hennion 1983; Hirsch 1991), and thus to a Western audience.[1] Basically, it is a story of raï rising from a position of transient value in Algeria (cf. Thompson 1979) to a potential position as a durable commodity, an art product, in the West. The point of the story is not that raï has been adopted in a number of contexts, but how it has been culturally redefined and put to use (cf. Kopytoff 1988: 67).

ON THE PRODUCTION OF RAÏ[2]

The basic form of raï comes from a performative context – weddings, cabarets, etc. – in which the singers, on the basis of an ongoing dance rhythm, choose a catchy key phrase to which they repeatedly return. They have a range of standard phrases or formulas at hand to keep the movement going during the course of the song; but they sometimes improvise by entering into a dialogue with the audience. They comment on those present, they flatter them or make dedications – the whole idea being to touch people, which of course is at the center of all professional musical entertainment. This can subsequently prompt the listeners to donate a banknote to the orchestra. These consumers, for their part, use the singers – by means of money – as a medium for competitive games, or for making dedications to people present among the audience, accompanied by a favorite song.

This performative context has a long history in Algeria, but the actual breakthrough of raï came in the late 1970s in western Algeria. It started in the cabarets of Oran with a new generation of singers, the sons of workers, craftsmen, etc., most of them with no high school degree, originating from Oran's densely populated districts. They borrowed part of their verbal stock from the repertoire of an older performative context, e.g. that of *shikhâs*, female singers and male entertainers at weddings, in brothels or at *basTas* (pleasure parties). The cabarets are a continuation of these male pleasure parties with "free women" and constitute social spheres in which boundaries between gender roles tend to be altered – women display such traditionally male behavior as drinking and smoking; men express a public pleasure for the opposite sex that is not displayed elsewhere (cf. Schade-Poulsen 1993b).

A number of song lines from this period, sung in the local dialect, dealt quite openly with men's relationship to – and problems with – "free women" and the consumption of food, alcohol, and sexual services at such parties. Other lines ventured into descriptions of the problems of crime and alcohol abuse – and often invoking the name of God – bemoaning that the "milieu" leads men away from the proper path in life.

It was these themes that were brought into the recording studios by producers who had noted their success in the cabarets; and in the years to come, a business developed in which singers, producers and professional songwriters sought out new key phrases with which to touch their listeners. In the studio the singers maintained the principles of the live performance by improvising, joking and making dedications to people present in the studio or to acquaintances outside. The original scene was thus transferred to the studio context and intertwined with it, and this synthesis was in turn made available to consumers.

In the late 1970s, the cabaret scene was, moreover, the place where musicians versed in Western rock and pop would fuse with acoustic raï ensembles by way of a process of "improvised analogy." Drum sets, drum machines and bass guitars replaced acoustic percussion; later on, synthesizers replaced reed flutes, trumpets, accordions, or violins. The new instruments opened up new musical possibilities which, in short, allowed for the integration of Western musical formulas into the local rhythmic scheme and, hence, of references to such Western contexts for music consumption as discos and private parties. The recordings were made with a modest input of capital in an informal and improvised atmosphere.

Finally, the period coincided with the "death" of the vinyl record in Algeria and the rise of the cassette tape in its place. The latter opened up the possibility for a widescale production of music and an extension of consumption in time and space, leading a new generation of producers into the business, many of them with a social background similar to that of the singers. The cassettes were distributed on a "parallel market," where major earnings were and are generated by evading taxes and neglecting to declare the products to the national copyright agency. One of the implications of this practice has been that Algeria is now closed to foreign commercial musical interests. The competition among producers is also tough, evidenced by pirate recordings, copying and remakes of successes – commonplace phenomena that maximize profits by taking minimal investment risks.

ON THE CONSUMPTION OF RAÏ

With the onslaught of cassette tapes, the cabaret themes were taken outside the spheres they were originally intended for. They have since provoked a debate in Algeria centering on the socio-moral organization of the family.

This organization addresses the notions of reason (*`aql*), respect (*qder*), and modesty (*hashâm*). Basically, it involves not smoking, drinking, or speaking of matters of love and sexuality in front of family members and is practiced according to the members' position of power. The weaker thus displays modesty in front of those more powerful: young men in relation to their fathers; wives in relation to their husbands; sisters in relation to their brothers, etc., the exception being that sons might deal with these matters in front of their mothers, who, in acts of caring, strengthen the mother–son bond and thus their long-term position in a male-dominated society.

The organization of the family is linked at a number of points to Muslim doctrines concerning notions of purity and impurity. However, the socio-moral organization of the family tends to be contextual, i.e. what one does not do in one context, may be permissible in other contexts. The formal Muslim doctrines are on the other hand all-encompassing, i.e. what you do not do in one context, you should not do in other contexts either. By and large, raï seems to have been consumed according to the contextual logic. It has taken place mainly within groups divided according to age or gender, except at weddings, where families listen to raï in each other's company.

The wedding parties are inversions of the everyday moral and sexual norms of family life, and they are in this sense akin to the raï cabaret performances. In both places one finds the same competitive games and transactions regarding words for money. Both places also situate sexuality at center stage: in the cabarets, via men's acquaintances with "free women," at weddings, by way of the consummation of the sexual contract.

None the less, there are significant differences. In the cabarets, for example, one frequently hears dedications made to women who are mentioned by name, whereas this would be unheard of at weddings. Naming women in public opens up the possibility of unchecked sexuality; it also calls attention to women in public life. Thus, cabarets are spaces for male competition; they emphasize limitless leisure and lust, where male as well as female roles are altered. The wedding party, on the other hand, confirms male unity and re-enacts a regulated sexuality in which male and female roles are reinforced.

The reception of raï can be quite diverse. For example, the statement "She loved to drink Ricard and walk the boulevard" (cf. Schade-Poulsen 1993a) can be extremely embarrassing in the family context because of its reference to overt sexuality; at the wedding, however, it can be a joking reference to a world turned upside down; in the cabaret, it is simply a description of what goes on. Finally, the peer group can interpret it as a touching scene from the life of a prostitute, or a commentary on the meetings of men and women in the public spheres of Algeria's major cities.

On the whole, the very success of these cabaret lyrics, young voices and amplified Western electric instruments, all of which have gone far beyond their origins and are now materialized on the mobile and democratic tape cassette, surely suggests that raï has tapped into elements of vital concern among Algerian youth, bringing issues of sexuality and lifestyle to the fore. I have argued elsewhere that the concerns might indeed have to do with a shift in gender roles in post-independence Algeria, including changes in the family structure, the focus on the couple as a unit, and the important arrival of women in the public spheres (Schade-Poulsen 1993b); but such genre labels as "raï reggae," "pop raï" and "disco raï" also indicate that Algerian youth have an eye on Western spheres for gender encounters and leisure life.

Due to its reputation, raï was nonexistent on national radio and television in the early 1980s. In 1982, however, Medi 1, a commercial radio in Tangier, began playing raï songs on the air. In December 1984, the French-language Channel 3 in Algeria followed suit, partly to compete with Medi 1. And in July 1985, a raï group participated in the "Festival of Youth" at a newly opened one billion francs trade and museum center in Algiers. Two months later, the national party, FLN, sponsored an offical raï festival in Oran, which was followed by two concerts in the first half of 1986 in Paris.

Transferring raï from wedding parties and cabarets to the concert stage meant a decisive media breakthrough not only in Algeria but in the West. The stage performance alone meant that the former exchange of money for an emotional interplay between performers and audience would be less visible, producing a performative context similar to those found in westernized show business.

In the following years raï would spread to the entire Algerian territory as well as to Morocco and Tunisia. New groups of listeners came along, enjoying raï exclusively for its musical references to Western leisure spheres. New singers were constantly emerging and, along with them, new cassettes. Many public concerts were held, and eventually raï had reached such official standing that in 1989 the raï stars Sahraoui and Fadela performed at a meeting of the five leaders of the Maghrebian states.[3]

None the less, Algeria's history through the 1980s also entails the catastrophic rise in economical and social problems that led to the October revolt in 1988. Important democratic changes were borne of this revolt, and the country experienced in the ensuing years a more open and prolific press, which, for the sake of further argument, did not lead to new perspectives on raï. Free elections to the municipalities were held in 1990, followed by the Islamist party takeover of the country's major cities (except for Kabylia), and consequently, a defunding of non-religious cultural activities. Not until the army crushed the Islamists would concert activity be revived.

At the time of my field work, raï was the main pop genre of the country and no longer dealt primarily with lust and free-form sexual behavior, but more with youthful love stories in Algeria's urban public spaces. The songs have never revolted against the sacredness of the parents' generation or against brothers' power over their sisters, nor have they ever questioned the basic notions of purity, impurity and the whole complex of respect.

One of raï's basic ideals is to overcome fundamental problems in issues of love and daily life by achieving a material status that permits one to *master* the basic values, not to break them. Most listeners I knew were perfectly aware of the formulaic character of the songs and did not see any contradiction in identifying with music that referred to Western as well as Algerian party contexts, or in identifying with singers of their own age and social background who sang about problems of love and lust and the Islamist idea of regulating these problems by segregating men and women in the public sphere.

RAÏ IN THE WEST

In 1985, raï singers were already performing in Oriental cabarets and at weddings in France; raï cassettes had long been known in the North African community thanks to community radios, plus the informal distribution network for cassettes that was fast becoming worldwide.[4] Western audiences encountered raï in various press reviews of stage concerts in Algeria and France, and in 1986 raï had made its appearance on the international market. In Paris, leading singers such as Cheb Khaled and Cheb Mami were managed by people who had experience with both the Arab and the Western music business; a local immigrant, Cheb Kader, was also "created" as a raï singer. All three were furnished with backing bands (rarely found in Algerian raï). Meanwhile in London, Island Records signed a contract with the leading studio in Algeria mainly to promote Sahraoui and Fadela; several discotheques in London and Paris featured raï; and by 1990, the four premiere names of raï had given concerts in Europe, North America and Japan.

Out of this has come a number of records and CDs intended for the Western market. Many were tracks recycled from master tapes for the Arab cassettes, but a number of them were produced specifically for a Western audience; two of these were created in collaboration with Western producers known for their cooperation with Third World musicians.[5] According to the reader profile of *Actuel* and *Libération*,[6] raï's main promoters, the Western raï audience was made up of young, upwardly mobile, urban consumers of travel and leisure products, on their way to becoming decision-makers in French society. The most detailed descriptions of raï outside France – and outside the specialized music press – are to be found in *The Face* and *Art Forum*, both of which are in the business of "cross overs" between fine art, photography, pop music, and documentaries from "hot spots" around the world (cf. Walker 1987). This would seem to indicate that we are not far from having located what Bourdieu (1979) would call social stratas possessing high symbolic (rather than high economic) capital.

When I started my work in Paris in 1990, there was a division between such large cultural-commodity supermarkets as FNAC and Virgin, and the local retail dealers in, e.g., Barbes. The latter were mainly selling low-quality cassette tapes for half the price marked at FNAC and Virgin, who mostly sold the records and CDs in the World Music section. However, raï's expected breakthrough into a wider Western context failed to come about in 1990. A number of people knew about raï yet they still weren't buying it. The (unofficial) sales figures for raï recordings were extremely low, rarely reaching more than 20,000 copies sold, and the two "international" recordings had not found the large audiences expected, except as Hebrew remakes in Israel.[7]

In 1991, *Libération* dropped its monthly review of raï cassettes and replaced it with a World Music review. In 1992, neither Mami, nor Kader, nor Sahraoui and Fadela were in the international record business. Instead, they performed in Western towns and suburbs with a high concentration of North Africans, or at concerts featuring Third World music. The scene in France, though not unimportant, seemed primarily to be a matter of weddings, local community concerts, Oriental cabarets, some discotheques, local community and World

Music radio stations, a few larger concerts in Paris and occasional features on state radio channels, e.g. France Inter.

Khaled is perhaps the exception to this tendency. In 1991 he represented France at a large open-air concert in Central Park, New York. In 1992 he was decorated as *Chevalier de l'ordre des Arts et des Lettres*. The same year, after having signed a contract with Barclay and agreeing to distribution by the multinational Polygram, he was the first Arab to make it to the French Top Ten, doing so with the hit "Didi" (Khaled: Barclay). Today, it seems he is popular in India, Turkey, Israel and Egypt as well. I shall return to this potential success story. But having touched on the flow of raï from the Oranian cabarets to the concerts in New York, I shall now elaborate on its valorization by the press and Western music creators. First the press story.

THE PRESS STORY

One of the first articles to mention the phenomenon of raï was written in *Algeria* in 1981.[8] It established that raï had become extremely popular, and that all family members listened to it, though not in each other's presence; moreover, raï had provoked a fierce opposition. The article reported how the opponents viewed raï as a destructive deviation from the bedouin poetic tradition, drawing its substance from a jaded and vulgar jargon that signalled an impending moral decay.

Its perspective, however, was that raï had to be seen as a social phenomenon – with its initiates, its detractors, its unabashed peddlers, and, no less, its substantial audience. It stated that for those more informed and eager to analyze, raï music could be seen as a scream of revolt and a desire to break down taboos and prohibitions.

The article described how the bedouin music tradition had been modernized in the 1950s in Oran, leading to other innovations in the 1970s. It also mentioned that raï probably was inspired by seemingly immoral and subversive interpreters such as the above-mentioned *shikhâs*. Raï had grown out of the social environment of a rural population coming to the cities, impoverished and crowded together in scanty houses, where unemployment and illiteracy created an atmosphere of violence, crime, and sexual inhibition, and the brothels formed the center of a marginalized society with its own codes and secrets.

A selection of songs transcribed from cassette recordings was also analyzed. The songs appeared as broken lines – interspersed with dedications to people termed as marginals – from which one could deduce the identity of potential raï consumers: single men of poor origins, nostalgic immigrants, mentally disturbed, divorced, urbanized peasants in search of supernatural solutions, people with a pronounced male machismo who competed for females who were presented as simple sexual objects.

In sum, then, raï was seen as the main expression, though ambiguous and blurred, of the most deprived in Algeria. It was placed on a par with the gypsy music of the European cabarets and with the blues that had come out of New Orleans. The famous *shikhâ*, Remitti, could be compared to Edith Piaf, and the forceful young Fadela sang like the hard rock of Janis Joplin.

The second lengthy inquiry into raï appeared two years later with three articles headlined: "*The maquis of raï*," "*All we need is raï*" and "*Raï, blues and psychoanalysis*."[9]

They confirmed a number of facts from the first article and also added that opponents of raï complained about the lack of decent, more elaborate lyrics. The journalist argued that the subjects raï touched upon were not any more immoral than many a classical Arab poem and, moreover, the lack of good texts might be due to the fact that raï's rhythm and atmosphere were what mattered.

The articles in 1983 proclaimed that raï was the music of young people who had turned against the older generation. Raï was a way of saying that youths were willing to accept the consequences of their age, including their lack of experience. The articles posed the question of whether the music perhaps could be referring to such situations as young men lustfully observing the neighbor's 17-year-old daughter, jealously eyeing the cousin's car, mischievously watching the achiever's villa, and awaiting the future with confusion.

These articles also ventured into the history of raï, but went a step further by making extensive references to the writings of Miliani,[10] who assigned only a marginal status to the singers and producers and did not see these as being in opposition to the norms. Still not convinced by Miliani's analysis, the journalist proceeded to analyze raï as a (self-) expression of sexual forces in which the notion of the scream was central:

> but you may ask yourself if it [raï] doesn't signify "being", a being which has surrendered to destiny by means of its weakness or by the forces of desire. . . . Anyhow most of the texts in raï are interspersed with apostrophes, similar to the scream or complaint.
> (*Algérie Actualité*, 2–8 April 1981)

Finally, the journalist produced a first-time interview with the singer, Khaled. The journalist, impressed by Khaled's personality and popularity, gave this description: "A monument of sympathy. . . . It was as if I was in the local café with an old friend from the local area" (ibid.).

Khaled's life was then sketched out: how he felt stifled in school, how he started playing Moroccan music, how he had been rejected as a musician on the radio and subsequently went into raï. Khaled apologized for his lack of good song lines, admitting that if raï was to follow up on its success, it needed better lyrics. He went on to explain raï's success, attributing it to the fact that it offered a style different from those played on the radio. He knew that some of the lyrics could not be listened to in the midst of one's family, however this didn't apply to all the songs. The article concluded: "You come to raï as you go up in the maquis. A maquis of music without iron collars" (ibid.).

The third major inquiry into raï was published in the program for the Raï Festival in Oran, August 1985. Here, the roots of raï were traced all the way back to pre-Islamic, post-Islamic and later classical texts derived from Muslim Andalusia. The program described raï's development into colloquial Arabic, the famous *melHun* of the bedouin poets, stating that the latter was appropriated by the rural indigenous elite, many of whom had close relations with the colonial administration.

Shepherds and minstrels simplified the *shîkh's* poetry, which was in turn embodied by the *shikhâs* in the public bars and brothels established by the colonial power. The thematics of raï changed in the 1920s and 1930s, however, propagating themes of social misery created by the colonial regime. Musically, this tradition was eventually modernized in the 1970s, a period when the bedouin poets had run out of innovations, handicapped as they were by their mercantile egoism.

According to the program, it was in the late 1970s that raï made itself felt throughout the whole Algerian territory – and without any official help. Boasting as it did a new generation of singers, it was ushered in by the advent of the cassette tape and the introduction of the synthesizer from rock, disco, and reggae. It was fast becoming an independent musical genre and a way of expression for youth.

THE NARRATIVE

The following three magazine articles represented sophisticated attempts to describe raï and present factual elements concerning its forerunners and current state of being. They also broke with a previous ideological consensus regarding a coherent and healthy civil society based on sound peasant values (Virolle-Souibès 1989: 58). Sexual problems were addressed, as were such topics as social tensions, the many brothels, and the everyday life of young people. Thus, the articles produced a biography of raï, anticipating nearly all the topics that would be debated in the Algerian press in the years to come.

Up to this day, one of the trends in the Algerian press has been to pursue the idea of raï having a disruptive effect on its consumers,[11] and in the course of raï's spread to the West, one branch of this trend has developed the idea of raï being an instrument for political or occult powers,[12] or for cultural-imperialist forces attempting to destabilize Algerian society and secularize the second-generation immigrants in France.[13]

A more predominant approach, however, has defined the debate in terms of being "for or against" raï lyrics. In discussions as these,[14] the issue of raï's vulgarity has been constantly stressed, as has the problem of oversimplified lyrics or the lack of poetic content. A good deal of well-intentioned advice has been given to raï performers, while extremely harsh attacks have been launched against the music publishers.[15] Nevertheless, a central element in the three inquiries has persisted: the idea of situating raï in the context of the oppressors and the oppressed.

In the 1981 version, raï was the scream of revolt issuing from the poor and disrupted peasantry who had been confronted with the post-independence politics of the Boumedienne regime, along with the sexual taboos of Algerian society. In the 1983 version, raï became the expression not only of sexuality but of young people reacting against the older generation, against the newly rich of the Chedli regime, and against the national media, the latter story being "headlined" by the powerful reference to the war of liberation (i.e. "the maquis of music"). In the festival feature, raï, as part of the national cultural heritage, proved its vitality in opposition to the colonial regime, to mercantile *shîkhs* and to a cultural invasion from abroad.

All in all, a heterophonous master narrative,[16] as formulated by Bruner (1986), was established in the sense that raï became the hero in "a past of oppression" and "a present of resistance." But unlike in Bruner's account, the future was not explicated, the end of the story was not known, and is still not known today.

Up to the present time, however, the "hero status" of raï has persisted in the struggle to define Algeria's moral, cultural, and political identity. Several articles dealing with raï have criticized the government's neglect of cultural policies.[17] Other articles have seen raï as a vital representative of Algerian youth and of national cultural vigor, now endangered by the rising Islamist forces.[18] Both tendencies have been strengthened by the propagation of raï in the West. Many articles have reported on raï singers' success abroad;[19] some have compared the opportunities of artists in Algeria with those offered in the West,[20] and other articles have involved the raï singers (valued because of their success in the West[21]) in the conflict with the Islamists.

However, the master narrative, its basic structure and main motives were also transferred to the West. Issues of sexuality, youth, the scream, the family, the history of raï, the opposition to the radio, etc. all crossed the Mediterranean;[22] but by crossing the sea, the story was now surrounded by new fields of interpretive associations.

THE PORTRAYAL OF RAÏ IN THE WEST

The key example is provided by an article in *Libération*[23] published on the occasion of the first raï concert in Paris. It summed up all the previous elements from the Algerian press and added a whole range of facts to the biography of raï. What is interesting, however, is that it was accompanied by an editorial headline proclaiming "Raï: The Enraged 'New Wave' of Oran" (*Libération* 22 January 1986), and referring to pinball machines as well as the liberation war:

> Born on the threshold of the 1980s, raï is much more than a rhythm; it is a way of being . . . while distancing themselves from classical lyricism, the chebs [youth] rehabilitate sex, alcohol and realism by singing about flirts, pinball machines and cars . . . ; the kids of the Mazda . . . make a symbol out of raï. The authorities think it's a disease . . . but . . . raï keeps moving. The chebs know they have won their Battle of Algiers.
>
> (Ibid.)

And finally, it reviewed the first long-playing record in the history of raï:

> [Khaled] is a night hawk: he never sings before . . . four o'clock in the morning, and this record brings forth a prudent testimony of the "folly of Khaled", confronted with his audience of crazed people in love. . . . The piercing complaints of this inspired singer and pleasure seeker recalls the great moments of blues, or Salif Keita's psalmody; but Ray Charles is too a source of inspiration.

> The instrumental accompaniment of the synthesizers and the rhythm box, the accordion blending with the synthesizer, the heavy sounds of the electric bass and the arabesques of the electric guitar backed up by traditional percussion, produce a sound which cuts through everything you might have heard before. It's a universal music like rock and reggae.
>
> (Ibid.)

It seems clear that the master narrative has been transferred into a field of knowledge, interest, and perspective different from that found in the Algerian press. The most enlightening accounts of what took place were presented in three articles in the monthly review, *Actuel*,[24] which together with *Libération* sponsored the first raï concerts in Paris.

ACTUEL

Actuel was actually the first to introduce raï to a Western audience with a travel report from Algeria in 1983. Here it described Khaled as representing an underground movement. The journalist described the music as follows:

> a song of broken hearts, a complaint, a fado. It is inspired by Andalous singing and by local music, the Oranian rhythm mixed with an electronic sauce . . . , with a sound as cheap and beautiful as a Colombian cumbia.
>
> (*Actuel* 50, 1983)

He went on to describe his experience of raï in cabaret: "[the words] of raï are raw; when it speaks about love, it goes on, it sings a kind of blues, though joyous and sensual . . . , an assertion of sexuality" (ibid.).

The major part of the article, however, dealt with growing Islamicist attacks on women and described at length the economic, demographic, and political problems that Algeria faced as a result of the Boumedienne era. It suggested that changes were slowly underway under the Chedli regime due to its anti-corruption policies, democratization, and liberalization. And as a part of all these changes, raï music was seen as an essential phenomenon.

Young girls were now seen dancing in the cabarets – marginal girls, to be sure, but nevertheless a sight unimaginable under the Boumedienne regime. The writer described how he had spent two lonely years as a teacher in Algeria that were only rarely spiced with open passions. Now things were changing:

> I saw a couple kissing. Even if the man hurried away with a look of guilt, there was an earnest anticipation of freedom.
>
> (Ibid.)

Two years later the same journal described raï as follows:

> Raï is at one and the same time Algeria's punk, blues, reggae and funk . . . . Oran is the Kingston of this secret and lyrical underground explosion. Cheb Khaled is its Bob Marley, but because he is considered too beastly a person, there is no mention of raï on television.
>
> (*Actuel* 68, 1985)

The article, like others before it, included a "fascinating" description of the cabarets of Oran. It described the changes in instrumentation that had taken place since raï's acoustic beginnings, along with the crude recording techniques and the disputes between the publishers and copyright bureaus; it also described as a hypocrisy the fact that family members did not listen to raï in each other's presence.

On the whole, however, the article dealt with Khaled as an oppositional figure, and as a bohemian everyone told stories about. It is in fact interesting how the approach to Khaled differed from the one in *Algérie Actualité*:

> Two years ago, he was driving, dead drunk, with a whore in a stolen car. The two of them had been fighting and he ended up hitting a guy with the car. Khaled was taken to prison for 3 months.
>
> (Ibid.)

The article concluded by describing an encounter with Khaled which ended late one night in an apartment. Khaled, his girlfriend, two musicians, an officer from the army police, and some tradesmen were all listening to Khaled's latest cassettes while watching an X-rated film and consuming huge quantities of wine.

The third article was entitled "Raï – Algeria Wants to Make Love, the Arab Blues Against Fundamentalism."[25] It predicted, "In the year 2000 there will be 30 million young North Africans. What will they support? Fundamentalism or raï?" (*Actuel* 115, 1988). Here, raï was described as the scream of desire of Algerian youth, the idea being that France had been waiting for a break in the media's Arab–Islam–veil–Koran–fundamentalist image of the Arab countries. The article went on to analyze how Algerian society conceals its phantasms and sexual frustrations, suggesting that it was precisely this state of being that raï was consciously reacting against.

> Weary of masturbating, Raï is claiming the right to fuck when you want, where you want, and how you want.
>
> (Ibid.)

In this light, the article concluded that raï can only be compared to the '68 reaction against the morality of Catholic France.

What was it, then, that had taken place in the *Libération* article? First, it is obvious that overlaps occur between the Algerian and French version; furthermore, by crossing the sea raï did not lose its hero status in the narrative, one of the reasons being that journalists tend to use previous articles as a main source of documentation. Second, the press releases sent out to journalists by record companies and concert promoters tend to be . . . just that. Third, a number of journalists were also personally involved in promoting raï as such.[26] Moreover, there exists a trans-metropolis Oran–Algiers–Paris network of people who know one another, and who in turn are the main source of information for writers outside this network.[27] Many of these people share a common background: a university degree founded on the French left-wing intellectual tradition; and their main perspective, an opposition to totalitarian cultural tendencies in Algeria as well as in France.

Yet despite these similarities it is also obvious that our narrative was guided into a new field of knowledge – a field in which drinking and rock were associated with a notion of liberal and modern Islam seen in opposition to intolerant, archaic Islam and a totalitarian state. This whole construction was seemingly homologous to associating the consumption of "sex, drugs, and rock 'n' roll" with a critique of the morality of bourgeois middle-class Western society!

Headlines such as "Rock against Islam," "Rather Elvis than FIS," "He Talked to Paul Sweeney about Fundamentalism and Fun"[28] are examples of how raï – with a touch of popular orientalism[29] – was related to the myths of youth and subcultures in the West.[30] References to Liverpool, Elvis Presley, Jim Morrison, Detroit, the Bronx, punk, and reggae came up regularly.[31] "Rebel" was another code word referring to James Dean (not to mention the Rolling Stones). And the October events in Algeria in 1988 were referred to as the revolt of the "raï generation" as if it were another '68 generation. Finally, with the Islamist takeover of the communes in Algeria, raï came to be a main representative of the liberation struggle against Islamism, with the singers as the main protagonists.[32]

All the doubts and uneasiness attending the story of raï's origins in Algeria had disappeared in the West.[33] Instead, the vulgarity discussed in Algeria became a virtue.[34] Further differences became noticeable: first, it is highly uncommon in Algeria for the press to go into detail about a singer's personal life, in accordance with the above-mentioned notions of respect. Singers are described "front stage" as conforming to Algerian codes of normal family life and as practicing a serious artistic endeavor. In the West, the press has focused on the cabaret scene and on the life of the singers in their leisure time. Second, the simple-mindedness of the lyrics has not been discussed in the West. Whereas the Algerian press tends to discuss this in the framework of high vs. low culture, in the West the lyrics – if indeed they are translated and understood – have been regarded and valued as factual statements of self-expression.

Third, whereas the commercial aspect of raï has been heavily criticized in Algeria, with a dividing line running between the singers as the creators and the publishers as the profit-seekers, the Western press tends not to launch any critical inquiries into the Algerian or Western promotion strategies. The music-recording aspect is shown a great deal of interest (which is not found in the Algerian press), but more as an interesting sociological fact of Third World conditions.

Musically, the main difference is that raï, in Algeria, is placed within a field of possibilities made up of – at the center – Moroccan, Egyptian, and Algerian musical genres. At the same time, it is compared with genres valorized in the West.

In the Western press, raï music slips out of the Arab and Middle Eastern landscape to be integrated with such syncretic musical styles as New Orleans blues, Argentinian tango, West African juju, Greek, Turkish, and Flamenco melodies, Portuguese fado, and reggae,[35] many of which originated in milieus steeped in prostitution and drug use. Since 1987, more and more of these have been labeled as World Music – a notion rarely used in the Algerian press.

Finally, the musical aspect of raï has rarely been described in the Algerian press. In the West, an introduction seems to have been necessary. The main tendency has been to stress raï's dual character as being somewhere between modernity and tradition, between bedouin music and rock, and the critics have primarily expressed a fascination with the voice in raï, since the language barrier prevents the Western listener from understanding the text.

DIDI, DIDI

Despite the differences, though, it seems there exists what we might call a mediascape of raï[36] (Appadurai 1990: 299) whose transnational point of view fluctuates between seeing it, on the one hand, as the scream of pain of uprooted peasants and, on the other hand, as the scream of James Dean's rebellion.

It is the mediascape of raï that has structured the relationship to raï as well as to the singers, and not the opposite. In Algeria the singers have been confronted with questions as to the vulgarity of raï and, later, as to their political opinions on the Islamist movement. In the West they have been questioned about their lifestyles and their relationship to the FIS. To address the singers' relationship to the press goes beyond my errand here. Suffice it to say that they have tended to answer situationally, strategically, in accordance with the role of an artist, stage performer, and songwriter.

The mediascape seems to have had its impact in Algeria in the early 1990s: most people described the singers as songwriters, relating how raï dealt with the social problems of young people, and did so in such a formulaic way that it seemed as if the story had been learnt by heart from the press. Many people could also recount the story of raï from the *shîkhs* and the *shikhâs*. Furthermore, they recounted – without using the label of World Music – how raï had conquered the world, i.e. Europe, Japan, the United States. They thereby transmitted the idea that raï was a part of the Western world of leisure without an awareness that raï's primary audience abroad was composed of North Africans.

In the West, the mediascape has promoted raï. Nevertheless, raï has had difficulties in attaining commercial success. It has been suggested in the press that this has been mainly owing to the *de facto* absence of raï on the commercial radio stations and television prime time, in addition to a latent French racism. On the whole, it seems difficult to "sell an Arab" to a Western audience.[37] Another reason, however, lies in raï music itself and in the main themes of the promotion by the press. The story of Khaled's successful record will serve as an illustration.

By and large, the musical components of raï have been altered in records produced for a Western audience. In Western pop, for example, it is just as important as it is in raï to have a refrain, a formula, to sing along to – and Arabic is not the ideal language for a Western audience. In Western pop, it is also important to dance, to move your body. However, raï is based on a binary, often poly-rhythmic, principle in which the 4-beat strokes are much less emphasized than in Western pop music. In raï the bass tends to stress the triplets, related to the popular form of dancing in Algeria in which the hips (following the triplets) lead the body, rather than the feet (following the 4 beats). This particular use of bass tends to make Western dancers lose the "feeling," as they are accustomed to letting their feet be guided by a bass accentuating the 4 beats. Moreover, it brings them off beat with the singer, so they won't have a "body" to move in identifying with the images of sex, alcohol, raï and youth.

Thus, on Khaled's record that was produced in the US and Belgium, the only thing left of Algerian raï consists of its stock phrases, the sense of phrasing melodic lines, and primarily *the voice* of Khaled. The major hit formula is *Didi*! Many of the tunes on the record are accompanied by a heavy, funky bass, and polyphonous background choirs have been added (previously unheard of in raï). The dedications, the informal atmosphere, i.e. the Algerian primal scene, has of course been left out.[38] Consequently, raï produced for a Western audience cannot be recreated in Algeria. Not only do the aesthetics differ, the Algerian studios do not possess the capital and equipment to reproduce the sound.

But Khaled's record company has ventured further than this. With a budget of two million francs, it has appropriated the songs Khaled has recorded for Algerian producers and declared him as the songwriter of several hundred songs to the French copyright bureau.[39] They have thus privatized a part of Algerian oral folklore and the work of Algerian musicians and popular songmakers. Together with the multinational Polygram company they succeeded in obtaining press coverage for the album, which was unparalleled for raï. A substantial amount of TV time was purchased for airing a video of *Didi*. The record cover shows Khaled photographed at the same angle as Stevie Wonder on one of his records. Inside the sleeve the lyrics are printed in Arabic – for the first time in the story of raï – but with no accompanying translation, i.e. their purpose is strictly aesthetic. (In Algeria the titles are written in Latin letters.) And, finally, they have introduced a change in Khaled's image. In an interview film, Khaled is seen describing his career as a musician in a Parisian museum of art, while his American producer is comparing him to Bob Dylan.

The press material is graced with a Magritte-inspired headline: "Ceci n'est pas un Arabe," and the raï lyrics are interpreted as follows:

> Indeed, we owe him beautifully surrealistic poems . . . which neither the French poet Apollinaire nor André Breton, the founder of surrealism, would disown.
>
> (Press release, Barclay, 1992)

However, with the release of the *Didi* record, Khaled seems to have had to resolve a difficult situation. In an interview in *Le Monde* (20 February 1992), Khaled was asked why he represented France at the New York concert of 14 July 1991, and also to comment on the release of his album in Israel. He replied that he was born under the French flag in 1960, that his godmother was French, that his bass player was Jewish, that his group consisted of Jews, Arabs, and French, and that Jews and Arabs were cousins.

The answers given by this "liberal Arab" representing a multicultural France did not at all please a number of people in Algeria, nor the Algerian press.[40] In an interview in *Le Matin* (18 March 1992), Khaled disavowed his statements: "Me, I'm not an intellectual. I speak, as they say, in 'Arabic French.'" It was a wise answer by a singer who has been involved in a game for which his voice lacks training.

CONCLUSION

Music does not flow freely in the world, the world's music does not weaken the logic of the market, and the creolization of music is not a story of simple "cuts 'n' mixes." The flow of raï from Algeria to the West reveals boundaries and differing political, economical, moral, and ideological perspectives. It also reveals that raï is not only embedded in several contexts, it is also *embodied*, since the story of the flow of raï is one which basically starts with dancing and leisure in the Algerian cabarets and ends with another kind of dancing in Western discos, or on stereo racks.

In Algeria, the flow of raï relates to places and moments for enjoying music and leisure, organized according to notions of family, gender, and power. Furthermore, the liberation of raï from its original place of performance, its modernization and transfer onto cassette tapes, opened up new imaginative spaces lodged in between the cabaret, the wedding, and the family, revealing the existence of meeting places for men and women in Algeria that relate to Western concepts of leisure.

All in all, this is the story of a cultural commodity which attained new meanings among Algerian youth while being distributed in Algeria and France by a parallel commercial circuit with a Maghrebian clientele.

Two crucial transformations were subsequently added to "the social life" of raï: a wider societal project of freedom, equality, and creativity as expressed by the Algerian press and, equally importantly, the official stage concert.

Both these transformations made it possible to convert raï to a form that would pique the interest of the Western press and the music media. New contexts arose, as exemplified by the backing bands that were furnished and by the first raï record releases and, later, CDs. One could say that raï entered into a new commercial and performative sphere, symbolized by the difference in price and actual distance between FNAC, Virgin and Barbès in Paris.

New fields of interests were also added to the social life of raï: preoccupations with the Western problems of racism and totalitarianism, where the image and status of the Arab or Algerian were at stake. At the same time, raï was pulled away from an Algerian and Arabic musical context in favor of the so-called "root musics" (Feld 1988: 31) of the world, which focus, according to the Western press, on sexual excessiveness and "vertigos" (drugs, alcohol, etc.).

In other words, raï was mixed with particular notions regarding youth cultures, Islam, sex, and alcohol (similar to old European ideas of the Orient [cf. Saïd 1978; Rodinson 1982], all of which were linked to a concrete political involvement against racism, Islamism, etc.

The final transformations affecting "the life of raï" disengaged it from its embodied specificity as well as its political context: first, the musical transformation gave the hypothetical Western listener the opportunity to be in time with the performer and to enter into a relationship with him; second, the most well-known singer was presented as a "pure artist," i.e. as being above or outside all practical endeavors except the one of creating art.

Here, then, we have at least three points of view on raï, each in their own field of interest: the perspective of Algerian raï producers and consumers, the perspective presented in the press, and the perspective of multinational interests. They seem to have confirmed one another in posing the existence of a relation between music, consumption, sexuality, and politics, but without recognizing how differently organized this is from place to place.

As for the notion of World Music, the description of raï in the Western press proves interesting and indeed leads to the tentative suggestion that, rather than a global ecumene connected to the established category of World Music, there is an audience consisting primarily of Western urban intellectuals and artists, etc. This audience is engaged in a dialogue with Third World colleagues, and consumers of one or several non-Western musical genres, each of which is perceived as having a specific appeal in terms of musical communicative devices, socio-political involvement, vertigos, and cultural imagery.[41] The people involved with World Music function as mediators of Third

World music to a broader Western community, facilitating the many stage concerts plus record and CD releases. Moreover, they seem to serve as agents for the multinational companies and their appropriation of local musical creativity.

It is not yet clear just where the latest transformation of raï will lead – to the world of those singing "We are the World," or to the world of those involved in World Music. What seems most striking at the present time is the increasing discrepancy between how raï is produced on the multinational level and how it is produced locally in Algeria, exemplified by the impermeability of the Algerian music market for foreign interests, by the West's advanced CD and studio technology, and by the political appropriation of raï artists in the West.[42]

In this sense, the notion of World Music is not innocent; it involves a particular set of power relations through which to describe the world and label it as "World." The elements the Western press has had to deal with are similar to those mentioned in the anthropological debate today[43] (i.e. cultural products being westernized without becoming Western, cultural products crossing borders, etc.). For anthropologists concerned with such labels as cultural complexity, globalization, etc., an obvious task must be to present the world in ever more subtle ways.

ACKNOWLEDGMENTS

This chapter is based on ten months' field work in Algeria and four in Paris, carried out between 1990 and 1992 and financed by The Danish Research Council for the Humanities. I have additionally drawn on a collection of about three hundred press articles from the Francophone Algerian press and other sources around the world, as well as from my experiences with the Parisian media and my participation in Scandinavian World Music radio programs. Events that have taken place since 1993 are not included in this discussion.

NOTES

1 I will concentrate on the Algerian, Anglophone, Francophone, and Scandinavian press. My field schedule did not allow a closer study of the consumption of raï among broader Western groups nor among Maghrebins and second-generation immigrants in France. This wider perspective must therefore be left out of the present chapter.

2 Raï (*rray*) means literally: an opinion or point of view. My description of raï in Algeria is seen from the male point of view.

3 *El Moudjahid* 16 June 1989.
4 For an early report see Bariki (1986).
5 Cheb Khaled and Safi Boutella: *Kutché*, Sterns; Chab Mami: *Let me raï*, Totem Records.
6 *Libération*, "le Topo – Libé," Paris 1990. "Actuel Général Médias" 1990.
7 Problems such as the Gulf War and internal disagreements in the musical sphere are not without a cause. The article by Regev (1989) indicates that Western-based raï may function as a mediator between Oriental and Western socio-musical spheres in Israel.
8 *Algérie Actualité* 2–8 April 1981.
9 All translations from French in this chapter are mine.
10 Miliani wrote the first academic essay on raï (1981).
11 Either by stating it directly or by means of interviews with persons representing (or claiming to be in line with) the *shîkh*s. Cf. *Algérie Actualité* 12–18 April 1984; *El Moudjahid* 7 July 1985; *El Moudjahid* 12 August 1985; *Révolution Africaine* 23–9 August 1985; *El Moudjahid* 22 May 1992; see also Schade-Poulsen 1992, 1993a; Virolle-Souibès 1989.
12 Cf. Virolle-Souibès 1989; *Algérie Actualité* 26 November to 4 December 1985; *El Moudjahid* 6 Feburary 1986.
13 *L'Evènement* 8–14 September 1991; *El Moudjahid* 1 January 1992.
14 *Algérie Actualité* 14–20 November 1985; *Algérie Actualité* 4–10 September 1986; *Parcours Maghrébin* 1988; *Horizons* 10–11 February 1989; *Horizons* 9–10 June 1989; *El Moudjahid* 14 June 1989; *Révolution Africaine* 9–15 August 1990; *Alger Républicain* 30–1 August 1991.
15 *El Moudjahid* 10 October 1985; *Révolution Africaine* 12–18 September 1986; *Algérie Actualité* 28 May to 3 June 1987; *Algérie Actualité* 1–7 September 1988; *Parcours Maghrébin* 1988; *Algérie Actualité* 2–8 March 1989; *Horizons* 12 September 1989.
16 Here, along the lines of the arguments in Bruner's article, I am using a metaphor characterizing Arabic music in which the musicians, together, each play their variations on a common theme of musical progression.
17 *Algérie Actualité* 29 May to 3 June 1987; *Algérie Actualité* 15 February 1986; *Algérie Actualité* 5–11 January 1989.
18 *El Moudjahid* 10 October 1985; *Algérie Actualité* 4–10 September 1986; *Révolution Africaine* 2–8 August 1990; *Algérie Actualité* 11–17 October 1990; *Horizons* 5 May 1991; *El Moudjahid* 11 August 1991.
19 *Horizons* 7 Feburary 1989; *Horizons* 9–10 June 1989; *El Moudjahid* 3 August 1989; *Algérie Actualité* 26 July to 1 August 1990; *Le Soir d'Algérie* 30 September 199; *Le Soir d'Algérie* 20 May 1991.
20 *Algérie Actualité* 28 February to 3 June 1987; *Algérie Actualité* 17 September 1988; *Algérie Actualité* 27 October 1988 (however not without a critical perspective on Western "showbiz").
21 *Horizons* 4 July 1990; *Algérie Actualité* 26 July to 1 August 1990; *Révolution Africaine* 9–15 August 1990; *Le Soir d'Algérie* 20 May 1991: *Algérie Actualité* 12–18 December 1991; *Horizons* 1 January 1992; *Le Soir d'Algérie* 16 March 1992.
22 At first through reports from the Youth Festival of Algiers and the Raï Festival of Oran: *Libération* 8 July 1985; *Le Monde* 23 July 1985: *Libération* 23 August 1985; *Jeune Afrique Magazine* September 1985.
23 *Libération* 22 January 1986. For a similar version see *Afrique Asie* 24

February 1986 and the more exotic writings of Rabah Mezouane, 1992 and the LP cover: "Le monde du raï, Mélodie."

24 *Actuel* 50, 1983; *Actuel* 68, 1985; *Actuel* 115, 1988.

25 Translated for *The Face*, June 1988, under the title "Sex and Soul in the Maghreb."

26 For example, one member of the Oran Festival Committee would be a former director of the locally controlled radio station in Oran in addition to being a songwriter. Another was the head of the FLN-controlled association of artists. A journalist in Algeria would arrange raï concerts in Morocco, two journalists in France would owe their jobs to their knowledge of raï, a third would write the sleeve notes for raï records and the promotion articles for a promoter, the latter having a family link to the former Jewish community of Oran, etc. And a fourth would write for a journal which controlled a local radio station specializing in "World Music." The role of journalists as gatekeepers within the promotion circuit of musical products is acknowledged by producers just as well as it is known in academic literature, see Peterson and Berger (1972); Hennion (1983); Hirsch (1991).

27 Thus the daughter of a member of the Oran Festival Committee was a well-known artist in Paris, another member would be a friend of an Algerian journalist in France who would be working on the same journal as a French reporter who had written a song for Khaled, plus an Algerian colleague who would have participated in the promotion of raï on the local community station, Radio Soleil. There, a French music enthusiast would later work for an Algerian raï producer and help him to introduce his records in London, etc. All of these would know a journalist in Oran who, in turn, would have contacts in Algiers and to a journalist working on the Algerian Channel 3, etc.

28 Respectively, *Nouvel Observateur* July 1985; *L'Evènement du Jeudi* 5 March 1992; *Independent* 3 September 1992.

29 A number of LP records produced for the Western market have camels or veiled women as cover motifs – motifs never used in Algeria.

30 *Le Nouvel Observateur* 26–30 January 1986; *Africa Beat* no.6, 1986; *Libération* 9 October 1986; *Libération* 19 October 1986; *Folk Roots* May 1989; *Newsday* 6 August 1989; *Slitz* no.1, 1990.

31 *Q Magazine* December 1986; *Le Monde* 24 January 1986; *Africa Beat* no.6, 1986; *Observer Report* 13 September 1987; *Jyllands Posten* 27 December 1988; *New Musical Express* 4 February 1989; *European* 9–12 April 1992.

32 *Libération* 1 August 1990; *Le Monde* 20 February 1992; *L'Evènement du Jeudi* 5 March 1992; *Middle East Report* March/April 1991 and September/October 1992; *Independent* 3 September 1992; *Le Figaro* 11 May 1992.

33 With the exception of many articles in *Libération*, which maintained a critical view of the topics discussed below.

34 Miliani's statements on the conformity of raï were forgotten in both Algeria and in the West.

35 *Le Matin* 23 January 1986; *Le Monde* 24 January 1986; *Africa Beat* no. 6, 1986; *International Herald Tribune* 23 December 1988; *Libération* 12 February 1989; *Art Forum* September 1991.

36 I use the term only in so far as Appadurai's definition fits the case story presented.
37 *Algérie Actualité* 26 July to 1 August 1990; *Libération* 7 January 1991; *Libération* 27 February 1992; *Libération* 12 May 1992; *Le Soir d'Algérie* 10 May 1992; *Pulse* November 1989; *Rock & Folk* June 1992.
38 Which implies nothing about the quality of the music.
39 *Le Monde* 20 February 1992; *L'Etudiant* June 1992.
40 Cf. *Le Soir d'Algérie* 4 March 1992; *El Moudjahid Quest* 8–14 March 1992.
41 Frith (1991) has argued likewise in terms of Britain.
42 Cf. Malm and Wallis (1992) for a similar point of view.
43 For example in Appadurai 1988 and Hannerz 1989.

REFERENCES

Appadurai, A. (ed.) (1988) "Introduction", *The social life of things*, Cambridge: Cambridge University Press.
—— (1990) "Disjuncture and Difference in the Global Cultural Economy," in M. Featherstone (ed.) *Global culture*, London: Sage.
Bariki, S. (1986) "Les effets culturels de l'émigration, un enjeu de luttes sociales," in *Nouveaux enjeux culturels au Maghreb*, Paris: CNRS.
Barthes, R. (1987) "The Grain of the Voice," in S. Heath (ed.) *Image, Music, Text*, London: Fontana Press.
Bourdieu, P. (1979) *La distinction*, Paris: Minuit.
Bruner, E. (1986) "Ethnography as Narrative," in E. Bruner and V. Turner (eds) *The anthropology of experience*, Urbana and Chicago: University of Illinois Press.
Chambers, X. (1994) *Migrancy, Culture, Identity*, London: Routledge.
Comité d'organisation du 1er Festival (1985) *1er Festival de la chanson "ray"*, Wilaya d'Oran: République Algérienne Démocratique et Populaire.
Fairley, J. (1989) "Out of the Archive and Into the World of Music," *Popular Music* 8, 1: 101–7.
Feld, S. (1988) "Notes on World Beat," *Public Culture Bulletin* 1, 1: 31–7.
Frith, S. (1983) *Sound Effects – Youth, Leisure, and the Politics of Rock*, London: Constable.
—— (1991) "Critical Response," in Robinson et al. (eds.) *Music in the Margins*, London: Sage publications.
Geertz, C. (1983) *Art as a Cultural System, Local Knowledge*, New York: Basic Books.
Hannerz, U. (1989) "Culture Between Center and Periphery: Toward a Macroanthropology," *Ethnos* 54: 200–16.
—— (1992) *Cultural complexity*, New York: Columbia University Press.
Hebdige, D. (1979) *Cut 'N' Mix – Culture Identity and Caribbean Music*, London: Comedia.
Hennion, A. (1983) "The Production of Success: An Antimusicology of the Pop Song," in R. Middleton and D. Horn (eds) *Popular Music 3*, Cambridge, London, New York: Cambridge University Press.
—— (1990) "J'aime Bach," stencil. Paris.
Hirsch, P. (1991) "Processing Fads and Fashions: An Organizing-set Analysis

of Cultural Industry Systems," in C. Mukerji and M. Schudson (eds) *Rethinking Popular Culture*, Berkeley, Los Angeles, Oxford: University of California Press.

Kopytoff, I. (1988) "The Cultural Biography of Things," in A. Appadurai (ed.) *The Social Life of Things*, Cambridge: Cambridge University Press.

Langer, S. (1953) *Feeling and Form*, New York: Charles Scribner's Sons.

Malm, K. and R. Wallis (1984) *Big Sounds from Small Peoples – The Music Industry in Small Countries*, London: Constable.

—— (1992) *Media Policy and Music Activity*, London and New York: Routledge.

Manuel, P. (1988) *Popular Musics of the Non-Western World*, New York and Oxford: Oxford University Press.

McMurray, D. and T. Swedenburg (1991) "Raï Tide Rising," *Middle East Report*, March–April: 39–42.

Mezouane, R. (1992) "Génération raï," *Autrement*, série monde, 60: 64–70.

Miliani, H. (1981) "Les représentations de la femme dans la chanson populaire oranaise dite raï," *G.R.F.A.-document de travail, 8*, Ronéotype, Oran: Université d'Oran.

Nettl, B. (1985) *The Western Impact on World Music*, London: Collier Macmillan.

Patterson, O. (1994) "Ecumenical America – Global Culture and the American Cosmos," *World Policy Journal* Spring: 103–18.

Peterson, R. and D. Berger (1972) "Three Eras in the Manufacture of Popular Music Lyrics," in R. Denisoff (ed.) *The Sounds of Social Change*, Chicago: Rand McNally & Co.

Regev, M. (1989) "The Field of Popular Music in Israel," in S. Frith (ed.) *World Music, Politics and Social Change*, Manchester and New York: Manchester University Press.

Rijven, S. and W. Straw (1989) "Rock for Ethiopia," in S. Frith (ed.) *World Music, Politics and Social Change*, Manchester and New York: Manchester University Press.

Rodinson, M. (1982) *La fascination de l'islam*, Paris: Maspéro.

Saïd, E. (1978) *Orientalism*, London: Routledge & Kegan Paul.

Schade-Poulsen, M. (1992) "Mit hjertes ulykke – om analysen af algiersk popmusik," *Tidsskriftet Antropologi* 26: 59–76.

—— (1993a) "Essai d'analyse d'une chanson raï – côté hommes," in F. Colonna and Z. Daoud (eds) *Etre marginal au Maghreb*, Paris: CNRS.

—— (1995) "The Power of Love – Raï Music and Youth in Algeria," in V. Amit-Tala and H. Wulff (eds) *Youth Cultures*, London: Routledge.

Thompson, M. (1979) *Rubbish Theory*, Oxford: Oxford University Press.

Virolle-Souibès, M. (1989) "Le Raï entre résistances et récupération," *Revue du Monde Musulman et de la Méditerranée* 1, 51: 47–62.

Walker, J. (1987) *Cross-Overs*, London and New York: Methuen.

Waterman, C. A. (1990) *Juju – A Social History and Ethnography of an African Popular Music*, Chicago and London: University of Chicago Press.

4 Seeking place

Capsized identities and contracted belonging among Sri Lankan Tamil refugees

Ann-Belinda Steen Preis

> Les places, comme fragments d'identité, sont un ancrage précaire dans l'origine . . .
>
> (Daniel Sibony, *Entre-Deux* 1991: 232)

In this chapter I wish to draw attention to a distinctive phenomenon of deterritorialization and displacement that I have only recently begun to explore in more detail: the production, circulation, and consumption of video films among Sri Lankan Tamils, some of whom live as refugees in a number of Western countries. These films raise certain questions that are linked to the current anthropological interest in theorizing the relationships between "space," "place," and "identity." More specifically, the videos form part of a problematic which Malkki (1992: 24) has recently described as the complexity of "notions of nativeness and native places . . . as more and more people identify themselves, or are categorized, in reference to deterritorialized 'homelands', 'cultures' and 'origins'." Furthermore, the very themes of the films touch directly upon the question of "how to deal with cultural difference while abandoning received ideas of (localized) culture" (Gupta and Ferguson 1992: 7). The first film that I present in this chapter is, as we shall see, a creative answer to a political problem that has engendered displacement and "refugeeism"; the second is less analytically accessible in its complex linkage between video, culture, and politics.*

The notion of "Sri Lankan Tamil refugee" was introduced to the international public for the first time in connection with the violent anti-Tamil riots that occurred in the Sri Lankan capital of Colombo in late July and early August 1983 (Tambiah 1986: 21–6; Kapferer 1988: 29; Hyndman 1987: 55). Since then, Sri Lankan Tamils – many

* Please note that Tamil orthography is not used in this article.

of them single young men of Vellalar (high caste) origin from Jaffna – have been arriving in various West European countries and North America, applying for political asylum. The little-known struggle of the Tamil minority in Sri Lanka for an independent homeland, and against discrimination by the Sinhalese majority, came to the fore in the European media in the mid-1980s because of extremely critical exchanges between governments, non-governmental agencies, and UNHCR officials on Tamils' eligibility for political asylum. Discussions initiated and measures taken in connection with the Tamils at a certain point turned them into something of a test case for EC refugee policy prior to the elimination of internal frontiers between the European Community member states, and the realization of the "single market" in 1993 (Gels 1989; Rudge 1987; Steen 1993). The production of video films should thus be seen against the background of a continuous political conflict in Sri Lanka, and the consequential displacement of Tamils (now approximately 200,000) to different Western countries.

At this point it is important to stress that videos obviously have nothing "essential" to do with Sri Lankan Tamils; they belong to a much broader category of globalized cultural products yielded by an advance in technological sophistication about two decades ago (Appadurai 1991: 198). Furthermore, the production of video films is now part of a much more general "diaspora practice", which anthropologists have perhaps accorded too little attention so far: exiled Asians (visibly those hailing from the cinema-happy continent of India) have in recent years begun to produce, and exchange among themselves, a number of private "family" and "community" videos on social and cultural events. This practice seems, at least in part, to reflect the increasingly restrictive immigration and visa policies of Western governments that prevent people from joining their relations on the European territory.

However, the videos produced by Sri Lankan Tamils deserve attention for yet other reasons: a remarkable feature of the films is that they primarily depict weddings of family members, Jaffna temple festivals, and important lifecycle rituals; they hence treat the question of social and cultural *recreation* in a diaspora situation. In general, the films are made by hired Sri Lankan Tamil cameramen, whose knowledge of the combinations of sound and image, and on the technicality and effects of a right focus, is surprisingly sophisticated. The films subsequently enter a system of circulation, within which the original videotape is initially sent by mail to close relatives – e.g. to and from parents and their children or to and from brothers and sisters – who then copy them and redistribute them among more distant *contakkarar* (bilateral kindred), from among whom they enter increasingly encompassing circles of copy and exchange. The films thus operate in a space between the Tamil "homeland" and Tamil "diaspora culture." In a context of displacement and connection they articulate the paradoxical possibility of "being there without being there."

REFUGEE PLACES

What emerges from this brief outline is that the videotapes in circulation among Sri Lankan Tamils are clearly not like the many Indian-produced industrial films that now exist on videotape and can be bought or rented in a number of Asian-owned shops in London, San Francisco, Sydney, or Copenhagen. Nor are they films about Sri Lankan Tamil culture in the sense of a "sum total" (Barth 1989) or a "unified corpus" (Clifford and Marcus 1986:19) that could be aptly used as teaching material in an upper secondary school. They do not represent "standard" culture, but they still resemble it. They are different and yet similar. The question is in what way?

While groping for an answer to this question I recently came across a very inspiring work of the French mathematician and psychoanalyst, Daniel Sibony. Though probably not so well known in anthropological circles, his recent book, *Entre-Deux – L'Origine en Partage* (1991), in fact shares a number of concerns with modern anthropology. Sibony's starting point – and major argument – is that the idea of "difference" is unsatisfactory when set up against the contemporary whirlwinds of identity. Up to now, he argues, we have been living and thinking under the sign of difference; there has always been a trait, a boundary, separating the whole with its "here and there," thus in and by itself *making* the difference. However, there is something about the facts, the events – extremely lively these days – which increasingly urges us not to remain satisfied with the reference (mark) of difference. Sibony proposes that in the current malaise of identity, both subjective and collective, where boundaries vacillate and identity sometimes collapses, sometimes condenses, the idea of difference is no longer satisfactory to account for this stir; it is too simple and too congealed.

A particular proposition seems to emerge from Sibony's reflections: there is a growing need in anthropology for more subtle explorations of how the very notion of cultural difference can be *put to work* in the present context of globally unfolding "mutations" of identity. This is not to say that the idea of difference has suddenly become false; it is (still) correct but limited, relevant but minute; rather like a reduced range of action, a feeble freedom of movement. Faced with the contemporary myriad of bolting identities, it merely sets about the demand for a closer examination of the very "space" through which people pass in order to become different and attempt to live their difference; in short, the very gesture of "seeking place" (Sibony 1991: 225–34).

ABSENCE AS PRESENCE

Consider this first video film that I once saw together with Saraswati,[1] a Sri Lankan Tamil woman refugee living in Denmark. The film is more than two hours long and has been made precisely for viewing in Saraswati and her family's apartment in a middle-sized industrial Danish town in Jutland, called Herning. It deals with the celebration of Saraswati's sister's second son's birthday in Sri Lanka (1989) and many of Saraswati's family members, whom she has not seen for several years, appear in it. For the present purpose we may call the film "The Empty Chair".

To the evocative tones of classical Tamil music, the first 15 or 20 minutes of the film show beautiful scenery along sandy beaches with swaying palm trees and colourful flowers in full bloom: Jaffna romance *par excellence*. Next it turns towards a vast terrain of light-green paddy fields, with distant villages on the horizon. One particular village is selected and approached. The film stops at Saraswati's sister's house, which is situated near Saraswati's parents' house, a fact that makes her exclaim "this is my house, this is my house" several times. A number of prestigious cars are parked in front of the sister's house where the party is supposed to be held; they are filmed from various angles and for quite some time. The house itself has been decorated and a big banner with "welcome" written upon it put up at the gate. The guests are arriving and Saraswati knows them all. "This is my sister's husband's sister and her two children, here comes my father's sister and her husband, this woman is my . . . " etc. It is all very confusing, but we soon agree that there are all Saraswati's *contakkarar* – and a few neighbors.

When all the guests are assembled inside the house, its various advantages are highlighted in the film: the modern fan in the ceiling, the television set and radio, the exquisite furniture. The children are playing a small electrical piano, a prestigious toy indeed (Saraswati later buys a smaller copy of the instrument for her daughter). The boy whose birthday is being celebrated cuts the birthday cake and puts small pieces of it into the mouths of his parents, with his right hand, as one often sees couples do at their wedding. At a certain point, all the guests, who are sitting in two long rows along the walls of the room, are filmed individually. There is plenty of time to discuss who they are, how they look, to whom they are married, how many children they have, and especially to emphasize their education and the kind of occupation in which they are presently engaged. Suddenly, the camera focuses on an empty chair. The film stops, there is a break, a pause, and a black and white photograph of Saraswati, her husband and two children appears for a while; they have been "inserted" in the film. Then the photograph disappears, the film starts again, and the camera continues to move slowly from individual to individual.

Saraswati's film suggests one thing above all: if one says deterritorialization one apparently also has to introduce the notion of *re*territorialization. For various (good) reasons, "essentialist" perspectives in anthropological cultural analysis have in recent years been increasingly submitted to criticism. However, non-essentialist theorizing has tended to leave too little space for the occurrence of often simultaneous, or parallel, processes of "essentialization." In Saraswati's case, since she is "here" and her *contakkarar* "there," the videotape becomes a sort of "concentrate" of family unity, which is in actual fact described as one of the many consequences of being a refugee: acute physical separation of people. Although privately produced video films form part of a much broader (diaspora) practice, they may thus be of a different, and more precarious significance to refugees. Saraswati's film seeks to maintain family "oneness" through images that evoke a sense of "belonging" in a context of geographical dispersal of family members. The video thus not only brings evidence to Appadurai's argument about fantasy as a social practice and social lives as constructions or fabrications (1991: 198), but perhaps gives even more support to the recent proposition that "Where the very notion of 'home' as a durably fixed place is in doubt – aspects of lives remain highly 'localized' in a social sense" (Peters in Gupta and Ferguson 1992: 11).

This further suggests that the "empty chair" does not so much symbolize or represent the fact that Saraswati and her family are *missing* in Sri Lanka, as one could at first be tempted to assume. It is not just used in the film as a sort of symbolic question mark as to their current whereabouts, but rather as the indication of an empty space in which Saraswati and her family can find their place, precisely *while* living in exile. By integrating their physical displacement technically in the film, they are at one and the same time absent *and* present, or rather, present as non-present. Absence is introduced as *a mode of* presence.

BREAKS AND CONNECTIONS

Similar dynamics are apparently at work in other such family films. Apart from children's birthdays (particularly the first of the first-born), a closer look on the shelves of Tamil refugees reveals videotapes on various important temple festivals in Jaffna. In nearly every case, ownership of the temple is invested not in the Brahmans who perform the complicated rites of the *akama*[2] temple's daily and annual calendar, but in one or several of the Vellalar lineages – *cantati*[3] (Banks 1960: 67). Such Vellalar-owned *akama* shrines of Jaffna are in fact shrines of the elephant-headed Pillaiyar (Ganesa), who is deeply loved for his great partiality to those who honour him; a partiality which is believed to translate very easily into material benefit. Despite several years in exile, many Vellalar Tamil refugees thus regularly send considerable sums of money to temples in their original villages and receive festival videos (and Pillaiyar's blessings) in return.

The majority of the video films, however, depict the weddings of beloved family members, the rites carried out on the occasion of "the 31st living day of a newborn child" which marks the lifting of the *tutakku* pollution period (birth, death, menstrual pollution), and those of *camaatiya vitu*, the rites of first menstruation that parents carry out for their daughters. Many Sri Lankan (Hindu) Tamils would consider the stage set for a happy and prosperous life when a family has been properly installed in a good, spiritually well-ordered home.[4] However, this state must be maintained through auspicious household ceremonies, since the continued happiness and prosperity of the family depends in large part on the commitment to maintain purity in the home. The rites of the lifecycle protect the well-established home from periodic "weaknesses" due to blood releases at birth, puberty, and menstruation, and from the sundering of the family by the grace of the gods during times of such *tutakku* affliction. Moreover, the auspicious rituals carried out after female puberty and marriage are intended to protect women from attacking, mystical agents that might afflict them with infertility. Hence, the household becomes the repository of chastity and of greatness (Pfaffenberger 1982: 209; Hart 1973).

The point is, however, that life continually poses the threat of pollution; the aforementioned *tutakku* as well as *tittu* or *tuppuravu illai*; uncleanliness from touching or imbibing some defiling substance. The former is the more serious of the two (Pfaffenberger 1982: 195) and is precisely the one being addressed, and subsequently "removed," in the video films. These films are then sent, or exchanged between, relatives, moving to and from England, Canada, Australia, France, Germany, Sri Lanka, and several other geographical locations. Circulating among Tamils around the world, they are watched, as in Saraswati's home, with immense pleasure over and over again in the evenings. In a highly pragmatic way, the films thus appear to be "social reproduction" films which in a wider sense address, and are the vehicles of, the precarious question of Tamil community in a diaspora context. Through their images, the continuation of (Tamil) social life becomes possible: in one film, long-distance temple services keep a Vellalar *cantati* "intact"; in another, *contakkarar* members are informed that impurity has been correctly "removed." Faced with real and ongoing social fragmentation, sometimes aggravated by the factual disappearance or death of people in the Sri Lankan civil war(s), these films thus insist upon the continuity, saliency, even reinforcement, of certain places of belonging.

IMPOSSIBLE COMMUNITY

What obviously follows from this small excursion into the reproduction of Jaffna Tamils' lifecycle rites on videotapes is that the young unmarried Tamil boys or men – the "typical" refugee from the Lanka – are in no position to have these films made. Since they are unmarried, they generally do not have children, and in particular no daugthers for whom they can celebrate *camaatiya vitu*, the puberty rites, which, next to a marriage, provide a man with the best means to demonstrate his wealth and commitment to the values of the Tamil Hindu community, and of whom it may be said: "His family is a good one; those people are of good caste, they keep their women well bound. They are good people to get married with" (in Pfaffenberger 1982: 206). The unmarried and unsettled Tamil refugee is prevented from participation in these attempts to recompose "identity" through "belonging." He cannot make these films, and he cannot send them to, or receive them from, anyone, for the simple reason that he has so little to film. Without a wife, a family, a house, and "order" of his own, he has no place in the social network through which these films move and is, consequently, both socially and culturally marginalized from it.

Social reproduction, hence, community, is here, at least momentarily, disturbed. As Saraswati's husband says: "These boys sit four or five persons and they drink and have a party and lovers and all that; believe me, they are not going to send this kind of film home."

Bachelor refugees thus experience a double mode of refugeeism: they live in a different and limited world of action; they occupy a different place. However, this is not simply a place of victimized non-action; it merely opens the possibility of participating *differently* in the cultural construction of Tamil identity in exile. Young, unmarried men are faced with the very real choice of stressing their commitment to one of the fundamental ambitions of their community which, since colonial times, has been almost its precondition: higher education and professionalism. They can demonstrate their participation in the strategy for social mobility adopted by the (Jaffna) Tamil minority during British colonization (subsequently forming an important concomitant of post-Independence Tamil migratory patterns), generated by the "need to concentrate on white-collar and professional niches as the only way to progress and prosperity" (Tambiah 1986: 66). And they can do this by having films made that bear witness to their specific educational and professional achievements in exile. Like Sivakumar, who, when he received his certificate of completed apprenticeship in a local school of typography, arranged for the document, his teacher and his fellow students to be "shot" on the very examination day, whereupon he proudly sent the videotape to his parents in Jaffna for (cultural) integration: "Look how I qualified; I succeeded in educating myself."

In this geographically remote place where the young student appears most "strange" to his parents – having staged himself in a Danish institution, with a Danish teacher, and a Danish certificate – he is in fact remarkably "at home." It is as if he is saying: "look at my new place, you cannot say that you do not recognize it, that it is not a place in *our* universe of representations." Danish refugee authorities would perhaps be tempted to see the film as a clear-cut proof of successful "assimilation" (or even better: acculturation), so prominent on the West European political agenda these days. Yet higher education and professionalism are places *that exist already*, as we have seen in Saraswati's film. The interesting question is how they are "homeized." Thus, when seeking place – a crucial gesture for refugees – the difference lies not so much between being placed or not, but on the *movement* between two places that is set about by displacement, by the memory of places, and the displacement of the memory. That which operates is the space where it produces itself, where it invents itself, where one can create it – the difference that differs (Sibony 1991: 14). Yet, as we shall see, power is not absent.

EXILE POWER

In 1988, the first Sri Lankan Tamil died in Herning. The news spread like wildfire among Tamils resettled by the Danish Refugee Council in various places all over the country. Many believing Tamil Hindus would agree with Pfaffenberger's interpretation (1982: 101) that the career of certain ghosts and spirits (who despise and seek to destroy human happiness) begins when, for some reason, a person is unable to get a decent funeral (*cettu vitu*), the "death house" rite. Ideally, the soul should go on to the realm of the manes (*pitir-s*) – thought to maintain a fairly benign exisistence in the realm of death (*Yama*) – but it can only remain there so long as the family performs the proper funerary rites, plus the annual obsequies for the deceased in which they are offered balls of rice or rice meals (*pintam/matai*). The purpose of the funeral is thus not only to console the bereaved, but also to speed the soul of the deceased into the next world. The funerary rites are designed to sever the bonds of the soul with this world, so that it may proceed to the realm of the *pitir-s* and enjoy a fairly benign afterlife; hence, it is the duty of loving children of the deceased to see that the rites are correctly performed. In the case of the first Tamil who died in Denmark, however, things took a slightly different turn.

The deceased had come to Denmark under the family reunion scheme to stay with his three married daughters in Herning. When he died of a heart attack, only a couple of weeks after his arrival, his two sons immediately turned up; one from Canada, another from the Middle East. There was total confusion about the rituals. How were the funeral rites and post-funeral rites to be carried out? And who should do it? Where could arrangements for a correct cremation be made, and when? After some negotiation with the authorities in the local municipality and the hospital, the sons were given permission for the body of the deceased to be exhibited for one whole day in the mortuary near the local Protestant church. Someone knew a person in Germany who kept a book with the *mantirams* (invocational verses), and it was quickly sent for. Yet other necessary elements were still lacking.

A Hindu funeral would generally involve the services of various castes: the (untouchable) Paraiyars announce the death, Barbers tend the pyre, the (Sudra) Koviyar carry the bier of the deceased, and the Washerman ties white cloths on the rafters of the head room where the corpse is being kept. None of these people were present in Herning; hence, their services could not be obtained. Most importantly, there was no Saiva Kurukkal (non-Brahmin priest) to carry out the rites, so the sons turned to a recently arrived Brahmin and requested him urgently to prepare some of the recipes for the rituals in his apartment (he never went to the mortuary). In the end, a person who knew the *mantirams* volunteered, under similar pressure, to recite them. In the total confusion of having to act quickly, the Brahmin "did a lot of things wrong," as rumours subsequently had it. For instance, he carried out the post-funerary rites before the actual funeral had taken place. When I later discussed the funeral incident with him, he confessed that he would never be able to officiate as a temple priest in Jaffna again.

At this point in the incident "power" begins to pervade Tamil (religious) "culture": the funeral had been filmed and the videotape sent to the man's relations in Valvetettiturai in Jaffna. Apart from showing the deceased lying on a bier, the cameraman had decided to focus for a long time on various items that had been in the man's possession: his identity card, his library card, his official stay permit, and his public health insurance (!). Just before he died, his voice had furthermore been recorded on a special mail-tape that one can buy in Danish post offices. When people die in Jaffna, different kinds of people (and castes) from the locality would be likely to attend the funeral; high caste members take a "purifying" bath afterwards. However, those who put oil on the head of the deceased, and participate in the symbolic feeding of the soul before its departure for the *pitir-s* are, as Tamils say, "only the very, very close," i.e. the *cantati* members, who, because of their affiliation to the deceased, are afflicted by *tutakku* pollution (in the case of Vellalars for thirty-one days). What this particular film now shows is not only that several hundred Tamils from all over Denmark have displaced themselves to pay homage to the deceased but, even more surprisingly, that many of them in fact approach the deceased and participate directly in the above rites. Most of these people do not even know the deceased at all, yet they willingly submit themselves directly to this threat of pollution. Why? My assistant with whom I watch the film answers this question very quietly, as if he does not like it at all: "Veliampalam asked them all to come; he gave the order: 'all must do it.'" The next thing one hears is that Veliampalam is the leader of the LTTE guerillas, the Liberation Tigers of Tamil Eelam, in Denmark.

The funeral incident is an example of cultural *bricolage* composed by a Hindu funeral in a Christian mortuary, by Tamil *mantirams* and Danish mail-tapes, and by LTTE supporters who ought to have been *cantati* members; hence, by many lacking things and persons – things and persons out of place. Primarily, however, the incident is about an "empty space" created by the death of a man; by a rupture that releases the reorganization of places in which, until then, each and every person had believed themselves to be. Of course, the transcendence of religion by politics is by no means anthropological news. The funeral incident nevertheless suggests that in a refugee context such processes may be differently constituted and acute. When Veliampalam challenges and renegotiates existing, fixed places of status, caste, and purity difference, the political order is not only about "the political" – otherwise almost an "ecological" framework for refugees (Steen 1993: 126) – but about the continuation of Tamil unity at a crucial moment of potential dissolution. Obviously, the LTTE leader acts from his position of power, but his intervention is less a call for the "army" than an interpretation. It is an attempt to seize identity *as it fragments*; to insist upon connection *in* fragmentation. This is, indeed, the more invisible message sent by Tamils "abroad" to those "at home" in the funeral film.

And more than that. Films about funerals are never sent *from* Sri Lanka because, as my assistant says, "no person will ever say yes to photograph it." The hidden truth of this statement is, however, that *if* everybody had been in place in Denmark, the funeral would not have been filmed. The funeral video is clearly to be viewed in the context of the many other, more easily understandable, films that Sri Lankan Tamils produce. Yet, in this particular case the LTTE leader uses the video differently and more problematically by recomposing culture, politics, and power. He shows that in certain circumstances of refugeeism, places will have to be modified, and even disregarded: Brahmins must risk pollution, high castes must become low, and "all must do it." The video thus becomes a real break with "tradition"; it represents a different "out of place" culture. In the final analysis, the funeral incident and the filming of it suggest that there are perhaps never any real, fixed, or solid places; "a place is a *potential* of displacements" (Sibony 1991: 308; emphasis mine).

CONCLUSION: ABOUNDING DIFFERENCE?

Sri Lankan Tamil video films, streams of cultural capital, teach us about the mobility, the flexibility, the changeability, and, more than anything else, the *impossibility* of Identity. They announce that *the*

Place does not exist, but its question is at work in displacement; that *Identity* does not exist but its question is at work in the mutations of origin; and that *the* Origin does not exist, but is always ready to set itself up, to test itself, to play itself out, through action (Sibony 1991: 23). This is why the notion of "belonging" is important. Belonging is a catalogue from which people can draw selective aspects, elements, and characteristics of Identity. Belonging allows for cultural similarity within difference; it makes space for cultural heterogeneity within "a group"; it allows us "to see 'culture' as a product of shared historical processes that differentiates the world as it connects it" (Gupta and Ferguson 1992: 16).

This is precisely why the idea of cultural "difference" seems unsatisfactory for confronting the questions that anthropology increasingly poses and that touch upon the mutations of origin and identity: the fact that difference is not a wall, but a vast area of an "in-between" where that which operates is not the trait of difference, symbolized by the characteristics of "One," but the very space-making of human memories; a passage through the "places" of memory and origin, from which unknown energies of inventiveness and contraction are drawn (Sibony 1991: 11). The critical point is not the "difference" between them, but the double movement of that which happens between them. The in-between is a process, a dynamic, a vehicle between oneself and one's origin; a game rather than an "end product." It is the space where the movement takes place.

A word of caution must be inserted here: by introducing the notion of "in-between" in connection with recent Sri Lankan Tamil displacements, one obviously runs the risk of exaggerating its significance for the modern refugee category and its predicaments. The theoretical implications of the term are, of course, much broader. With regard to Sri Lankan Tamils alone, they obviously involve, and have involved in the past, several other, differently conjugated, "in-betweens," which could be explored in more detail. The most obvious example emerges from recent attempts to tackle the issue of communal violence in Sri Lanka, revealing that the Sri Lankan crisis can hardly be portrayed as a conflict between two homogeneous "ethnic" groups, Sinhalese and Tamils, standing on each side of the ethnic divide. Such representations are based on primordialist, essentialist notions of culture, portraying the conflict grossly as a result of age-old ethnic hatreds. A similar argument could be applied to particular in-between spaces of the British administrators and the middle-class, English-educated "elite" Tamils (and Sinhalese) during the colonial period in Sri Lanka. The in-between might equally enhance analysis of particular narratives of "immigrant superiority" and "assimilation into the British upper-class," which were generated subsequent to the first, visible post-Independence departure of Tamil professionals (doctors, engineers, accountants) for England. In their current versions, these narratives stress Sri Lankan Tamils as exemplars of the British colonial success, while largely omitting the ongoing Sri Lankan conflict.

However, video films in global circulation among Sri Lankan Tamils suggest that the trait of difference establishes too simple an account of the (post)modern situations imposed by the movement of things and people. Difference is a much too feeble in-between; it is almost a stereotype of the in-between, a limited borderline case, surrounded in its "pure" acuteness. It cannot account for the dynamics, nuances, fragments, and micro-aspects of difference between Tamils in Denmark and those in Sri Lanka, between young bachelors and married adults, between *cantati* members and LTTE supporters, etc. These "identities" do not join or oppose each other along the trait that separates them. On the contrary, there is a vast space between them where the integration is flexible, mobile, and rich in differentiated games. The idea of a boundary or of traits, with an inside and an outside, a here and a there, seems insufficient. It is the space in-between which imposes itself as a reception place for differences at play. The study of contemporary "jet" refugees establishes this more general argument in an instant, radical, and sometimes almost crude manner – because of displacement, because of lacking places, and because of the vital necessity of constructing new ones. In short, because refugees are always at the heart of the matter; intensely, vividly, and acutely in the act of re-questioning, re-interpreting, and renegotiating their lives.

ACKNOWLEDGMENT

I am grateful to Associate Professor Michael Whyte, Institute of Anthropology, University of Copenhagen, whose comments on an earlier version of this chapter helped clarify some of its most difficult issues.

NOTES

1 In the present chapter all the names of Sri Lankan Tamil informants are pseudonyms.
2 The term "akama koyilkal" means "shrines (built according to) the temple's scriptures (*akama's*)" (Cartman in Pfaffenberger 1982: 60).

3 A *cantati* is a group of agnates, their wives, and their unmarried daughters, perceived to constitute "one body" (*ore otampu*) (Pfaffenberger 1982: 154).

4 On specific house rituals, see Pfaffenberger (1982: 131–4), and Daniel (1984: 105–62).

REFERENCES

Appadurai, Arjun (1986) "Theory in Anthropology: Center and Periphery," *Comparative Studies in Society and History* 28, 2.

—— (1991) "Global Ethnoscapes. Notes and Queries for a Transnational Anthropology," in Richard G. Fox (ed.) *Recapturing Anthropology. Working in the Present*, Santa Fe, New Mexico: School of American Research Press.

Barth, Frederik (1989) "The Analysis of Culture in Complex Societies," *Ethnos* 3–4.

Banks, Michael (1960) *Caste in Jaffna. Aspects of Caste in South India, Ceylon and N.W. Pakistan*, London: Cambridge University Press.

Baudrillard, Jean (1992) *L'illusion de la Fin ou La grève des événement*, Paris: Editions Galilée.

Clifford, James and George E. Marcus (1986) *Writing Culture. The Poetics and Politics of Ethnography*, Berkeley: University of California Press.

Daniel, Valentine E. (1984) *Fluid Signs. Being a Person the Tamil Way*, Berkeley: University of California Press.

David, Kenneth (1973) "Until Marriage do us Part: A Cultural Account of Jaffna Tamil Categories for Kinsman," *Man* 8, 4.

Gels, Johan (1989) "Responses of European States to De Facto Refugees," in Gil Loescher and Laila Mohannan (eds) *Refugees and International Relations*, Oxford and New York: Oxford University Press.

Gupta, Akhil and James Ferguson (1992) "Beyond 'Culture': Space, Identity, and the Politics of Difference," *Cultural Anthropology* 7, 1.

Hannerz, Ulf (1992) *Cultural Complexity. Studies in the Social Organization of Meaning*, New York: Columbia University Press.

Hart, George L. (1973) "Woman and the Sacred in Ancient Tamilnad," *Journal of Asian Studies* 32, 2.

Hyndman, Patricia (1987) "The 1951 Convention Definition of Refugee: An Appraisal with Particular Reference to the Case of Sri Lankan Tamil Applicants," *Human Rights Quarterly* 9, 1.

Kapferer, Bruce (1988) *Legends of People. Myths of State. Violence, Intolerance, and Political Culture in Sri Lanka and Australia*, Washington: Smithsonian Institution Press.

Malkki, Liisa (1992) "National Geographic: The Rooting of Peoples and the Territorialization of National Identity Among Scholars and Refugees," *Cultural Anthropology* 7, 1.

Pfaffenberger, Bryan (1982) *Caste in Tamil Culture. The Religious Foundations of Sudra Domination in Tamil Sri Lanka*, Foreign and Comparative Studies/South Asian Series, 7. Maxwell School of Citizenship and Public Affairs. Syracuse University.

Rosaldo, Renato (1988) "Ideology, Place, and People Without Culture," *Cultural Anthropology* 3, 1.

Rudge, Philip (1987) "Protection and European Asylum Policy," *Third World Affairs*, Third World Foundation for Social and Economic Studies.
Sibony, Daniel (1991) *Entre-Deux – L'Origine en Partage*, Paris: Editions du Seuil.
Spencer, Jonathan (1990) "Writing Within. Anthropology, Nationalism, and Culture in Sri Lanka," *Current Anthropology* 31, 3.
Steen, Ann-Belinda (1993) *Varieties of the Tamil Refugee Experience in Denmark and England*, Minority Studies, University of Copenhagen & The Danish Center for Human Rights, Copenhagen.
Tambiah, S. J. (1986) *Sri Lanka. Ethnic Fracticide and the Dismantling of Democracy*, London: I. B. Tauris & Co., Ltd.
Underwood, Kelsey Clark (1986) "Image and Identity: Tamil Migration to the United States," *Kroeber Anthropological Society Press* 65–6, 4 December 1993.

Part II

The culture and politics of place

5 The nation as a human being – a metaphor in a mid-life crisis?

Notes on the imminent collapse of Norwegian national identity

Thomas Hylland Eriksen

THE ISSUE

What kind of metaphor is a nation, and what are the sources of its symbolic power? In the relevant literature, the nation has been likened to a growing tree, a family or lineage, a village or homestead, a farm or an individual person. Handler (1988) cites one of his Quebecois informants to the effect that the nation is "like a friend." Like a person, the nation is endowed with a biography by its imaginers, and it is presumed to have gone through phases of self-development. Its past, like that of the individual, is being fashioned so as to make sense of the present and, like the ideal bourgeois individual, it is being symbolically represented as sovereign, integrated, and inhabited by a soul. In the following discussion, I propose to see the high modern disintegration of the bounded, self-sustaining individual in relation to the ever-growing questioning of the nation, conceptualized as a community of culturally similar individuals with shared political concerns. I shall argue that there is an intrinsic connection between the two processes.

THE CONCEPT OF CULTURE

In an important recent debate over the nature of ethnicity, Yelvington (1991) defines it as a form of fictive kinship, criticizing Bentley's (1987) suggestion, inspired by a reading of Bourdieu, that ethnic differences have their origin in differences of *habitus*. In Yelvington's view, the idea that ethnic identity is an aspect of *habitus* is better regarded as a "native" concept than an analytical one. Other scholars (e.g. Southall 1976; Fardon 1987; cf. Eriksen 1993c: ch. 5) have pointed out that anthropological conceptualizations of ethnic groups, tribe, etc. seem to owe more to European notions of nationhood than to the actual social boundaries and identity labels extant in the areas in question at the time of ethnographic field work. Ironically, European ideas of nationhood and ethnic identity have gradually been appropriated by the members of these "tribes," "nations," or "ethnic groups," and as a result, a social world which initially consisted of many minor, negotiable differences has increasingly developed into one consisting of but a few major and more solid ones – those designating ethnic groups or nations and their boundaries. A traveler from Bergen to Stockholm prior to the implementation of nationalist ideology, say, in the mid to late nineteenth century, would notice that each and every valley had its own dialect. However, he would be unable to say where the Norwegian dialects merged into Swedish ones. Today, the dialectal variation within both Sweden and Norway is much less significant, and it has also become possible to point out where the linguistic boundary goes. It follows the national boundary, and the development (from many small differences to a few major ones) is obviously connected to the standardizing power of national mass education and national mass media. Differences have become digitalized: they are now sharp and easily definable, and are seen to correspond to the red lines on the map.

A related discovery is nowadays being made in the comparative study of culture, especially regarding its use in the definite and plural form (*a* culture; culture*s*). The anthropological concept of culture is, in other words, shown to have the same origin as the concept of nationhood, and suffers from the same analytical shortcomings: "cultures" are, at bottom, neither clearly bounded, essentially unchanging nor traditionally conceptualized as "cultures" in "native" representations. Today, however, reifying notions of culture are increasingly common among the world's peoples, and this fact (like analogous facts concerning nationhood and ethnicity) has doubtless contributed to the present anthropological impasse concerning the concept of culture.

It may be the case, in other words, that the current attempts at refashioning traditional concepts of culture are more or less directly caused by the uncomfortable and intellectually difficult fact that "culture is loose on the streets" – I refer to the politically motivated appropriation of anthropological concepts of culture by a variety of social movements. Not only have these movements – most of them ethnonationalistic – compromised and parodied classic concepts of culture; they have also made it difficult for outsiders to describe themselves in terms of anthropological concepts of culture since they employ the very same concepts as native terms. As Hviding remarks in a paper dealing with "indigenous essentialism" in Melanesia

(Hviding 1994), his Solomon Islander informants claim, implicitly referring to ethnographic sources, that nothing would have distinguished them from other peoples in the world if it hadn't been for the fact that they had their *kastom* (cf. also Sahlins 1994). In a remarkably short time, reified and reifying ideas of historically and socially continuous cultures have moved, from being among the most central *defining concepts* of anthropology, to forming part of the *defined space* (cf. Ardener 1989) – to be accounted for, necessarily, by other defining concepts.

However, there may also be other important reasons for the presently widespread attempts to discard classic conceptualizations of culture, and they may be viewed both in relation to contemporary trends in social theory (notably the interest in semantics and deconstruction) and in relation to changes in the immediate social world itself. Could it simply be the case these days that the daily experience of anthropologists (as well as, possibly, their informants) fails to confirm the traditional notions of culture seen as a system of symbolic meaning shared by the members of a community? This is the horizon I wish to explore with direct reference to Norwegian nationhood.

The case has not been chosen arbitrarily: Norway is widely considered one of the most nationalist countries in Europe, one where the processes of cultural homogenization and legitimation of the state through invented national symbols are generally perceived, locally and among comparativist scholars, as a unanimous success. Words referring to Norway (*Norge* and *norsk*, meaning "Norway" and "Norwegian") are, if added together, only preceded by the words "and" and "in" in the Norwegian frequency dictionary, which is based on newspaper language (Heggestad 1982). If, therefore, I succeed in arguing that Norwegian nationhood may be on the verge of collapse, there is a strong probability that this too would be true of other nations.

NORWEGIAN NATIONHOOD

Nationalism, the textbook wisdom goes, is a kind of ideology which holds that the political boundaries should be coterminous with the cultural boundaries of a given territory; in other words, that a state (a "country") should only comprise people *of the same kind* (Gellner 1983; Smith 1991; cf. Eriksen 1993c: ch. 6). The idea of the Norwegian nation was born the moment a few people decided that (1) the area contained a *distinct culture*, (2) the area should have political self-determination, i.e. should be a sovereign state. Neither of these assumptions was obviously or "naturally" true at the time, that is in the early decades of the nineteenth century. Norway had been a Danish province for four centuries, and had, immediately after the Napoleonic Wars, entered an imposed union with Sweden. The symbolic construction of the nation was therefore directed towards two main targets: Denmark (the problem of cultural distinctiveness) and Sweden (the political dimension).

During the formative stages of Norwegian nationalism in the mid-nineteenth century, Norwegian nationalists had to compete with Scandinavianists, who regarded all of Scandinavia (or at least Norway and Denmark) as a single cultural area. (Mazzini, the great Italian nationalist, would later argue that Scandinavia was really a single nation, considering the cultural similarity of Norwegians, Danes, and Swedes.) The fusion of a cultural identity with a state implied in nationalism is not in itself "natural" either, as several recent writers on the history of nationalism have reminded us (Gellner 1983; Anderson 1991; Hobsbawm 1992 and Smith 1991 being the most frequently cited ones). Before (and indeed after) the French Revolution in 1789, few states were nation-states: they were multi-ethnic states. At the court of the Ottoman Empire, to mention but one example, three different languages were spoken – Arabic, Turkish, and Farsi (Persian). At the royal court in Copenhagen – the capital of Denmark–Norway until 1814 – German, French, and Danish were used.

Nationhood is a social fact in so far as the inhabitants of an area believe in the existence of that imagined community which is proposed by the nationalists. Accordingly, they hold that they have something profound in common – which could be described as *metaphoric kinship* – with a great number of people whom they will never know personally. It is in this sense that the nation may be spoken of as an imagined community. It is neither more nor less "imaginary" than other kinds of communities, but it is abstract and depends on ideological justification – it must be "imagined" by its members – in order to exist. In the case of Norway, Norwegianism would eventually win out over Scandinavianism and, by now, surely, few Norwegians claim that they belong to the same nation as Danes, or Swedes, for that matter.

Nationhood need not be strongly related to "objective cultural traits," although nationalist ideology tries to persuade people that it is. So even if it could be argued that people from southeastern Norway still, in the mid-1990s, have more in common culturally with people from western Sweden than with people from western Norway, such a similarity has little consequence in so far as people from eastern and western Norway insist that they belong to the same nation and exclude Swedes from it (cf. Eriksen 1993b).

HISTORY AND EXPERIENCE

A critical look at the historical sources of any nationalist project will quickly reveal that they are ambiguous. Norway is certainly no exception. For example, the history – or histories – of the Nordic region may just as well be used to justify a Scandinavian or regional identity as a Norwegian one. The history of each country is intertwined with that of the other Scandinavian countries and, at a lower level of integration, people from, say, Sunnmøre (northwestern Norway) may frequently feel that they have little in common with people from Oslo. It is only retrospectively that their ancestors could be described, anachronistically, as "Norwegians." Of course, the reified history of any community is a product of the present intending to make sense of the present and is not produced by the past. Any past contains material sufficient for the potential construction of a variety of "presents." The contemporary view of the Viking era (c. AD 800–1050), for example, is quite different from the view that prevailed in the sixteenth century and, in this sense, the history of the Vikings has actually changed quite radically. Today the nation – as a community of citizens regarding themselves as culturally similar – depends on ideological justification in order to exist. Further, since nations are historical products, the definition of nationhood may also change. There can be no doubt that if the nineteenth-century project of a unified Scandinavian nation had succeeded, the earlier history of the region would have been written differently from the way it has been; the past would have *meant* something different. There is no end to fruitfully ambiguous raw material in the past(s). In the light of continuously emerging new "presents," the past may be seen to bifurcate endlessly at innumerable points in time.

At this point, we should take notice of the analogy to individual biographies. The projected view of the nation as a metaphoric person developing through time (from an embryonic stage through infancy to maturity and on, perhaps, to old age and death) is perfectly analogous to the classic bourgeois view of the individual as a cultural organism unfolding through time.

The question to be posed at this point is whether the idea of the nation, imagined as "inherently limited and sovereign" (Anderson 1991: 6), still corresponds to, and helps to make sense of, the everyday experience of Norwegians. As Anderson says (1991: 5), nationalism is perhaps more appropriately likened to such phenomena as kinship and religion than to ideologies such as fascism or liberalism. In this, Anderson wishes to draw attention to the sensuous, emotional aspects of nationhood – as does Kapferer (1988: ch. 1) when he speaks of nationalism as a kind of ontology. What needs to be kept in mind is that such an ontology, granted that it does not form an irretrievable part of *habitus*, requires ideological justification. And for this to be successful, studies of ritual and social cohesion have taught us (e.g. Turner 1969), the ritual symbols (in this case symbols of nationhood) must not only have an effective ideological pole, but a sensuous or emotional one as well. In other words, their validity and, thereby, the political structure must be continuously affirmed through the everyday practice of the members of its target group for the ideology to retain its legitimacy.

Before considering the current pressure against the Norwegian concept of nationhood (i.e. the native idea of shared culture in a classic anthropological sense), another, related, aspect of nationhood must be mentioned. This is its postulate of continuity as well as potential conflict between *individual* and *society* – an endemic feature of modern ideologies pre-eminently represented in the idea of the nation, which is, in Dumont's words, simultaneously conceived of as a collective individual and as a collectivity of individuals (Dumont 1980). It is, in many countries of today, the corporate metaphor *par excellence* – a synonym for the societal body. When, as I shall eventually argue, the idea of the individual as "inherently limited and sovereign" collapses, the nation is doomed to follow suit, since its very conceptualization feeds on the concept of the individual. If the individual can be shown to have several histories, so can the nation – and the two concepts collapse simultaneously when the consequences are fully worked out.

THE NATIONALIZATION OF CHILDHOOD

In Norway as in many other countries, historians, ethnologists, and writers have made important contributions to the creation of nationhood. The history of the nation is usually so fashioned as to resemble the history of an individual from childhood to maturity; the past, as mentioned above, is being reconstructed in order to make sense of the present. One important function of such myths has also been to connect the history of the nation with the history of the individual so that childhood recollections become symbolically attached to the national memory (cf. Connerton 1989: ch. 2). Thus, fond memories of experiences from childhood and adolescence are being transformed into *national* memories. The tree beneath which one first kissed becomes, in this way, a *Norwegian tree*; the parental house becomes a *Norwegian house*, and so on. One is expected to feel a profound commitment to the nation because one's childhood experiences have become nationalized: the tree, the house, the smells, the rites of passage one went through, one's parents and so on were first and foremost *Norwegian*. The biography of individuals is thus appropriated by the nation and connected to the national narrative. Personal identity becomes synonymous with national identity, and not only the genealogical past, but even the experiential past, is read through a nationalizing filter.

Rituals are also important in this sense of linking personal experience, and particularly childhood experience, with nationhood. Thus, Norwegian Christmas trees are decorated not with angels, but with small Norwegian flags; the main annual public ritual, Constitution Day, is dominated by ice-cream eating children carrying little national flags; and even cross-country skiing, which is enforced upon children through school, has an explicit national content. The activity of skiing makes the children more Norwegian, and they are told that much.

Its great emotional power, and its unabashed linking up with the intimate sphere, suggests one important sense in which nationalism has more in common with kinship or religion than with, say, liberalism or socialism. This example also indicates that the stability of national myths is dependent on the stability of childhood recollections and their connection to kin genealogy. When childhood memories become ambiguous and contestable, they are no longer able to support the objectified image of the nation. With the ongoing pluralization of society, the shared experiences which form the foundation of the legitimacy of the nation cease to be shared. This important point will be elaborated below.

CONTESTING THE PAST

Critical voices have in recent years increasingly added their versions of Norwegian history to those explicitly or implicitly contributing to nation-building. The national myth of the heroic resistance of the Norwegian people during World War II, largely created by historians and others writing on the period, could serve as an example. Several historians have in more recent times filled in this picture with new facts and interpretations of this heroic era (for two recent contributions, cf. Dahl 1991–3, Sørensen 1991). For example, they have argued that Norwegian Nazis, many of whom died for their fatherland on the Eastern Front, may actually be regarded as devoted patriots. Parallels between certain aspects of Nazi politics and social democratic politics have also been pointed out. Further, it has been shown that although many Norwegians actively resisted the German occupation from 1940 to 1945, many indeed did not. In order to understand the controversial character of such new facts and re-interpretations of history, one must understand the role of the Second World War in the contemporary national definition of self. A very great number of books have been published on the war, and most of them depict Norwegian resistance as heroic. This resistance highlights sacred aspects of Norwegian nationhood: it shows the willingness of Norwegians to sacrifice their lives for their country, the importance of patriotism in times of hardship, and finally the divine destiny of the territory, as it were, as an independent country. Read diachronically as part of the nationalist script, the German occupation represented a low ebb in the development of Norwegian nationhood; it was a severe threat against the nation, from which the latter eventually emerged victorious. It is not surprising, then, that re-interpretations offering alternative perspectives on Norwegian achievements during the war can still be controversial.

Other central nationalist ideas have also been tampered with recently. The transition from the heroic age of Norwegian nationhood (notably the Viking age) to the "four-hundred years' night" under Danish rule has been rewritten by historians lacking the nationalist bias which was formerly part and parcel of the historiographical profession, and it has become possible to argue that there was no "necessary" continuity between the medieval Norwegian state and the Norwegian nation-state which was created in 1814, and gained full independence in 1905. This presumed continuity, evident in the name of the king elected in 1905 (Haakon VII), suggesting that modern Norway was really the same country as the medieval kingdom, must be regarded as an ideological construction, neither more nor less. The king himself was originally a Danish prince, and spoke Danish till the day of his death.

In an important book on the doctrine of national self-determination, regrettably not available in English, the political scientist Øyvind Østerud (1984) reminds his readers that many "typical" aspects of Norwegian culture were really quite recent imports from the European continent at the time when they were discovered and fashioned as national symbols by the early nationalists. This proves true for "traditional" Norwegian handicrafts, musical instruments, and folk costumes. Most of the regional *bunads*, an important type of national costume, were self-consciously invented in the early decades of the twentieth century (many of them designed by writer and suffragette Hulda Garborg, the wife of the novelist Arne Garborg), and the patterns were openly inspired by costumes in continental Europe.

The very idea of Norwegian culture and society as a "natural" and stable entity evolving according to its internal laws for over a thousand years, is gradually becoming completely untenable to a growing number of people. Norwegian culture and society have developed through crucial, if sometimes sporadic, contact with continental Europe, and the changes have been dramatic. It could easily be argued that in terms of shared notions, contemporary Norwegians have less in common with the Wergelands of the nineteenth century (famous Norwegian nationalists) than with contemporary Germans or even Brazilians.

The "tradition" on which nationalism and national identity feeds has been deconstructed in this way, and the great tradition of nationhood is increasingly being fragmented into several lesser histories which point out the ambiguities involved in interpreting the past, and which reveal nationalist versions of history as compounds of fact, myth, and interpretations which are open to discussion. With the increased influence of these counter-hegemonic interpretations of the past, it has become more difficult for the nationalists to expropriate the childhood recollections of the citizens: formerly doxic truths have been moved to the realm of opinion. And, it must be added, when it is shown in this way that the biography of the nation is negotiable, it becomes evident that so, too, is the biography of the individual citizen.

Since Norwegian history can be re-interpreted, the content of Norwegian collective identity can also be changed; indeed, some have argued that it may eventually collapse under the burden of an excessive and bewildering number of epicycles. This, some have argued, is even needed in our day and age, which is marked by two strong tendencies running counter to currently held conceptions of the substance of Norwegian nationality. They are, in short, the emergence of a poly-ethnic Norwegian society and the globalization of culture.

THE EFFECT OF THE MINORITY PRESENCE

Approximately 100,000 non-European immigrants and refugees and some 40,000 Sami comprise a small percentage of the country's population, but in recent years they have increasingly demanded formal equal rights and the acknowledgment of an official minority status. A continuous reminder that nationalist ideology does not conform perfectly with social reality, ethnic minorities constitute a thorn in the eye of many governments. Norway is no exception, and problems arising from the presence of minorities go to the naked core of nationalism seen as a cultural system: What is the actual content of the national identity? Who should be included in the nation and who should be excluded from it? And what kinds of demands should be placed on inhabitants who are not, culturally speaking, members of the nation?

The Sami, that sub-Arctic ethnic group who were formerly known as the Lapps, are Norway's oldest ethnic minority. In all probability, they have lived in what is now Norway for at least as long as the Germanic-speaking tribes and their descendants, the ethnic Norwegians. Until the late 1950s, Sami identity had been strongly stigmatized, and the transhumant Sami served as a defining Other to Norwegians, who thereby could define themselves as "civilized." Many Sami living in ethnically mixed areas chose to undercommunicate their ethnic origins – that is, they publicly pretended not to be Sami (Eidheim 1971) – and, to be sure, there has been considerable permanent assimilation to Norwegian identity, particularly among the coastal Sami. From the early 1960s on, but particularly since 1980, the country has seen the growth of a powerful ethnic revitalization movement investing pride and dignity into the formerly despised Sami identity; they have taken self-conscious measures to glorify and re-codify half-forgotten Sami customs, while at the same time making certain that they receive their share of the national welfare. This ethnopolitical movement has enjoyed considerable success. The Sami language, threatened by extinction as late as the 1960s, has been revived, and it is now the main administrative language in those parts of Finnmark county defined as Sami core areas. Substantial government subsidies ensure that Sami literature is published, and national radio provides a certain measure of programming in Sami. In 1989, a Sami parliament with limited but real power, *Sametinget*, was inaugurated by the late Norwegian King Olav V.

The fact that the Sami achieved political, cultural, and linguistic rights within the institutional framework of the Norwegian nation-state also indicates that there need be no serious conflict between an ethnic majority and a minority living in the same country. However, the avoidance of conflict seems to require that the minority be granted cultural self-determination in respects defined as important by its leaders. This may entail demands for religious and linguistic rights that may not be accepted by the nation-state, which for its part proclaims the essential cultural homogeneity of its inhabitants. Indeed, if we look at the more recent immigrants to Norway, it becomes evident that the rights successfully claimed by the Sami are not automatically granted by a national majority. During the election campaign of 1991, for example, leading politicians in Oslo suggested that immigrant children should be deprived of the right to be taught in their mother-tongue in primary schools, and strong political lobbies fought for years against the building of a mosque in the city, although Muslim organizations were willing to fund it themselves.

The overtly anti-immigrant groups, some of which are openly racist, are numerous but small and politically marginal in the country. However, suspicion, fear, and myths abound, especially targeting Muslim immigrants (who make up around 1 percent of the population). Many Norwegians exaggerate their numbers if asked; many believe that Muslim women have an average of ten children each; there is a widespread idea to the effect that all Muslims are "fundamentalists," and so on. In general, the very presence of Muslims in the country is seen as a threat against Norwegian identity by some zealous patriots, who reject that "mix of cultures" presumedly imposed by migration, and who would prefer that Norwegian society conformed firmly to nationalist doctrine; namely, that it should only comprise people "of the same kind."

In the 1990s, it is possible for a person to identify him- or herself both as a Sami and a Norwegian. It is so far much less common for a person to identify him- or herself as a Pakistani-born Muslim and at the same time as a Norwegian, even if the person in question is a Norwegian citizen. The idea of Norwegianness, as it is produced and reproduced in public discourse, appears incompatible with Islam.

Perhaps the future will see an increasing polarization between Norwegians and immigrants; perhaps many of them will leave, or perhaps many will be assimilated. It is, however, also quite conceivable that the Asian, African, and South American immigrants and refugees will succeed along the same lines as the Sami; that they will be able to assert their minority identity while simultaneously becoming integrated into Norwegian civil society. In this case, classic nationalism based on notions of cultural similarity and shared descent will have to be abandoned.

GLOBALIZATION AND THE IMPLOSION OF CULTURAL DIFFERENCES

The relationship between *isolation* and *contact with others*, or introverted and extroverted tendencies, is highly ambiguous in Norwegian history as in the history of any European country. The relative isolation of the society, which among other things entailed the absence of a powerful landed gentry after the Black Death (1348–50), has clearly had substantial effects on its ideology, social organization, and self-definition. On the other hand, Norwegians are also proud of their large merchant fleet (which, it is sometimes claimed, can be traced back to the Viking age), and during the past century Norwegians have apparently been a very extroverted people; they are well-traveled, have sent off a great number of Protestant missionaries to Africa, India, the Far East, and Madagascar, and are among the strongest supporters of the United Nations. Through incoming migration, Norwegian society has come closer to the rest of the world in a different way; it has been confronted *at home* with customs and beliefs radically different from the endemic ones.

In another sense, too, Norwegian society is much less sheltered from the rest of the world than it used to be. This concerns the globalization of culture; the spread, through modern media of mass communication, of symbols, images, and messages which know of no national or cultural boundaries, and which are dislodged from the spatial dimension, or, to use Giddens's term, disembedded. Ours is the era of the jet plane and the satellite dish. The world has shrunk, and some of its internal boundaries are vanishing. The impact of globalization on Norwegian identity – leading as it is to an increased tension between homogenization and fragmentation, between isolation and integration – has been described at length in my recent collection of essays on culture in Norway (Eriksen 1993a; cf. also Eriksen 1993b). The main point here is that globalization (and the accompanying, reflexive localization), along with the increased visibility of cultural minorities, creates an acute crisis in the traditional depiction of the nation as historically continuous and culturally homogeneous.

In the face of technological change and the fact that formerly discrete societies have become intertwined, it would seem difficult to maintain the idea of a bounded, historically continuous Norwegian culture. Since processes of cultural homogenization relativize cultural differences, and since increased geographical mobility severs the connection between territories and "cultures," one might expect the distinctiveness to vanish gradually. At a certain level, such an "implosion" of cultural difference is doubtless taking place. Like virtually every other prosperous ethnic group in the world, Norwegians nowadays watch Sylvester Stallone on FilmNet and Madonna on MTV; the pizza has become a local staple; an Oslo flat may be furnished and decorated in the same way as a flat in Milan or Berlin, and so on. In terms of consumption and lifestyle, there is less and less to distinguish Norwegians from any other Western European people.

On the other hand, as is well known from the literature on ethnicity, cultural self-consciousness and concerted delineations of boundaries may actually be a more or less direct outcome of an ongoing process of cultural homogenization. As a general rule, it is when the self-professed carriers of an identity feel that it is threatened from the outside that it becomes most important to them. To the Norwegian farmer of the 1840s, there was no reason to define his social identity. He felt no obligation to ask questions about who he was. To people living in modern, complex societies, the situation is quite different. Their way of life is different from that of their forebears, but the feeling of a continuity with the past may still remain important. They are now constantly brought into contact with people whom they define as different (foreigners, immigrants, etc.), and are thus brought to reflect on their identity. They must be able to explain *why* they describe themselves as Norwegians and not as Swedes, Pakistanis, etc. Furthermore, the shrinking of the world imposed by globalization seems to lay pressure on their identity as something distinctive: the old and familiar is replaced by the new and foreign and seems to threaten one's uniqueness. In this way, the pressure from cultural complexity and globalization is at the root of the modern identity crisis, where ethnic identification and the concomitant politicization of culture are often seen as solutions in the face of the disappearance of boundaries (cf. Friedman 1992). As Anglicisms enter the language, new shopping malls with enormous car parks replace the old family-run groceries, and the video machine replaces the storytelling grandmother, the individual may react by reaching toward that which seems constant and secure in a sea of accelerating change: the nation, seen as a pseudo-*Gemeinschaft*, a metaphoric family or a metaphoric individual, often becomes the focus of such longings. This process of cultural nation-building, I shall argue, is nonetheless soon coming to an end simply because too many everyday experiences fail to fit the model expected to account for them. However, globalization and the minority presence do not by themselves lead to the dissolution of national identity: on the contrary, they may contribute to its revival, at least in the short term.

Changes in the mass media situation are also important and need to be mentioned, however briefly. As is well known, Anderson (1991) and several other theorists of nationalism (e.g. Karl Deutsch) have stressed the importance of mass communication in the development of shared representations and subjective nationhood. In the second edition of *Imagined Communities*, Anderson has added a chapter on maps, which can be seen as excellent condensed symbols of the nation. The map shows the nation as a fixed entity, as an abstraction (a product of imagination), and inhabitants are taught its contours daily through the national educational system and mass media. Every classroom has a map of Norway in front of the blackboard, which can be rolled down whenever necessary. Until recently, further, the majority of Norwegians had access to only one TV channel. The most widely seen programme was, as in many countries, the evening news. Immediately following the news, the national weather forecast served as a daily reminder of the geographical extent of the nation; most of the households were told of the weather in distant areas, but no mention was made of the weather in neighboring countries. The weather map itself showed only Norway. Since the mid-1980s, however, cable television and the emergence of private Norwegian television channels have destroyed this hegemonic situation. No longer is everyone compelled to follow the same programmes, and different households increasingly relate to different discourses. The daily weather map is no longer seen by the majority of households. The consequences may not be dramatic, but this development fits well with the other changes mentioned, and certainly adds to the impression of cultural fragmentation. The "overarching cultural categories" of Norwegian society, accurately defined by Marianne Gullestad (1992: 140) as "categories which are used to justify without themselves needing justification," are, as a consequence, becoming less doxic. Popular debates about "what is typically Norwegian" reveal a growing reflexivity and analytical distance to phenomena such as "peace and quiet" (*fred og ro*; Gullestad's example), "going for a walk" (*å gå tur*), cross-country skiing (which is codified as a national activity), and other notions and practices formerly considered as self-evidently shared and therefore scarcely considered at all.

THE ADAPTABILITY OF INDIGENOUS ESSENTIALISM

The cultural differences of the world were for a brief period in the twentieth century regarded, by anthropologists and others, as spatial, demographically fixed, and historically stable. They have by now reached a point of theoretical implosion. It is becoming increasingly difficult to uphold the idea of the nation as an "inherently limited and sovereign" state founded on shared culture. I have mentioned several tendencies which, taken by themselves, might suggest the imminent break-up of the Norwegian nation, which, in a European context, is if anything more homogeneous and less problematic to justify vis-à-vis its inhabitants than most other nations. Notably, I have mentioned the growing questioning – by erstwhile nation-building disciplines like history and ethnology – of official myths of origin, the widely perceived creolization and differentiation of ideas, identifications, and ways of life, the discovery of cultural minorities and their assertion of specific cultural rights within the compass of the nation-state. In addition, we could mention other, no less important and no less widespread processes such as the globalization of capital (which seems to turn nationalism into a form of "false consciousness" in a Marxian or left-Hegelian sense) and the globalization of political issues (which seems to make nationalism obsolete as a political project). These kinds of development, familiar to any contemporary anthropologist working in a complex society, do not, nevertheless, call for a strong revision of the concept of culture. It would suffice to add a few extra epicycles in a more or less Parsonian manner; add a mitigating concept of differentiation, one of relationality with respect to identification, and one of change – and the concept of culture as shared meaning at the level of a community of individuals remains more or less intact. Clifford Geertz himself, the main proponent of the "culture as shared meaning" notion in anthropology, has suggested that perhaps culture is less tightly integrated than he formerly held; in other words, it is integrated like an octopus rather than like a fugue by Bach (Geertz in Shweder 1984).

As we have seen, moreover, the *native* concepts of culture as a thing and of the nation as a bounded community are alive and kicking more than ever before, and indeed they sometimes seem to be inversely related to actual cultural uniformity and stability. For this reason, Eric Hobsbawm's suggestion to the effect that nationalism is in the throes of death is less than convincing, given his argument. In the second edition of his *Nations and Nationalism since 1780*, published after the break-up of the USSR and Yugoslavia, Hobsbawm (1992: ch. 6), intriguingly, is actually even more insistent than earlier in prophesying nationalism's imminent decline. His reasons are purely instrumentalist: since nationalism will not do as a tool for rational governance, it will eventually have to go. Although the future may prove Hobsbawm right, it is at present difficult to see his optimistic linkage of ideology with reason confirmed in contemporary identity politics anywhere in the world.

Voltaire said of the Holy Roman Empire that it was "neither holy, Roman nor an empire"; with respect to the Norwegian nation-as-a-human-being, it could be said that it is neither limited, sovereign, nor integrated. In addition, I shall now argue, its symbolic relationship to the individual is becoming problematic since the integrated bourgeois individual is increasingly a creature of the past.

THE INDIVIDUAL – NO LONGER "INHERENTLY LIMITED AND SOVEREIGN"

My own main argument, although it leads to a conclusion similar to Hobsbawm's, follows a different line from his. Rather than focusing on the political shortcomings of nationalism, I would argue that its *emotional* impact is becoming difficult to maintain because a central source of its symbolism is about to disappear in many societies, including Norway: the bourgeois individual, the integrated person with his or her "value-orientation," stable "personal identity," and sense of continuity with the past as well as the surrounding society. Although many social theorists have by now proclaimed the "death of the individual," the empirical evidence is still frequently absent (as in Giddens), whimsical (as in Baudrillard), or difficult to understand (as in Strathern). Yet there are good reasons for believing that the on-going implosion of cultural differences and the concomitant explosion of new communication technologies, to mention but two of the most important features of this era, have profound and lasting effects on the concept of the individual. It is here, in the cultural construction of the person, rather than in the "objective" changes of cultural boundaries and content, that the battle over political identifications is being fought. Globalization and the collapse of history as a single master narrative contribute to this development, but it should primarily be understood in its own terms, from within. It is certainly no coincidence that the most characteristic literature of our era thematizes uprootedness, exile, and creolization and that some of the most important imaginative writers, at least in the English language (for example V.S. Naipaul, Salman Rushdie, Ben Okri, but also French-language writers like Patrick Chamoiseau), write from a creolized vantage-point. Homi Bhabha's celebrated essay, "DissemiNation," opens with the confession that although his title owes something to Jacques Derrida (himself an "uprooted" Jewish *pied-noir*), it owes something more to his own experience of migration. "I have lived that moment of the scattering of the people that in other times and other places, in the nations of others, becomes a time of gathering" (Bhabha 1990: 201). On the other hand, it has been argued that this kind of concern is characteristic of a certain breed of intellectuals but not of contemporary societies as such. Of course, most citizens do not possess the vocabulary and conceptual framework of a Bhabha, a Todorov, or a Bauman, but it can be shown not only that the experience of post-individualism is not confined to middle-class intellectuals, but also that institutional changes can be identified which contribute to explaining this situation.

The collective orientation of pre-bourgeois societies once gave way to the individualism of early modernity; now, it seems appropriate to suggest, this development continues and we are left with a social space of *dividuals* (Strathern 1992a) who tend to conceive of themselves in relational and dynamic terms. Because of an obsolete epistemology, social research has largely failed to identify these processes. Comparing the present situation with ideas of "integrated, stable individuals in societies," conservative theorists may label the current situation as one marked by "uprootedness," "anomie," "differentiation," etc. – using concepts firmly embedded within the parameters of the individual–society dichotomy (cf. Ingold 1989). Research on phenomena such as multi-channel television, consumption, serial monogamy, large-scale migration, and youth culture in European cities nevertheless suggests (albeit usually implicitly) that the old dichotomy between individual and society, and thus the old idea of the nation as a collective individual, may be breaking down simply because the bounded and self-determining individual is being transformed into a set of potential relationalities, a chameleon, an "onion," to paraphrase Ibsen's Peer Gynt, "layer upon layer but no core." The branching out of the nation's past into several possible pasts, described above, runs parallel to the discovery that people, too, have several possible pasts. (It is never too late to acquire a happy childhood, just as it is never too late to acquire a glorious history.) A related argument is represented in Strathern's work on the new reproductive technologies (1992a, b), where she argues that parenthood and notions of the family as a natural entity are threatened and that, as a consequence, both individual and society vanish. A main metaphoric source for the nation, in other words, is under threat.

SOME IMPLICATIONS

This argument has many possible implications. First, and most obviously, social theory must move – and indeed does move – towards relational and processual perspectives, endorsing programmatic statements such as Leach's old remark to the effect that the smallest "unit" studied by social anthropologists is the dyadic relationship – or, slightly more radically, supporting Bateson's acquaintance whose car carried a bumper sticker saying "Down with nouns!" (Bateson 1972). Second, by implication, culture must be – and again, is being – rethought as process and as a prerequisite for communication rather than as a field of shared meaning. Third, anthropology seems to assume a new political responsibility in this situation: rather than preaching the gospel of cultural relativism, anthropologists now become engaged in the task of disengaging ideologies which reify culture (which are, incidentally, frequently inspired by cultural relativism) from the political sphere. The field of social relations itself – rather than the opposition between individual and society and, by metaphoric extension, the opposition between the nation and foreign nations – will have to be the starting point of enquiry.

What of the nation? The very fact that people discover that identities can be negotiated – they learn to see themselves as relational – casts doubt on its future as a cultural source of "natural emotions." The deconstruction of the nation and the dissolution of the individual are mutually reinforcing processes. And at this point it is easy to agree with Hobsbawm that the future of the nation is really very uncertain and that current ethnonationalistic revitalization movements – from the Solomon Islands to Norway – may be plausibly seen as desperate expressions of death throes. If the nation dies, this will among other things strengthen the relevance of the metaphor of the nation of the human being, since people have to die.

REFERENCES

Anderson, Benedict (1991) *Imagined Communities*, 2nd edition. London: Verso.

Ardener, Edwin (1989) *The Voice of Prophecy and other Essays*, Oxford: Blackwell.

Bateson, Gregory (1972) *Steps to an Ecology of Mind*, New York: Bantam.

Bentley, G. Carter (1987) "Ethnicity as Practice," *Comparative Studies in Society and History* 29, 1: 24–55.

Bhabha, Homi K. (1990) "DissemiNation," in Homi S. Bhabha (ed.) *Nation and Narration*, London: Routledge.

Connerton, Paul (1989) *How Societies Remember*, Cambridge: Cambridge University Press.

Dahl, Hans Fredrik (1991–3) *Vidkun Quisling*, vols 1-2. Oslo: Aschehoug.

Dumont, Louis (1980) *Homo Hierarchicus*, TEL edition, Chicago: University of Chicago Press.

Eidheim, Harald (1971) *Aspects of the Lappish Minority Situation*, Oslo: Scandinavian University Press.

Eriksen, Thomas Hylland (1993a) *Typisk norsk. Essays om kulturen i Norge*, Oslo: C. Huitfeldt.

—— (1993b) "Being Norwegian in a Shrinking World," in Anne Cohen Kiel (ed.) *Continuity and Change. Aspects of Modern Norway*, Oslo: Scandinavian University Press.

—— (1993c) *Ethnicity and Nationalism: Anthropological Perspectives*, London: Pluto.

Fardon, Richard (1987) "'African Ethnogenesis': Limits to the Comparability of Ethnic Phenomena," in Ladislav Holy (ed.) *Comparative Anthropology*, Oxford: Blackwell.

Friedman, Jonathan (1992) "Narcissism, Roots and Postmodernity: The Constitution of Selfhood in the Global Crisis," in Scott Lash and Jonathan Friedman (eds) *Modernity and Identity*, Oxford: Blackwell.

Gellner, Ernest (1983) *Nations and Nationalism*, Oxford: Blackwell.

Gullestad, Marianne (1992) *The Art of Social Relations. Essays on Culture, Social Action and Everyday Life in Modern Norway*, Oslo: Scandinavian University Press.

Handler, Richard (1988) *Nationalism and the Politics of Culture in Quebec*, Madison: Wisconsin University Press.

Heggestad, Kolbjørn (1982) *Norsk frekvensordbok*, Oslo: Scandinavian University Press.

Hobsbawm, Eric (1992) *Nations and Nationalism since 1780*, 2nd edition. Cambridge: Cambridge University Press.

Hviding, Edvard (1994) "Indigenous Essentialism? 'Simplifying' Customary Land Ownership in New Georgia, Solomon Islands," *Bijdragen tot de Taal-, Land- en Volkenkunde* 131, 4: 802–24.

Ingold, Tim (ed.) (1989) *The Concept of Society is Theoretically Obsolete*, Manchester: Group for Debates in Social Anthropology.

Kapferer, Bruce (1988) *Legends of People; Myths of State*, Baltimore: Smithsonian Institution Press.

Østerud, Øyvind (1984) *Nasjonenes selvbestemmelsesrett*, Oslo: Scandinavian University Press.

Sahlins, Marshall D. (1994) "Goodbye to Tristes Tropes: Ethnography in the Context of Modern World History," in Robert Borofsky (ed.) *Assessing Cultural Anthropology*, New York: McGraw Hill.

Shweder, Richard (1984) "A colloquy of culture theorists," in Richard Shweder and Robert A. LeVine (eds) *Culture Theory*, Cambridge: Cambridge University Press.

Smith, Anthony D. (1991) *National Identity*, Harmondsworth: Penguin.

Sørensen, Øystein (1991) *Solkors og solidaritet*, Oslo: Gyldendal.

Southall, Aidan (1976) "Nuer and Dinka are People: Ecology, Ethnicity and Logical Possibility," *Man* 11, 4: 463–91.
Strathern, Marilyn (1992a) *After Nature*, Cambridge: Cambridge University Press.
—— (1992b) *Reproducing the Future*, Manchester: Manchester University Press.
Turner, Victor (1969) *The Ritual Process*, Chicago: Aldine.
Yelvington, Kevin (1991) "Ethnicity as Practice? A Comment on Bentley," *Comparative Studies in Society and History* 33, 1: 158–68.

6 Paradoxes of sovereignty and independence

"Real" and "pseudo" nation-states and the depoliticization of poverty

James Ferguson

There is a joke, which is said to be told (in various versions) by residents of Tijuana, Mexico. A "gringo" tourist walks into a Tijuana bar, and finds himself getting the cold shoulder from the locals who are drinking there. He approaches a Mexican drinking at the bar for an explanation, asking if they could not have a beer together. The Mexican refuses, saying: "Look, you gringos came here in 1840 and stole half our country. Now you sit up there with your cars and your swimming pools and your skyscrapers, while we sit here in our poverty. Why should I have a drink with you?" The gringo responds: "You mean, 150 years later, you still can't forgive us for taking half of your country?" "No," the Mexican replies. "I can forgive that. It is not easy, but I can forgive that you took half of our country. But there is one thing that I can't forgive." "What is that?" asks the gringo. "What I *can't* forgive, is that you didn't take the other half, too."[1]

The joke is not very funny. Even when told by Mexicans, it is vaguely embarrassing to a liberal political sensibility. At the end of a century dominated by anti-colonial nationalist struggles for sovereignty and independence, we can hardly help but see national independence as almost synonymous with dignity, freedom, and empowerment. This, I will suggest here, may be in some respects a trap. A comparison drawn from the recent political history of southern Africa may be a way of illuminating this.

In particular, I will briefly describe the way poverty and powerlessness have been apprehended and written about in Lesotho, a nation-state whose political independence and territorial sovereignty are universally acknowledged. I will then compare this with the way that very similar realities have been apprehended in the pseudo nation-state of Transkei, a South African "Bantustan" whose claims to national independence and sovereignty were fiercely contested, and ultimately denied (cf. Figure 1). I will argue that the very

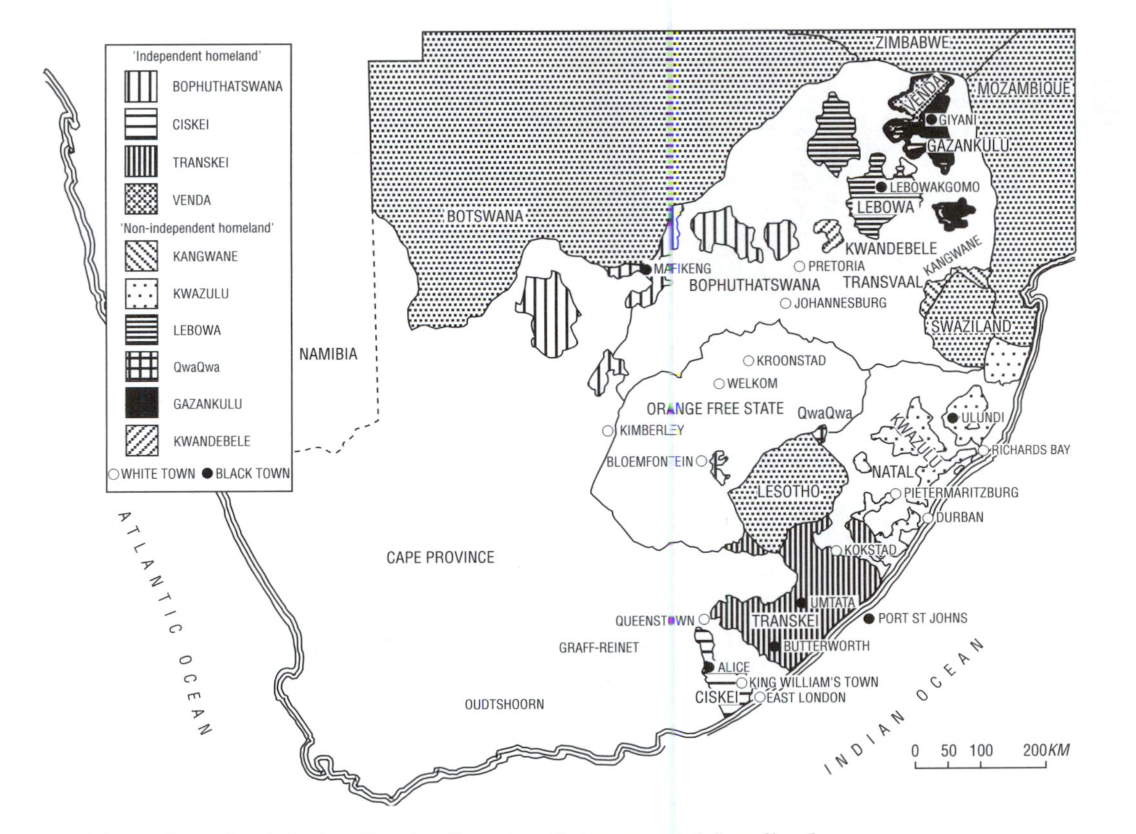

Figure 1 South Africa's "homelands;" also showing Lesotho, Botswana, and Swaziland
Source after Roger Omond (1985) *The Apartheid Handbook: A Guide to South Africa's Everyday Racial Policies*, Harmondsworth: Penguin,

weakness of Transkei's claims for sovereignty facilitated a radical, politicizing analysis of the roots of poverty and underdevelopment that can be usefully extended to the predicaments of the impoverished "real" nation-states of the world. Particularly at a time when the nation-state form is under unprecedented strain all around the world, with naturalized national mappings of peoples onto places more and more widely challenged and contested both in scholarship and in the wider world, there may be much to be gained from exploring political and analytical alternatives to the sovereign nation-state frame of reference. A close look at the southern African experience may help us to do just that.

In a final note, I will also reflect on some parallels between the dominant anthropological vision of the world as an assemblage of separate and unique "cultures" or "societies" and the dominant "development" vision of the world as an assemblage of "national economies." I will argue that anthropological ideas of culture, society, and "the field" tend to localize and depoliticize our understandings of global inequality and cultural difference in the same way that the idea of the sovereign nation-state localizes and depoliticizes our perceptions of poverty.

LESOTHO: A "REAL" NATION-STATE

As I first prepared to travel to Lesotho for field research in 1982, it was necessary to assure many friends and acquaintances in the United States that Lesotho was, as I said, "a real country." With much discussion in the press of South Africa's attempt to establish bogus ethnic "Bantustans" as supposedly "independent states," it was necessary to insist on this. Given Lesotho's precarious position as a small enclave completely surrounded by South Africa, confusion was perhaps understandable; in any case, it was necessary to emphasize that Lesotho was not a phony ethnic "homeland," but a former British colony that had received its internationally recognized independence in 1966. And that, of course, to me and to my friends, made all the difference.

It was history that had made Lesotho "a real country." Through the resistance of its people and the canny diplomacy of its nineteenth-century founder, King Moshoeshoe I, Lesotho was not incorporated within South Africa, but was (like Swaziland and Botswana) brought into the British Empire as a so-called protectorate (then known as Basutoland) under the jurisdiction of a High Commission. Spared the overrule of the South African settler state, Lesotho and the other so-called High Commission territories attained independence in the mid-1960s, along with the rest of the British-held colonies in Africa. Free and independent, one of the "front-line states" in the struggle against apartheid, Lesotho stood proudly apart from South Africa and its ethnic Bantustans (whose supposed "independence" Lesotho defiantly refused to recognize).

When I arrived in Lesotho, however, this categorical difference began to seem less absolute. Thoroughly dominated, economically and politically, by South Africa, Lesotho's "independence" proved difficult to locate. Migrant labor to South Africa was the predominant form of employment, South African firms dominated local banking, manufacture, and commerce, and the South African Rand was the everyday currency. One of the few gestures toward economic independence, in fact (if only a symbolic one), was the introduction of a Lesotho currency, the Loti, at par with the Rand. Yet few seemed to take to the nationalist gesture; currency continued to be insistently spoken of as "Rands," and South African notes were actively preferred. Worse still, many informants compared their own situation unfavorably to that of the residents of South African Bantustans like the Transkei. Indeed, one of my most articulate and politically sophisticated informants shocked me by wishing openly that Lesotho might become a Bantustan – for in the Bantustans, he insisted, taxes were lower and government services better than in Lesotho. The distinction between "real" and "pseudo" nation-states, so important back in the United States, seemed much less so here on the ground.

To an economic historian, this would perhaps be unsurprising. For in economic terms there is not a great deal to distinguish Lesotho's history from that of the "Native Reserves" within South Africa (i.e. the territories reserved for "native" black South Africans, which would later become the foundation of the supposedly independent "Bantustans"). To begin with, the Basotho subjects of King Moshoeshoe, like other African farmers in the region, lost most of their best agricultural land in a series of wars with encroaching white settlers, between 1840 and 1869. On this diminished land area, the peasant farmers of Basutoland nonetheless managed to respond to new markets with the production of surprisingly large crops of surplus grain throughout the late nineteenth century (Murray 1981), a pattern which has also been documented for black peasant farmers in the South African "Native Reserves" (cf. Wilson and Thompson 1971; Bundy 1979). At the same time, increasing numbers of Basotho travelled to work in South Africa after the discovery there of diamonds in 1867 and gold in 1876. Over the years, however, agricultural production slumped, as more and more people cultivated a small and deteriorating land base, and as the once-lucrative South African markets for agricultural produce were closed off. Families came to depend more and more on cash remittances from men employed in South Africa, most commonly in the mines. By the time of independence in 1966, Lesotho was little more than a labor reserve for the South African economy (cf. Murray 1981). This economic trajectory displays striking parallels with that of the "Native Reserves" of South Africa, and of the Transkei[2] in particular (Wilson and Thompson 1971: 69).[3]

Yet if Lesotho's economic history was surprisingly similar to that of "Native Reserves" like the Transkei, its political trajectory was strikingly different. For when the British decolonized in the 1960s, Lesotho, along with the other southern African protectorates, achieved the status of an internationally recognized, sovereign nation-state, notwithstanding its precarious geographical position entirely encircled by South Africa (see Figure 1).

As a small, economically dependent, geographically surrounded labor reserve, British Basutoland was perhaps an odd candidate for national independence. In the debates surrounding decolonization, certainly, there were some who claimed that such a territory would be economically neither independent nor (as it was said) "viable" (Spence 1968). Politically, too, it was not clear how "independent" an independent Lesotho could be, being completely surrounded by such a powerful and domineering neighbor. Indeed, such fears proved well founded in the early years of independent Lesotho, which saw not only continuing economic dependence, but repeated and unsubtle South African interference in electoral processes and a substantial presence of white South Africans in key government positions.[4]

Yet such reservations never seriously challenged Lesotho's legitimacy and acceptance within the international community. The new nation-state was received as simply one of a number of former British colonial territories acceding to independence. Indeed, it seems clear that Lesotho's sovereign status was accepted by the international community more as a response to its status as a British ex-colony than as an endorsement of any internal capabilities to function economically or politically. Unlike the case of Transkei, Lesotho's accession to statehood was received as a routine decolonization, not as part of a cynical ploy to strip black South Africans of their citizenship (see below). It was this political context, rather than any objective features of the territories involved, that made Lesotho, but not Transkei, "a real country."

TRANSKEI: CHRONICLE OF A PSEUDO NATION-STATE

The roots of the South African Bantustans are to be found in the old "Native Reserves," formally established under the terms of the Land Act of 1913, which reserved about 7 percent of South Africa's land (later increased to 13 percent) for exclusive African settlement, while setting aside the rest – the overwhelming majority – for the whites. But with the rise of the Nationalist Party and its policy of "apartheid" in 1948, the rural reserves acquired a new political importance. For as the master plan of apartheid unfolded through the 1950s and 1960s, it became clear that its central strategy was to translate the facts of racial domination and segregation (already well established in South Africa) into the terms of *national* difference. With discriminations of color rapidly losing legitimacy both inside and outside South Africa, the planners of apartheid aimed to redefine black South Africans as ethnic citizens of "their own" (as they said) "national states" or "homelands," to be constructed and consolidated mainly out of the pieces of the old Native Reserves. As these new "Bantu states" or Bantustans attained "independence," their African citizens would indeed enjoy the political rights and voting privileges that the world was demanding – but only *within* these states. There they would be able to (as it was usually put) "develop freely along their own lines." But within the 87 percent of the country designated "white South Africa," Africans would be foreign citizens. Even Africans born and raised in so-called "white" areas would be assigned citizenship on the basis of their ethnicity in one of the "Bantu states," thus becoming foreigners in their own land. Citizens of the Bantustans might, of course, be allowed within "white South Africa" as workers, with the proper permissions, but they would be no more entitled to political rights there than are foreign workers in other countries (such as Turks in Germany, or Mexicans in the United States). Through this sinister and ingenious plan, the "race problem" (so-called) would be solved at a stroke, for there would be no more black South Africans. Instead, the problem would be re-posed as a problem of nationality, and of migration between independent national states.

A very considerable amount of energy and money was put into this improbable plan. Literally millions of people, as is now well established, were forcibly relocated, and dumped within the boundaries of the new Bantustans-to-be (Platzky and Walker 1985). And supposedly independent governments were indeed set up, starting in 1976, for the Bantustans of Transkei, Bophutatswana, Venda, and Ciskei. Ultimately, it was envisaged that all ten ethnic "homelands" (see Figure 1) would become independent, to be linked together with so-called "white South Africa" in what the South African president, P. W. Botha, liked to call "a constellation of states," something like the British Commonwealth. Planners also harbored hopes (from as early as 1954) that the former High Commission Territories of Lesotho, Swaziland, and Botswana, might also eventually be brought into such a constellation (Spence 1968: 74).

As all this was happening, an extraordinary effort was being made to establish the legitimacy of the supposed national states, both within South Africa and beyond. National governments were established with all the trappings, complete with ambassadors, embassies, and limousines. Moveover, national symbols were self-consciously fashioned for the new states. Anthems, flags, crests, mottos, etc. – all were being churned out at a record clip in the early 1970s by Pretoria's Department of Bantu Administration and Development. The new "Republic of Transkei" was given not only a national flag, but a national crest (in the incongruous style of medieval European heraldry) displaying a bull's head (said to symbolize "not only the vital role of animal husbandry but also the importance of bulls in the ritual life of the Xhosa people"), along with the unintentionally ironic motto, "Unity is strength" (Malan and Hattingh 1976). Transkei's supposed "independence" in 1976 was accompanied by a tremendous flurry of such nationalist symbol-waving, including an elaborate and expensive independence ceremony, and the publication of a glossy coffee-table book celebrating the new "Republic of Transkei" and its cultural heritage. Never was Hobsbawm and Ranger's somewhat cynical phrase "the invention of tradition" (1983) more literally appropriate.[5]

It is now clear, of course, that these various attempts to secure legitimacy for the Bantustans were more or less a complete failure. In spite of vigorous lobbying, no nation outside of South Africa ever extended formal diplomatic recognition to the supposedly "independent" states. And in spite of a dizzying combination of carrots and sticks thrust at them, the supposed "citizens" of the Bantustans were never well sold on the idea that "independence" for impoverished and scattered patches of African reserves constituted their political deliverance. In the end, the Bantustan strategy was abandoned as a total failure. Today, under the new interim constitution, the former homelands have been completely reincorporated within a unitary South Africa, with a provincial structure that preserves none of the old homeland boundaries or institutional structures. The era of "independent Bantustans" ended up being a short one.

But it is worth remembering that such an outcome was not always obvious or inevitable. When Transkei was put forward as the first of the new "independent" Bantu states, many observers – black as well as white – regarded it as a not implausible new entry into the world of nation-states. It was, as its defenders noted, larger, richer, and more populous than its internationally recognized neighbors, Lesotho and Swaziland (see Figure 1). It was better consolidated, and larger than the other proposed "national states" – and if its territory was not entirely contiguous, well, neither was that of many other well-established nation-states, including the United States, for example. Moreover, the legal case for Transkeian statehood (in formal, constitutional terms) turned out to be surprisingly strong (Southall 1982: 5–6). Transkei's poverty and lack of resources made it vulnerable to arguments about its economic "viability"; but as Mlahleni Njisane (who would later become Transkei's non-accredited ambassador to the United States) observed (correctly), Transkei was "neither the smallest nor the poorest of countries in Africa." On the contrary, he claimed: "The simple fact is that Transkei will not be any worse off than half the Third World" (BCP 1976: 16, 17).

Internationally, too, it was not immediately obvious that the Transkei's independence would fail. The Republic of Transkei, let us remember, appeared on *National Geographic*'s world maps as an independent country from 1976 until at least 1981.[6] And although formal diplomatic recognition was withheld, many informal and business contacts were established with foreign countries, especially with such internationally spurned states as Israel and Taiwan. And we may never know how close the Reagan Administration may have come to extending formal recognition to the Bantustans; some Reagan advisors, at least, were not prepared to dismiss the "independent national states."

Ultimately, the legitimacy of Transkei was arbitrated both in the international "community of nations," and in vigorous domestic political debate. Arrayed against the formidable propaganda apparatus of the South African state were powerfui oppositional political movements (ironically, "anti-independence" movements), which stripped away the coating of flags and anthems and nationalist rhetoric to attack the underlying political maneuver they concealed. A few quotations will give a bit of the flavor of the anti-independence campaigns.

The Black People's Convention, in 1975, declared that the independence of Transkei

> is a cunning manoeuvre by the racist regime of Vorster to give National and International credibility to the abhorrent policy of apartheid, precisely at a time when the process of liberation has shown itself to be inevitable in Africa, and also at a time when the subcontinent has dramatically changed in favour of the struggle for National liberation. . . . The so-called independence is nothing but yet another manoeuvre to "legalize" the alienation of the people of the Transkei from the rest of Azania, which is their motherland, so as to give the denial of their rights in Azania a legal and constitutional backing.
>
> (BCP 1976: 39)

For Steve Biko, the Bantustans were "the greatest single fraud ever invented by white politicians" (Biko 1978: 83). Some black politicians thought they could use Bantustan independence to press for black liberation – "quick," as Biko said, "to see a loophole even in a two-foot-thick iron wall" (ibid.: 36). "But if you want to fight your enemy you do not accept from him the unloaded of his two guns and then challenge him to a duel" (ibid.: 85).

> These tribal cocoons called "homelands" are nothing else but sophisticated concentration camps where black people are allowed to "suffer peacefully". . . . [W]e black people should all the time keep in mind that South Africa is our country and that all of it belongs to us. The arrogance that makes white people travel all the way from Holland to come and balkanise our country and shift us around has to be destroyed. Our kindness has been misused and our hospitality turned against us. Whereas whites were mere guests to us on their arrival in this country they have now pushed us out to a 13% corner of the land and are acting as bad hosts in the rest of the country. This we must put right. Down with bantustans!!!
>
> (Ibid.: 86)

POLITICS AND POVERTY: TWO DISCURSIVE LANDSCAPES

The difference in the positions of Lesotho and Transkei in the world of legitimate nation-states has resulted in strikingly different treatments of the realities of poverty and powerlessness that the two territories so evidently share. In the "development" discourse that dominates discussions of Lesotho, poverty has inevitably been treated as an attribute of Lesotho's *national economy*. As I have shown elsewhere (Ferguson 1994), historical and structural causes of Lesotho's predicament have been largely obscured from view, as the "nation-state" frame of reference has displaced a wider, regional perspective. Through what I have called the "anti-politics machine" of "development," persistent poverty has been constructed as a product of Lesotho's rather unfortunate geography and lack of resources (taken as givens), together with the technical fact that these meager resources have not been fully "developed." The actual causes of poverty in Lesotho were, as I have suggested, very much like those in the Transkei; but discussions of poverty in Lesotho have rarely made any reference to South African state policy, enforced low wages, influx control, or apartheid. For poverty in the independent nation-state of Lesotho has been insistently formulated in national terms, as "*Lesotho's* poverty" – and, thus, implicitly, Lesotho's problem (Ferguson 1994).

The apartheid experiment involved, among other things, an attempt to deploy this same maneuver internally: to transform the political problem of poor and racially oppressed South Africans into a question of international relations with "developing countries." Indeed, South African planners always claimed that "apartheid" really only meant "separate development," and that they were eager to help "the Bantu" to "develop" within their own independent "Bantu-states" (*Bantustans*). Along with the invention of national flags and crests, then, went a parallel emphasis on the "development" of each homeland, guided by its own government, but with the paternalistic assistance of the South African state. National development plans were solemnly drawn up for each homeland, even the tiniest ones like Lebowa and QwaQwa. Consultants and academics argued earnestly over the merits of different "national development strategies." Development projects were drawn up and implemented; their failures were analyzed and lamented.

Transkei was thus very much caught up in the web of "development" discourse. Like Lesotho, it was the object of a distinctive mode of knowledge, which sought to identify "problems" within the national economy, and to prescribe technical solutions to them. In at least some respects, then, the "illegitimate" and internationally despised "development" activities in Transkei and the "legitimate," internationally beloved "development" initiatives in Lesotho – so different in the view from afar – looked a good deal alike when seen closer up.

But beyond these similarities, I argue, lies a crucial difference. For the *reception* of the "developmental" constructions I have described, both inside and outside of the territories in question, was strikingly different in Transkei than has been the case in Lesotho. While "development" discourse in Lesotho has largely succeeded in depoliticizing poverty, constructing it in technical (and national) terms as a lack of some combination of skills, inputs, and resources, in the case of Transkei "development" discourse encountered an acute, vigorously politicizing critique. Rather than accepting "Transkei" as a bounded economic unit, critics from the start relentlessly insisted on connecting the Transkei's economic predicament with a wider economic order, and on linking, in a quite direct way, rural black poverty with urban white wealth.

Hector Ncokazi, who led the resistance to Transkei's independence until his detention by security forces in 1976, declared, for instance,

> The people of the Transkei who are so shabbily and callously ill-treated by the South African socio-political system are the selfsame people, who have built the South African economy which the government boasts of abroad. They have suffered most as a result of mine disasters that have riddled this country in the past. They now want the fruits of their labours and compensation, by the granting of human rights, for their sufferings.
>
> (BCP 1976: 22)

Hlaku Rachidi, of the Black People's Convention, observed for his part,

> [In the Bantustan plan], Blacks must be pushed off and made so-called citizens of dummy states all around South Africa, to reduce their claim in broader metropolitan South Africa. One notices immediately that this is a sophisticated version of the same 'Native Reserves' created during the Smuts era. The so-called dummy black states now envisaged will have no elaborate industrial infrastructure calculated to give jobs to the millions of Blacks who are supposedly their citizens. Neither are they seriously meant to have this by their white creators because the white man has decided that although he certainly does not want the black man's vote in the broader metropolitan South Africa, he certainly wants the black man's labour to man the white man's factories, to build for him, to sweep his streets, to make his garden and to care for his babies. Thus migratory labour will eventually be at the heart of the entire relationship between the so-called dummy states and the broader metropolitan South Africa. . . . [The Bantustans] will be used as

> dumping grounds for the unwanted black vote . . . [and] will serve as convenient labour reservoirs without the other complicating factors arising out of having to recognise the permanence of black labour in metropolitan South Africa.
>
> (Ibid.: 42–8)

Such a radical political critique, coupled with effective political mobilization, eventually had its effects at the level of policy discourse as well, as the whole Bantustan strategy began to be more and more seriously questioned in the mid-1980s. The Development Bank of Southern Africa, for instance, was an official lending agency charged with "development" investment in the homelands. The early issues of the DBSA's house journal, *Development Southern Africa*, reveal a broad acceptance of the "separate development" framework, and showcase various attempts to hammer out "development" policy for the new "national states" (e.g., for Transkei, Nkhulu 1984). By 1986, however, it is possible to find quite fundamental questioning of this framework within this policy discourse. Thus one author critiqued a proposed "Rural Development Strategy for Lebowa," observing that its authors "have failed to examine the nature and circumstances of poverty in Lebowa and, in particular, the structural dependence of Lebowa, with its largely 'locked in' population, within the South African political economy" (Cobbett 1986: 309–10). On the contrary, he claimed,

> by treating Lebowa in effect as a self-contained country and not critically examining its position within the South African economy, the authors have chosen to wear ideological blinkers. Thus, for example, the impact and implications of the migrant labour system on the development options for Lebowa are not examined. The document studiously avoids any political analysis both of the causes of rural poverty and of the possibilities which political reform might or could present
>
> (Cobbett 1986: 317)

Another author writing at about the same time finds that discussions in the journal have come to a broad agreement on the existence of "one functional integrated South African economy" (as opposed to a set of distinct "national" economies corresponding to discrete "homelands"). He proceeds to argue that

> the acceptance of a functional integrated economy and its implications for policy is so totally "opposite" from previous thinking,

> that a simple adaptation of existing structures and strategies to this "new" paradigm may lead to somewhat muddled thinking
>
> (van der Merwe 1986: 464)

This sort of rejection of the idea that a small, dependent labor reserve could be analyzed as a national economy, and the questioning of the whole ethnic–national frame of reference, was – as I have argued at length elsewhere (Ferguson 1994) – conspicuously absent from official "development" discourse in Lesotho during this same period. Precisely because the legitimacy of Lesotho as a sovereign, independent nation-state was not in question, economic structures were insistently conceived in national terms ("Lesotho's economy"), and questions of poverty, growth, wages, etc. were treated as matters of national policy ("Lesotho's development problems"). In the case of Transkei, on the other hand, the formidable political challenges to the very existence of the Bantustans created a very different discursive landscape, in which questions of poverty, economic policy, and "development" could be posed in a way that made questions of wider regional economic and political structures more visible. This was true both of radical oppositional political discourse and, at a later stage and in a watered-down form, of some official development discourse.

DEPOLITICIZING POVERTY: A CONSTELLATION OF STATES

The Bantustan strategy attempted to depoliticize the disempowerment of rural Africans by hiving them off in independent states. But the refusal of critics inside and outside South Africa to accept this spurious separation has repoliticized the poverty of the rural reserves by reconnecting it to the system that created it.

The insistence on maintaining a strict distinction between this situation and the case of Lesotho – insisting on treating Lesotho as a "real" (i.e., sovereign and independent) nation – ironically depoliticizes its powerlessness by unintentionally performing a similar separation. Through its very international respectability, Lesotho is rescued from P. W. Botha's envisioned "constellation of states," but is simultaneously incorporated into a much larger constellation, the world community of nations, within which it occupies an equally powerless position (cf. Malkki 1994). This may suggest the relevance of the joke with which I began, which is in fact very serious. For the joke suggests that – as in the case of South Africa's magnanimous acceptance of Lesotho's formal independence – there may be a certain cunning involved in "taking only half." After all, is it not precisely by *acknowledging* Mexico's sovereignty, even while politically and economically dominating the country, that the United States manages to contain the political implications of the massive poverty of *its* labour reserve within the ideological borders of "Mexico's problems"?[7]

I would emphasize here that I do not mean to deny that national independence, in southern Africa and elsewhere, has often had progressive and empowering consequences. I mean only to point out that conceiving liberation in terms of national independence has had certain ideological effects that we would do well to keep within sight. In particular, where the national frame of reference has enjoyed an unquestioned legitimacy, economic grievances have tended to be seen as "problems" essentially local and internal to a national economy, and economic critique has been largely channeled into discussion of whether or not "the nation" is pursuing "the right policies." In this way, the wider system of economic relations that is constitutive of many of these "problems" is removed from view, thus depoliticizing the discussion in a very fundamental way from the start. This fact becomes especially visible, I have suggested, when the politics of poverty in a legitimate nation-state like Lesotho is contrasted with a case like that of Transkei, where the national frame has fundamentally lacked legitimacy and a much more radical critique has been possible.

The Bantustan experience has given the world a rich lesson in the treacherous traps of national sovereignty. The politicization which ensued through the debate over the Bantustans has resulted in the wide dissemination of a radical and clear-sighted analysis of the systemic roots of poverty in the region. Lesotho stands out as a clear counter-case, in which the introduction of an uncontested national sovereignty has largely succeeded in obscuring regional connections and localizing responsibility for poverty within national borders.

But Lesotho, even if it is a particularly clear case, is not unique. For none of the impoverished nations of the world are truly "sovereign" or "independent"; and nowhere do we find a true "national economy." By being all-too-respectful of nationalist myths of sovereignty and independence, we who study the Third World have often unwittingly aided at a global level that very depoliticization that P. W. Botha failed to accomplish at the regional level through his envisioned "constellation of states." For what is the international order of nations if not just such a "constellation of states" which segments off the exploited and impoverished regions within discrete national compartments with "their own problems," thereby masking the relations that link the rich and poor regions behind the false fronts of a sovereignty and an independence that have never existed?

The line between "real" and "pseudo" nation-states is more fragile than we have yet realized, and South Africa's experience with ethnic "homelands" has more to teach us than we have yet acknowledged. There may be much to be gained by bringing the conceptual and political clarity that has characterized recent analysis of South Africa's "pseudo" nation-states to our understanding of the international constellation of so-called "real" nation-states as well.[8]

EPILOGUE: ANTHROPOLOGICAL APARTHEID? A CONSTELLATION OF CULTURES

In this brief final section, I wish to suggest some parallels between the way the idea of a national economy works to localize and depoliticize perceptions of poverty and the way conventional anthropological ideas about "cultures," "societies," and "the field" act to do the same to our understanding of cultural differences.

Let me begin by suggesting, uncontroversially, that just as there is no "national economy of Lesotho" separate from an encompassing set of relations with a wider South African (and ultimately global) system, so, too, there can be no local "cultures" apart from the wider and encompassing relations within which they are defined. Just as the economies of what world-system theorists refer to as "core" and "periphery" demand to be understood via their interrelations, so, too, the forms of life and systems of meaning that are found in the different parts of the post-colonial world demand to be understood relationally, as they inflect and constitute one another. Recent theorists (e.g., Gilroy 1991, 1993; Bhabha 1994; Wright 1985) have shown that such things as Englishness and Europeanness require to be understood in relation to the colonial encounter: that whiteness is constructed on the ground of colonial non-whiteness; that rationality is built against the presumed irrationality of the savage native; Enlightenment against the imagined blackness and ignorance of the Dark Continent. Cultures of the colonized, meanwhile, are constructed in a similar, if inverse, fashion; thus "*sesotho* culture" in Lesotho is explicitly built up as a contrast and point of resistance against a dominant "white culture," locally styled "*sekhooa*"[9] – and that which counts as "local culture" (thus that which is "anthropological" enough to get into most ethnographic accounts) is constituted by this uneven encounter.

The conventional anthropological idea of "a culture" that forms "a system" which can be known "holistically," however, tends to push such constitutive relations from view.[10] The holistic vision of culture as system is usually based on some sort of analogy with language, with language presumed to be uncomplicatedly unitary and systemic. Yet even for language this may be a dubious way of proceeding, as Mary Louise Pratt has recently demonstrated (1987). Pratt argues that dominant models of language (in structural linguistics and elsewhere), rely on the fiction of a homogeneous and undifferentiated "speech community," in which all speakers are equal players, and all share a set of common meanings and codes. Since actual speech situations are more often characterized by *partial* sharings, hierarchical power relations, and different and conflicting understandings on the part of differently situated actors, Pratt refers to the counterfactual linguistic model as a "linguistic utopia," serving to imagine a very particular type of community. Against this "linguistics of community," Pratt counterpoises what she calls a "linguistics of contact," a linguistics that places at its center the workings of language across rather than within lines of social differentiation, of class, race, gender, age.

Anthropological conceptions of "the field," too, I have argued elsewhere,[11] help to reinforce the anthropological weakness for seeing cultures as the property of separate "societies" or "communities" rather than as phenomena of hierarchical relation and interconnection.[12] The ethnographer's still-familiar tropes of entry to and exit from "the field," the images of "heading out to" or "coming back from" the field, powerfully suggest two separate worlds, bridged only at the initiative of the intrepid anthropologist. Such images, of course, push to the margins of the anthropological picture precisely those connections that link the two places, and situate them within a common, shared world. Deborah D'Amico-Samuels (1991: 75) has put it well:

> Because the notion of the field current in anthropology allows that removal to take place symbolically and physically, the real distancing effects of the field are masked in the term "back from the field". These words perpetuate the notion that ethnographers and those who provide their data live in worlds that are different and separate, rather than different and unequal in ways which tie the subordination of one to the power of the other.

The distancing and relativizing move that allows us to even-handedly contrast one "culture" (the one we study) with another ("our own") thus has some of the same hidden dangers as the nationalist move that sets up formally symmetrical relations between substantively unequal and mutually constitutive national economies. In this sense, the familiar anthropological claim that "they have their own culture" carries something of the same effect in cultural analysis as the development planner's claim that "they have their own economy" does in economic analysis: namely, the closing off from view of those connections and relations that would allow for a very different analysis.

Refusing the spatial localization and insulation that is created by a "fielded" concept of culture, on the other hand, does something analogous to what the challenging of the sovereign nation-state did in the case of Transkei: it problematizes the "givens" and demands an accounting of why cultures are "different," "exotic," "isolated," or what have you, and of how they got to be that way. Placing a central analytic focus on the connections and relations that constitute national economies as national, or local cultures as local, can combat the dehistoricization and depoliticization that both developmentalist analyses of economies and anthropological analyses of cultures, in their different ways, promote.

NOTES

1 I am grateful to Ricardo Ovalle Bahamón for telling me a version of this joke, and for a stimulating discussion of its significance in a southern African context.

2 I use the phrase "the Transkei" to refer to the pre-1976 territory, in its days as a "Native Reserve." I speak instead of "Transkei" when the reference is specifically to the supposedly independent "Republic of Transkei."

3 On the economic history of Lesotho see, in addition to Murray (1981) and Wilson and Thompson (1971) cited above, Leys (1979), and Palmer and Parsons (1977). On the history of the Transkei see Wilson and Thompson (1971), Bundy (1979), and Southall (1982) for overviews, and Beinart and Bundy (1987) for a very stimulating set of more detailed studies.

4 See Ferguson (1994: 105–7) and references cited there.

5 See Anonymous (1991) for an excellent account of similar processes in Ciskei.

6 The *National Geographic* maps contained a note in small print observing that the homelands' independence was not internationally recognized. But Transkei and the other "independent" homelands were nonetheless depicted as "countries," each in its own contrasting color.

7 A related argument has been made in Köhler (1993).

8 On the imagined international community of nation-states cf. Malkki 1994.

9 Jean and John Comaroff have written about the closely related contrast among Batswana between *sekgoa* and *setswana*. See Comaroff and Comaroff 1987, 1991.

10 This is an argument that I develop at some length in a forthcoming article, "Open Systems and Closed Mines: The Limits of Anthropological Holism on the Zambian Copperbelt."
11 See Akhil Gupta and James Ferguson (in press).
12 This section of my argument I have developed jointly with Akhil Gupta. See Gupta and Ferguson (1992), Gupta and Ferguson (in press).

REFERENCES

Anonymous (1991) "Ethnicity and Pseudo-Ethnicity in the Ciskei," in L. Vail (ed.) *The Creation of Tribalism in Southern Africa*, Berkeley: University of California Press.

BCP (Black Community Programmes) (1976) "Transkei Independence," *Black Viewpoint* 4, Durban: Black Community Programmes.

Beinart, William and Colin Bundy (1987) *Hidden Struggles in Rural South Africa: Politics and Popular Movements in the Transkei and Eastern Cape 1890–1930*, Berkeley: University of California Press.

Bhabha, Homi K. (1994) *The Location of Culture*, New York: Routledge.

Biko, Steve (1978) *I Write What I Like*, New York: Penguin Books.

Bundy, Colin (1979) *The Rise and Fall of the South African Peasantry*, Berkeley: University of California Press.

Cobbett, Matthew (1986) "Review Article: A Rural Development Strategy for Lebowa," *Development Southern Africa* 3, 2: 308–17.

Comaroff, John L. and Jean Comaroff (1987) "The Madman and the Migrant: Work and Labor in the Historical Consciousness of a South African People," *American Ethnologist* 14: 191–209.

—— (1991) *Of Revelation and Revolution: Christianity, Colonialism, and Consciousness in South Africa*, vol. 1, Chicago: University of Chicago Press.

D'Amico-Samuels, Deborah (1991) "Undoing Fieldwork: Personal, Political, Theoretical and Methodological Implications," in Faye Harrison (ed.) *Decolonizing Anthropology*, Washington, DC: Association of Black Anthropologists.

Ferguson, James (1994) *The Anti-Politics Machine: 'Development', Depoliticization, and Bureaucratic Power in Lesotho*, Minneapolis: University of Minnesota Press.

—— (1995) "From African Socialism to Scientific Capitalism: Reflections on the Legitimation Crisis in IMF-ruled Africa," in David B. Moore and Gerald J. Schmitz (eds) *Debating Development Discourse: Institutional and Popular Perspectives*, New York: St. Martin's Press, pp. 129–48.

Gilroy, Paul (1991) *There Ain't No Black in the Union Jack*, Chicago: University of Chicago Press.

—— (1993) *The Black Atlantic: Modernity and Double Consciousness*, Cambridge, MA.: Harvard University Press.

Gupta, Akhil and James Ferguson (1992) "Beyond Culture: Space, Identity, and the Politics of Difference," *Cultural Anthropology* 7, 1: 6–23.

Gupta, Akhil and James Ferguson (eds) (in press) *Anthropological Locations: Boundaries and Grounds of a Field Science*, Berkeley: University of California Press.

Hobsbawm, Eric and Terence Ranger (eds) (1983) *The Invention of Tradition*, New York: Cambridge University Press.

Köhler, Gernot (1993) "Global Apartheid," in Robert J. Gordon and William A. Haviland (eds) *Talking About People: Readings in Contemporary Cultural Anthropology*, Mountain View, CA: Mayfield Publishing Co.

Leys, Roger (1979) "Lesotho: Non-Development or Under-Development: Towards an Analysis of the Political Economy of the Labor Reserve," in T. M. Shaw and K. Heard (eds) *The Politics of Africa*, London: Longman and Dalhousie University Press.

Malan, T. and P. S. Hattingh (1976) *Black Homelands in South Africa*, Pretoria: Africa Institute of South Africa.

Malkki, Liisa (1994) "Citizens of Humanity: Internationalism and the Imagined Community of Nations," *Diaspora* 3, 1: 41–68.

Murray, Colin (1981) *Families Divided: The Impact of Migrant Labour in Lesotho*, New York: Cambridge University Press.

Nkhulu, W. L. (1984) "Regional Development in Transkei," *Development Southern Africa* 1, 3–4: 333–42.

Omond, Roger (1985) *The Apartheid Handbook: A Guide to South Africa's Everyday Racial Policies*, Harmondsworth: Penguin.

Palmer, Robin and Neil Parsons (eds) (1977) *The Roots of Rural Poverty in Central and Southern Africa*, Berkeley: University of California Press.

Platzky, Laurine and Cherryl Walker (1985) *The Surplus People: Forced Removals in South Africa*, Johannesburg: Ravan Press.

Pratt, Mary Louise (1987) "Linguistic Utopias," in Nigel Fabb, Derek Attridge, Alan Durant and Colin MacCabe (eds) *The Linguistics of Writing*, Manchester: Manchester University Press.

Southall, Roger (1982) *South Africa's Transkei: The Political Economy of an "Independent" Bantustan*, London: Heinemann.

Spence, J. E. (1968) *Lesotho: The Politics of Dependence*, New York: Oxford University Press.

van der Merwe, A. F. (1986) "The Policy Implications of an Appropriate Development Strategy for Southern Africa," *Development Southern Africa* 3, 3: 462–5.

Wilson, Monica and Leonard Thompson (1971) *The Oxford History of South Africa*, vol. II, New York: Oxford University Press.

Wright, Patrick (1985) *On Living in an Old Country*, London: Verso.

7 The experience of displacement

Reconstructing places and identities in Sri Lanka

Birgitte Refslund Sørensen

INTRODUCTION

In the mid-1970s the government of Sri Lanka embarked on a large and costly development project which involved the displacement of more than 100,000 Sinhalese farmer families, primarily from the central and southern regions, and their resettlement in the north-central and eastern dry zones. Apart from a few minor urban centers these areas were only sparsely populated before, but by diverting the water from the Mahaweli Ganga, the longest river in the country, the government envisaged their transformation from barren, remote areas into fertile centers of growth based on the cultivation of paddy, chilies, and other cash crops. Once the necessary clearing of jungle and construction of access roads and water canals had been completed by the Mahaweli authorities, the first Mahaweli settlements were ready to be ceremonially inaugurated in the late 1970s.

Some fifteen years later, in the beginning of 1991, I moved into one of these early settlement project areas in the North Central Province in order to carry out my doctoral field research on social and cultural consequences of displacement and resettlement. Out of the ten new settlements, a new township, and a few old (*purana*) villages which constituted that particular project unit, I selected a single settlement for my study. Later, however, I expanded my research to include the adjacent *purana* village, because it turned out that social meanings, to a large extent, were created in the interface between the settlers and the villagers.[1]

The settlement in which I worked consisted of 156 households at the time of my stay. It was a rather heterogeneous community with members from almost every district of the country. The majority had settled there during the first years of the settlement's existence, and although land was no longer available, newcomers had continued to arrive and thus contributed to the heterogeneity of the area. Finally, the settler community also showed a considerably larger diversity in terms of caste than more traditional Sinhalese villages.

The purana village situated less than a mile from the settlement was both smaller and socially more homogeneous. In 1991 the core of the old nuclear village counted a little less than 80 households. Except for a few intermarried individuals and a single temporary resident, all inhabitants were born and bred in the village, belonged to the same caste, and were interrelated through kinship. The total number of people of village origin who were living in the vicinity was considerably higher, however. A number of families of village origin were living in a village expansion project that had been implemented just outside the old village boundary in the 1940s in order to reduce the impact of the increasing population. Others, primarily young couples, were living in the new settlements which offered better housing facilities and in some cases even land for a small agricultural production.

The main question that guided me in my work in the settlement and the purana village was: How does displacement and relocation influence people's lives? I was interested in examining how social relations had been influenced by the major change in agricultural production, i.e. the shift from kinship-based subsistence production to individual commercialized production which had taken place in the wake of the project implementation. I also wanted to explore what exactly the increasing social heterogeneity of the local community meant for the construction of social and personal identity. As my discussion will show, these issues all touched upon the interrelationship between space, place, culture, and identity.

In a discussion of the production of ethnography, Bruner argues that ethnographies are guided by implicit narrative structures which order the data in *temporal sequences* defined by systematic relations, and at the same time *give meaning* to experiences (1986b: 139–41; my emphasis). The same point could be asserted with regard to the complex body of sociological and psychological theories which I shall collectively refer to as "relocation studies."[2] Relocation studies represent a particular kind of narrative which, as I shall show later, defines *a priori* the methodological and conceptual components of the analysis as well as the course of events in the lives of displaced persons.

In this chapter I shall argue that this particular delimitation of our subject matter is inadequate, and that it often prevents us from discovering and identifying the dynamic, creative aspects of displacement, and thus from understanding how people really *live with* and continue to *reinterpret and elaborate on* their experiences, depending on context and purpose. I shall try to demonstrate that people are not simply victims of change, but social agents taking a keen and active role in the ongoing process of social engineering. In order to do so, the focus will be shifted from the conventional analytical narrative and its particular staging of displaced lives and redirected to the narratives, or accounts, constructed by and communicated between people themselves.[3]

In a thought-provoking article on nostalgia, Kathleen Stewart states that "to narrate is to place oneself in an event and a scene – to make an interpretive space . . . which is relational and in which meanings have direct social referents" (1992: 252). "Individual life narratives," she continues "dramatize acts of separation – freedom, choice, creativity, imagination, the power to model and plan and act *on* life" (ibid.: 253). Shifting our focus then, from the external analytical narrative of displacement to the internal one anchored in actual social interaction is, I will suggest, a more favorable approach for comprehending how people experience displacement and how they express these experiences in social actions, and thus it is a more useful approach for the identification and understanding of its social and cultural implications.

As my discussion will demonstrate, people's own narratives clearly stressed the social, cultural, and political dimensions of displacement. Rather than being personal stories about pathological suffering, these accounts treated displacement as an event, or "an experience" (Bruner 1986a: 6), which served as a frame of reference for the reinterpretation and reorganization of history, culture, society, and identity in a broader sense.

The local accounts also raised important questions concerning the appropriate spatial and temporal contextualization of displacement. As I shall argue below, studies of relocation tend to focus on the local level exclusively, and thus to ignore the wider political and social context in which displacement takes place. They furthermore dehistoricize the event by focusing on the general psychological dimension of it. Lack of space prevents me from elaborating at length on this issue, but I shall try to demonstrate how the contemporary project of the Sri Lankan nation-state, which is both framed and challenged by internal "ethnic" conflict and globalization, has generated particular ideological interpretations of the Sri Lankan citizen, the local village community, and of cultural identity. I shall then show how these interpretations and definitions penetrate the local level and how they are used by different competing parties to lend authority to their particular interpretations of events. The local narratives thus locate displacement in the complex interface between a local community and the world at large, placing it in a particular historical context.

NARRATIVES OF DISPLACEMENT

The conventional analytical narrative of displacement and resettlement, if one may make such a generalization, follows a "home–out–home" structure. The temporal and spatial point of departure is the home area of the displaced person, where she lived prior to displacement. Although the home area as a social and cultural locality is rarely given much attention as such, it nevertheless plays a significant role in the narrative as a point of reference, or a contrast, to the present. "Home" is the socially and culturally familiar environment in which the displaced person has developed a sense of integrity and identity. In the analysis it comes to assume the role of an idealized and harmonious past which has been lost, and which now exists exclusively in the nostalgic longing of the displaced person.

The main point of concern in relocation studies is the present, which is both temporally and spatially separated from the "past home." The present is often conceptualized as a kind of anti-structure, a "topographical site between two fixed locales" (Gupta and Ferguson 1992: 18), or a liminal phase (Westen 1985: 382), which is marked by uncertainty and a lack of coherence. For the individual arriving in this borderland, the immediate experience is one of anxiety, distress, and nostalgia, the seriousness of which is often assumed to be proportional to the relative "cultural distance" between the two locales (Furnham and Bochner 1989). The encounter with the unfamiliar, it is argued, threatens to dissolve the displaced person's sense of integrity as it confronts her with her incapacity in the new social and cultural relations. The existence as a displaced person is thus conceptualized as a kind of social non-being. As argued by Malkki – and exemplified by countless scientific publications on the phenomenon – this is a state of being which is understood as "an inner pathological condition" (1992: 31) or "a categorical anomaly" (1990: 33).

The narrative of displacement – like the Western narrative of fiction – requires that the displaced person leave the liminal borderland and enter a new space (defined as such by its orderliness), so as to develop a new identity. If the displaced person fails to grow new roots, she will remain uprooted, marginalized, and pathological in a space in-between. As in other narratives reflecting "the regime of modernization," this narrative shows a "clear valuation on the re-establishment through whatever process of the coherence and stability of identity" (Marcus 1992: 312). The future in the narrative, in other words, promises the reconstitution of "home" and identity either by means of "cultural and social skills training" or "psychotherapy" (Furnham and Bochner 1989). Well integrated (read: assimilated, acculturated, adapted), the displaced person has re-entered the category of "normal subjects." Displacement has become an event of the past, and this marks the end of the story.

This sort of narrative temporally demarcates displacement as a historically limited experience running from uprooting to integration, and at the same time it expresses a particular conceptualization of space and place which in short can be characterized as a merging of territory, culture, and identity; a relationship which explains the anxiety assumed to result from being situated "between places." "The idea of culture," as stated by Clifford (1988: 388), "carries with it an expectation of roots, of a stable territorial existence."

Recent anthropological writings have eagerly debated the assumed homogeneity and consistency of cultures and societies, the confusion of society with already completed processes, the confinement of cultures within bounded territories, as well as the consequent conceptualization of personal identity as derived from these structures. Challenged by an apparent increase in the flow of people, goods, information, and ideas within and across borders, a new ethnographic narrative is emerging in which culture and society are regarded as the ever-changing outcome of practice rather than a pre-existing structure (Rosaldo 1989: 106; Foster 1991: 235; Barth 1992: 23; Ortner 1984). This new philosophical mood perceives changes, inconsistencies, and paradoxes as a natural and integral part of people's reality. Personal identity, according to this view, is a complex sense of being or belonging not derived from one local structure, but actively and strategically constructed in relation to multiple spaces and for a variety of purposes (Marcus 1992; Giddens 1991).

This point of view has far-reaching implications for our understanding of displacement and resettlement since it deconstructs the static spatial and temporal conceptual entities on which the conventional narrative was based. Moreover, it urges us to be more attentive to social processes and the particular conditions and circumstances under which patterns of order and difference develop.

The new ethnographic narrative furthermore directs our attention to the individual, not as a typical representative of a culture whose point of view should be voiced, but as a human being and as a social individual (Barth 1992, 1994). Applied to the narrative of displacement, this means that the displaced person no longer simply plays the role of the pathological victim in our story, but has become a creative agent in the construction of the story herself. It is the displaced persons themselves, engaged in actions in a complex social reality, who define the course, the components, and the context of the narratives.

With these theoretical and methodological reflections in mind, let us now return to the Sri Lankan local scene briefly introduced above, and examine more carefully some of the narratives of displacement which dominated at the time of my stay. It should be mentioned that for quite some time I did not detect any pattern or even consistency in the stories people narrated. Each story seemed to have its own unique focus and particularities. However, a kind of pattern gradually emerged in which narratives of displacement could be divided into two main categories: one consisted of the villagers' narratives, the other of the settlers'.[4] Although alternative interpretations and divergent perspectives were continuously voiced by members of the two communities, they had not yet been transformed from individual perspectives into collective, social narratives. Nonetheless, the younger generation, i.e. the children of villagers and settlers born and bred within the settlement structure, was becoming ever more visible as a distinct social group with its own interpretations, meanings, and interests. Elsewhere, in my analysis of the settlement project, I have included the youth as an "emerging identity," and it is important to emphasize that categories or identities which are dominant at one moment, or in one context, may disappear and give way to new ones in other instances (see Sørensen 1993a, b).

As I shall reveal below, the two narratives bore significant differences in their conceptualizations of time and space, and consequently ascribed different roles and identities to villagers and settlers respectively. It is worth noticing, however, that they also shared some perspectives which I suggest originate from shared circumstances. First of all, both narratives were an outcome of the conceptualization of displacement as more than just "inner experience." To both settlers and villagers, it was "an experience" (Bruner 1986a: 6), an event that stood out from the ordinary flow of social life and compelled them all to reconsider existing categories of identity and social relations in the context of that event.

Second, both narratives could also be seen as expressions of resistance to the experienced or anticipated implications of the project, which not only necessitated an encounter with strangers and the unfamiliar, but also seemed to substitute "difference" with "in-difference." As part of the Sri Lankan nation-state's efforts to create a homogeneous national culture, and at the same time expressing the ideals of a national citizen and a capitalist individual, the project could be said to express egalitarian ideology in different guises. And it was often criticized, particularly by the villagers, for ignoring the existing criteria of differentiation such as caste and family and treating all as if equals (Sørensen 1993a: 118–19).

CULTURAL DISPLACEMENT: THE PERSPECTIVE OF LOCAL VILLAGERS

The voice of the host population is often excluded from analyses of displacement, and all the attention is given to those who have been physically relocated; but as I have argued elsewhere, the host population, in this case the villagers, may feel no less displaced than the settlers (Sørensen 1993a: 27). Although the villagers remained in the ancestral village, they had experienced a profound transformation of the physical and social space around them, and this had generated a sense of cultural displacement. For instance, the villagers often discussed the appropriateness and efficiency of their ancient agricultural rituals – were they still effective in the era of technology and chemicals, after land had become a commodity? (See also Malkki 1992; Gupta and Ferguson 1992.) Moreover, it is important to stress that the host population constitutes a part of the total social field in which displacement takes place and is interpreted, and their experiences and responses are equally significant for understanding the social generative processes unfolding in the wake of displacement; they too are involved in the re-interpretation and reconstruction of places and identities.

Whenever the Mahaweli project and the present conditions were the topic of conversation, the elder villagers expressed their points of view by making comparisons with the pre-project past. In those days, they said, village life had been more harmonious and peaceful. One reason for this state of affairs, according to the villagers, was that everyone was related to each other as kin. The customary preference for cross-cousin marriages had created a strong sense of continuity and belonging, and also protected family land against enterprising outsiders who wished to profit from cultivation and trade in dry-zone crops. At the same time this custom had ensured the survival of caste purity, an issue of great importance to the high-caste villagers. The old village community was furthermore described as having been unified in terms of production and distribution. Although paddy land had never been equally distributed among the villagers, there was now a general consensus that a greater sense of equality previously existed among the villagers. This was due in part to the fact that landowners were obliged to help those relatives who were less fortunate and, likewise, the fact that swidden cultivation (*chena*) of the forest lands, to which all had usufruct rights, had played a significant role in the dry-zone village economy. As Kloos has argued, it was the *chenas* rather than the paddy fields that had been the main source of income in dry-zone villages having rain-fed tanks (1988: 57).

The account the villagers produced of the past was one which created a merging of history and landscape (Foster 1991: 244) – and of bodies, one might add. The past was rarely recalled in terms of particular events, chronologically ordered, but rather as lived experiences. The social activities that had bound people together in intimate relationships had also linked them to the land and given the locality its particular identity as a place. Villagers' accounts of past hunting expeditions, of cultivation practices related to swidden cultivation, or of rituals performed for the village deity to secure protection from the evils of the jungle, were all expressions of embodied experiences. The past identity of the locality had left its scars on nature as well as on the bodies of the villagers and could not be easily forgotten. The area was full of signs remembering the past, as it were (Stewart 1992: 260), and when the villagers narrated their story, they would re-imagine themselves in that space (Okely 1994: 5). It was no doubt hard for them to watch the newcomers arrive and build homes on the lands where they used to go hunting or collectively cultivate their *chenas*. Indeed, the villagers were painfully aware of this new life which reorganized space and imposed its particular signs and meanings, threatening to displace or having already displaced the old ways which formed the core of their pride and identity.

Affluence and harmony had become qualities of the past, and this was seen as a direct result of the project. With the implementation of the Mahaweli project and the new government's commitment to a market economy, agricultural production had been reorganized in several ways. First of all, the old ancestral landholdings had been confiscated by the Mahaweli authorities and redistributed together with the newly developed areas in plots of equal size to all farmers regardless of status and previous social position. During this process the earlier *chena* lands had also been lost, as they were transformed into irrigated paddy land or included in the residential zones which were established to house the newcomers. Second, cultivation had been commercialized and specialized in such a way that farmers were now producing mainly for the market and consequently were forced to buy most of their food there as well. The integration into market economy was not a recent development, however. As early as the 1940s some villagers had already begun to cultivate cash crops on the *chenas* for trade with merchants from the south. But with the implementation of the Mahaweli project the production of cash crops had expanded considerably. Furthermore, new scientific and capital-intensive cultivation methods had been introduced. In short, the villagers felt, to their great annoyance, that an individualistic, selfish, and more competitive personal character had replaced the former collective, social ways, and that class and wealth had become the criteria of local status at the expense of caste and personal character (Sørensen 1993a). The traditional leadership, based on personal character and social standing, had also been undermined. As one villager put it, "Now we can't even break a branch of a tree without having to ask permission from the Mahaweli authorities." Or as one of his friends said: "To get influence you do not need a good personality, you only need good connections with the police and in Colombo."

To summarize the villagers' narrative of displacement, one can say they conceptualized the past as a time when they were in control, i.e. that they alone defined the meaning of the surrounding space in relation to which they defined their own identity. To accept their story as a "truth" about the past, in the sense that it reflects things as they really were, would be too rash, however. It has often been pointed out that such "mythical" accounts of the past are selective interpretations and representations which perhaps tell more about the present context of narrating than about the past, and this goes for the present case as well. Then again, historical objectivity is no appropriate criterion for measuring the pain of displacement. To the villagers' minds the present was indeed a liminal phase, a time out of order in which outside forces (the government, the Mahaweli authorities, and the settlers) were eradicating old meanings of space and identity and replacing them with new ones. The villagers were living in "a place whose meaning [was] dying out" (Stewart 1992: 260).

The acknowledgment of the outsiders' increasing influence was rarely interpreted or articulated as an indication of the villagers' own incapacity, however, and consequently the recent loss of power and autonomy did not seem to have resulted in an extensive loss of self-esteem, as one might have expected. This was very clear both in verbal accounts and in actions. One example of these efforts to maintain or regain a positive and strengthened sense of identity was the frequent interpretation of the present situation as evidence of Lord Buddha's prediction: that the world would enter a phase of decay after 2,500 years of development, the turning point being in the year 1956. According to this point of view, the villagers identified themselves as the protectors of the ancient values of generosity and compassion, whereas the outsiders and modern society in general were regarded as the exponents of moral decay and defilement.[5] The outsiders' present prosperity was only a short-term benefit which would soon be lost, as it had not been gained from "right conduct."

PHYSICAL DISPLACEMENT: THE PERSPECTIVE OF SETTLERS FROM OUTSIDE

Relocation theories commonly assume a dramatization of the disjunction of past and present with a nostalgic emphasis on the past, but this was not the case among the Sinhalese settlers, who were remarkably silent about the past. Only on very rare occasions did the settlers make any explicit references to life in a past space and time, and when they did so they were not all that specific or detailed in their accounts. In this way the usual analytical approach was challenged, i.e. of having at the core of the analysis a comparison between "before" and "after," "then" and "now," or "there" and "here." Consequently, different questions came to the fore. First of all: Why did the settlers seem unconcerned about the past? And second: What were their experiences of displacement and how were these experiences expressed?

When I began my field research in the settlement, I had no previous knowledge of the villagers' interpretations of the events, and for some time the settlers' representations dominated my own interpretations of relocation. When I interviewed the settlers to gather some basic information about their socio-economic backgrounds, I always wound up with a request to tell me something about their experience of moving to the dry zone, establishing a new home, etc.

Like the villagers, the settlers seemed to share an experience, or at least they shared some kind of collective narrative about that experience, to which all except the youngest settlers who were born and bred in the village contributed. This narrative never began in a distant time and place, but began at the moment the person had arrived in the settlement. The typical account opened with a description of how the area had looked at the time of the person's arrival as compared to the present.[6] One woman told me: "When we arrived here, there was jungle all over. This garden was covered with thick jungle. It was not like today where the area is developed." Others simply said that when they arrived in the settlement "there was nothing here." Some would include a characterization of the inhabitants who already lived in the area. The original villagers were described as primitive, uncivilized, ignorant, or like Veddas (the "aborigines" of Sri Lanka). According to most settlers, the villagers used to dress in a very simple way, the women often bare-breasted, and they had used a very crude and obscene language. Some men told me that they did not allow their female kindred to walk alone because of the "bad environment."

This conceptualization of the population of the dry-zone village was not in any sense special to this group of settlers. As Brow has shown, the category of Vedda is commonly used by Sinhalese to describe those among them "who lack the cultural attributes that collectively define a civilized and distinctively Sinhalese identity. Thus those who are ignorant of Buddhist teaching, or who live by foraging in the jungle or even from swidden cultivation rather than wet-rice agriculture" (Brow 1990a: 11; for another example of a similar usage see Spencer 1990: 144). In other words, the settlers only used pre-existing cultural categories to render their new environment meaningful.

It was indicative of the settlers' self-perception as well as their perception of space that they tended to ignore completely the fact that village communities already existed in the area when they themselves arrived. If they did acknowledge the villagers' prior occupation, they often described them as primitive and thus distinct from themselves. Their arrival in this remote area not only marked a change in their personal life, but also the creation of this area as a "place." It was only when they arrived that a transformation of nature into social space – or into place – had transpired, and they themselves were the pioneers and catalysts of this process. They played the role as civilizing agents, an identity they illustrated by relating how they had taught the villagers to speak a "civilized" language, how to dress properly, and cultivate paddy according to the new scientific methods rather than relying on old traditions and rituals.

The settlers did not experience displacement primarily as a loss of meaning, or as "meaning emptying out," as was the case among the villagers, but rather as an encounter with a space that was still almost empty of meaning. And the settlers perceived themselves as being a creative force in filling that space with meaning. This was one reason, I would argue, why the settlers seemed to be preoccupied with the present, and notably the future, rather than with the past.[7] But their temporal focus also reflected the fact, I would argue, that they did not share any past time and place. Since they came from various places they had no shared experiences, events, or signs in space to which they could relate their interpretation, and hence they could not easily transform their individual experiences, as did the villagers, into a collective, standardized narrative of the past that was based on embodied knowledge (Okely 1994: 7). The villagers' past to a large extent resided in shared practices and experiences which were now interpreted collectively and pieced together to form a coherent construction of past space and time (Stewart 1992: 261; Alonso 1988: 35, 49). The settlers' past, on the other hand, was located in disconnected spaces which were more difficult to piece together. And to this should be added the fact that the social relations between the settlers were often tinged with distrust and a wish for distance and privacy. Whenever I asked them about their relationships to other neighbors or to the villagers, I was often given the answer, "It is of no use. It is better to keep them at an arm's distance." In the case of the settlers, the past was, in other words, largely filtered through individual memory (Marcus 1992: 317) and embedded in diffuse communication.

In the settlers' narrative of displacement we then find a valuation of the past as either neutral or, in cases where people had strongly wished to leave home, even as negative. For the settlers it was the present and particularly the future which symbolized and promised "golden days." The settlers' view also differed from that of the villagers with regard to the conceptualization of the locality. To them it was only just emerging as a place, i.e. it was not a place possessing an embodied meaning which was being challenged, threatened, and therefore slowly dying out.

THE SITES OF STRUGGLE

In a discussion of historical discourses in Mexico, Ana Maria Alonso states that "in analyzing the construction of social memory, it is important to pay attention to the sites where it is produced and disseminated" (1988: 49). Sally Falk Moore seems to share this view when she argues in favor of a processual analysis because "it identifies both the locus of certain struggles . . . and the particular terms in which those are conceived" (1994: 370). Although Alonso's discussion concentrates on the hegemonic relations between a dominant memory and subordinated counter-histories, her point is applicable, I would argue, to situations where the struggle is between narratives "at the same level," as in the present case.

Interpretive narratives of the kind I have presented here were never told as coherent completed stories; they consisted of bits and pieces revealed in many different ways and contexts, and they were continuously modified and elaborated upon. The relatively coherent form they are given here is to a great extent a result of my collection and putting together of such bits and pieces. When on some rare occasions I was presented with a story of displacement in a rather coherent form, this was generally a result of my own direct questioning (see also Hastrup 1992: 121). A second factor that is relevant to the identification of the form and locus of the struggle is that the different individuals and communities did not have equal access to the arenas of communication. The villagers, who lived in a nuclear village and were related through kinship, had a much closer interaction than the settlers, who were spread over a larger area on their individually owned and separated plots of land, and who considered close social associations as potentially harmful. This meant that the villagers had more opportunities to transform individual perspectives into collective narratives than the settlers. This being said, the important question remains, however, where and when the villagers and the settlers exchanged their points of view. Where and how did the negotiations of identities and meanings of space take place? I was often told that in the early days of the settlement there had been more direct confrontations between the villagers and the newcomers, as the villagers tried to prevent the outsiders from obtaining land for agriculture or residence. But in recent years their social relationship had been rather marked by mutual avoidance. When I asked people about their relationships to those of "the other community" they would often respond by saying "we do not go there. It is of no use. We only go there if there is a need." But although the relationship between villagers and settlers had to some extent developed into what Long terms a "socially constituted system of ignorance" (1992: 13), the different narratives about the experiences of displacement were not only recounted within each group in order to reinforce its sense of shared identity; they were meant to be played out in communication between the groups, and to become part of social life.

So far I have focused on the verbal accounts as social expressions, but in a social environment marked by occasional and limited interaction between the "opponents," verbal accounts have a limited effect since they depend upon face-to-face encounters. As I am not fluent in Sinhala I may be misinterpreting this point, but I got the impression that the verbal accounts of displacement most often came to the fore when there was a dispute over land or another kind of disagreement between families belonging to different communities, etc. Still, it is possible to make a statement and disseminate meanings without the help of words. The variety of expressions used to signal and communicate the experiences of displacement was substantial, ranging from the very explicit and compelling to mere tacit indications, for which symbols, cultural products, behavior, practices and actions were employed. Let me give some examples of how the two dominant competing narratives were manifested in signs or actions (see Sørensen (1993a) for a more exhaustive discussion of these and other examples).

The first example illustrates a very explicit and powerful expression of identity. After I had been in the area for some time, the villagers told me one day that they had established a village Buddhist Society whose primary aim was to build a new temple in the old village. At that time the villagers had only a simple hall for sermons and a Bo tree, which could hardly encourage a monk to reside there and serve the community on a permanent basis. Although the existence of a temple always enhances the identity of a community, I was still somewhat surprised by their decision, knowing that they had a very close and long-standing affiliation with a temple in the vicinity. When asked, the initiators of the temple project told me that a dispute had arisen with the monk at their temple. The cause of it had been the monk's sudden decision to rename the temple, a measure the villagers regarded as a serious insult. Not only had the monk failed to consult the villagers, which would have been the appropriate thing to do considering that they had been the patrons of the temple for many generations; he also intended to give the temple a name which indicated a close link between the temple and a low-caste village in the vicinity that had prospered from the Mahaweli project. The villagers tried to reach an agreement with the monk, but after several unsuccessful attempts they decided to build their own temple. Although I understood their reaction to this assault on their status and pride, I did not yet fully understand why they had decided to invest so much time and money in the construction of a new temple when – in my eyes – they had other and more convenient options available to them. When the policy for the Mahaweli project had been decided, a great emphasis had been placed on the support and improvement of the "cultural infrastructure." Therefore the construction of Buddhist temples in the new settlements had also been both encouraged and financially supported by the government. The settlement discussed here had also benefited from this policy and now had a relatively large temple. Why did the villagers not want to use this temple which was located just next to the village itself? The details regarding their decision will be left aside here, but let me select a few important arguments that came up during a conversation with representatives of the new Buddhist Society.

First of all, the temple in the settlement was a new one, which meant that it lacked the historical continuity and tradition that is part and parcel of a temple's authority and reputation. Second, the head monk had not been installed on request of the local population as an expression of their wish to have him as their teacher and guide. He had come to the area on his own and had built up the temple mainly with the help and financing of the project administration – not from local contributions. Though most people liked the monk's personal character and also acknowledged his great insight into the Buddha's teachings, he had not achieved his present position "according to the tradition."[8] The villagers were hoping to install a monk in their future temple "according to the tradition" by asking a monk who also happened to be a relative and lived in a nearby town to send one of his disciples to the village. There may have been one other thing that influenced the villagers to reach their decision: the monk in the settlement apparently was of a lower caste background than the villagers, and this may have caused some of them to prefer another temple and another monk though none of them said so (see Gombrich (1991) for a discussion of the issue of caste within the Sangha).

At the immediate level, the villagers' project was a clear reaction to and statement about their experience of deteriorating social relations and status, but it also entailed a vision and strategy for the restoration of identity. To use Stewart's words, the project could be seen as "a resurrection of time and place, and a subject *in* time and place" (1992: 252). First of all, the temple would improve the villagers' status in relation to the settlers and the nearby low-caste village by inscribing them in the cultural tradition and by giving them the facilities to improve their religious life. Second, the project was also a strategic use of space (Munn 1992: 108), as it would leave an eternal or at least a long-lasting mark on space, which would restore their close link to the land.

The villagers also tried, in less grandiose and costly ways, to hold on to the world that was deserting them, for instance by cultivating some of the crops they formerly cultivated in the *chenas*. At the time when the villagers still had access to forest lands for cultivation, millet (*kurakkan*) rather than rice had been the primary staple food. Millet was usually eaten with vegetables and meat from the jungle, but now the jungle as well as the *chenas* had been lost, and the villagers had to do without both millet and meat for their meals. The pleasures of hunting and the delight of a good and satisfying meal were recalled with a measure of nostalgia and, indeed, they were issues that often came up in accounts of the past. But, I would argue, it was not merely an expression of nostalgia when some villagers continued to separate a small corner of their field for the cultivation of millet. Rather it was yet another way of making a culturally significant place by "making further inscriptions on the landscape of encoded things" (Stewart 1992: 257). When they prepared the millet for a meal it was no longer an everyday event related to village subsistence economy; it was a rare occasion and a celebration of identity. As Stewart asserts, even consumption is a production (ibid.: 259).

The settlers also expressed their identity and conceptualization of the locality by consuming products that were invested with particular meanings. The settlers, especially the youngest, often staged their identity as a lifestyle involving products which they associated with modern life, and their savings were often spent on television sets, furniture, the latest fashion, and going to the movies, etc.

Such practices can be characterized as "interpretive practices," and when one expresses one's identity to the world by means of these practices and objects, it can be seen as a way of creating "interpretive spaces" (Stewart 1992: 252) where people can stage their different projects (Long 1992: 10) and perhaps even direct other people's actions towards these spaces. When the villagers began the construction of the new temple, and when the settlers marked the landscape with their television antennae, both communities were making important inscriptions on space. They were not simply coping with sorrow and distress, but constructing places and identities. Compared to the space occupied by the verbal accounts, the interpretive space that these practices and products generated seemed to be more insistent due to a visible presence and a presence over time, although one should not ignore the fact that verbal accounts also had a reality and influence beyond the moment of narrating.

THE NATIONAL INFLUENCE ON LOCAL LIFE

So far I have focused my discussion on the construction of local place as a struggle between local competing communities and individuals, but it is important to emphasize that non-local voices interfered in the process as well, with still other conceptualizations of place and identity. So even though people were making their own histories, this was done under conditions not of their own choosing (cf. Rosaldo 1989: 105). Of particular relevance here are the national interpretations of local community, which seemed both to lend support to some of the views inherent in the two local narratives and to challenge them at the same time.

The Mahaweli project plays a significant role in the Sri Lankan nation's construction of a national history and a cultural identity. The new project is based on ancient irrigation schemes, which are commonly believed (some would say proved) to have been the foundation of an early Sinhalese civilization and hence of Sinhalese supremacy on the island. The Mahaweli project is therefore seen by many as a symbol of Sinhalese national identity. In the ceremonial openings of settlements, in political speeches, in the national media, etc., the project is thus often represented as the Sinhalese people's means of self-realization, and likewise the Sinhalese paddy farmers are represented as patriotic citizens who will make the glorious past realizable in the future (Tennekoon 1988: 297).[9]

In this process, local histories are "departicularized" (Alonso 1988: 45) and subsumed under the totalizing national history, which considers the Sinhalese people to be homogeneous, and defines the Sinhalese in opposition to the Tamil minority of the north and the east, and secondly to the Western world. In a more thorough discussion of the villagers' temple project I have argued that it could be seen as an indication of the dissemination of nationalist ideology, as the villagers were creating the village according to the official image, i.e. as consisting of paddy fields, a tank, and a temple (Sørensen 1993a; see also Spencer 1990; Woost 1990). But although they were thus reproducing the symbols of a homogenizing narrative, making it possible and obvious for others to conceptualize them as "nationalists" or "patriots," they also resisted its implications in their insistence on being different from the settlers. They subsumed the notion of one Sinhalese nation under that of local difference, using the temple project to reaffirm their own superiority by linking the village and its history to the mythical past. Such links were for instance established in the view shared by some villagers that the village had played a central role in the ancient kingdoms. In this way the villagers sought to use roots and traditions as the decisive criteria of local status and thereby "displace," or exclude, the settlers who could never claim such ancient links to the land. By exploiting the historical past the villagers managed to obtain the moral and discursive support of the nation for their own project of social and cultural differentiation.

Besides being a symbol of the glorious past, invoked by patriotic and opportunistic politicians alike, the Mahaweli project is also represented as a powerful symbol of the modern future. Together with other development projects, it is envisaged by the government as a means of including Sri Lanka in the group of newly industrializing countries before the end of this millennium. In that perspective, which is profoundly inspired by the international economic development discourse, local communities are first of all seen as potential centers of growth and the population as industrious, rational, and enterprising. Not surprisingly, the settlers usually identified themselves with this interpretation, which harmonized with their self-perception as pioneers, civilizing agents, and entrepreneurs. They too, in other words, could obtain support from national agents and discourses creating the local place in their image.

Although the narratives of the "glorious past" and the "glorious future" were interconnected, they also expressed values which were in principle incompatible. The past was basically associated with Sinhalese culture, which, like other Eastern cultures, is perceived (by its own people as well as by Westerners) to be essentially spiritual in contrast to the materialistic West (Foster 1991). But the glorious future, which was to be achieved by means of development – including aid from Western countries – was often associated with materialism. Tennekoon (1988) has made this point clear in a fascinating article about the Mahaweli project, and concludes that only by presenting modernization in the guise of tradition, or reinterpreting traditions as modern is it possible to overcome this dilemma, which in fact is what the villagers as well as the settlers are trying to do.

Local events often expressed such multiple meanings without any overt discrepancy, but at the same time the ambiguity inherent in the national project always seemed to pose a danger of further displacement or marginalization for the groups seeking its support in the construction of places and identities. The villagers' adoption of and partial assimilation to the national narrative was a threat to their "embodied past" as *chena* cultivators because of the narrative's emphasis on paddy cultivation as the basis of the Sri Lankan national identity. In speeches as well as in concrete projects the government has repeatedly condemned swidden cultivation as primitive and as the prime cause of erosion. The settlers' commitment to modernization processes and symbols, on the other hand, was likewise a potential source of further social displacement or critique in so far as it exposed the settlers to identifications as immoral, materialistic, selfish, non-Buddhist, etc. Though a large number of "modern products" had already been introduced and integrated in the local community there was a constant debate about their acceptability, and it happened that a product, a practice, or a way of behaving or dressing was condemned or ridiculed as an imitation of "Colombo-7 people" (a wealthy quarter of Colombo); and Colombo-7 people in turn were seen as imitators of Western lifestyles.

Although displacement is always primarily a local event or process, we must not neglect the different contexts that influence and condition the local scene. In the present case, the fact that Sri Lanka is still in an ongoing process of forming the post-colonial state – caught in-between sub-national conflicts and the increasing importance of supra-state institutions and structures – is thus of great significance for understanding the particular conditions, circumstances, and interpretations of experiences of local displacement (Sørensen 1993a: 35–7).

DISPLACEMENT AS EVENT AND PROCESS

I hope that these brief glimpses of daily life in various neighborhoods of a Sri Lankan settlement scheme have been persuasive in showing the need for a more open-ended, flexible, and actor-oriented approach to displacement and relocation than the conventional relocation studies have provided us with.

Relocation, I have argued, is not simply experienced as an inner condition, although the suffering created by separation can be overwhelming and temporarily paralyzing. Relocation is also, and perhaps more than anything, a social event which compels all within its scope to reconsider and renegotiate their identities. The settlement scheme discussed here changed the physical environment drastically and forced the villagers to use it in new ways. This was a change that drove them to reflect on religious traditions, customary ways of agriculture, and on the nature of community life.

The fact that new inhabitants made competing claims on the same environment only exacerbated this process, as the settlers exposed the villagers to new practices and offered them alternative perceptions. The presence of the settlers in the area created a new context or condition for the construction of village identity. As the discussion showed, the fact that there existed an old village community also played an important role for the settlers, although a somewhat different one. The settlers rarely perceived the villagers as a threat, though they had at times been a serious hindrance to the acquisition of land; but rather, they saw them as a primitive or old-fashioned population whom they should try to educate. The villagers' presence was thus an important factor in the construction of an identity as progressive entrepreneurs.[10]

Within the framework of a discussion of place and identity, it is of particular interest to note how people not only let themselves be defined by the surrounding space, but actively try to create that space and thus to exercise at least some control over the definition of their own – and others' – identity. This is an action which involves spaces, times, and objects far beyond what we would normally consider relevant for the analysis of local experiences of displacement. In following this case, the experience of displacement and relocation cannot be rendered as a linear process with a final termination, but must be understood as a multiple process that stretches its influence in many directions and continues to include new aspects in an ongoing process of identifications. The analysis of displacement, in my view, should aim at an identification of these processes, the actors, their intentions, conditions, and options, and should demonstrate how particular identities and places are continuously being created by people in their efforts to gain control over their own lives.

ACKNOWLEDGMENTS

This chapter was first presented in a preliminary form at the workshop "Finding a Space and Place for Culture," Magleaas, Denmark, and I wish to express my gratitude to the other participants for their stimulating responses. I also wish to thank Danida's Research Council, who funded the field research on which this chapter is based.

NOTES

1 Norman Long has defined the "interface situation" as a "situation where different life-worlds interact and interpenetrate" (1992: 6). The analysis of interfaces "stresses the reproduction and transformation of social discontinuities inherent in interface encounters" (ibid.).

2 For a more comprehensive review and discussion of some of the principal contributions to this genre, see Sørensen (1993a: 22–44).

3 In the present discussion of people's experiences of displacement, the term "narrative" refers not only to verbal accounts, but also to actions that serve as statements or commentaries on the social situation.

4 When I categorize people as either villagers or settlers I use the distinction that was employed by people themselves. The category "villager" refers to those who are born and bred in the village, regardless of whether they still live in the village or have moved to one of the new projects in the area, while "settler" refers to those who have moved to the area after the implementation of the Mahaweli project. The category of outsider was broader than settler and referred to all individuals not born and bred in

the village; for instance it included the few individuals who had married a villager and lived in the area. The terms "village" and "settlement" refer to the administrative units demarcated by the Mahaweli authorities.

5 This interpretation in many ways echoes the national critique of modernization and Western culture. In the summer of 1991 the Sri Lankan government closed the casinos in the capital and confiscated all the gambling machines that free enterprise had brought to most small towns in the country as they were regarded as the source of the Sinhalese people's corruption. This decision and its implementation received a relatively wide coverage in the English-language press, where it was described as a battle between good and evil, or between Sinhalese and Western cultures. A similar message was clearly conveyed in a headline crowning an article about the increase in violence: "Alien Materialistic Ideologies Responsible for Country's Crisis, says President" (*Daily News* 15 July 1991).

6 As the settlers have arrived over a period of about ten years the descriptions given by early and later settlers were different in many respects. Still they shared many common perspectives. In this section I refer only to the early settlers who arrived in the first two to three years after the settlement scheme was opened.

7 In this discussion I have emphasized the role of the present context for the settlers' focus on the present and the future, but as I have argued elsewhere, it might be equally important to look at the settlers' past and their reasons for moving to the Mahaweli settlement (1993a). According to the settlers themselves, the move to the new settlement was often an escape from poverty, social conflicts, marginalization, etc., and hence they had good reasons for not dwelling on the past.

8 See Michael Carrithers (1986) for a discussion of the founding of Buddhist community temples and their role in the community.

9 The Tamil minority often refers to the Mahaweli project as a colonization project because Sinhalese farmers resettle in areas that the Tamils consider their homelands. When Sinhalese politicians use allegories of the kind just mentioned it thus contributes to the Tamil population's sense of marginalization. It should be mentioned, however, that I never heard the settlers or the villagers speak of themselves as patriotic farmers trying to restore the Sinhalese nation.

10 The villagers also played another important role which I have not discussed here, i.e. as guides to local religious life. Though the settlers generally focused on material progress, they still belonged to the "overall Sinhalese cultural world" and conceptualized their lives within that framework. As none of them were familiar with its particular local expressions, however, they had to rely on the guidance given by the old villagers in times of crisis and celebration.

REFERENCES

Alonso, Ana Maria (1988) "The Effects of Truth: Re-Presentations of the Past and the Imagining of Community," *Journal of Historical Sociology* 1, 1: 33–57.

Barth, Fredrik (1992) "Towards Greater Naturalism in Conceptualizing

Societies," in A. Kuper (ed.) *Conceptualizing Societies*, London: Routledge.

—— (1994) "A Personal View of Present Tasks and Priorities in Cultural and Social Anthropology," in Robert Borofsky (ed.) *Assessing Cultural Anthropology*, New York: McGraw-Hill.

Brow, James (1990a) "The Incorporation of a Marginal Community within the Sinhalese Nation," *Anthropological Quarterly* 63, 1: 7–17.

—— (1990b) "Notes on Community, Hegemony, and the Uses of the Past," *Anthropological Quarterly* 63, 1: 1–6.

Bruner, Edward M. (1986a) "Experience and Its Expressions," in V. W. Turner and E. M. Bruner (eds) *The Anthropology of Experience*, Urbana and Chicago: University of Illinois Press.

—— (1986b) "Ethnography as Narrative," in V. W. Turner and E. M. Bruner (eds) *The Anthropology of Experience*, Urbana and Chicago: University of Illinois Press.

Carrithers, Michael (1986) [1983] *The Forest Monks of Sri Lanka*, Delhi: Oxford University Press.

Clifford, James (1988) "On Orientalism," in *The Predicament of Culture*, Cambridge, MA: Harvard University Press.

Foster, Robert (1991) "Making National Cultures in The Global Ecumene," *Annual Review of Anthropology* 20: 235–60.

Furnham, Adrian and S. Bochner (1989) *Culture Shock. Psychological Reactions to Unfamiliar Environment*, London: Routledge.

Giddens, Anthony (1991) *Modernity and Self-Identity. Self and Society in Late Modern Age*, California: Stanford University Press.

Gombrich, Richard (1991) [1971] *Buddhist Precept and Practice*, Delhi: Motilal Banarsidass Publishers.

Gupta, Akhil and James Ferguson (1992) "Beyond 'Culture': Space, Identity, and the Politics of Difference," *Cultural Anthropology* 7, 1: 6–21.

Hastrup, Kirsten (1992) "Writing Ethnography," in J. Okely and H. Callaway (eds) *Anthropology and Autobiography*, ASA Monographs 29. London: Routledge.

Kloos, Peter (1988) "Land Policy and Agricultural Underproduction in a Sinhalese Village in Sri Lanka," *South Asian Anthropologist* 9, 1: 55–65.

Long, Norman (1992) "From Paradigm Lost to Paradigm Regained?" in Norman Long and Ann Long (eds) *Battlefields of Knowledge. The Interlocking of Theory and Practice in Social Research and Development*, London: Routledge.

Malkki, Liisa (1990) "Context and Consciousness: Local Conditions for the Production of Historical and National Thought among Hutu Refugees in Tanzania," in R. G. Fox (ed.) *Nationalist Ideologies and the Production of National Cultures*, Washington: American Anthropological Association.

—— (1992) "National Geographic: The Rooting of Peoples and the Territorialization of National Identity Among Scholars and Refugees," *Cultural Anthropology* 7, 1: 24–44.

Marcus, George (1992) "Past, Present and Emergent Identities: Requirements for Ethnographies of Late Twentieth-Century Modernity Worldwide," in Scot Lash and J. Friedman (eds) *Modernity and Identity*, Oxford: Blackwell.

Moore, Sally Falk (1994) "The Ethnography of the Present and the Analysis of Process," in Robert Borofsky (ed.) *Assessing Cultural Anthropology*, New York: McGraw-Hill.

Munn, Nancy D. (1992) "The Cultural Anthropology of Time: A Critical Essay," *Annual Review of Anthropology* 21: 93–123.

Okely, Judith (1994) "Vicarious and Sensory Knowledge of Chronology and Change: Ageing in Rural France," in K. Hastrup and P. Hervik (eds) *Social Experience and Anthropological Knowledge*, London: Routledge.

Ortner, Sherry B. (1984) "Theory in Anthropology Since the Sixties," *Comparative Studies in Society and History* 26: 126–66.

Rosaldo, Renato (1989) *Culture and Truth. The Remaking of Social Analysis*, Boston, MA: Beacon Press.

Spencer, Jonathan (1990) *A Sinhala Village in a Time of Trouble*, Delhi: Oxford University Press.

Stewart, Kathleen (1992) "Nostalgia – A Polemic," in G. Marcus (ed.) *Rereading Cultural Anthropology*, Durham and London: Duke University Press.

Sørensen, Birgitte Refslund (1993a) "Relocated Lives. Experiences of Change and Continuity in a Sri Lankan Settlement Scheme," Ph.D. dissertation, Institute of Anthropology, University of Copenhagen.

—— (1993b) "Changing Reasons for Ritual Performance. A Discussion of a Sinhalese Harvest Ritual," *Folk* 35: 65–89.

Tennekoon, N. Serena (1988) "Rituals of Development: the Accelerated Mahaweli Development Program of Sri Lanka," *American Ethnologist* 15: 294–311.

Westen, Drew (1985) *Self and Society. Narcissism, Collectivism, and the Development of Morals*, Cambridge: Cambridge University Press.

Woost, Michael D. (1990) "Rural Awakenings: Grassroots Development and the Cultivation of a National Past in Rural Sri Lanka," in J. Spencer (ed.) *History and the Roots of Conflict*, London: Routledge.

8 Localizing the American dream

Constructing Hawaiian homelands

Ulla Hasager

> We don't want to make the Hawaiians rich, we want to make them work.
>
> (McCarthy, Governor of Hawai'i, 1921)[1]

In 1921, the Hawaiian Homes Commission Act was passed by the United States Congress and signed into law by the President. The stated purpose of the Act was to "rehabilitate" Kānaka Maoli (indigenous Hawaiians),[2] who were living under extremely severe conditions. By the end of the nineteenth century they had experienced a depopulation of genocidal dimensions as a direct result of their steadily declining social and economic conditions. They were generally landless and many were crowding in tenements in Honolulu, or trying to survive on small parcels of land (*kuleana*) in rural areas that were otherwise occupied by large ranches or sugar cane plantations. The general health situation was alarming. Rehabilitation was supposed to be accomplished by returning people to the land.

Following the passing of the Act, selected public lands were labeled and set aside as "homeland" by territorial legislation. The "homeland" created by the Act actually became the homeland of the Kanaka Maoli homesteaders, but not in the sense the American congressmen had envisioned when they codified their American ideals of homesteading into a law intended to benefit a limited group of Kānaka Maoli. These American ideals concerned securing an industrious and happy life for the "Hawaiian race," thereby, supposedly, protecting "the race" from dying out.

This chapter outlines and juxtaposes the declared intentions of the Act with its actual implementation by the institutional bodies of the federal and state governments and by the corporal bodies of the homesteaders. It explores how the people of the Ho'olehua Homestead area on the island of Moloka'i came to regard the desolate, windy, barren and dry plain as their homeland. The analysis is based on data collected during field work in 1992–3, and on historical documents.

The first section of the chapter traces the visions and intentions of the three parties that were influential in creating the Hawaiian Homes Commission Act. The second section analyzes the actual implementation of this law. It outlines how the institutions of the federal and state governments administered it, and how the homesteaders, while living under the conditions framed by the law, envisioned and used it. The analysis focuses on questions of usage, attachment to place and creation of a viable community. It demonstrates how the implementation of the homesteading program by the homesteaders created ways of using the available homestead area, perhaps more akin to the old Kanaka Maoli ways of living on the land than to the American dream of small-scale independent farmers. This is discussed in the third section of the chapter, which also points to some consequences of this realization for the politics of the institutions administering the "Rehabilitation Act." The discussion of the creation of a homeland touches on certain issues concerning the concept of culture within anthropology, a concept that is currently subject to critical debate. These issues will be addressed in the final section.

VISIONS AND POLITICS

The American dream – the vision of federal and territorial institutions

The idea behind the Hawaiian Homes Commission Act was explained to me by a homesteader as the "American idea of creating a good society by giving everybody forty acres and a mule." In 1920, homesteading was certainly a thoroughly tested tool in US policy. A federal Homestead Act of 1862 was intended to encourage small farmers to go west and settle. Still earlier homesteading regulations had offered the possibility of registering one's home as a homestead. This was meant to secure the home and land in question in case of bankruptcy.[3] The purposes of the eighteenth-century American homesteading laws were, first, to "open up" new land, "expand the frontier" and settle so-called "empty" land, and second, to prevent development of large landholdings by creating a strong community of hard-working small farmers. In Hawai'i, at the beginning of the twentieth century, there was very little land to "open up," but there were many large landholdings (that is: leases of public land) to break up. As it turned out, the large landholdings were protected by the Hawaiian Homestead Act.

Half a century before the American takeover of the government of Hawai'i in 1893,[4] homesteading programs had been considered here. The Scotsman and future minister of foreign affairs, R. C. Wyllie, interviewed all the influential congregationalist missionaries (in writing) as to what might be done to better the deteriorated conditions of Kānaka Maoli. Most of the missionaries stressed the desirability of Kānaka Maoli "owning their own lands which they might farm" (Wyllie 1848: 52–7). Again in 1884, the government considered homesteading laws as necessary for the betterment of the "Hawaiian peoples' social and economic position," according to Judge Sanford Dole. When Dole later became president of the so-called "Republic of Hawaii," he and his government introduced the Hawaiian Land Act of 1895. This law favored homesteading by "opening up" the public lands for this purpose.

The United States finally fulfilled the aspirations of the members of the "provisional government," annexed Hawai'i in 1898, and made it into an American territory by the year 1900. Congress decided *not* to apply the more extensive homesteading laws of the US to the new territory, because they felt that the 1895 Land Act gave sufficient priority to the settlement of small-scale farmers. They did, however, make some changes in the land laws. They reduced the length of the general leases from twenty-one to five years, and the "Organic Act"[5] specified that no corporation could acquire and hold real estate in Hawai'i in excess of 1,000 acres.[6] Other amendments in 1910 made it possible for land to be homesteaded on public demand, wherever leases of the public lands expired. These provisions, however, completely failed to prevent further concentration of land ownership. From 1900 to 1920 the average size of the sugarcane plantations almost doubled (McGregor 1989: 41ff.).

The committees of Congress dealing with Hawaiian matters were very supportive of homesteading. They viewed it as a means of "Americanizing" the Islands (Vause 1962: 20). A local newspaper put it this way:

> The insistent demand has been heretofore for the Americanization of the Islands – for the building up of an independent, prosperous, intelligent middle class, which would be bound to the country and identified with its best interests – in a word, a growing democracy.
>
> (*Garden Island*, 23 March 1920: 2)

The debate in Congress before the passage of the Hawaiian Homestead bill focused on two aspects of the situation in Hawai'i. The moral considerations of the need to take care of Kānaka Maoli, "our wards," on the one hand, were reinforced by efforts to solve the "political" question of the "oriental peril," on the other (Vause 1962: 45–7). The American Congress and the ruling American business elite in Hawaii feared that the second-generation Japanese – sons and daughters of the imported labor force for the sugar plantations – would soon become the voting majority and thereby assume political control of the Islands. One way of counteracting this was to please the present Kanaka Maoli voters and secure their loyalty and numbers for the future. The basic ideas and concerns of Congress found resonance in the territorial administration and among the leaders of local society.

"Rehabilitation" and land rights – the vision of the Kanaka Maoli leaders

Alarmed by the general health situation and living conditions, 200 Kanaka Maoli leaders in 1914 formed the 'Ahahui Pu'uhonua O Na Hawai'i, the Hawaiian Protective Association (McGregor 1989: 327ff.). It was a political organization dedicated to social and educational work in order to "uplift" Kānaka Maoli. They urged people to save, "to buy their own home and to look after the health of their families" (ibid.: 247). Members of the Association drafted the "rehabilitation solution," which eventually became the Hawaiian Homes Commission Act. Rehabilitation was envisioned to be achieved by living the traditional "Hawaiian fish-and-*poi*" way, which indicates a way of life based on cultivating the taro gardens and fishing. *Poi* is produced from the taro corm and has been the staple for Kānaka Maoli for centuries.

In 1917, the Kanaka Maoli leaders sent out appeals for funds to the *haole* (White)[7] elite. In these they expressed what they expected the *haole* in powerful positions might want to hear in order to support Kānaka Maoli financially and politically.

> [The Hawaiian] must wake up and fully realize that he is "nobody" and that he has "nothing"; that he must start a new life, by going back to the soil and by fishing, as his ancestors did; That he must work hard every day, or else he will be a thief, stealing, to keep his lazy body alive; . . . That . . . it is only by bettering his condition, pulling himself up to the standard of the other more

> enlightened and earlier civilized races that he can ever expect to be their equal.
>
> (Hawai'i State Archives, Delegate Kalanianaole Petitions File, quoted in McGregor 1989: 240–1)

This quotation shows how rehabilitation is believed to occur through living a life not only "as [the] ancestors did," but also according to the virtues of the Protestant ethic: modest life and hard work (cf. Weber 1958). The excerpt invokes paternalistic attitudes, which indeed reflected the reality of the political and economic distribution of power in the Territory of Hawaii (Kent 1983).[8]

Congressional delegate Prince Kūhi'o Kalaniana'ole, who was influential in getting the rehabilitation bill through Congress,[9] circulated a letter in the Senate, in which he outlined how the extinction of Kānaka Maoli might be avoided:

> The Hawaiians were a seafaring and agricultural people. Their entire life was spent in the outdoors. But with the coming of civilization conditions were changed, the Hawaiians . . . were forced into the crowded tenements of the cities and towns and were subjected to all the evils of modern civilization. . . . Disease and the change in their living conditions weakened their vitality to such an extent that today they are susceptible to all diseases and their resistance being very low the death rate is high. Under the provisions of this bill, by placing the Hawaiians on the soil, away from the cities and towns, it is certain they will again retain their former vitality and in the course of years the race will increase, and become a majority element in the land of their birth.
>
> (Hawai'i State Archives, Delegate Kalanianaole File, quoted in McGregor 1989: 267)

The Prince presented a somewhat different attitude when he discussed the rehabilitation bill in a speech in Honolulu in 1920. Here, at home, he emphasized the *rights* to the land, besides describing the poor living conditions.

> I introduced this bill to set aside for the Hawaiian people lands that originally belonged to the Hawaiians. We find that the people who live in the tenement houses in this city [Honolulu] are nearly all Hawaiians. . . . These Hawaiian families . . . do not own an inch of land in their own country. The majority of their children are feeble-minded, so the board of education experts tell us; they are poor in mind, spirit and industry, because they live in tenements. In the morning their mothers send them to the little Chinese coffee

> shops to buy coffee – I hate to think what kind of coffee they get there – poor bread and stinking butter. This is their food. How can they grow up robust and healthy and survive? That is why the race is fast dying out. These conditions stare the Hawaiian people in the face.
>
> (*Pacific Commercial Advertiser* 24 September 1920: 1)

These quotes explicitly link rehabilitation of Kānaka Maoli with "placing them back on the soil." The quote from the Association emphasized the work ethic and the necessity of a change of attitude as well. "Rehabilitation," which could have been accomplished in various other ways, had become synonymous with getting parcels of land to work in a healthy out-of-door lifestyle.

"A political accident" – the politics of the local business elite

The developing land laws in Hawai'i were a serious threat to the large sugar planters. They leased half of the arable public lands, and many of the leases were due to expire between 1917 and 1921. Before the amendments of 1910, the planters had been successful in countering the homesteading initiatives, but by way of federal policy and American democratic and liberal ideals, their businesses and power were now threatened. Therefore, the local business elite supported the Hawaiian Homes Commission Act as a means of amending and in some cases cancelling the basic land laws of the Territory – aside from whatever "idealistic" motives they might have had concerning rehabilitation, Americanization and "progress." The Act allowed the sugar planters to keep a firm grip on their extensive areas of leased public lands and at the same time their support made a good impression on the Kanaka Maoli voters. Had the Act *not* been passed, Kānaka Maoli would in effect have had access to some of the most productive lands in the Territory (*Ka Mana O Ka 'Āina* 1989: 11).

The federal and territorial bodies were pursuing the American dream on behalf of the homesteaders. They meant to secure democracy and good living conditions by creating conditions intended to resemble private ownership of land – in moderate parcels. The local Kanaka Maoli leaders, on the other hand, saw the law as a means of protecting the continued existence of Kānaka Maoli and of regaining control of some of the lands lost since the introduction of private ownership of land in the mid-nineteenth century. The third policy-making party, the local ruling business elite, had its own political agenda in regard to changing the land laws. They sought a way out of being caught between liberal ideals and paternalistic practices. The three forces joined their divergent motives and secured the Hawaiian Homes Commission Act through a "political accident" uniting the issues of land and rehabilitation (Vause 1962: iii). In the view of historian Marylyn Vause, who has analyzed the Hawaiian Homes Commission Act, there were only strategic reasons and no logical grounds for this union.

LIFE AND ADMINISTRATION

The Hawaiian Homes Commission Act set aside about 200,000 acres of public land for homesteading by "Native Hawaiians" – defined by Congress as only Kānaka Maoli of 50 percent or more "Hawaiian blood."[10] The burden of proof rested with the would-be beneficiaries. The land was taken out of the 2.4 million acres of so-called public lands that had been "ceded" by the Republic of Hawaii to the United States in 1898 upon annexation.[11]

Under the Hawaiian Homes Commission Act as amended, "Native Hawaiians" were entitled to apply for ninety-nine-year leases of land at a dollar a year for residential, pastoral, or agricultural purposes. According to the Act, beneficiaries were also entitled to services, for example in the form of financial and technical aid in establishing their homesteads.

The lands set aside to be returned to the people were marginal and of such poor quality that a contemporary agricultural expert wrote the following:

> I can not refrain from writing you my views in relation to H. R. 13,500, a bill which according to its sponsors is for the purpose of rehabilitating the native Hawaiians. . . . This bill was not conceived for that purpose, but rather for the purpose of rehabilitating a few sugar companies and Hawaiian politicians. If this bill was conceived in honesty of thought and purpose, those behind it would have selected lands better adapted for the purpose than those named in this bill.
>
> I am quite familiar with all of these lands and I have no hesitancy in stating that they are wholly unsuited for the purpose. These lands have for years been available to the capitalistic element of the Territory but who have passed them by for the very good reason that those parts having fertile soil but no water would require such a large expenditure to bring water to them that

> compensating returns would not follow. How public officials can so far forget their obligation and duty to their Hawaiian constituents as to try and put through such a measure is beyond my ken.
>
> (A. Horner to Senator Miles Poindexter, letter, 18 November 1920, quoted in full in Vause 1962, Appendix X: 184–7)

Only about 10 percent of the lands selected for future homesteading could at best be classified as first-class pastoral land. None of the land could rightfully be labelled prime agricultural land (*Ka Mana O Ka 'Āina* 1989: 4). This poor quality of the land was not seen to be a problem, because it would help to foster the work ethic, which law-makers felt would turn Kānaka Maoli into good Americans.

> It was not the wish . . . to give the Hawaiians the highly developed lands for if this was done the main object of the measure would be defeated as the Hawaiians would not work the lands themselves but would have the work done by Japanese.
>
> (Governor McCarthy, quoted in Vause 1962: 103–4)

Water could improve large areas of the selected lands, but the prospects of getting the necessary water to the homelands were "dim and unattainable" – according to engineer John Wilson (1920, quoted in Vause 1962: 118). Furthermore, very poor financing provisions combined with administrative problems obstructed the actual implementation of the Act.

Over the years, the trust obligations inherent in the Hawaiian Homes Commission Act have been grossly neglected by the United States' government and, from 1959, the State of Hawai'i and its Department of Hawaiian Home Lands.[12] In 1991, after seventy years, only about 17.5 percent of the lands had been homesteaded, while 62 percent were being used by non-natives, often in cheap long-term leases (Hawaii Advisory Committee to the United States Commission on Civil Rights 1991b: 1).[13]

"Forty acres and a mule"

The first lands in the Territory to be opened up for agricultural homesteading were the Kalaniana'ole Settlement in 1922 and the Ho'olehua area in 1924. Both are located on the Island of Moloka'i. They were chosen for a five-year probation period.

Most of the 25,306 acres of land managed by the Department of Hawaiian Home Lands on that island are located in the dry plain of Ho'olehua and on the equally dry southwestern slopes of the eastern mountain range. Ho'olehua was divided up into homestead lots consisting of neat squares of 40 acres each, irrespective of gullies and other natural dividers. No consideration was given to the direction of the prevailing winds that blow incessantly.

Before 1924, the western part of Moloka'i, including the Ho'olehua Plain, does not seem to have been inhabited, except for temporary sheltering (de Loach 1970: 40–1, 66f.). Though uninhabited, the West End did play a role in the life of the Moloka'i people. It was famous for its adze quarries, and was renowned for its fishing, hunting, and gathering. Some areas were known as good for cultivating sweet potatoes. But Kānaka Maoli had chosen to live in the eastern part of the island. Fertile valleys, stretching from the mountains to the sea, provided everything needed within close reach. These valleys, called *ahupua'a*, supported the traditional Hawaiian socio-economic system. The basis of this system was destroyed when undivided use-rights to land were changed to private ownership during the land reforms, the Māhele or "Division," in the mid-nineteenth century. In a short period of time most of the lands of Hawai'i passed into the hands of a few people, primarily non-Kānaka Maoli (Kelly 1956, 1994; Levy 1975). On Moloka'i, extensive lands in the West End, formerly owned by kings,[14] ended up in the hands of a *hui* (corporation) of businessmen who created the Molokai Ranch. By 1897[15] they controlled three-fifths of Moloka'i's land. One-third of the *hui*'s land was leased from the government. When these leases expired in 1918, the lands were turned over to the government for homesteading (Cooke 1949: 13).

Cattle raising seemed to be the only venture with a potential for becoming a major industry in Moloka'i. Again and again attempts at truck-farming failed (de Loach 1970), as did attempts to establish sugar plantations. One agro-industry, however, turned out to be very prosperous: production of pineapple – now synonymous with the Hawaiian Islands, especially Moloka'i and Lāna'i, for people all over the world. From 1923 to the mid-1970s, when it "phased out," the pineapple industry was extremely decisive for the social, political, and, of course, economic life of Moloka'i. The Moloka'i Ranch itself stuck to the cattle business and various other enterprises, but leased out extensive areas of land to large pineapple-growing corporations.[16] The pineapple plantations expanded their areas of production into the homestead area (detailed below) and created "camps" for workers which turned into little towns.

By 1935, 74 percent of the population of Moloka'i lived in the western half of the island (de Loach 1970: 123). The pineapple industry and the homesteading program had completely shifted the center of population of the island from east to west. The two enterprises had, furthermore, turned a devastating decrease in population into a sky-rocketing 500 percent increase. By 1920, a little more than a thousand people were living on Moloka'i, almost all of them Kānaka Maoli (de Loach 1975: 93). This was one-fifth of what the population of the island had been a hundred years earlier. Due to the importation of a plantation labor force for the pineapple industry, the ethnic composition of the population also changed radically: of the 5,677 persons living on Moloka'i in 1935, 23.6 percent were Filipino and only 42.2 percent Kānaka Maoli (de Loach 1975: 93, 106), but the Kanaka Maoli population had doubled. This was mostly owing to the homesteading program.

Constructing homelands

The homesteaders, as a general rule, were expected to build their homes and settle one family on each lot, at a distance from their neighbors. And they did. Some of the first settlers were selected from among people who had been approached and encouraged to apply for homesteads, because they were experienced farmers and were expected to be particularly suited for this rural lifestyle (Hawaiian Homes Commission 1925: 8; Keesing 1936: 36–41). Among the first to settle in Ho'olehua was a group of families of farmers and fishermen who all came from the same area on the island of Maui and were members of and leaders within the same church. They had been encouraged to apply for homesteads and came to Moloka'i, where they stayed – in spite of the initial discouragement caused by the local conditions and facilities offered:

> [O]ne of our members of the church . . . was assigned to issue out applications for homestead. So he called our . . . family together, and . . . told us, we are the right kind of people to come here to instruct others how to live on the land. But many coming from the city and they don't know anything about taro or growing, about farming. We know about farming. So how about we come here and we can help our people become . . . farmers, self-sufficient, not to depend on working under somebody else. Because of that, we all came. But we didn't know anything about this place. We thought that everything was here. We thought water was available but there was no water for farming. . . . So, we had a tough time when we came here. . . . We are farmers, we are fishermen, we are

> hunters. . . . So we . . . came well prepared. We came here with food enough for two years, and we came here with net for fishing, we came with rifles, shotguns, with ammunition.
>
> (Homesteader interview in Brigham Young University 1981: 5–6)

When the Commission in 1922 was ready for the first homesteaders, Governor Wallace Farrington, chairman of the Hawaiian Homes Commission, gave an address on "What Rehabilitation Means to the Hawaiian People":

> [The initiative of Congress] to me signalizes the day for the Hawaiian to step forward to assume the responsibilities and privileges of his broader American citizenship and destiny. . . . Hard work, self-denial, study, sincerity, enthusiasm, and determination are all essential to success and we must bring these to bear in this Territorial and national enterprise. Can the Hawaiians do it? I know they can if they will make up their minds to it. . . . These soldiers of the soil must have as sincere support as has ever been given soldiers of military warfare.
>
> (Ibid.: 22)

The same official report from the Hawaiian Homes Commission also applauded the accomplishments of the administrators in preparing for the first settlers to move onto the land. The Commission had been "building roads, clearing, providing for water, fencing. . . . Plans for neat and attractive bungalows have been adopted" (Hawaiian Homes Commission 1922: 9–10).

The first years looked promising. In 1925, the executive officer of the Commission described the "Moloka'i Miracle" as a completely rational result of the willingness to work of the "splendid types of Hawaiians and part-Hawaiians" (Hawaiian Homes Commission 1925: 10, 15). By the end of the probation period, an investigator from the US Department of the Interior was supposed to evaluate the program. In spite of the celebrated hard work of the homesteaders, a serious drought threatened to jeopardize the whole program. The Commission's ignoring of the water problem barely escaped an embarrassing exposure.

> The crops were already planted: corn, watermelon, pumpkin, and drought was getting drier and drier, see. . . . So all these elders got together and . . . had three days fasting at my daddy's home [for rain]. . . . When they released, the rain started drop. And the rain came three days, day and night, day and night. . . . And all this

wilted corn and watermelon they all came up. So when the investigator came down here, this food was all matured. [All] the Mormons took all their crops up to the warehouse as a gift. We called that the *ho'okupu* [ceremonial gift-giving to a chief as a sign of honor and respect]. *Ho'okupu*, a gift to the Department of the Interior.

(Quoted from Brigham Young University 1981: 12–13)

The continuation of the Hawaiian Homes Program was therefore secured, not only by experienced and hard-working farmers, but also, it is said, by the help of God. Nevertheless, the problem of water persists to this day. Few crops can be grown in the Ho'olehua area without irrigation. The Kalaniana'ole Settlement in Kalama'ula early on repeated the lesson learned by the American Sugar Company some twenty years earlier; the irrigation water from the low-lying wells turned saline.[17] Of course, the salt became infused in the land and the homesteaders, after the hard work of clearing, could no longer cultivate their crops in it. These unfortunate farmers were offered new agricultural land in the Ho'olehua area.

In Ho'olehua, the homesteaders started out to farm their lands in the modern "truck-farming" style. The relatively large size of the lots in the Ho'olehua area – 40 acres – was initially decided upon because it was calculated that there was sufficient rainfall for dryland agriculture. The stated objective was to use the lands for diversified agriculture. But the reports of the Hawaiian Homes Commission to the legislature at this time reveal that the administrators had pineapple production on their minds for the homesteaders. They were discussing agreements with the pineapple companies and involving them in the planning before people ever moved on the land.

The lands of Molokai . . . are well adapted for pineapple culture. . . . Letters have been sent to every pineapple corporation in the Territory, requesting that each submit a statement outlining a method by which to undertake to assist the homesteaders, financially and otherwise, in the cultivation of their lands. . . . According to present plans, the best scheme would be adopted and put into effect.

(Hawaiian Homes Commission 1925: 15–16)

It was suggested that the homesteaders should work their holdings themselves and receive a daily compensation for their labor. The plans were already very specific concerning "devoting" 30 to 35 acres of each 40-acre agricultural lot to growing pineapples (1925: 16). This was presumably not known to the homesteaders, many of whom tried other crops under great hardship. Problems such as difficulties with marketing, the climate, and pests caused many of them to give up diversified agriculture, and pineapple cultivation provided a welcome alternative. The homesteaders made agreements similar to the ones suggested by the Hawaiian Homes Commission with two pineapple companies, which, from 1927, were leasing their lands. After a few years, it became obvious that the system of planting little squares, corresponding to seven-eighths of a homestead, in crop rotation, was ineffective and made it very difficult to control pests. A new system was invented consisting of large blocks of contiguous parcels of homestead land. The farmers were no longer responsible for weeding and taking care of their own specific lot (Keesing 1936: 71–84). After 1931, the homesteaders hired Korean and Filipino workers to take care of their portion of the crop, or they paid plantation work gangs to do it (ibid.: 76).

From the 1940s onwards, all but 90 percent of the homestead families had leased their lands to one or the other of the two pineapple corporations. This policy was strongly encouraged by the Hawaiian Homes Commission (Spitz 1964: 33–5). The Commission was well aware that if the lands were not used for pineapple production, the problem of irrigating the fertile but dry soil had to be solved. However, this was a financial and thereby political problem beyond the commissioners' capabilities to solve.

The opinions among the homesteaders about the pineapple business were and are diverse and similar to the range of opinions displayed today concerning so-called "third-party leases." Some felt that the pineapple was destroying the land; one informant described a former pineapple area as "raped" land that needed to be "nurtured back into life." Some have been fiercely protecting their rights to control what happens to their lots, and some have felt that they have been prevented by the Commission from working the land. In a statement before a hearing on the administration of Hawaiian Home Lands a third-generation homesteader explained:

> Our original pineapple contract with Libby . . . was paying $20 a ton. My Dad made at least $3,000 a year – and for those times, the Hawaiian Homesteaders were considered very rich – I remember my dad having a new car. . . . The Homesteaders were getting their "value" from their land. . . . So what did the Commission people do? – they demoted the Homesteaders down to "peon" level; had them sign a new pineapple contract, giving them only $70.00

> pr. month. . . . Even now, as I review this story, my eyes get wet; little as I was, I knew what they were doing.
>
> (Administration of Native Hawaiian Home Lands 1990: 144, 448–9)

Others, such as one of the early Ho'olehua homesteaders, felt that the pineapple was a blessing, because it was too hard to work the farms. Her mother, for instance, was too busy in the fields to even see her grandchildren, "that's why the people took pineapple. The people who said the Homesteaders up here never work, they should have been here. . . . I can tell you that was work" (interview, ca. 1978, *Nā Mana'o O Nā Kupuna* n.d.: 25).

Another point of contention between the Hawaiian Homes administration and the homesteaders is the administration's ambition of "neat attractive bungalows." The county's and the Department of Hawaiian Home Lands' regulations concerning housing standards have, for example, prevented some homesteaders from moving onto land that was allotted to them during the acceleration program in 1984–7. Furthermore, homesteaders are prevented from insuring their houses and, thereby, from obtaining utilities like water and electricity, if their houses are not in accordance with county regulations. The discrepancy in opinion about proper housing between authorities and some homesteaders can be illustrated by a description of the problem given by a witness in the People's International Tribunal, Hawai'i, 1993. Talking about a tent city on Hawaiian Home Land, this witness coined the term "affordable houselessness," and criticized the assimilation efforts, beginning 170 years ago, pressuring Kānaka Maoli to build "regular" houses:

> It is a conspiracy to keep the Hawaiian people afraid of the rain. You spend your whole life putting up four walls, investing in a stationary coffin, so afraid of the elements that you spend all your money and miss half your life. There is no need to fear the rain.
>
> (Onekahakaha, Hawai'i, 18 August 1993)[18]

Home, land – homeland

By living on the land the homesteaders have made the Ho'olehua Plain their home and created a viable community there. Today, oldtimers and their descendants have family ties to many different lots in the homestead area. This situation has come about due to intermarriage and through applying for homesteads in the area. Even though the lots as a general rule stay in the families, they do not necessarily pass in direct line from parent to child. For various reasons lots are often passed down directly to grandchildren or to nieces and nephews, when youngsters take over a lot that the older generations are unable to take care of. Also the practice of *hānai*, the giving of a child to – most often – the grandparents, extends bonds of relationships throughout the neighborhood. This is combined with a practice of children staying away from their parents for extended periods of time to spread the sense of belonging to the greater part of the homestead area.

> And so the homestead life, here, I must say, has been a wonderful life for each one of us. Regardless of the hardship. . . . We took [up homesteading] with [the] spirit . . . that we were coming to make the best of it and we stuck with it until this day. . . . We [made] our home here and [will] be buried here.
>
> (A homesteader speaking in an interview with Mary Kawena Pukui, 8 March 1961, transcribed by the author)

When asked if and how they came to feel at home in the windy and barren Ho'olehua, most informants explained that this was the land they lived on, the place where their children had been born and where they themselves were going to be buried. They furthermore established that this was the land that they took care of, and that it was from here they went out to fish, hunt, and gather.

The frequent mentioning of subsistence activities illustrates the importance homesteaders attach to the possibilities of fishing, hunting, and gathering, which have continued to be very important throughout the years. Recently, this priority has been acknowledged by the Hawaiian Homes Commission through an agreement that a group of homesteaders is to take care of the lands and waters of Mo'omomi, located along the northwest coast of Moloka'i (*Ka Nūhou* 1994: 6). It was the result of years of persistence and research by third-generation homesteaders. "We have to *hānai* [adopt and take care of] our own *'āina* [land]," one of them said. These observations are confirmed by the findings of the "Subsistence Task Force Group," established by the state administration. The task force made a survey in June 1993 of the Moloka'i community regarding the extent and importance of subsistence activity. They found that it was widespread and constituted a major factor in the economy (Governor's Subsistence Task Force Group 1993).

Questions about the understanding of the concepts of home and place of belonging frequently initiated talks about *'āina*, in very general terms, usually stressing the importance of taking care of the land, *mālama 'āina*. Teachings such as "You take care of the land, and it takes care of you," "Never take more than you need," "Give back what you take" are repeated again and again. One of the early homesteaders told me that what she was taught as a child, and what had always been true to her, was the wisdom of the words "Take care of the land with love, then it will give to you." There has recently been a scholarly tendency to ascribe this attitude, phrased in the concept of *aloha 'āina*, to a recent invention. My research indicates that this cultural model of the relationship between man and land is in fact widespread and traceable back in time to early historical sources. The above-mentioned homesteader explained that even though the expression might be new (it (re)appeared with the upsurge of the movement for indigenous rights from the mid-1970s) the concept is old. Oldtimers repeatedly stress the importance of sharing, "share everything you have, take only what you need." The literature on the traditional Kanaka Maoli relationship to land stresses this "family" relationship, the importance of living in harmony (*pono*) with the surroundings. As the younger sibling, you respect and take care of the land (*mālama 'āina*), which in turn provides for you (Kame'eleihiwa 1992: 19–49).

The points raised above suggest some reasons for the relative lack of attachment to an individual home,[19] or a homestead lot, and the relative importance conferred on the environment of the homestead area and land in general. The sense of belonging encompasses a larger area, often including the borderlands.[20]

CONTINUITY AND CHANGE

Grid or *ahupua'a* – cultural models of the relationship between man and land

Kanaka Maoli "localizing" strategies show that their perception of use of the land differs from the intended "rehabilitation" through "ownership" of private parcels of land. Several different co-existing cultural models of the relationship between land and man can be outlined on the basis of the foregoing analysis. They range from federal and territorial administrators' "property type" concept of land as something which can be divided up in exclusive categories, owned by humans, bought and sold (Bohannan 1966: 101–2), to the more general concept of responsibility to love and care for the living land.

Preliminary analyses – only outlined in the above examples – show that the cultural models invoked by the Department of Hawaiian

Home Lands in their deliberations with the homesteaders have been basically paternalistic, embracing ideas of taking care of wards, knowing better, and trying to convince the homesteaders of the value and moral requirement of hard work. Individual responsibilities and rights are stressed. Repeatedly, the homesteaders have been reacting to the implementation of such models which limit their activities. An interesting pattern is revealed by the recent point of contention as to whether claims by the homesteaders should be individual, as the Department states, or collective, as homesteaders maintain (cf. "Hawaiian Home Lands Trust Individual Claims Review Panel").

At the risk of oversimplification, I will argue that the cultural models discernible in the homesteaders' ideas of land use, in the way they live and actually use the land, and the way they have created a community in a former uninhabited place, are akin to the cultural models describing the *ahupua'a* system of land use. This becomes convincing if we imagine the Ho'olehua Plain with its cherished borderlands and coastal area as an *ahupua'a*. One hundred years ago, the *ahupua'a* system was described as a socio-economic system with its integrated system of gathering, hunting, agriculture, aquaculture, and fishing, all of which rendered the population of an *ahupua'a* self-sufficient on the whole.

> The *unit* of land, so to speak, seems to have been the *Ahupuaa*. . . . The Ahupuaa ran from the sea to the mountain, theoretically. That is to say the central idea of the Hawaiian division of land was . . . radial. Hawaiian life vibrated from *uka*, mountain, whence came wood, kapa, for clothing, olona, for fishline, ti-leaf for wrapping paper, *i.e.* . . for ratan lashing, wild birds for food, to the *kai*, sea, whence came *ia* fish, and all connected therewith. Mauka [towards the mountain] and makai [seawards] are therefore fundamental ideas to the native of an island. Land . . . was divided accordingly.
>
> (Lyons 1875: 104)

The land division usually included fishponds and the ocean as far as the reef. Running from the seashore up into the mountains, the *ahupua'a* thus included fishing rights, cultivable lands and uplands. *Mauka–makai* is still a central orientation to Kānaka Maoli.

The daily practice of the homesteaders reveals striking similarities with the basic features of the *ahupua'a* system. This is evident in the patterns and importance ascribed to "subsistence" activities – activities involving the whole environment and leading to patterns of exchange and bonds of attachment covering the entire Ho'olehua area. Dynamic extensive family networks and the emphasizing of collective rights, claims, and activities also point in this direction. Some aspects of resemblance are readily created by the administrative institution's implementation of the Homes Commission Act. This is true, for instance, for the multiple undivided rights to the same lands, the existence of an office taking care of the land on behalf of the "true owner," and the establishment of communal pastures.[21] This interpretation is supported by other "modern/traditional" conjunctures, for instance the use-right that was introduced to prevent the Kānaka Maoli from selling their homesteads. The history of pineapple on the homestead lands might, in its own ironic way, have contributed to this professed cultural continuity by "disturbing" any creation of bonds of "private ownership" between man and land – if such were indeed being formed. In a sense, the "modern" pineapple production has reinforced the "overlaying" of the grid of squares of individual "ownership" with the large "triangle" of the *ahupua'a* social and economic system.

The Ho'olehua homestead area is, thus, a prime example of the "creative survival" of simultaneous continuity and change. The categories invented by legislators and interpreted and implemented by the central institutions of the federal and state governments defined certain limits – physical and judicial – within which the homesteaders constructed new ways of living with or on the land. Following Sahlins (1993), I will suggest that in the actual daily practice of "creating" Hawaiian Homelands – a completely new category and reality – the continuity with the past has played a significant role.

A localized dream

It was clear in the debates during the first decades of the century that the dream of a homesteader Hawaiian style, a "rehabilitated Hawaiian," was the "Americanized" industrious, hard-working farmer.[22] Like any other American, he would be the head of a happy, healthy, and hard-working nuclear family living in a home on a plot of land, fenced in, and tilled with the help of "1920-modern" truck-farming methods. The original understanding of the need to "go back to the soil" – agreed upon by local Kanaka Maoli leaders – was based on concepts of individual families having the incentive to work the land out of a feeling of responsibility and satisfaction stemming from "ownership" and attachment to a specific piece of land. A similar understanding was recently expressed in an interview with the 1993 Director of the Department of Hawaiian Home Lands, Mrs. Hoaliku

Drake, who believes that happiness is "ownership" of a piece of land and to take care of the family (interview, 22 October 1993).

As the story went, this part of the dream did not come true. In fact, it was hardly tried out for a variety of reasons such as limited funds (for prospective farmers and administrative bodies alike), poor quality of the land, and lack of water, infrastructure, storage facilities, and markets. Furthermore, the neat grids, transferred from the drawing tables of the surveyors to the 40-acre square lots carved out of the lands of Ho'olehua, were, in the course of history, overlaid by another grid of much larger square meshes, encompassing all but a few of the homesteads in a system of large pineapple fields grown in rotation. After fifty years, when the pineapple production had moved to better grounds and cheaper labor forces, the homesteaders and their descendants had another chance of living up to the old dream of the legislators. In the meantime, they had created and involved themselves in the Moloka'i society in multiple ways. Farming became a challenge and great opportunity to some and a burden to others. Many have taken up the challenge[23] but many others had already established lives based on other occupations. For the older homesteaders, the intervening fifty years had taken their toll. No longer were they young and vigorous.

Today, the total population of Moloka'i is 6,717 persons – 48.9 percent Kānaka Maoli, 20.5 percent Filipinos, 17.6 percent Whites and 8.9 percent Japanese (calculated on the basis of information in DBEDT 1993). This composition of the population testifies to the fact that Governor McCarthy's prophecy came true: "the Hawaiians would not work the lands themselves" (quoted above). But the prophecy came true because the land was too bad, not because it was too good: without irrigation, the lands seemed only suitable for pineapple. These completely changed preconditions were the responsibility of the Hawaiian Homes Commission itself.

The above population figures not only indicate that the "Americanization" aspect of the Hawaiian Homes Commission Act failed. They also indicate that the "rehabilitation" aspect succeeded. The number of Kānaka Maoli on Moloka'i has tripled. This is, of course, due to several factors, but there is no doubt that the strong Kanaka Maoli communities of the homestead areas – also a testimony to success – are decisive. In the end, Kānaka Maoli certainly did not become rich. And as present statistics show, they did not become that healthy either (Blaisdell and Mokuau 1994: 53–5). But in spite of much hardship and economic, social, and health problems, the Kānaka Maoli of Moloka'i do not need "rehabilitation" in the moral sense as defined by the instigators of the Hawaiian Homes Commission Act. They neither need nor want to be wards of the state.

The viability and creativity of the homestead communities does not stem from an implementation of the American concept of home(steads). It stems from the fact that the land is there and that the Kānaka Maoli have the right to it. If "rehabilitation" is taken to mean increasing the numbers and vitality of Kānaka Maoli and their communities, the union of land and rehabilitation issues, criticized by Vause, turned out to be quite logical anyway.

The American dream of the legislators of Congress and the Kanaka Maoli need for land merged in a law, the passing of which was fuelled by the economic and political interests of the White business elite in the Territory of Hawaii. What was created through political games and hidden agendas continued to be fraught with problems based on the inherent opposition in the goals of the three involved parties. The fragile co-existence of federal democratic ideals, the paternalistic plantation economy as embodied in the political leadership of the Territory of Hawaii, and the homesteaders' particular lifestyle continued.

The central institution of the State Department of Hawaiian Home Lands still tries to "raise" its beneficiaries as good citizens, "American" style as identified above, through paternalistic attitudes and procedures. Though it might not be obvious to the agency itself, its numerous acts and regulations support efforts to keep complete control over how and when the lands are going to be used by the homesteaders. Many controversies and misunderstandings between Kānaka Maoli occupying the homelands and the central administration could be avoided if the Department would realize that the homesteaders in the processes of localizing have created ways to perceive of and use the lands which are different from the American dream that first promoted homesteading.

PRACTICING PLACE – AND ANTHROPOLOGY

Space is constructed as place[24] or locality by processes such as "structures of feeling" (Gupta and Ferguson 1992: 8) and everyday practice, including actual physical action. The above analysis of various ways of "practicing place" of peoples and institutions begs further research into questions concerning the power of classification and the shaky relationship between land rights and the practice of identity. The homesteaders' way of creating a homeland and community indicates that attachment to actual physical places is significant for the creation of human identity – and thereby culture. Representations of symbolic places are important enough to kill for, but the actual environments and land(scapes) within and with which human beings live are indispensable to the construction of identity. At the same time, the physical environments themselves are constructed through classification and action (cf. Hasager 1991: 125ff.; Bourdieu 1977). The two forms of belonging – living and feeling at home in one place while having strong emotional ties to another place, which one might never see – do not preclude each other. On the contrary, the study of the way these processes interplay might create significant new understandings of human beings' relationship to place.

Constructing a homeland does not merely concern construction of identity and, thereby, society, relating to the memory or dream of a place where you do not live. It is also and primarily concerned with a construction of an actual physical place to live. This might account for the strong emphasis here on the physical relationship to the lived-in place compared to contemporary anthropological theories of globalization and deterritorialization, which focus on structures of feelings directed towards the places displaced people have *left*, whereas the present study focuses on the relationship to places people are moving *toward*.

The identity of humans, the social and physical space, and the construction, maintenance and transformation of identity and space are thoroughly interwoven processes. Cultural values are often connected with a place. And belonging somewhere seems to form a vital part of strategies of identity. But this "somewhere" does not mean that new homelands cannot be constructed, nor that it is impossible to belong in several ways to several places at the same time. The lesson of cultural models tells us that human beings have the capacity of living sane lives with many different, even conflicting, models or perceptions of the world – and of homelands – at the same time. By understanding culture as process, we might be able to embrace an understanding of a simultaneously continuing and changing multiple attachment to places.

Powerful social institutions must be analyzed to reveal the false credibility that they acquire by employing legitimizing metaphors precisely building on connection with place. But we must be careful not to sweep out, along with the despised institutions and models, insights into the relationship of human beings to the land, to the environment, to the surrounding space.

As anthropologists we are always in a learning process, constantly building up understanding: rejecting old "truths," trying new theories, rejecting or improving them, and so on. Considering the effect that our theories may have on the conditions of life for human beings, we must be mindful that our power, in a sense, is greater than our knowledge. Therefore, the responsibility of contextualizing our research extends to the publication of our findings as well.[25] What anthropologists publish, backed up by the authority of the academic tradition, becomes part of real life, always liable to be utilized in political debates or legal arguments (cf. Trask 1994: 272–3).

When we are theorizing about the meaning of place and space for human beings in the present-day world, we also have to be aware that what we are talking about is the identity as well as the basic living conditions of the people with whom we are working. To put it squarely: at the same time that indigenous peoples all over the world are beginning to make some headway in having collective and territorial rights acknowledged in international fora, such as the United Nations, anthropologists are presenting theories that might be (mis)understood as stating that attachment to place is pure illusion.

As was the case with the lands of the Hawaiian Homes Commission Act, it often happens that what from the outset was considered poor land and, therefore, allocated to the indigenous peoples, later on became, for reasons of investment and resource development, valuable lands that state agencies as well as private persons and corporations very much wished to get their hands on. Without careful moral and ethical considerations concerning contextualization of research and publication in practicing anthropology, I am afraid, a theory of deterritorialization might come in handy for nation-states neglecting the collective rights of, or even finding subtle genocidal ways of getting rid of, the indigenous peoples within their borders.

Perhaps anthropologists should be more concerned with finding a place and space for human beings than with rescuing the "traditional" concept of culture?

ACKNOWLEDGMENTS

This chapter is based on a paper presented to the International Workshop "Finding a Place and Space for Culture" arranged by the Institute of Anthropology, University of Copenhagen, 1–3 December, 1993, at Magleås Kursuscenter, Denmark. It is part of the research project, "The Lands of Hawai'i between Localization and Globalization," which deals with Hawaiian Homeland on Moloka'i, Hawai'i, under the research program, "Complex Cultural Processes," at the Institute of Anthropology, University of Copenhagen. Research was carried out on Moloka'i and in Honolulu, Hawai'i, in 1992–3, funded by the Institute of Anthropology, University of Copenhagen, The Danish Research Council of the Humanities, and the Danish Research Academy.

NOTES

1. Quoted in Vause (1962: 72).
2. Kanaka Maoli (pl.: Kānaka Maoli), the true people, is used throughout this chapter for people who consider themselves native to the Hawaiian Archipelago, Ka Pae'āina. Even though there is some discussion as to whether these terms are traditionally "correct" – not only among anthropologists and historians – I have chosen to use them for three reasons: (1) because many local people themselves use them, (2) because the term "Hawaiian" has too many meanings – even aside from federal definitions, see below, and (3) because it is a simple tool to remove the mind-set from the stereotypes affixed to Hawai'i and Hawaiians. References and official names are kept in their original language usage.
3. The concept inspired a lot of interest in European countries, where several governments were discussing possibilities of following the American example.
4. In 1893 a small group of American businessmen supported by the US Navy overthrew the Hawaiian Queen and government in "an act of war," as the American President later that year labeled it in his "Message to the Congress," calling for righting of the wrong (Cleveland 1994: 134). Extensive areas of government and crown lands under the kingdom of Hawai'i were "ceded" to – that is: taken by – the US government and became labeled "public lands."
5. In 1900, the Organic Act made Hawai'i a territory of the United States. It served as the "constitution" of the Territory up through 1959, when Hawai'i became the fiftieth of the United States of America, after a ballot vote that failed to provide the choice of independence.
6. Existing vested rights were not to be affected, and none of the plantations were prosecuted for circumventing the 1,000-acre limitation (McGregor 1989: 41ff.).
7. The terms "White" and "Western" relate to the cultural models, actions, and politics of the people in power, whether in the US or in Hawai'i. It is not meant to indicate an overall encompassing, cohesive Western culture.
8. Reverend Akana, a member of 'Ahahui Pu'uhonua O Na Hawai'i, promoted going "Back to the soil and work! work! work!" as the prescription for "racial development" (Akana 1918: 50–1). In his monograph entitled *The Sinews for Racial Development* (1918), he outlined various courses of action for lifting the people out of their "physical and moral destitution." Akana was later appointed as one of the first members of the Hawaiian Homes Commission in 1921.
9. The full story of the creation of the homestead areas is of course far more complicated and Prince Kūhi'o's role and motives are strongly debated.
10. Fifty percent was a compromise between the original suggestion that all Kānaka Maoli with 1/32 or more Hawaiian blood were eligible and the

view that only *piha* Kānaka Maoli, "pure" Kānaka Maoli, should benefit – because they were the only ones threatened with extinction. How the 20,000 Kānaka Maoli of pure blood and thousands more part-Hawaiians of the 1910s could be returned productively to 200,000 acres of the least valuable lands of the Territory, is a question that was not discussed (Vause 1962: 114, 128, 132; *Ka Mana O Ka 'Āina* 1989: 2).

11 The Department of Hawaiian Home Lands today manages a somewhat reduced area of 187,413 acres of land on five different islands.

12 This is documented in the several studies that have been carried out in the course of the last fifteen years, for example: *Administration of Native Hawaiian Home Lands* (1990); *Federal-State Task Force Report on the Hawaiian Homes Commission Act* (1983); Native Hawaiian Study Commission (1983). Some of the titles of the reports constitute in themselves a continuing story: *Breach of Trust? Native Hawaiian Homelands* (Hawaii Advisory Committee to the US Commission on Civil Rights 1980); *A Broken Trust. The Hawaiian Homelands Program: Seventy Years of Failure of the Federal and State Governments to Protect the Civil Rights of Native Hawaiians* (The Hawaii Advisory Committee to the United States Commission of Civil Rights 1991a); and finally, the State of Hawaii's Office of the Governor, Office of State Planning's *Federal Breaches of the Hawaiian Home Lands Trust* (1992). The reports reveal an interesting attempt from each of the two levels of administration – federal and state governments – to prove that the trust responsibility rests with the other. Also within the federal government there is disagreement as to which department is responsible. Disagreements of this kind have played a major role in preventing "beneficiaries" from pursuing their rights (Hawaii Advisory Committee to the US Commission on Civil Rights 1991a Appendices; Office of State Planning 1992, *passim*).

13 Some of the most suitable lands for development of homes are still used by the United States government for military and other public purposes with virtually no compensation paid to the trust (Hawaii Advisory Committee to the United States Commission on Civil Rights 1991a; Hasager and Prejean 1992).

14 The brothers, Kamehameha IV (1853–63) and Kamehameha V (1863–72).

15 "One reason for its formation at this time was that after annexation, under the terms concerning territorial lands, no corporation could be formed which owned over one thousand acres," as George P. Cooke straightforwardly stated it in his account of forty years as a leader of the Moloka i Ranch (1949: 2). To this day the Ranch is a very influential factor in the daily life of the people of the island. The Ranch is now owned by a foreign company. They have had several huge so-called development projects planned – often unwanted and repeatedly resisted by the local community. The demonstrations in 1975 of a group of ¯naka Maoli for access rights to the west coast across the lands of the Ranch is considered a key event in the initiation of the present upsurge in the Hawaiian Rights Movement (Minerbi 1994: 8).

16 Libby, McNeill, and Libby to the west and the California Packing Corporation to the east of Ho'olehua.

17 There is no doubt that the administrators knew about the dangers of

salination of the Kalaniana'ole Settlement irrigation water. Some of them were involved in both ventures (Cooke 1949: 2,76ff.).

18 The tent city is at Onekahakaha Beach, Keaukaha, on Hawai'i Island. The major part of about 150 testimonies heard during the tribunal addressed the question of homelessness and the problems and concerns in relation to the administration of Hawaiian Homelands. This shows the central importance of Hawaiian Homelands for beneficiaries, people on the waiting lists, and other Kānaka Maoli (author's notes).

19 The Hawaiian translation of the English "home" is: "Home, kauhale. *Also*: kinana hale (*including the house grounds*)." "Home" is derived from English. "Kauhale" means "Group of houses comprising a Hawaiian home," lit. plural house (Pukui and Elbert 1981: 73).

20 In this case, the category of home cannot be thought of as an exclusive category of a fenced home(stead). A broader, prototype-like definition will prove more useful (cf. Hasager n.d).

21 The headman or *konohiki* can be compared to today's Department of Hawaiian Home Lands, while the true owner, *akua*, the God, finds its parallel in the State of Hawai'i.

22 A man, according to much of the language of the reports, newspaper articles and speeches. In reality a large proportion of the homesteaders and people on the waiting lists are women. This has historical and practical reasons, as explained by Felix Keesing (1936: 38), but probably also has to do with a tradition for a strong social position of women.

23 Some felt forced to do it, because the Department of Hawaiian Home Lands for a period during the 1970s tightened up control of the land by implementing regulations stipulating occupancy and actual farming of the homesteads.

24 This follows Gupta and Ferguson (1992: 8). Michel de Certeau talks about space as "practiced place." Space (*espace*) is "caught in the ambiguity of an actualization, transformed into a term dependent on many different conventions, situated in the act of a present (or of a time), and modified by the transformations caused by successive contexts," whereas place delimits a field. "A place (*lieu*) is the order (of whatever kind) in accord with which elements are distributed in relationships of coexistence" (1984: 117). This terminological and philosophical discrepancy might be encompassed in a double understanding of space as the physical reality (whatever that is) that together with time is the basic constituent of reality – as least as we human beings represent it to ourselves. The open field of possibilities which space signifies is transformed into specific places or localities by human social practice, by physical actions as well as through categorization and other actions of representation. Practicing this specific place, human beings create specific physical space – but also social space, space of identity (Hasager 1991: 138ff.) and space of experience (Friedman n.d.: 10).

25 It can be as simple as a question of timing, as demonstrated by the debate between the Kanaka Maoli director of the Center for Hawaiian Studies at the University of Hawai'i, Haunani-Kay Trask (1991), and the late Professor in Anthropology, Roger Keesing (1989, 1991).

REFERENCES

Administration of Native Hawaiian Home Lands (1990) "Joint Hearings before the State Committee on Indian Affairs, United States Senate and the Committee on Interior and Insular Affairs," House of Representatives, 101st Congress, 1st Session, Washington: US Government Printing Office.

Akana, Rev. Akaiko (1918) *The Sinews for Racial Development*, Honolulu: Board of the Hawaiian Evangelical Association.

Bitterman, Mary G. (1963) "A Brief History of the Hawaiian Homes Commission," Working Paper WP72–031, Hawaii Environmental Simulation Laboratory, University of Hawaii. Draft.

Blaisdell, Kekuni and Noreen Mokuau (1994) "Kānaka Maoli, Indigenous Hawaiians," in Ulla Hasager and Jonathan Friedman (eds) *Hawai'i – Return to Nationhood*, IWGIA Document 75, Copenhagen: International Work Group for Indigenous Affairs.

Bohannan, Paul (1966) "'Land', 'Tenure' and 'Land-Tenure'," in Daniel Biebuyck (ed.) *African Agrarian Systems*, Oxford: Oxford University Press.

Bourdieu, Pierre (1977) *Outline of a Theory of Practice*, trans. Richard Nice, Cambridge: Cambridge University Press.

Brigham Young University – Hawaii Campus (1981) Oral History Program. Interviewer K. W. Baldridge. Laie: BYU, Behavioral and Social Sciences Division.

Cleveland, Grover (1994) "A Friendly State Being Robbed of Its Independence and Sovereignty" (President's Message Relating to the Hawaiian Islands, December 18, 1893), in Ulla Hasager and Jonathan Friedman (eds) *Hawai'i – Return to Nationhood*, IWGIA Document 75, Copenhagen: International Work Group for Indigenous Affairs.

Cooke, George Paul (1949) *Moolelo o Molokai. A Ranch Story of Molokai*, Honolulu: Honolulu Star-Bulletin.

DBEDT, Department of Business, Economic Development and Tourism (1993) *General Population and Housing Characteristic for the State of Hawaii: 1990*, Hawaii State Data Center Report 6, Honolulu: DBEDT, Information Resource Management Division.

de Certeau, Michel (1984) *The Practice of Everyday Life*, Berkeley: University of California Press.

de Loach, Lucille Fortunato (1970) "Moloka'i: An Historical Overview," in Henry Lewis (ed.) *Molokai Studies. Preliminary Research in Human Ecology*, Honolulu: Department of Anthropology, University of Hawaii.

—— (1975) "Land and People on Moloka'i: An Overview," MA thesis.

DHHL, State of Hawai'i, Department of Hawaiian Home Lands (1992) "Historical Overview of the Hawaiian Homes Commission Act," State of Hawai'i, Department of Hawaiian Home Lands. 7 December 1992.

—— (n.d.) "Helu Waiwai 'Aina," Land Inventory.

Friedman, Jonathan (n.d.) "A Reflection Upon Re-Presentation," unpublished manuscript.

Garden Island (1920) 23 March.

Governor's Subsistence Task Force Group (1993) Minutes, June to October.

Gupta, Akhil and James Ferguson (1992) "Beyond 'Culture': Space, Identity, and the Politics of Difference," *Cultural Anthropology* 7, 1: 6–23.

Handy, E. S. Craighill, Elizabeth G. Handy and Mary Kawena Pukui (1972) *The Polynesian Family System in Kā'u, Hawaii*, Rutland, Vermont and Tokyo: Tuttle.

Hasager, Ulla (1991) "Kulturel identitet i global historisk-antropologisk sammenhæng - mod en metode til studium af identitet," Magisterkonferens, Institute of Anthropology, Thesis Series vol. 42, Copenhagen.

—— (1994) "Ka Ho'okolokolonui Kanaka Maoli, Peoples' International Tribunal, Hawaii, 1993," *Indigenous Affairs* 1: 4–11. The International Work Group of Indigenous Affairs.

—— (n.d.) "Land and Territorialization," paper prepared for Seminar by the Institute of Anthropology, University of Copenhagen, "Studying Processes," Egebjerg, May 1994.

Hasager, Ulla and Kawaipuna Prejean (1992) "Hawaii: Administering Hawaiian Homelands: A Trust Broken – Civil Rights Denied," *IWGIA Newsletter* 2, The International Work Group of Indigenous Affairs.

Hawaii Advisory Committee to the United States Commission on Civil Rights (1980) *Breach of Trust? Native Hawaiian Homelands*. A summary of the proceedings of a public forum sponsored by the Hawaii Advisory Committee to the US Commission on Civil Rights.

—— (1991a) *A Broken Trust. The Hawaiian Homelands Program: Seventy Years of Failure of the Federal and State Governments to Protect the Civil Rights of Native Hawaiians*, December, Washington: US Government Printing Office.

—— (1991b) "Federal Government Accused of Failing Native Hawaiians," press release, 12 December.

Hawaiian Homes Commission (1922) *Rehabilitation in Hawaii*, Bulletin of the Hawaiian Homes Commission 2.

—— (1925) *Report of the Hawaiian Homes Commission to the Legislature of Hawaii*. Honolulu Office of the Hawaiian Homes Commission, Territory of Hawaii.

Ka Mana O Ka 'Āina (1989) "The Hawaiian Homes Program," Bulletin of the Pro-Hawaiian Sovereignty Working Group, May/June.

Ka Nūhou (1994) "Information and Community Relations Office of the Department of Hawaiian Home Land," August, 20, 6.

Kame'eleihiwa, Lilikala (1992) *Native Land and Foreign Desires – Pehea Lā E Pono Ai*? Honolulu: Bishop Museum Press.

Keesing, Felix M. (1936) *Hawaiian Homesteading on Molokai*, University of Hawaii Research Publications 12, University of Hawaii Publications 1: 3. Honolulu.

Keesing, Roger M. (1989) "Creating the Past: Custom and Identity in the Contemporary Pacific," *Contemporary Pacific* 1, 1 and 2: 19–42.

—— (1991) "Reply to Trask," *Contemporary Pacific* 3, 1: 168–71.

Kelly, Marion (1956) "Changes in Land Tenure in Hawaii, 1778–1850," unpublished thesis, University of Hawaii at Mānoa.

—— (1994) "The Impact of Missionaries and Other Foreigners on Hawaiians and their Culture," in Ulla Hasager and Jonathan Friedman (eds) *Hawai'i – Return to Nationhood*, IWGIA Document 75, Copenhagen: International Work Group for Indigenous Affairs.

Kent, Noel J. (1983) *Hawaii – Islands under the Influence*, New York: Monthly Review Press.

Levy, Neil M. (1975) "Native Hawaiian Land Rights," *California Law Review* 63, 4: 848–85.

Lyons, C. J. (1875) "Land Matters in Hawaii 1," *The Islander* 1, 18: 103–4.

McGregor, Davianna Pomaika'i (1989) "Kupa'a i Ka 'Āina: Persistence on the Land," Ph.D. dissertation in History, University of Hawaii, December 1989.

—— (1993) "'Aina Ho'opulapula/Hawaiian Homesteading." Testimony submitted to Ka Ho'okolokolonui Kanaka Maoli/Peoples' International Tribunal, Hawaii, 12–21 August 1993.

MacKenzie, Melody Kapilialoha (1991) *Native Hawaiian Rights Handbook*, Honolulu: Native Hawaiian Legal Corporation and Office of Hawaiian Affairs.

Minerbi, Luciano (1994) "Native Hawaiian Struggles and Events, A Partial List 1973–1993," *Social Process in Hawaii* 35: 1–14.

Nā Mana'o O Nā Kupuna. An Oral History of Hawaii (1980) Kaunakakai: Pu'u o Hoku Media Service Inc.

—— (n.d.) Kaunakakai: Pu'u o Hoku Media Service Inc.

Pacific Commercial Advertiser (1920) 24 September.

Pukui, Mary Kawena (1961) "Interview with Mitchell Pauole, Gertrude Pauole and Eleanor Williamson," 8 March, Ho'olehua, Moloka'i. BPBM audio tape HAW 107.6.

Pukui, Mary Kawena and Samuel H. Elbert (1981) [1971] *Hawaiian Dictionary. Hawaiian–English, English–Hawaiian*, Honolulu: University Press of Hawaii.

Sahlins, Marshall (1993) "Goodbye to Tristes Tropes: Ethnography in the Context of Modern World History," reprint from *The Journal of Modern History* 65, 1: 1–25.

Spitz, Allan A. (1964) *Land Aspects of the Hawaiian Homes Program*, Legislative Reference Bureau Report No. 1b, Honolulu: University of Hawaii.

State of Hawaii, Office of State Planning, Office of the Governor (1992) *Federal Breaches of the Hawaiian Home Lands Trust* Part 1, April 1992. Honolulu: Office of State Planning.

Trask, Haunani-Kay (1991) "Natives and Anthropologists: The Colonial Struggle," *Contemporary Pacific* 3, 1: 159–67.

—— (1994) "Politics in the Pacific Islands: Imperialism and Native Self-Determination," in Ulla Hasager and Jonathan Friedman (eds) *Hawai'i – Return to Nationhood*, IWGIA Document 75, Copenhagen: International Work Group for Indigenous Affairs.

United States Congress (1921) *Hawaiian Homes Commission Act 1920*. 9 July 1921, ch. 42, 42 Stat. 108. Washington DC: Government Printing Office.

Vause, Marylyn M. (1962) "The Hawaiian Homes Commission Act: History and Analysis," MA thesis, University of Hawaii at Mānoa.

Weber, Max (1958) *The Protestant Ethic and the Spirit of Capitalism*, trans. Talcott Parsons, New York: Charles Scribner's Sons.

Wyllie, R. C. (1848) *Answers to Questions... Addressed to All the Missionaries in the Hawaiian Islands, May 1846*, Honolulu: Hawaii Department of Foreign Affairs.

9 Picturing and placing Constable Country

Judith Okely

PAINTING PLACE

In this chapter I shall consider the interconnections between the iconic, national representation through art and its mechanical reproduction (Benjamin 1992) of a specific place in rural England. The space has been given and made a place-name through a cultural artefact. Tourists and local planners assist in dreaming or designing the place through the artist's legacy. Residents respond differentially to his art. The painter is John Constable, who received limited recognition in his lifetime (1776–1837), but who, in the late twentieth century, is designated as the recorder of an archetypal rural "Englishness." The context, interests, and practice of the nineteenth-century artist and the significance of the original landscape which inspired the artist are in crucial respects very different from the late twentieth-century context. The landscape was not, in Constable's day, perceived as an icon of England.

Drawing on my participant observation residence from the mid-1980s, I shall discuss both the tourist encounter and the experience of some of the long-term aged inhabitants of this space. The voices of the latter speak of how Constable Country is variously lived over an extended time span. The experience of strangers and residents in the locality is in part constructed for them by aesthetic history and local commercial concerns. Acquaintance with the painter's representations affects a person's perception of the locality. This may not coincide with the painter's concerns. The experience of the long-term inhabitants may seem less immediately and vividly affected. Instead, the iconic representations have some long-term implications: they provide not only a pleasurable backcloth, but are also open to appropriation by the powerful. The iconic legacy is used in controls over residential and aesthetic space.

The distinction between representation and "reality" has been problematized by postmodernism. Baudrillard has posited the notion of "A hyperreal henceforth sheltered from the imaginary, and from any distinction between the real and the imaginary, leaving room only for the orbital recurrence of models (and the simulated generation of difference)" (1988: 167). Many of his examples are entirely "man-made." Other postmodern examples are drawn from urban settings, indeed the term postmodern was originally taken from architecture (Jameson 1991). In the case of Constable Country, we have a rural, cultivated context, where not only buildings and farm work are part of the vision, but also natural vegetation, wild birds, the sparsely populated river, fields, trees, and great cloud-puffed skies. While the image of the countryside is becoming "an ever more attractive object of the tourist gaze," this has, according to Urry, "little to do with post-modernism" (1990: 97). The countryside has been considered the antithesis to postmodernism, with the former's apparent traditional virtues. However, such values are belied by the daily practice of the owners, workers, and inhabitants of the countryside. The rural landscape is not as traditional as some representations would convey; it is also structured and cultivated. It is inhabited, changed, and experienced. The differences between rurality and the metropolis have little to do with geographical distance. The example of the rural landscape in this chapter is created and imagined in part by an urban gaze.

Constable Country, so named after the great national painter John Constable, is on the north Essex and southern Suffolk border in East Anglia. It is some 50 miles from the metropolis of London. The main villages within this locality are East Bergholt, Dedham and Langham. Constable's most popular and mass-reproduced paintings have links with this geographical and aesthetically bounded locality. They are principally *The Haywain* (1821) displayed in the National Gallery, London; *The Leaping Horse* (1825) in the Royal Academy, London; *The Cornfield* (1826) in the National Gallery, London; *Flatford Mill* (1816–17) in the Tate Gallery, London; and *Dedham Vale* (1828) in the National Gallery of Scotland, Edinburgh, followed by *The White Horse* (1819) the Frick Collection, New York, *Dedham Mill* (1820) in the Victoria and Albert Museum, London, and *Glebe Farm* (1830) in the Tate Gallery, London. There are many earlier oils, studies, and sketches in various collections.

The Haywain reveals a horse-drawn cart with two men crossing a shallow mill pond. A dog watches them in the foreground. To the left is a red-tiled, white-walled cottage half hidden in shrubbery. A woman kneels, possibly washing clothes in the water. A fisherman is half hidden in the reeds. Tall elm trees, their leaves and branches painted in delicate detail, stand beyond the water, and fringe the flat meadows beyond. There are dots of men haymaking on the horizon. As in the manner of Ruisdael whom Constable admired, there are pools of sunlight next to shadow on the grass. Almost a quarter of the picture consists of sky. White clouds billow. There is a patch of blue. But to the left, above the trees, the layers of cloud are darker. The picture conveys an atmosphere of languidness.

Constable also painted other localities, for instance, Hampstead Heath, Salisbury Cathedral and the Lake District. Although his style and subject matter in these other paintings have been influential in the popular imagination and the ideology of Englishness, he has come to be associated primarily with the rural landscape of this small area of East Anglia. A century later, a generalized and abstracted vision of "real England" emerged from this specific and chance location. The image was circulated by means of mass-produced reproductions which appear as imitation oil paintings, and as ornamentation on plates, tins, and table mats. The choice of a nineteenth-century rural image excludes the "dark satanic mills" and continues William Blake's longing in his poem "Jerusalem" for "England's green and pleasant land." Both in the past and the present, the urban and agricultural working class are rendered near invisible in Constable's images. Today, the icon in England also implicitly privileges a white rural culture from which non-whites tend to be excluded (Gilroy 1992). *The Haywain* as icon has been reworked for political posters (cf. Daniels 1989: 216–17). For example, nuclear cruise missiles were placed by photo montage in the hay cart, thus drawing attention to the fact that East Anglia as an imagined rural idyll has been dotted with US airbases from which US planes flew to bomb Gadafi's Libya in the 1980s.

In other contexts, *The Haywain*, when exported, has no national image, and instead may represent a European rural idyll. When doing field work in France and lunching in Rouen with a family brought up in rural Normandy, I noticed a china plate displayed on their dresser. It was a reproduction of *The Haywain*. No-one present had known it was by an English painter, nor that it was of a part of England. Nor did the back of the plate made in France reveal this. My host had liked it when he saw it on sale in Rouen.

To give the context of the production of Constable's paintings, I draw on the scholarly insights of art historians. In the early nineteenth century, the paintings were both created and viewed very differently from the ways in which they are reproduced and viewed in the late twentieth century. They were not symbols of a national identity. Moreover, landscape *per se* was not a genre of great significance. It was a backcloth for mythological or heroic human activity. Today the landscape itself is mythologized.

Constable chose this locality not because it was associated with classical landscape concerns but for more grounded and personal reasons; he was connected to it from his childhood. Constable's father owned Flatford Mill and had connections with Dedham Mill and East Bergholt. He shipped grain and imported coal. "Just as it is unusual for an artist to establish an imagery so potent that advertisers still exploit it, so they seldom give their names to particular regions. What Constable's pictures established as 'Constable Country' was where his family lived" (Rosenthal 1987: 9). He "was one of the very few to have discovered anything worth painting in the Stour Valley. . . . Constable's choice of this area to paint was idiosyncratic and almost provocatively anti-fashionable, for along the Orwell valley, but a few miles from East Bergholt, lay scenes of proven beauty which had the benefit of a powerful association with the name of Thomas Gainsborough" (ibid.: 9–10).

Both Constable's location, and his decision to concentrate on landscape were unusual at the time. "Landscape was considered 'an inferior genre'. . . . History painting was the most exalted expression of public ideas" (ibid.: 41). Landscape was downgraded because, according to the painter, Reynolds, "such work could communicate only limited and particular ideas, not morally elevating ones" (ibid.: 41) in its detail. Constable's parents had "urged him to abandon landscape for the more lucrative portraiture" (ibid.: 31). But he was resolute; "Landscape is my mistress – 'tis to her I look for fame, and all that the warmth of imagination renders dear to man" (ibid.: 31). Constable was only grudgingly recognized in British art circles towards the end of his life. He frequently faced financial hardship.

After painting and studying beyond his home territory, the artist expressed his intention of returning to Bergholt, one of the villages in the locality, "where I shall make some laborious studies from nature – and I shall endeavour to get a pure and unaffected representation of the scenes that may employ me" (ibid.: 35). This plan remained central. Contrary to other traditions at the time, he was concerned with "actualities." The paintings of his home territory, known and experienced by the artist through many years, bear the mark of minute, informed observation. Constable painted his early landscapes "not by going on a picturesque tour" (as was the tradition), "but by discovering landscapes around East Bergholt" (ibid.: 39). Paradoxically, those same locations are now viewed as "picturesque" and are part of the tourist's itinerary in recent decades. Constable's paintings and the locations are, contrary to Reynolds (quoted above), now open to "morally elevating" ideas about a vanishing rurality and national heritage.

CULTIVATED LAND

The locality retains many of the geographic and "natural" beauties of the early nineteenth century. There are the distinctive skies, the willows, and oak trees. Poplar trees have increased and elms have diminished. The river Stour winds its way through the water meadows. Here, appearances may be deceptive. Landscape has always been open to cultivation, just as views may have been constructed. The agricultural cultivation is as intensive as in many other places. The locality has, like much of East Anglia, been used as the grain basket of England, and has been especially vulnerable to the effects of agri-business and the EC Common Agricultural Policy. Since the 1980s, modern farming in Britain has become one of the most mechanized and technologized in Europe. Granted, there were considerable earlier changes in 150 years. In this chapter, I am more concerned with those changes of the past ten to fifteen years, after Britain joined the Common Market and when farmers, with the support of the ministry of agriculture, precipitated capital-intensive changes, receiving gross subsidies of the like not seen by urban heavy industries such as steel and coal mining. Through a decade, the anthropologist was able to witness considerable transformations in agriculture and the rural economy. All the while I was able to enjoy the natural and cultural landscape while living in the locality, on the fringes of a large village and half an hour's walk from Flatford Mill.

Much of the farm land in the locality of my field work is owned by two or three farmers. As elsewhere in East Anglia, grants were available in the 1980s and earlier, to uproot hedges, cut down copses, drain and plough meadows, and use potentially dangerous amounts of fertilizers and pesticides. Some had chemical similarities to Agent Orange, used by the United States to defoliate Vietnam. Wild flowers, as elsewhere in England, have all but disappeared from the meadows. Grass variety is replaced by a uniform rye, and some of the fields have taken on the appearance of a green baize "snooker table," to use the naturalist Miriam Rothschild's vivid comparison. Farm labourers have been replaced by capital-intensive machinery in a region once known for its labour-intensive agriculture. Mixed farming, including the growth of fruit and vegetables, has given way to a monoculture of grain, which has contributed to the EEC surplus. Now that the policy has reaped its own problems, some of the enlarged fields have been reconverted to intensive sheep grazing and short-term fattening of beef cattle. The slurry from crowded cow sheds leaks onto public paths. Where once there were high hedges affording animal shelter and wildlife habitats, the sheep are cordoned off by electric fencing. Some of the traditional public footpaths have suffered the same aesthetic fate and the unguarded walker may be jolted by the occasional electric shock.

It seems that the icon of rural England is no more respected by the farmers than some piece of scrubland elsewhere. Farmers have been permitted to erect huge metal silos and other modern buildings without the need for planning permission, from which agriculture is exempt. A resident who had joined a local conservationist society resigned when she realized that farmers could build what they liked, whereas there were rigid restrictions on, for example, minor extensions to private houses.

Some residents have expressed an active involvement with the landscape. The Footpath Society has engaged in a continuing struggle with the large landowners. The Society achieved the erection of concrete signposts for key paths, although some posts point bleakly towards vast expanses of uneven ploughed terrain. One former employee of the wealthiest farmer, who had been made redundant in the 1970s, led the twenty-odd walkers of the Society, including myself, in trampling down waist-high barley where his former employer should have left a path. Another member of the Footpath Society explained to me that she no longer walked down a particular track towards the celebrated Flatford Mill (a key Constable subject which adjoins "Willy Lott's Cottage" in *The Haywain*), because she did not want to be reminded of the lost hedgerow where she used to collect blackberries and watch for birds.

No member of the Footpath Society explicitly volunteered comments to me about Constable. The members engaged with the landscape as a place through which they had rights to walk. It was not, seemingly, a place for dreaming contemplation. None of the Society's monthly walks which I completed and which were selected by a different member at each meeting, took us in the direction of the tourist "honey pots." The paths in the vicinity of Constable landmarks were already much trampled. Instead, we skirted the edges and found less frequented paths. This was also in line with the Society's policy of protecting footpath rights by affirming regular usage. In this case residents of the locality who are members of the Footpath Society had a generalized interest in protecting the rural landscape, regardless of Constable's cultural icon which has come to be linked to only one or two reified places.

Despite the general technologization of the landscape, more dramatic interventions by the agricultural and industrial lobby have been subject to controls, precisely because of the national Constable iconography. In the mid-1980s, the landowning farmers sought, with the aid of EEC subsidies, to drain the meadows either side of the Stour river between the village of Dedham and Flatford Mill, a mile or two downstream. There was a possibility that the meandering river would also be straightened in the course of this development. The landowners claimed that they wanted to extend cattle grazing for longer periods of the year by reducing flooding. Others suspected that the draining was in preparation for ploughing and for the more lucrative grain production. Even the council official, ostensibly employed as a conservationist, was sympathetic at a public meeting towards the farmers' commercial demands. His compromise solution was to negotiate a "gentlemen's agreement" whereby the farmers would agree, without legal sanctions, not to plough for fifteen years.

These plans to alter this celebrated valley caused a national controversy played out in the media. Constable was brought into the argument at this juncture. Public figures aired their objections to the draining and river-straightening scheme. If even this locality could not be protected, it was argued, then there was no hope for the English landscape. The Vice Chancellor of Essex University and lecturers in the Art Department added their objections to an emergent campaign against ploughing. In contrast to other campaigns against development where the locality could not be so visibly linked with a cultural artefact and icon of Englishness, the plans were eventually dropped.[1]

"JUST LOOKING"

When fortuitously the financial returns through EEC subsidies for grain production fell, the farmers' interest in draining subsided and the meadows were sold to the National Trust. This charity was founded in 1895 to protect the British heritage, including "natural scenery." Generally, since the 1930s, the Trust has tended to direct its funds towards the upkeep of large country houses rather than landscapes and humble abodes. The purchase of the meadows was exceptional in view of the Trust's major priorities. Again, it seems that the Constable icon had influence. Soon, the meadow paths were clearly marked with the Trust's distinctive oak-leaf logo. This same national institution had, some years previously, acquired the thatched cottage and tea house near Flatford Mill in the vicinity of the scene of *The Haywain* and other paintings. In the 1940s, the Trust had already been bequeathed the Mill and what is always referred to as "Willy Lott's Cottage" (Constable's painting had identified it as such). All of these buildings operate as a field centre, with residential courses on such subjects as wildlife or outdoor painting. The cottages have, for decades, been used as a place to serve afternoon teas, with rowing boats for hire at that point of the river.

But the tea house was once a less regulated place. In the early 1980s, the thatch was in shreds and the roof was askew; all very much like a Constable painting (see *The White Horse*). The souvenirs on sale were decidedly tacky: distorted Constable reproductions in plastic or glittery frames and crude *Haywain* ash trays. After the National Trust takeover, the cottage was straightened up. The huge tree beside it was removed and municipal bushes were placed between the river and tea tables, presumably on the grounds of safety, or to provide a hygienic barrier from the tourist-friendly ducks. Tasteful china mugs, plastic floral aprons, and more accurate Constable reproductions are now on sale, along with the standard "good taste" National Trust kitchen goods' nostalgia and pot pourri. Nearby, there remains a wooden kiosk of long standing that continues to sell the tacky souvenirs and postcards. Its junk food of sweets and factory drinks contrasts with the National Trust brown scones and afternoon tea.

Another Trust cottage is devoted entirely to Constable's work. Large reproductions of his paintings indicate the presumed positioning and viewpoint of the painter along the river and by the Mill. There are quotes from his letters and a replica of his palette. Realism is elicited in order to convert the painted image back into the local landscape. The "culture" of oil painting and watercolour creates for the spectator a vision of "nature." Thus the visitors are encouraged to confront Constable's representations and to put themselves in his pictures as they stroll along the lock and by the mill pond.

The exhibition, with its mapped locations of each celebrated painting, presumes that Constable always painted exact replicas of locations. In fact, like other painters, he experimented with composition and in some of his paintings transposed objects and played with place. Although, in contrast to many other landscape painters, Constable's detail was grounded in long-term familiarity with place, he was no photographic realist. After sketches *in situ*, he painted many of his final great canvasses away from the countryside of his inspiration; in his Hampstead London studio. Thus any gaze upon the landscape of Constable Country is already mediated by the culture of representation and the painter's own selectivity. The landscape has in any case undergone subsequent agricultural changes. The towering metallic storage silos, modern machinery, and indeed the crowds of other tourists have to be blotted out. The semiotic and experiential concerns of the late twentieth-century visitor or inhabitant are various. Tourists may only partially make the link between picture and place. The inventive vacuum which exists for any persons in a place new to themselves can be filled with the vestiges of a lost rural England snatched in a selecting glance. Not all the visitors will have the same responses. Although the majority of visitors are white British, there are African-Caribbean and Asian British. Essex University arranges an annual visit for its foreign students.

The National Trust, which rescued these few water meadows, is doing so because this space is framed in now popular paintings and named as national heritage. Meanwhile, vast tracts of rural space throughout Britain and portions of the landscape in the very vicinity are suburbanized or laid waste by agri-business. The supreme irony is that the lock gates have recently been restored, thanks to a donation from RTZ, the multinational corporation with ecologically and politically controversial operations in over forty countries (Moody 1991). The focus on a minute space of rural England detracts from a loss elsewhere, both nationally and globally. Yet even this sanctified space is not free of planning scandals, as the following example reveals.

In the mid-1980s, the owner of a small bungalow and adjacent field directly behind Willy Lott's Cottage, obtained planning permission from a council official while, it was said, his superior was away, to create a "wildlife pond." In fact, he wanted to dig an extensive pit to extract lucrative gravel. Lorry after lorry thundered down the narrow lanes, shaking the foundations of the famous buildings. The ever-enlarging lake diverted water from the Flatford Mill pond. There were protests and critical articles in the national newspapers. Again, the English heritage was seen to be threatened. Considerable embarrassment was caused to the local authorities who had allowed this slip-up. But little could be done. So as to undermine the miscreant, the local postman let it be known to the souvenir kiosk man and hence the entire community, that this man was also drawing unemployment benefit, while profiting from the gravel. Publicly, the miscreant maintained the conservationist line that he was merely protecting wildlife and that the gravel waste was incidental. Today, the authorities have made amends by planting trees around the edge of what is now an artificial lake, and erecting a bird watchers' hide.

A walk around the lake affords a view of distant villages on the hill slope. While the immediate locality has been protected from residential expansion, 1980s Wimpey[2] housing estates at the nearby village of Lawford cover and crowd the landscape beyond. These are within walking distance of a commuter train to London. They were built at the height of the Thatcher speculative years. Some English villages can be protected from expansion and rendered "traditional" by planning restrictions, precisely because building is encouraged in others. The now-expanded village of Lawford has a stunningly beautiful Elizabethan manor, but it is tucked away and not iconized by any celebrated landscape painting.

That another landscape with a country-house estate was painted by Constable has been no guarantee of preservation. The Essex University campus was built in the 1960s on the site of Wivenhoe Park. Constable depicted a large house in the distance, foregrounded by lakes, ruminating cows, and luxuriant oak trees. The house remains, but one lake has been drained, and another one created in front of the Vice Chancellor's 1960s flat-roofed, concrete residence. The once bucolic landscape is now disrupted by grey concrete teaching blocks and high-rise modernist black towers. Incredibly, the campus was inspired by the architect's love of the Renaissance towers of San Gimignano in Tuscany, Italy. One commentator has noted that the campus was designed so that the occupants of the brutalist buildings would, as far as possible, be unaware of the scenes from nature beyond.[3]

By contrast, the Constable image of Flatford Mill draws on a cluster of popular themes in the reconstruction of English history. It is not just an association with rural nature, but is also a nostalgic relic of rural industry. Some of Constable's paintings show the barges that took the grain down river, although his image of active industry was selective. The coal which Constable's father imported upstream had few rural associations and was not therefore pictorially reproduced. The rural workers are present in reassuringly small numbers, despite the fact that agriculture was labour-intensive (Barrell 1980). In *The Haywain*, the haymakers are insignificant specks on the horizon. A lone boy shepherd is foregrounded drinking from a pool in *The Cornfield*. Constable admitted that his occasional and individualized insertions were a deliberate sentimental narrative ingredient, when he found that his unanecdotal and nature-intensive landscapes failed both in popular and establishment appeal. An earlier painting of

Dedham Vale is unpeopled. In a later version of the same painting, when faced with continuing rejection or indifference to his innovative style, Constable foregrounded a Gypsy woman breast-feeding her baby outside her bender tent. Here also was a link between nature as landscape and a Gypsy woman as the nearest to nature. She was not representative of the rural working class who were so visibly excluded from his work. Constable's sentimental and narrative insertions of individuals have, through the years, continued to capture the popular imagination.

As I have already suggested above, Constable's major rural landscapes are devoid of visible numbers of agricultural workers who, if realism were a priority, would in that era have populated the fields in a labour-intensive economy (Rosenthal 1983). At the time of his major paintings, there were agricultural riots which were sufficiently disturbing to Constable that he chose to exclude them from his present time. Instead, he looked back to a seemingly more peaceable era of his youth. Thus Constable helped to create the image of a sparsely populated and tranquil English countryside, with only a scattering of individual labourers. The sentimentalized selection of rural workers can be contrasted with the work of the French painter, Millet, who foregrounded peasants and showed them as very physical and unsentimentalized labourers. Constable's perspective was different. He had come to know the landscape through his experience of being the son of a middle-class landowner. Some aspects were emphasized, others were neither seen nor represented. The fact that the middle or upper classes as owners or persons at leisure do not dominate the scene (cf. Berger 1972: 106–8) nonetheless enhances Constable's modern, seemingly politically neutral image.

A closer inspection reveals not only the absence of class conflict, but also a very specific choice of what has come to mean authentic Englishness in the late twentieth century. This specific rural idyll from nineteenth-century England today excludes not only twentieth-century urban brutalism, but also the presence of a multicultural nation (cf. Gilroy 1992). Constable's East Anglian and Salisbury paintings, moreover, privilege architectural landmarks of the Church of England, the established religion. Salisbury Cathedral is the centerpiece of his Wiltshire paintings. The appeal of the Flatford locality in the popular imagination can also be explained by its association with a cluster of rural images: not only the two mills and a vanishing rural industry, but also the distinctive tower of Dedham Church which appears in so many of Constable's overviews. It is a focal point among man-made objects in the rural landscape. It is a symbol of the

Anglican religion and reminder of a specific idyll of village community. Today, the church and its village are a major stopping-off point on the tourist and coach party route.

The Constable connection has fitted conveniently with other attractions for the tourist gaze. Since the middle classes have shown a growing interest in rural residence and used their power in spatial organization and an architectural aesthetic, the "traditional village" has also become an attractive place for others to visit, not just reside in (Urry 1990). In this Constable locality, the village high street has been meticulously restored or reconstructed in the image of seventeenth- or eighteenth-century architecture. The nineteenth-century additions are majestically bourgeois, not in the shape of red-bricked working-class terraces elsewhere. The huge Congregationalist Church, in red brick with gothic-type turret, once in competition with the Anglican hegemony, has long lost its religious function. It is now an Arts Centre, selling paintings of the locality, pottery, woollens, bric-a-brac such as horse brasses, reproduction antique furniture, and vegetarian meals.

The village has been uniquely open to skilled reconstruction, due to the fact that it is also the office location of a nationally celebrated architect, Quinlan Terry, who is "best known for the implementation of the classical tradition in the form of private houses in pleasant countryside" (Urry 1990: 124). As a lay reader, he plays an active role in the Anglican Dedham Church. He was greatly influenced by his mentor, Raymond Erith, whose classical concerns were premature, coinciding with the high modernism of British architecture. One local resident described how "He had the job of upgrading number 10 Downing Street, but underestimated the repairs. We all thought 'bang goes Erith's knighthood.'" But he left his mark through Terry.

In the village today, new houses have been largely designed in accord with Terry's neoclassical designs. The site of a former set of small shops has been filled with a residential building which, to the amateur eye, looks exactly the same age as its surrounding eighteenth-century low-beamed cottages. Other twentieth-century additions are also deceptive, as one local resident confirmed:

> When the bus tours went round Coles Oak Lane they stopped at my friend's house. The operator said "There's a typical Essex cottage going back to the sixteenth century." It was this century!

The interest in this locality has coincided with other national changes, namely the decline of the seaside as holiday attraction (Urry 1990). The coastal resort is no longer sufficiently different, being less of a contrast with post-industrial living. There are now affordable, warmer, and more exotic Mediterranean alternatives. Where once the Constable village was a last resort on a rainy day for coach trips to Clacton-on-Sea or Frinton-on-Sea, the inland rural location now has greater attraction. The "typically English village" is also appealing to foreign visitors. Britain, challenged by the creation of tourist specialisms, now presents itself as a location of the historically quaint (Urry 1990: 108). Although the majority of foreign tourists rarely move out of the well-targeted cities such as London, Oxford, Cambridge, Bath, York, and Edinburgh, numbers of American and European, along with British tourists, find their way to the locality, increasingly packaged with nostalgia.

Visitors are fed and watered by several pubs, the Arts Centre and the Essex Rose tea shop. The beamed interior of the latter has again many paintings on the wall, either nineteenth-century reproductions of village lanes and thatched cottages or local watercolours of suitably bucolic scenes. The table mats have reproductions of *The Haywain*. The reproduction of rural delicacy is interwoven with the memory of the painter.

I have mingled with the tourists over the years in the shops, tea rooms, at Flatford Mill, or along the footpaths. They do not arrive dressed for walking in the fields. They are urban or suburban dwellers momentarily passing through the rural landscape, looking for difference or tradition. The high-heeled shoes are ungainly for mud, cow pats and uneven terrain. Many wear pastel-shaded clothing vulnerable to the first bramble or barbed wire fencing. Some walk from Dedham village along the river to the Mill. Most drive to the parking area five minutes from Flatford, from where they wander to Willy Lott's Cottage, and the Mill and then stop for the National Trust tea. Colonies of ducks and house sparrows, well acquainted with these friendly visitors, have learned to cluster near that part of the bank and nowhere else, up or down river. They are fed and domesticated by generous scraps. Their presence has now been iconized inaccurately on the mill pond, rather than the river, in a recent painting which is a pastiche of Constable and is on sale as a postcard at the kitsch-filled kiosk. The card, which is identified as "from a painting by" one W. C. Affleck, is the ultimate simulacrum. Constable's imagery has been defused and domesticated, having little connection with anything recognizable as the aesthetic of high culture.

The extent to which Constable's influence has been mechanically contrived is further exemplified in the painting by an incoming local resident originally from London. Tom Keating, a self-taught painter, who specialized in making oil copies or "attributions" to rural artists such as Samuel Palmer, had been the defendant in a celebrated forgery case. He embarked upon painting a reverse image of *The Haywain*, as seen from Willy Lott's Cottage and showing the frontal view of the carter, with the painter and any spectator standing on the other side. When Keating showed it to his local publican, the latter pointed out that from the reverse side Flatford Mill should have been in the background behind the cart. Instead, Keating had painted in an entirely tree-laden scene. He confessed that he had never visited the original site which was only two miles from his home. He had presumed an entirely "natural" context for the national icon whose famous location had not aroused his curiosity. He painted a picture about a picture. Keating's position has some parallels with those of other local residents in that for him the painting as icon had become detached from its geographical origins. Tourists, by contrast, are encouraged to gaze at the "real" place behind the picture.

Earlier in the 1940s, another painter and a notoriously conservative president of the Royal Academy, Alfred Munnings, was attracted to Dedham explicitly for its aesthetic legacy. Unlike Constable, who had ignored his father's advice to concentrate on portraiture, Munnings was extremely financially successful, mainly because he switched from painting landscapes to lucrative portraits of celebrated racehorse winners for their owners. Even then in the immediate post-war period, landscapes of rural England were not highly valued as saleable items to the wealthy.

THE APPROPRIATION OF CENTRAL SPACE

I shall consider ways in which the locality is experienced by some of its permanent inhabitants, with specific reference to the aged. I examine the appropriation of space in terms of both ageing and class.[4] Two detailed examples are given of elderly women residents.

This Constable parish has become a powerful enclave of wealthy middle- and upper-class residents, in greater proportion than many surrounding parishes. Seventeenth- and eighteenth-century Flemish weavers had a lucrative base for processing the wool, once a major product of the area. They have bequeathed aesthetically pleasing multi-beamed houses splashed with the traditional pink mix of ox blood and lime. The church is a central institution, with an endowed "lectureship," whereas other parishes have seen the decline in congregation and the spreading of one vicar over several parishes. The church magazine, delivered monthly to every house, permanently displays on its cover a Constable sketch of the tower. Already in Constable's time, the architecture from previous centuries would have later appeal to the conservationists of the mid-twentieth century. Nonetheless, I suggest that its preservation has been greatly validated by Constable's nineteenth-century cultural production and presence.

The village hall, unlike the practice in most other villages, is not democratically shared for the entire community. It was bequeathed in a special trust linked to the church and the trustees are relatively secretive about its funds. "You have to be in with the church to know. It's run by a clique." Part of this building is used as a private preparatory school, making a class divide from the state primary school near the council estate. Any village society using the hall for a meeting has to pay a considerable booking fee. This has immediate implications for the club for the elderly, the "Good Neighbours." Meetings cannot be held there regularly because of the hiring expense to the club. Evening bookings are the most costly. Usually, the Good Neighbours have their festive meals, such as Christmas dinner, in the restaurant section of a local pub and their annual summer garden party in the grounds and home of the middle-class club president. The afternoon meetings in the hall tend to be disrupted by the noisy private pupils in the adjoining rooms. Other better-financed village societies, for example the mainly middle-class Horticultural Society, hold regular evening meetings in the hall.

The hall bears the mark of Constable. To the right of the stage is a huge oil reproduction of Constable's *Cornfield*. Thus the icon intrudes into the village public space. Public parish council and election meetings are held there. At the 1985 election meeting with the local Conservative Member of Parliament, the Constable picture competed with a giant portrait of Margaret Thatcher; an icon in blue, her party's colour. Voting takes place within the portals of the hall in the shadow of *The Cornfield*.

The label "Constable Country" is good for estate agents, it enhances the aura and value of local property, ensuring a premium on both large residences and traditional cottages which are increasingly purchased as second homes for city dwellers. Constable's name has also been of use in the selective preservation and reconstruction of buildings. After the haphazard building of a large housing estate in East Bergholt in the 1960s, some anxiety was expressed about the newly suburbanized landscape. This village is on the other side of the valley and includes the house inhabited by Constable, as well as the former residence of Randolph Churchill, the son of Winston.

Objections to further building in what was identified as the Constable locality were consolidated in the 1970s, so that the entire valley was designated an "area of outstanding natural beauty." The village is therefore subject to rigorous planning restrictions. But the interpretation is flexible according to the interest group. One resident said of the Dedham Vale Society, "They love creating a fuss. There are sometimes disagreements about gates; it's something for them to do." The conservationists are not always so trivial. During the 1980s, with the high cost of land and a speculative boom, individual "executive" houses were erected on scattered infill sites. The lack of smaller, cheap houses for both young and old was eventually recognized as a serious problem by the parish council, but with few results. The symbolic power of Constable's name is thus open to partial interpretations by those who know how to exploit it.

The Constable village on which I focused my research and on whose outskirts I lived for a decade, consists mainly of a widely scattered parish with approximately 2,000 inhabitants. It has a relatively thriving center containing more than the usual facilities; once two groceries, now one, a bank, a chemist, a butcher, clothes shops, a hair-dressers', souvenir and antique shops. The parish is unusual for its number of large country houses, just one of which, set in huge grounds, might elsewhere pass as the local manor.

Whereas earlier research by geographers in both France and England has examined the migration of the elderly from urban centers to rural outposts, revealing how those with property can buy space and ostensibly the peace of the rural idyll, my study has concentrated on micro-residential movements within a rural locality (Okely 1986, 1991b). These micro-movements indicate the amelioration of problems for the privileged. Whereas the younger aged may choose to move from urban centres, the rural aged may prefer to stay *in situ*. But, with infirmity or widowhood, it may be necessary to move a small distance to a more practical location.

I traced movements by the aged from the outlying areas to the centre of the village where shops, medical facilities, and services were more readily available. As the availability of cheap hired domestic labour declined in the post-war period, the wealthier elderly have had to become more self-sufficient, without the pre-war army of servants to maintain the upkeep of large properties and to provide care. They have adopted the practice of selling their large houses and expansive grounds, in order to move to the centre. The gardens become burdensome and frailty threatens car usage. Thus the demand for central compact housing has increased among the elderly bourgeoisie. The demographic rise of the aged has increased this general demand for suitable housing.

The extent of economic resources and sometimes political influence affects the individual's access to the centre and to residential and general autonomy. Whereas all the elderly are subject by definition to the increasing physical frailty of ageing, not only are there health differences linked to class, but also social and economic differences which ensure that some are more protected and privileged than others with equal or even better health. In the micro-movements from the periphery, those who gain access to the centre are those with resources, e.g. private pensions, investment income, and property. They are able to retain relative autonomy. New architect-designed flats and maisonnettes at London market prices have been erected to fulfil the demand. At the centre, essential facilities are within walking distance. For the poor, residence at the centre is virtually blocked (cf. Okely 1990, 1994).

The centre of this Constable parish has been almost entirely "gentrified." Cottages, once rented by the rural working class, have been sold and modernized. Some of the parents of my aged working-class informants had passed their last days in this central accommodation. Other cottages have been pulled down to provide garden space or new extensions for adjacent larger houses. In the 1980s, only one working-class couple in their late seventies remained in the High Street. When they died, their house was sold at a high price to a middle-class couple. In the 1990s, two working-class widows survived in their rented cottages down a side lane.

The council-house estates and almshouses, with elderly working-class residents, are away from the centre. On the perimeter, the physically active aged offer mutual assistance and a number of aged working-class residents occupy their own small bungalows or tiny chalets built cheaply in the 1920s. Through their working lives they have grown their own produce on long strips of land. In the 1980s, the alternative was the local authority old people's home on the perimeter. At the time it was seen as a last resort, but after its closure, as part of council expenditure cuts, it is now looked upon with some nostalgia by those with no alternative but a nursing home miles from the locality.

The main almshouses, under the control of the local council, are a fair walking distance from the centre. They are tenanted by former house owners rather than poorer tenants, for even the money from their house sales on the perimeter would not be sufficient for anything at the centre. Access to the three new almshouses, recently built by the Anglican church off the High Street, depends more on political and social influence than on financial hardship. The wealthy can, as an alternative to moving to the centre, attempt to prolong their residence in their outlying mansions by continuing to employ for gardening and housework, their aged and frail "retainers" or any available younger working-class residents.

There are also restrictions in movement and transport. These reflect not only the effects of ageing and retirement poverty, but also the decline in public transport and the greater national dependence on the private motor car. Those of the elderly who own cars, cling to this privileged form of mobility (Okely 1991b). As throughout Britain, the vast majority of the elderly residents of the locality have no car.

Thus the elderly experience a reduction in spatial exploration. Trips beyond the village are curtailed. Some had previously walked or cycled considerable distances. Public space being subject to the priorities of private motor vehicles, including those of tourists, the carless elderly find themselves vulnerable as pedestrians with diminished vision, hearing and balance. As in other matters, the aesthetic legacy gives strength to a traditional image of the village. All municipal street lamps are banned. The members of the Good Neighbours complained about this to the appropriate authorities, but to no avail. At night, save for the illuminated shop fronts of the chemist and the Co-operative grocery, and the occasional small spotlight from a pub, the village is plunged into a romantic nineteenth-century darkness. Meanwhile, a retired school teacher walks the High Street at night wearing illuminated armbands.

INDIVIDUALS AND MNEMONIC SPACE

My study of the aged in both England and France emphasizes the wider social and geographical space and its significance to the aged's past history, its potential for reminiscence, continuing meaning, and re-creation (Okely 1990, 1991a, 1991b, 1994). Here, I combine the individual experience with the larger context of the specific locality. I give two examples of elderly women who have been able to stay in their original homes on the periphery of the parish. There they have experienced a reduction in bodily movement in space, but have retained significant symbolic and practical continuity with the locality. For both, the place is made meaningful and created through personal history. From the fixed point of their homes, they recreate the wider place through the memory of lived experience. The two women are at opposite ends of the class spectrum. I trace the extent to which Constable or his reification impinges on their daily existence. Class, age and gender are significant.

Emily is a relatively wealthy woman, a graduate and former fruit farmer. Over 90 years old, she moved to Constable country in the 1950s when she and her husband sold their farm in a nearby county. She and her husband migrated from Scotland in the 1920s when land was relatively cheap in East Anglia. Emily has lived in a single-story prefabricated house since the late 1970s when she was widowed and moved from a large detached mid-war mansion in several acres of woodland and gardens down the road. Her current house is a strange legacy of Britain's colonial past. Erected between the wars, it has a line of rooms each leading into the other: "It's an old colonial army commander's hut. After the empire collapsed no-one wanted them. That's why there's a verandah." Such a design sits curiously with the neoclassical concerns of the planners and privileged architect.

Emily last visited Flatford Mill some twenty years ago with her grandchildren: "People brought their children to feed the ducks." Before she moved to the village, Emily had heard of it "as a very pretty place because of the countryside and the river. You could get a boat and row up the river. It would make an outing. There wasn't much to do in those days."

As for the village, "The natives say 'what on earth do these people come to do?' They wander up and down and look at the shops which are getting less and less. They have their tea or lunch and go home." She considers that it was not so well known before Constable's double centenary in 1976. That year there was a major exhibition at the Tate Gallery (which I happened to have seen).

Emily considered that "people aren't very conscious of Constable. The art group will mention 'Constable skies.'" None of her friends have reproductions of Constable in their houses; "You're more likely to find them in the cottages [*sic*]. People I know snobbishly prefer indifferent real paintings to replicas." Her walls have oils and water-colours by friends. Constable, she declared, "was never completely ignored. He will pop up in conversation. . . . I think Constable has left a certain aura. Artists come here to paint." Her interest in art developed since coming to the village. A friend encouraged her when in her eighties to join art classes. A lot of people did land-scapes and some still lifes. Some courses were held under the auspices of the Workers' Educational Association in the Munnings House. This Association was set up nationwide for the education of the underprivileged, but in this rural locality has been almost entirely appropriated by the middle classes. The topics are suitably adjusted to their interests. The extensive Munnings House was established as a museum by Munnings's widow, thanks to a considerable legacy earned from his racehorse paintings.

Since Emily arrived in the 1950s, the village has become "more a monied than an aristocratic place. The *nouveaux riches* are more snobby than the others who were almost feudal. . . . We often, I'm afraid, make jokes about the bookless houses." New executives of privatized industry have been refurbishing the larger houses. One council-run old people's home on the edge of the village has been closed and sold to a wealthy couple for their sole use.

In her nineties, Emily still drives but she may soon have to give it up and rely on friends or taxis. "You adjust to your abilities. I walk very badly. I can't go places and get out." What she most regrets about old age is not being able to garden. "It was my great hobby and exercise." Ten years ago, she tended the entire acre of garden, except the grass. Now she has a buggy "for tootling around and telling people what to do." She misses trips to the theatre at Ipswich. "That stage is over now. . . . The great secret of old age is to get what you can get. . . . I don't go for missing things, it's not very profitable."

She has depended on the same domestic cleaner for forty years. "You're in a very bad way if you lose your helpers. . . . You can't be cross with your menials." Since widowhood, she has had "a new life" with lots of friends "in different boxes; chess, bridge, art and drama." In an interview conducted by some school children, they remarked that she was the only one to put friends before family. "Your friends, they're immediate . . . in your life every day. Your family is from the outside looking in." Emily's dependence on local friends rather than family who are distantly scattered is consistent with the pattern for her social class. In contrast, members of the rural working class, such as Rose below, still tend to find relatives in the vicinity and ones who fulfil obligations of kinship.

Emily's doctor tried to persuade her to move from her house and the edge of the village. When she investigated residential homes for the elderly at Frinton-on-Sea, it was a "doleful place." Nor did she like the new compact housing in the village center. "All you could stare at was an outside wall." So she has preferred to stay with the familiar views of her large garden, now with fewer flower beds. With a private income, "it makes a great difference to live comfortably." Like the other elderly who remain as long as possible in their houses on the periphery, she can pay for adequate assistance for domestic work and shopping. She is surrounded by long-standing neighbors. "You get slower every day, so the days are easier to fill."

Every summer in the 1950s and 1960s, she and her husband would close up the house and drive around Europe for three months. This was the equivalent of the nineteenth-century gentleman's Grand Tour. Emily can recall the tiniest detail of place from her travels and advises younger friends of the best routes and sights. They in turn send her postcards on their trips. Her kitchen wall is plastered with these visual communications from around the globe. Her home has all her mementos and much-consulted books. She takes out her photographic slides and diaries from her many foreign trips.

By contrast, Rose, in her eighties, left school at 12, worked as a maid and graduated to being a "cleaning lady" after the Second World War. She also did piece-work on a mixed vegetable settlement. She was born in a neighboring village, but has lived in Constable Country since she was 10. Rose lives in the same small bungalow which she and her husband purchased upon their marriage in the 1930s. Later, an internal lavatory, bathroom, and kitchen extension were added. In those days, prices for prefabricated buildings on extensive strips of rough land were not beyond the reach of many of the rural working class. Moreover, planning restrictions were not severe.

Today, it would be virtually impossible to obtain permission to erect such a building. While her husband sold some of his land for the building of another bungalow in the 1940s, by the 1960s he was not given permission to erect another small bungalow on the remaining orchard. The arguments for rejection seemed hollow when permission was granted to build three extensive detached houses directly opposite. Again, there is a suspicion that neo-country houses for the privileged are acceptable in the spatial and residential aesthetics of the middle-class-dominated planning authorities.

Rose went to Flatford Mill recently by car with some neighbors. Before that, she had last gone in her teens. "More people go there than in them days. They've got transport now." In fact the Mill is no further away than the village centre to which she once regularly walked. In the 1930s, the meadows were regularly frozen. "They'd do them so they'd freeze." Her employers would go skating. Presumably some minor draining has occurred since, as the meadows are rarely if ever frozen today.

When prompted about the celebrated painter, she replied; "They'd talk about Constable, that was the whole idea of Flatford." In contrast to Emily, Rose knew no-one who did painting, except Keating (see above). She has a large framed reproduction of what she calls "The Wain" in her front room. She had seen it for £9 in the window of the village hardware shop, some twenty years ago. "I liked it because of Dedham." Again, she is not overly concerned to link the place with the representation. Unlike many visitors and the regular middle-class Sunday churchgoers, she did not link Constable and his paintings with the church: "I've never really thought about Constable and the church." This has instead a more personal spatial association. Rose was married there and her parents and husband are buried in its graveyard. She knows that she will be buried in her husband's plot.

Rose welcomed the tourists: "People come here because it's Constable's country. On a Sunday, the place is always thronging with people. The corner caf' never has a dull moment." Rose's description of the tourists contrasts with that of Emily who said disparagingly, "People still come in their hordes." Rose said she had always thought the village "was an outstanding place. There's so much going on." She is acutely aware of its past history of wealthy residents for whom she had worked from the age of 12 to her late seventies. "When I got married, everyone'd got a cook, parlour maid, housemaid; the lot, because the wages were so small. As soon as war started it had to stop." She recalled how there used to be a lot of working-class people in the centre of the village. "There was a lot of little cottages, they had them pulled down."

Like Emily, her life changed after widowhood. "I've had the happiest time sitting here." Relatives, some of whom she saw only a couple of times a year, now visit her daily. "Because I'm alone." Like Emily, she was passionate about gardening. But with the onset of arthritis, she had to grass over flower beds. Fortuitously, she inherited a large sum from her husband's years of secret savings, so she can pay friends, relatives, and others for odd jobs. When her niece tried to persuade Rose to move to another bungalow three miles away in her own village, Rose refused saying that she wouldn't know anybody there and there was "nothing to look out on from the window." As with Emily, the quality and nature of the immediate view is an absolute priority for someone in a fixed spot for days on end.

If she could not get anyone to do her lawn and remaining small flower borders near her windows, she would, if possible, move to one of the almshouses. "I couldn't stay here and let it get to be wilderness. I couldn't sit here and see it go to rack and ruin . . . looking back on all the hard work I've done." When she and her husband arrived in 1936, "it was a wilderness." Her husband pulled out the wild hawthorn hedge associated with the fields and replaced it with horticultural privet. She once created huge flower beds and now loves showing photographs of them.

Bent forward with arthritis, Rose still attempts weeding and delights in bonfires which affirm her control over untidy growth and decay. Her hands are swollen and bent, she has limited mobility in her arms, but finds ingenious ways of cleaning and dusting. She no longer goes to the Good Neighbours' club for the elderly. "I don't want people to see me like I am." She has resigned herself to restrictions in movement. She once depended on her bicycle:

> I had two warnings, you've got to be fairly nimble. I came home and put it in the shed. "Rose," I said "you've had your warning. That's not coming out no more." You've got to accept it. You see it's no good thinking that someone my age can do more. . . . I was a good walker.

Just five years ago, Rose would walk miles with her employer's dog. Her movements here were also gradually restricted and exacerbated by the farmer's decision to place at the entrance of a cart track a locked metal gate (for which he obtained an agricultural subsidy), which she was too frail to clamber over. When the Footpath Society asked the farmer if this track could be recognized as a right of way to replace another path that stretched incongruously across a bleak ploughed field, the farmer agreed, as long as the Society paid the legal expenses. These were beyond the Society's meager resources.

Like Emily, Rose has preferred to stay in her familiar living place. Both have thought about the alternatives, but have so far fended them off. Despite widowhood and increasing frailty, by chance both Emily (with inherited family trust money) and Rose (with the benefit of her husband's lifetime of frugality) have the financial resources for domestic support.

These women's houses and aspects of their cultivated gardens are their autonomous practical centre more than any wider scenery. As bodily frailty and the decline in public transport have reduced their movements, their homes have become a mnemonic space for the locality of their past. From here, they can imagine themselves further afield, and their visitors bring reminders and spatial continuity. Rose may not have walked in corners of the village for years, but she can conjure them up in words and in her imagination (cf. Okely 1994). This is different from outsiders passing through.

Like Constable nearly one hundred and fifty years earlier, these residents have thrived on long-term familiarity and incidental or narrative associations with place. Their past "sketches from life" can be used to paint larger compositions in the studios of their imagination. This form of imagining contrasts with that of the tourist where the lacunae in their dreams of place must be filled with grounded knowledge from elsewhere.

Neither Emily nor Rose engage with Constable's legacy in the same way that visitors are encouraged to. The site of *The Haywain* at Flatford Mill, so near to them, has also featured only incidentally in their lives. They have contrasting approaches to Constable's artistic legacy in ways which may be placed in the context of class and education, if not gender. Emily, a graduate in modern languages, and her middle- and upper-class friends are somewhat contemptuous of people who display reproductions of Constable's paintings in their houses. Instead, they are interested in trying out the art of oil painting and watercolours as amateur practitioners. They prefer original productions for display, however mediocre and unskilled. They have visited London art galleries to see the originals of celebrated artists.

Rose and others of the rural working class are enthusiastic about Constable reproductions on their walls. Constable is one of the few artists they recognize, precisely because of his link with their locality. They do not dabble in the art of amateur painting. The concept of an original work of art with its mystique and financial worth does not figure in their personal existence and aesthetic. Rose is more likely to side with those visitors attracted to the Flatford Mill kiosk selling reproductions on items such as ashtrays. Emily and her associates, on the other hand, are more sympathetic towards the study of Constable through the books and pamphlets on sale in the National Trust shop.

In Constable Country, these two elderly residents experience the consequences of selective planning aesthetics. Emily resigned from the Conservationist Society when she recognized how decisions were skewed. For example, one of her closest friends was refused permission to build a downstairs bathroom and bedroom when she was diagnosed as having multiple sclerosis. Planning controls have become both draconian and arbitrary in the name of a locality designated as one of "outstanding beauty." Constable's name is used selectively as a talisman by those with local political power. Such controls only rarely extend to the owners and custodians of the land in day-to-day agricultural practice. The most visibly dramatic developments, such as river drainage and gravel digging are curtailed, but then only after national protest.

TO CONCLUDE

Over a hundred and fifty years ago a painter happened to have been brought up in a relatively insignificant area of East Anglia. He insisted on choosing landscape as the major subject for his painting, even though the area was considered unremarkable and when landscape was considered an insignificant genre in high culture. With little recognition in Britain during his lifetime, Constable nonetheless had a significant influence on French painting. Today, his marvellous paintings, studies, and sketches are increasingly recognized. It was only in the late 1970s that his work became the focus for detailed fine art scholarship. At the same time, his paintings have been mass reproduced, popularized, and appropriated as a symbol of a vanishing and essential rural England. Constable's 1976 bicentenary exhibition at the London Tate Gallery coincided with the increasing transformation of the English landscape. This had been initiated by government in the post-war period when it was planned that the United Kingdom should become self-sufficient in food, rather than relying, as it had for centuries, on additional imports. Britain's entry into the EEC in the mid-1970s brought an even greater emphasis on subsidized and intensive food production, with little regard for the ecological consequences. There was therefore greater awareness and nostalgia towards a now idealized rural landscape.

Visitors to Constable Country are encouraged to view the locality as something special, as a rural dreamland. The sights are indeed a respite from some of the wider surroundings. For those who inhabit the locality, Constable also has varied meanings and implications. His name has been used for the appropriation of central village space by wealthy residents and tourist commerce. The latter has simultaneously ensured the continuity of the village centre for local shopping and facilities. Some residents welcome the bustle of tourists, others regard them with disdain.

Residents make sense of Constable in their own ways and depending on class, age, and gender. Middle-class elderly, especially women, are inspired to paint. Those of the rural working class, normally alienated from high culture, are inspired to display reproductions of Constable landscapes because they can claim an affinity of place. Enthusiasts of rural landscapes in general are keen to protect and walk the footpaths, whether or not Constable once walked and painted there.

Fortunately for the locality, Constable's legacy has been a powerful protection for portions of the landscape, despite the ravages of high-tech farming and new roads. As my account demonstrates, this locality has not been entirely free of the pressure from both agricultural development and suburbanized sprawl. It is also the case that the enclosure of designated areas "of outstanding beauty" may be achieved at the expense of other seemingly unspectacular localities which are not validated by an aesthetic and nostalgic icon. The reification of a little piece of England detracts from the more generalized and nationwide destruction of rural landscape and wildlife habitat. Constable Country exists through an accident of history. Other places without a Constable to save them have vanished from the map of the imagination. The humble hedgerow, pond, and copse have been removed in the name of agri-business and gross national product.

This chapter has posed questions about the notions of space and place to be studied. Anthropologists no longer focus on a spatial unit as a self-contained isolate. Colonial and capitalist interventions are part of the picture, as well as earlier migrations and histories. Globalization has made the notion of a neatly bounded isolate even more untenable. But the participant observer can in practice only cover a limited territory, unless she or he experiments with displaced fragments. The very practicalities of field work in a limited space may have misled the anthropologist into constructing social and historical isolates which were just a figment of his/her imagination. Instead, in this chapter I have done the very opposite. I started with a place that was recreated in the imagination by an artist and his viewers.[5] Then I put the paintings in anthropological context and on a map of sorts. The pictures emerged through processes of representation from a place and in turn have helped to create and conserve that place. Iconized in art, that place can be studied for its disparate and contradictory meanings not only for those who live there, but also for those who are just passing through, and for those who have never been there. A recognizable place is not made by parish boundaries and census returns, but through aesthetic vision, magnificent brushwork, and daydreams.[6]

ACKNOWLEDGMENTS

The concerns in this chapter have in part been influenced by my reading of Gupta and Ferguson (1992). I am grateful to Kirsten Hastrup and Karen Fog Olwig for inviting me to join the intellectually stimulating workshop near Copenhagen in December 1993.

My research was part of a comparative project financed by the Economic and Social Research Council (Okely 1986) and one in East Anglia (Okely 1991c).

NOTES

1 By contrast, the devastation of road building wreaked on Twyford Down in Hampshire in the 1990s was not prevented by the presence of ancient archeological sites. It is also significant that the development was led by government rather than by farmers, and for the purpose of road transport rather than agricultural profit. A similar devastation has occurred at Newbury.

2 Wimpey is the name of one of the most widespread building companies responsible for mass-designed private housing estates.

3 Perhaps paintings are not so easily used to iconize the grand houses of the landed gentry. The National Trust pours millions into their upkeep. But these are usually preserved because of their associations with their former owners – aristocrats and politicians – rather than through a great artist's representation and high culture.

4 For further details see Okely (1991c).

5 There is an autobiographical element (Okely 1992) to this approach of which I became conscious only after this chapter had been written. The 1976 Constable Exhibition (Parris *et al.* 1976), made such a vivid impression that when I was appointed as a lecturer at Essex University in 1982, I was drawn to living in Constable Country without "really knowing" it. I had visited Dedham and Flatford Mill, like any other tourist, for just one afternoon in the late 1960s. This chapter also plots my field work from tourist and gallery viewer to long-term resident.

6 Since this chapter was written, two further publications on Constable have emerged; Daniels (1993) and Bishop (1995). Both provide important historical contexts. Their content cannot be fully addressed at this stage, but their scope does not include contemporary ethnography of the locality.

REFERENCES

Barrell, J. (1980) *The Dark Side of the Landscape*, Cambridge: Cambridge University Press.

Baudrillard, J. (1988) *Selected Writings*, ed. M. Poster, Cambridge: Polity Press.

Benjamin, W. (1992) "The Work of Art in the Age of Mechanical Reproduction," *Illuminations*, London: Fontana.

Berger, J. (1972) *Ways of Seeing*, London: Penguin.

Bishop, P. (1995) *An Archetypal Constable: National Identity and the Geography of Nostalgia*, London: Athlone.

Daniels, S. (1989) "Marxism, Culture, and the Duplicity of Landscape," in R. Peel and N. Thrift (eds) *New Models in Geography*, vol. 2, London: Unwin Hyman.

—— (1993) *Fields of Vision: Landscape Imagery and National Identity in England and the United States*, Cambridge: Polity Press.

Gilroy, P. (1992) [1987] *There Ain't No Black in the Union Jack*, London: Routledge.

Gupta, A. and J. Ferguson (eds) (1992) "Beyond 'Culture': Space, Identity, and the Politics of Difference," *Cultural Anthropology* 7, 1: 6–23.

Jameson, F. (1991) *Postmodernism, or The Cultural Logic of Late Capitalism*, London: Verso.
Moody, R. (1991) *Plunder*, London: Partizans.
Okely, J. (1986) "The Conditions and Experience of Ageing Compared in Rural England and France," Report for the Economic and Social Research Council, Swindon.
—— (1990) "Clubs for le Troisième Age: Communitas or Conflict," in P. Spencer (ed.) *Anthropology and the Riddle of the Sphinx*, London: Routledge.
—— (1991a) "Defiant Moments: Gender, Resistance and Individuals," *Man* 26, 1: 3–22.
—— (1991b) "Age and Place in Rural Normandy and East Anglia," unpublished paper presented to the Department of Social Policy, University of Edinburgh.
—— (1991c) "The Ethnographic Method Applied to Rural Transport, Planning and the Elderly," Report for the Economic and Social Research Council.
—— (1992) "Anthropology and Autobiography: Participatory Experience and Embodied Knowledge," in J. Okely and H. Callaway (eds) *Anthropology and Autobiography*, London: Routledge.
—— (1994) "Vicarious and Sensory Knowledge of Chronology and Change: Ageing in Rural France," in K. Hastrup and P. Hervik (eds) *Social Experience and Anthropological Knowledge*, London: Routledge.
Parris, L., I. Fleming-Williams and C. Shields (1976) *Constable, Paintings, Watercolours and Drawings*, exhibition catalogue, London: The Tate Gallery Publications.
Rosenthal, M. (1983) *Constable: The Painter and his Landscape*, London: Yale University Press.
—— (1987) *Constable*, London: Thames & Hudson.
Urry, J. (1990) *The Tourist Gaze*, London: Sage.

Part III

Topical metaphors in anthropological thinking

10 Speechless emissaries

Refugees, humanitarianism, and dehistoricization

Liisa H. Malkki

INTRODUCTION

Massive displacements of people due to political violence and oppression and the sight – on television and in newspapers – of refugees as a miserable "sea of humanity" have come to seem more and more common. If these displacements, and media representations of them, appear familiar, so too does the range of humanitarian interventions that is routinely activated by the movement of people. The purpose of this chapter is to explore the forms typically taken by humanitarian interventions that focus on refugees as their object of knowledge, assistance, and management, and to trace the effects of these forms of intervention at several different levels.

One of the things that most immediately demands notice is that the forms of these humanitarian interventions appear to be so inevitable – as do the perennial impasses and systematic failures from which such interventions often suffer (Calhoun 1995: xii; Ferguson 1994). The contemporary crises of mass displacement – especially those of Rwanda and Burundi, which I will discuss here – offer an almost laboratory-like, tragic clarity of view into the larger question of humanitarian intervention.

My argument grows out of anthropological field research conducted with Hutu refugees from Burundi living in Tanzania (mostly in three very large refugee camps) since the "selective genocide"[1] of 1972 in Burundi. It also later addresses the 1994 genocide in Rwanda, and its aftermath. The chapter moves through a comparison of the social construction and uses of the refugee category in different social and institutional domains.

In the first section, I discuss the social significance of the refugee category for the 1972 Hutu refugees themselves – that is, for persons who have long been legally recognized and documented as "real," *bona fide* political refugees with a well-founded fear of persecution. I trace how the Hutu refugees in a particular context (many of whom still live in refugee camps) had come to appropriate the category as a vital, positive dimension of their collective identity in exile, and in what sense refugee status was a *historicizing condition* that helped to produce a particular political subjectivity.

The second section examines how the staff of the international organizations administering the Hutu refugees in Tanzania conceptualized the term, "refugee," in the course of their everyday discussions. While the legal claim to refugee status by the Hutu was acknowledged by these administrators, other, more elaborate normative expectations and definitions of "the refugee" lived – unstated but vigorous – in the shadow of the law. The net effect of the administrators' views, I will argue, was to depoliticize the refugee category and to construct in that depoliticized space an ahistorical, universal humanitarian subject (Barthes 1980; Malkki 1995a: 12–13ff.).

In the third section, the argument moves to a greater level of generality: the examination of the figure of the refugee as an object of concern and knowledge for the "international community," and for a particular variety of humanism. This exploration will suggest that refugee issues are one privileged site for the study of humanitarian interventions through which "the international community" constitutes itself (Ishay 1995; Calhoun 1995; Rusciano and Fiske-Rusciano 1990; Malkki 1994). The central purpose here is to examine some of the specific *effects* of the contemporary dehistoricizing constitution of the refugee as a singular category of humanity within the international order[2] of things. Much as in the case of the local refugee administrators in Dar-es-Salaam, one important effect of the bureaucratized humanitarian interventions that are set in motion by large population displacements is to leach out the histories and the politics of specific refugees' circumstances. Refugees stop being specific persons and become pure victims in general: universal man, universal woman, universal child, and universal family (Barthes 1980).[3] Of course, refugee populations usually consist of people in urgent need who have been victimized in numerous ways. The problem is that the necessary delivery of relief and also long-term assistance is accompanied by a host of other, unannounced social processes and practices that are dehistoricizing. This dehistoricizing universalism creates a context in which it is difficult for people in the refugee category to be approached as historical actors rather than simply as mute victims. It can strip from them the authority to give credible narrative evidence or testimony about their own condition in politically and institutionally consequential fora (cf. Balibar 1988: 724, 1995).

That humanitarian interventions tend to be constituted as the opposite of political ones has, of course, a long history and complex reasons behind it (cf. Zolberg *et al.* 1989; Loescher and Monahan 1989). But the purpose here is not to delve into that history; it is to emphasize the extent to which this opposition is taken for granted, and to ask: what are the effects of this conventionalized, depoliticizing, universalizing practice? A vital part of the answer must be, as I will try to show, that in universalizing displaced people into "refugees," in abstracting their predicaments from specific political, historical, cultural contexts, humanitarian practices tend to silence refugees.

A great deal of work has been done in recent years (in several disciplines) on the question of "voice" and representation, silencing and "ethnographic authority" (Clifford 1988: 21ff.). Some of this work has tended to move in heavily textualized domains where the potential political stakes in having or not having a voice have slipped beyond the immediate field of vision. It is in the horror of current events in Rwanda and Burundi, and in the massive displacements of people that have resulted (and that could well multiply in the near future), that the question of voice reveals its importance. There, the systematic disqualification of the refugees' own inescapably political and historical assessments of their predicaments and their futures has been (between the summer of 1994 and now, in February 1996) forming into a contestation between life and death.

It is my hope that an examination of the contemporary political tragedies of the Great Lakes region of Africa will help to make the case that familiar forms of humanitarianism, and of humanism, need careful, vigilant study especially now – that they should no longer be left to lie in their accustomed circuits of international policy science, but should, rather, be studied by scholars in many fields (especially in anthropology). The intent here is not to dismiss humanitarian interventions as useless. The alternatives to humanitarianism that come most easily to mind – utter, uninformed indifference or repressive, undemocratic, mercenary logics – are clearly terrible. But precisely because international interventions (humanitarian and otherwise) are increasingly important, we should have better ways of conceptualizing, designing, and challenging them. This is why it is useful to examine the idea of a universal, ahistorical humanity that forms the basis of much of contemporary progressive politics. This liberal, progressive politics, with its vision of a universal humanity, is hard-wired into the history of anthropology for powerful reasons. Perhaps anthropology is, therefore, an especially suitable site from which to begin questioning the workings and effects of these vital concepts and practices.[4]

REFUGEE STATUS AS LIVED BY HUTU REFUGEES IN MISHAMO, TANZANIA

The tens of thousands of Hutu refugees who fled the mass killings by the Tutsi-dominated army in Burundi in 1972, have for the most part been living in refugee camps[5] ever since. A much smaller group of these 1972 refugees (some 20,000–30,000) settled spontaneously in and around Kigoma township, and have thus had no experience of prolonged residence inside a refugee camp.[6] My field work (1985–6) was divided between Mishamo, a refugee camp with a population of about 35,000 in western Tanzania's Rukwa region, and the town and environs of Kigoma on Lake Tanganyika, next to the historical cross-roads of Ujiji. The biographical and social circumstances of the people in these two settings, the "camp refugees" and the "town refugees," were very different in exile, even though their lives in Burundi prior to 1972 appear to have differed much less. The most relevant contrast in the present context is that the social status of being a refugee had a very pronounced salience in the camp refugees' life-worlds, while in town it generally did not. That is, in Mishamo it was indispensable to understand something of the social and political meaning given collectively to refugeeness and to exile by the camp inhabitants. In contrast, for the people I have called the town refugees, refugee status was generally not a collectively heroized or positively valued aspect of one's social person. Insofar as it was considered relevant at all, it was more often a liability than a protective or positive status.

I have examined this contrast at length elsewhere (Malkki 1995a). But even in its simplest outlines, the case suggests that the elaboration of legal refugee status into a social condition or a moral identity does not occur in an automatic or predictable way, and that even people who fled originally from the "same place" can, and often do, come to define the meaning of refugee status differently, depending on the specific lived circumstances of their exile. In what follows, I will focus only on the "camp refugees'" social imagination of refugeeness because it was their definitions that most directly challenged the refugee administrators' visions of the same.

The most unusual and prominent social fact about the camp of Mishamo was that the refugees who had lived within its confines for so many years were still in 1985–6 continually engaged in an urgent, collective process of constructing and reconstructing a true history of their trajectory as "a people." This was an oppositional process, setting itself against state-approved versions of the history of Burundi.

The narrative production of this history in exile was sweeping. Beginning with what anthropologists and other students of mythology have called "myths of foundation," the Hutu refugees' narratives outlined the lost features of the "autochthonous," "original" nation and the primordial social harmony that was believed to have prevailed among the original inhabitants (the Twa and the Hutu). The narratives of the past then located the coming of the Tutsi in time and space: they were remembered as the pastoral "foreigners from the North" (sometimes as "the Hamites" or "the Nilotes") who came in search of new pastures for their cattle "only four hundred years ago." There followed the progressive theft of power from the "natives" (Hutu and Twa) by Tutsi ruse and trickery, and the emergence of an extractive, oppressive social hierarchy. The refugees' historical narratives went on to the colonial era, concentrating mainly on the period of Belgian administration, and defined the end of formal colonial rule as the defeat of the departing Belgians by Tutsi trickery. The culminating chapter in the refugees' historical narratives of the Burundian past amounted to a vast and painful documentation of the mass killings of people belonging to the Hutu category by Burundi's (mainly Tutsi) army, and, eventually, by Tutsi civilians, in 1972. So many years later, the historical and personal memory of the apocalyptic violence and terror of that era still had a sharp and shocking salience in people's everyday lives.

These historical narratives were ubiquitous in the camp, forming – as I have argued elsewhere with the benefit of more detailed evidence (Malkki 1995a) – an overarching historical trajectory that was fundamentally also a national history of the "rightful natives" of Burundi. The camp refugees saw themselves as a nation in exile. And they thought of exile as an era of moral trials and hardships that would enable them to reclaim the "homeland" in Burundi, at some moment in the future.

People in Mishamo tended to see their refugee status, then, as a positive, productive status and as a profoundly meaningful historical identity. Far from being a "mere" legal technicality, or a disabling problem to be endured, refugeeness was clung to both as a protective legal status and as a special moral condition – for it was only by together passing through a period as refugees that the Hutu as "a people" could effect their return to their rightful homeland.

Such a positive light on refugee status should not be taken to mean that the people in question did not notice or suffer under the large and small difficulties of being in exile. People in Mishamo were by no means unaware of their very considerable material and social hardships. But there were two important qualifiers to this. First, legal refugee status and UN-issued refugee identity documents were seen as offering at least some protection against possibly even greater hardship. More significantly, many in the refugee camp were of the opinion that embracing instead of escaping hardships was wise as the knowledge of difficulties would teach and empower people, making them worthier and more able to reclaim the homeland. As one man put it in describing the Tanzanian camp administrators who were often seen as exploitative and oppressive: "They begin to educate us as refugees" (Malkki 1995a: 222).

Conversations about refugeeness and exile with people in Mishamo began to suggest, over time, that refugeeness was seen as a matter of *becoming*. They often explained that in the initial stages of exile the Hutu had not yet been true refugees, refugees properly speaking. What they had to say strongly suggested that, socially, there was such a thing as a *novice-refugee*. True or mature refugeeness, then, entailed a cumulative process embedded in history and experience. It had to do, if I have understood correctly, with a certain level of self-knowledge, and the camp was a privileged site for the elaboration of such a knowledge.

Another indication that refugeeness had come to be interiorized as an aspect of people's identities in Mishamo was that it was considered to be inherited from one generation to another as long as the Hutu lived in exile. To quote one person,

> If I am a refugee here, of course my child is a refugee also – and so is his child, and his child, until we go back to our native country.

This vision, of course, fit well into the narratives of history and exile that were so central in the everyday life of the refugee camp, but it was quite different from the legal definition, and also from the ideal trajectory of refugeeness usually constructed by the staffs of the international aid organizations.[7]

Being a refugee also naturally suggested, even demanded, certain kinds of social conduct and moral stances while precluding others. Thus, for example, many refugees in Mishamo, in the camp, were continually angered by the conduct of those among them who engaged in commerce – those who had become "merchant refugees." (And, in fact, the most prominent Hutu "merchant refugees" mostly lived outside the camps, among the so-called "spontaneously settling refugees" in Kigoma and Ujiji, and other towns.) As one person exclaimed, "We have not come here to make commerce. We are refugees." This sense of outrage was echoed by another man also:

"[The merchant refugees], they became rich. They have cabarets, hotels, restaurants . . . *being refugees*!!" As we will see momentarily, the camp refugees and their administrators agreed on the point that a rich refugee was a contradiction in terms; but they came to this conclusion from different premises. The camp refugees recognized that wealth would likely root people in the here and now, making them forget that they were in exile *from elsewhere*, and thus properly rooted elsewhere. In a curious way, wealth and commerce made people "this-worldly" – while the "other world," of course, was the homeland. And refugeeness, ideally, was an integral part of the process of a future return – just as it was inevitably linked to the past. It should be noted, too, that commerce put Hutu in the position of exploiting other Hutu, thus challenging their corporate solidarity.[8]

This brief account of the social construction and moral imagination of refugeeness in Mishamo has, perhaps, been sufficient to show in what sense refugee identity can be shaped by historical and political context. Why the Hutu had to flee, what the history of political struggle had been in Burundi, how the refugees expected to help bring about a new political order in Burundi – all these were issues inextricably tied to the social meaning of exile. It would therefore have been impossible for them to concentrate only on life within the confines of their camp, as if the camp were not itself deeply within history.

THE SOCIAL IMAGINATION OF REFUGEE STATUS AMONG REFUGEE ADMINISTRATORS IN TANZANIA

Throughout my field research in Tanzania, I was offered crucially important assistance by the United Nations High Commission for Refugees (UNHCR) and the Tanganyika Christian Refugee Service (TCRS), that is, by the people in the agencies that – in addition to officials of the Tanzanian Ministry of Home Affairs – were charged with administering and assisting the Hutu refugees.[9] The UNHCR funded the greatest part of the refugee projects, while TCRS was the principal implementing agency. Linked to the umbrella organization of the Lutheran World Federation, TCRS was (and is) an organization with long experience of refugee work in Tanzania and one of the most effective of such groups in carrying out its mandate.[10]

When I had completed one year of field research in rural western Tanzania in late 1986, and returned to Dar-es-Salaam in preparation for my departure from Tanzania, the Director of the Tanganyika Christian Refugee Service invited me to his home to speak to TCRS staff about my research. To comply was a very modest way of acknowledging my debt to TCRS and the other organizations that had ferried my mail, given me access to their wireless radios, permitted their mechanics to sell me gasoline and fix my car, opened their library to me, submitted to interviews, furnished valuable maps, and rendered so many other similar services.

At the evening gathering on the terrace of the Director's Dar-es-Salaam home, I gave an account of what I had heard and thought in the course of the short year in western Tanzania, knowing that numerous people in my audience had much longer experience of living in Tanzania than I. I spoke about the fact that the Hutu refugees in Mishamo saw exile in Tanzania not first and foremost as a tragedy, but, rather, as a useful, productive period of hardships that would teach and purify them, and help them to grow powerful enough to return to their homeland on their own terms. That the refugees considered they had undergone hardship in Tanzania was evident, and I tried to give an account of this also. I spoke about the antagonisms that had developed in Mishamo Refugee Settlement as a result of the very hierarchical social organization within it, about resentment over practices that were considered extractive of the refugees' agricultural labor power, about the control of movement through Leave Passes, about the scarcity of secondary and higher education for refugee children, and so on. The most important point I was trying to convey was that the experiential reality of the refugee camp was powerfully shaped by the narrative memory of relationships and antagonisms located in the past in Burundi, antagonisms between the Hutu peasant majority there and the minority Tutsi category that at the time predominated in the military and government. That is, the camp was a site of intense historicity, and to be a refugee was a historicizing and politicizing condition. To study this historicity, I said, had become one of my main activities during the field work.

I knew as I spoke that my findings were in some measure incommensurable with the language of project evaluations and 'development' discourse in which refugee issues were so often framed (Ferguson 1994). The results of my research were listened to politely, but were clearly not received as particularly useful information by the TCRS staff who were my audience that evening. What I reported was not completely novel to them. Several among them – especially the Tanzanian staff – had previously heard aspects of the grand historical narrative of the Hutu as a people in exile. (In other organizations, too, there were individual staff members who were sometimes quite knowledgeable about the struggles over history in the region.)[11] But this historical knowledge, this narrative evidence, was, to all intents and purposes, irrelevant and unusable by the organization. Moreover, when it did become relevant to daily operations, it was as a potential trouble factor threatening to complicate the administering of the projects.

My presentation in the Director's garden provoked a spirited discussion of what a real refugee was, or ought to be – and whether the Hutu who had come to Tanzania in 1972 still fit the picture. One of the guests heard in my presentation evidence that the Hutu refugees were ungrateful recipients of international assistance, and was moved to challenge the refugee status of the Hutu on grounds of material, economic well-being:

> Nowhere else in Africa do these people [refugees] receive their own land to cultivate. Not in Sudan, not in Somalia. They say that these people are refugees; they should not have all the same rights as citizens.

Another TCRS employee added: "In fact, their standard of living is *higher* than in the Tanzanian villages!" While, clearly, both were referring to complex questions regarding the distribution of poverty, there was also an evident moral intent to say that a real or proper refugee should not be well off. Later in the same discussion, the Director of TCRS himself commented:

> I should show you a film the Norwegians made of the Burundi refugees when they first came. One was showing a bullet wound, someone else a cut, torn clothes, dirty. . . . They had *nothing*. . . . These people don't *look* like refugees anymore. If you go to Mishamo [refugee camp] as a visitor, you will think these are just ordinary villagers.

It was not uncommon to hear similar comments from other refugee administrators, whether of TCRS or the UNHCR. There was a pronounced tendency to try to identify and fix the "real" refugee on extralegal grounds. And one key terrain where this took place was that of the *visual image of the refugee*, making it possible to claim that given people were not real refugees because they did not look (or conduct themselves) like real refugees. This suggests that refugee status was implicitly understood to involve a performative dimension. For the administrators, the symbolic, social significance of the Hutu refugees' early wounds and physical problems emerged only gradually, in the course of numerous exchanges with TCRS and UN staff. It appeared that the staff – in an effort to do their jobs properly, and to direct assistance where it might be needed most – were in some manner trying to identify *exemplary victims*.

Frantz Fanon has observed that for "the native," "objectivity is always against him."[12] For the refugee, much the same might be said. In his or her case, wounds speak louder than words. Wounds are accepted as objective evidence, as more reliable sources of knowledge than the words of the people on whose bodies those wounds are found. So the ideal construct, the "real refugee," was imagined as a particular kind of person: a victim whose judgement and reason had been compromised by his or her experiences. This was a tragic, and sometimes repulsive, figure who could only be deciphered and healed by professionals, and who was opaque even (or perhaps *especially*) to him- or herself.

This set of expectations about the communicative efficacy (Tambiah 1985: 123–66) of corporeal wounds – and of the presumed unreliability of the refugees' own, narrative first-hand accounts of political violence – should be seen in relation to more general social expectations and interventions directed at refugees in Tanzania. What was conspicuously absent from all the documentary accumulation generated in the refugee camps was an official record of what the refugees themselves said about their own histories and their present predicament.

They were frequently regarded as simply unreliable informants. There was also a more general tendency among some (though by no means all) administrators to characterize the refugees as dishonest, prone to exaggeration, even crafty and untrustworthy. So, in a sense, they had to be cared for and understood obliquely, *despite themselves*. Their bodies were made to speak to doctors and other professionals; for the bodies could give a more reliable and relevant accounting than the refugees' "stories." I often heard the Hutu refugees characterized as persons who were always "telling stories."

Writing in the 1930s, Ernst Bloch defined "realism" as "the cult of the immediately ascertainable fact" (in Feldman 1994: 406). This useful phrase accurately describes how the figure of the refugee comes to be knowable: it is necessary to cut through "the stories" to get to "the bare facts." It is here that physical, non-narrative evidence assumes such astonishing power. It has all the authority of an "immediately ascertainable fact." In contrast, the *political and moral history of displacement* that most Hutu in Mishamo themselves insisted on constructing was generally rejected by their administrators as too messy, subjective, unmanageable, hysterical – as just "stories." Set against an ostensibly knowable, visible medical history of injuries or illness, a political history snaking its way from Burundi to Tanzania, from the past to the here and now, weaving people into complex loyalties and unseen relations, presented itself as unstable and unknowable – and as ultimately, or properly, irrelevant in the "practical" efforts to administer and care for large refugee populations.

In this manner, history tended to get leached out of the figure of the refugee, as imagined by their administrators. This active process of dehistoricization was inevitably also a project of depoliticization. For to speak about the past, about the historical trajectory that had led the Hutu as refugees into the western Tanzanian countryside, was to speak about politics. This could not be encouraged by the camp administrators (whether the Ministry of Home Affairs, TCRS, or the UNHCR); political activism and refugee status were mutually exclusive.

The conversation at the TCRS Director's Dar-es-Salaam home illustrates how the everyday language and practices of those very people who worked with the Hutu because of their refugee status continually acted to destabilize the solidity of the legal category, as documented in the refugees' identity papers. This destabilization occurred along several different axes. On the one hand, there was a continual, informal monitoring of signs of decreasing refugeeness. As the visible signs of a person's social refugeeness faded, one's worthiness as a recipient of material assistance was likely to decrease. But there was more to it than that. What emerges from this and other accounts is that the refugees were thought to be at their *purest* when they first arrived, and when their condition was visibly at its worst. So, instead of refugee status imagined as a state of being attained gradually (as the Hutu camp refugees themselves saw it), or as a legal status that one has or has not, the administrators tended to imagine it as a processual condition that was at its purest and most recognizable early in exile, and was thereafter subject to gradual adulteration over time. All this added up, in a subtle way, to the barely noticeable but nevertheless powerful constitution of the real or true refugee – an ideal figure of which any actual refugees were always imperfect instantiations.

REFUGEES AS AN OBJECT OF HUMANITARIAN INTERVENTION

The case of Tanzania in the mid-1980s facilitates the effort of identifying (even if tentatively) certain key features in the constitution of the archetypal refugee at the more general level of humanitarian policy discourse. I take as a starting point the observation that there has emerged, in the post-World War II era, a substantially standardized way of talking about and handling "refugee problems" among national governments, refugee and relief agencies, and other non-governmental organizations (Malkki 1995b). I would also suggest that these standardizing discursive and representational forms (or, perhaps more precisely, *tendencies*) have made their way into journalism and all the media that report on refugees. These developments have made it possible to discern transnational commonalities in both the textual and the visual representation of refugees around the world. Such transnationally mobile representations are often very easily translated and shared across nation-state borders. And because shared among the institutions that locate, fund, and administer refugee projects, these representations can reason-ably be expected to carry significant consequences. One of the most far-reaching, important consequences of these established representational practices is the systematic, even if unintended, silencing of persons who find themselves in the classificatory space, "refugee." That is, refugees suffer from a peculiar kind of speechlessness in the face of the national and international organizations whose object of care and control they are. Their accounts are disqualified almost *a priori*, while the languages of refugee relief, policy science, and "development" claim the production of authoritative narratives about the refugees.[13] In what follows, I attempt to look a little more closely at the systemic underpinnings of this form of silencing and speechlessness. I approach this phenomenon from several different directions, starting with a brief look at the complex effects of the visual representation of refugees, especially in the media of photography and documentary film.

The visual representation of refugees appears to have become a singularly translatable and mobile mode of knowledge about them. Indeed, it is not far-fetched to say that a vigorous, transnational, largely philanthropic traffic in images and visual signs of refugeeness has gradually emerged in the last half-century. Pictures of refugees are now a key vehicle in the elaboration of a transnational social imagination of refugeeness. The visual representation of displacement occurs in many arenas: among refugee administrators (as we have seen), in applied and other academic scholarship (Forbes Martin 1992), among journalists (Drakulic 1993; Kismaric 1989), in the publications of humanitarian and international organizations (UNHCR *Refugees* magazine), in television fund-raising drives, and even in fashion advertising. (I once saw a fashion spread in a Finnish women's weekly magazine, *Anna*, that was themed "The refugee look.") This global visual field of often quite standardized representational practices is surprisingly important in its effects. For it is connected at many points to the *de facto* inability of particular refugees to represent themselves authoritatively in the inter- and transnational institutional domains where funds and resources circulate.

The first thing to be noted about the mutual relationship between image and narrative, spectacle and self-representation, is that photographs and other visual representations of refugees are far more common than is the reproduction in print of what particular refugees have said. There are established institutional contexts, uses, and conventions for pictures of refugees, but not for displaced persons' own, narrative accounts of exile. Indeed, some of these visual conventions seem actively to help along the evaporation of history and narrativity.[14] The two examples described below of a "sea of humanity" and "women and children" are a case in point.

Mass displacements are often captured as a "sea" or "blur of humanity,"[15] or as a "vast and throbbing mass" (Warrick 1994: E1), especially in Africa, as illustrated by the many news photographs that portray groups of refugees, pressed together in a confusing mass. These are spectacles of "raw," "bare" humanity. They in no way help one to realize that each of the persons in such a photograph has a name, opinions, relatives, histories, or that each has reasons for being where they are now: inside the frame of the photograph.

Feldman's recent essay on "cultural anesthesia" explores these kinds of mass images.

> Generalities of bodies – dead, wounded, starving, diseased, and homeless – are pressed against the television screen as mass articles. In their pervasive depersonalization, this *anonymous corporeality* functions as an allegory of the elephantine, "archaic," and violent histories of external and internal subalterns.
>
> (Feldman 1994: 407; emphasis added)

This "anonymous corporeality" is a precise characterization of what happens to refugees in the regimes of representation under discussion here. No names, no funny faces, no distinguishing marks, no esoteric details of personal style enter, as a rule, into the frame of pictures of refugees when they are being imagined as a sea of humanity.

Of course, this anonymous corporeality is not necessarily just a feature of mass scenes; it is equally visible in another conventionalized image of refugees: women and children. This sentimentalized, composite figure – at once feminine and maternal, childlike and innocent – is an image that we use to cut across cultural and political difference, when our intent is to address the very heart of our humanity.

Elsewhere I have also suggested (Malkki 1995a: 11) that the visual prominence of women and children as embodiments of refugeeness has to do, not just with the fact that most refugees are women and children, but with the institutional, international expectation of a certain kind of *helplessness* as a refugee characteristic. In an article entitled, "The Refugee Experience: Defining the Parameters of a Field of Study," Barry Stein notes that "refugees are helped because they are helpless; they must display their need and helplessness" (1981: 327). This vision of helplessness is vitally linked to the constitution of speechlessness among refugees: helpless victims need protection, need someone to speak for them. In a sense, the imagined "sea of humanity" assumes a similar helplessness and speechlessness.

The bodies and faces of refugees that flicker on to our television screens and the glossy refugee portraiture in news magazines and wall calendars constitute spectacles that preclude the "involved" narratives and historical or political details that originate among refugees. It becomes difficult to trace a connection between me/us (the consumers of images) and them (the sea of humanity) (cf. Calhoun 1995: xiii).[16] Or more precisely, it becomes difficult to trace a connection, a relationship, other than that of a bare, "mere," common underlying humanity. "We are all human after all." "As a parent, my heart breaks when I see those dazed Rwandan orphans." These are very human and very decent reactions. One cannot help but feel horror and profound sadness, I think, in the face of such images or in the knowledge that such human circumstances do exist. But it is also possible and, indeed, useful to notice that in their overpowering philanthropic universalism, in their insistence on the secondariness and unknowability of *details* of specific histories and specific cultural or political contexts, such forms of representation deny the very particulars that make of people something other than anonymous bodies, merely human beings.

At first, it is difficult to see what might be so problematic in seeing the suffering of people with the eyes of "humanitarian concern" and "human compassion." It is surely better than having no compassion or simply looking the other way. But this is not the issue. The issue is that the established practices of humanitarian representation and intervention are not timeless, unchangeable, or in any way absolute. On the contrary, these practices are embedded in long and complicated histories of their own – histories of charity and philanthropy, histories of international law, peace-keeping, and diplomacy, histories of banishment and legal protection, histories of empires and colonial rule, histories of civilizational and emancipatory discourses and missionary work, histories of World Bank and other development initiatives in Africa, and much more. These humanitarian representational practices and the standardized interventions that go with them have the effect, as they currently stand, of producing anonymous corporeality and speechlessness. That is, these practices tend actively to displace, muffle, and pulverize history in the sense that the Hutu refugees in Mishamo understood history. And they tend to hide the political, or politico-economic, connections that link television viewers' own history with that of "those poor people over there" (cf. Calhoun 1995; Ferguson 1995 and Chapter 6 of this volume).

These processes were in grotesque evidence when the most recent large refugee movements from Burundi began to be photographed in the world's newspapers. In the 25 October 1993 issue of the *Los Angeles Times*, on what the *Times* calls its "Second Front Page," there was a large photograph of women and children laden down with bundles. Underneath there was a slim caption:

> Hutu tribe refugees cross the border near Rwanda after walking more than 37 miles from Burundi. Tribal violence is believed to have flared up between the Tutsi and Hutu after a Burundi military coup overthrew and killed President Melchior Ndadaye on Thursday. On Sunday, 4,000 people marched through the streets of Bujumbura, the capital, calling for the release of the bodies of the president and of others killed in the coup.
>
> (*Los Angeles Times*, 25 October 1993: A3)

The photo was a very large one, but there was *no story* to go with it.[17] It was as if this grouping of people – women clothed in colourful cotton wraps, children in ragged T-shirts and shorts, walking barefoot out of Burundi – had just become generic "refugees," and generic "Africans" in whose societies "tribal violence" periodically "flares up." It was as if this was all the context that might be required. Whoever got close enough to this cluster of people to take that photograph could have asked them to explain (if not in Kirundi, perhaps in French, or certainly through an interpreter) what had happened to them, and what they had witnessed. Instead, there was almost no news from Burundi at all – only this large Associated Press photograph.[18] And this small group of speechless emissaries was allowed to go on its way.

This newspaper photograph helps us to see how "the refugee" is commonly constituted as a figure who is thought to "*speak to*" us in a particular way: wordlessly. Just the refugee's physical presence is "telling" of his/her immediate history of violence. So we tend to assume, at any rate.

But it is not just that photographs displace narrative testimony. When there is testimony about refugees, it mostly does what the photographs do: it silences the refugees. For it tends to be testimony by "refugee experts" and "relief officials" (or even by those ever-ready "well-placed Western diplomatic sources"), not by refugees themselves. How often have we seen the media image of a (usually white) UN official standing in a dusty landscape, perhaps in Africa, surrounded by milling crowds of black people peering into the camera, and benevolently, efficiently, giving a rundown on their numbers, their diseases, their nutritional needs, their crops, and their birth and mortality rates? This mode of what may called a *clinical humanitarianism* looks for all the world like an exhaustive report on the displaced masses; and the official is surely trying to be informative, as well as to balance honesty and diplomacy. And yet the scene and the expert voice operate precisely to erase knowledge. In constructing a raw humanity and a pure helplessness, this spectacle all but blocks the possibility of persons stepping forward from the milling crowds, asking for the microphone, and addressing the glassy eye of the camera: "Now, if I may, Sir/Madam, there are numerous things that you have not considered, many details about our history and political circumstances that might assist you in helping us." Such details easily appear as mere quibbles, fine points, and posturing in the face of the other, very powerful narrative of emergency relief, humanitarian intervention, and *raw human needs*.

The visual conventions for representing refugees and the language of "raw human needs" both have the effect of constructing refugees as a bare humanity – even as a merely biological or demographic presence. This mode of humanitarianism acts to trivialize and silence history and politics – a silencing that can legitimately be described as dehumanizing in most contexts. And yet the mechanisms involved here are more complex than that. For one might argue that what these representational practices do is not strictly to dehumanize, but to *humanize in a particular mode*. A mere, bare, naked, or minimal humanity is set up. This is a vision of humanity that repels elements which fail to fit into the logic of its framework.

THE STAKES IN THE HUMANITARIAN INTERVENTIONS IN RWANDA, BURUNDI, AND BEYOND

The vast displacements of people that occurred in the wake of the fighting and the genocide of 1994 in Rwanda are a good example of what is at stake in the constitution of refugees as such passive objects of humanitarian intervention. The short section to follow will specifically address the effects of the disqualification of refugee knowledge in the matter of their repatriation to Rwanda from Zaire.

It would be impossible to give, in passing, in a single article, a thorough account of the complicated history that has culminated in the genocidal massacres of over half a million Rwandan citizens, overwhelmingly Tutsi, and the displacement of several million other Rwandan citizens, mostly Hutu, since April 1994. Important work on the genocide and its aftermath in Rwanda, as well as the contemporary political situation in Burundi, has been done by Reyntjens (1994); Prunier (1995); Lemarchand (1994a, b); Newbury and Newbury (1994, 1995); African Rights (1994); Mbonimpa (1993); Pottier (1994); Jefremovas (n.d.); Guichaoua (1995); Destexhe (1994); and others. The bare outlines, however, are as follows.

While, in Burundi, the minority Tutsi category controls the military and, effectively, the government, it is the Hutu majority that had been in power in Rwanda for all of its post-colonial history up until the RPF (Rwandan Patriotic Front) victory of 1994. The Hutu-led 1961 revolution that crumbled the monarchical system in Rwanda was violent; it resulted in the deaths of some 20,000 mostly Tutsi people and produced a sizeable exilic presence of Tutsi in Uganda (and elsewhere). It is largely from the ranks of these refugees and their descendants in Uganda that the RPF grew. In October 1990, the RPF attacked Rwanda from Uganda. "Following the attack," Amnesty International reports, "some 7,000 people were arrested, most of them Tutsi; virtually all were subjected to severe beatings and some were killed" (Amnesty International 1993: 1). Fighting between the RPF and the Rwandan government forces continued intermittently from 1990 to 1993. On 6 April 1994, the presidents of both Burundi and Rwanda were killed in a plane crash for which responsibility is still being debated. This touched off a nightmarish campaign of mass killings in Rwanda, a campaign made the more appalling because it involved planning and premeditation.[19] In the days following the crash, "death squads" were systematically eliminating political opponents of the hard-line faction of the Rwanda government (including both Tutsi and moderate Hutu). Then civilian militias were apparently given "a free hand to just kill every Tutsi in sight" (Lemarchand 1994a: 10). From Kigali, the killing spread to other regions of Rwanda. Eventually, many Hutu civilians began to kill their Tutsi neighbors.[20] In just a few months, hundreds of thousands of people, mostly Tutsi, were massacred. Most estimates of the death toll fall between 500,000 and 800,000. As the RPF forces made advances inside Rwanda, Hutu civilian communities took flight into neighboring countries for fear of retaliation. When the Rwandan army finally collapsed, over a million people moved in the space of a few days into Zaire (and also into Tanzania and elsewhere). The highest number reported for the Rwandan refugee population in the region was 2.2 million. These people have since become objects of world attention as the most awe-inspiring refugee population in the memory of the aid organizations and media working there.

The hundreds of thousands of people living and dying in awful conditions in the Rwanda–Zaire borderlands know better than anyone else on the scene what they have done, what has happened to them, why, and what they can hope for if they return to Rwanda. If anyone is an expert on the apocalyptic Rwandan political situation now, it is they. And yet, curious things are happening to their voices. They are either not heard at all and not quoted in earnest as real, "reliable sources" by the journalists visiting the Zairean camps, or their words are quoted in ways that they never intended (as symptoms of hysteria, evidence of brainwashing, and echoes of superstitious, gullible Africa). They are being rendered speechless in much the same way that the October 1993 refugees from Burundi's killings were.

This silence is the phenomenon to be understood. It is actually quite a riddle when we consider how much time, effort, and resources the refugee agencies and other aid organizations, journalists, politicians, UN peace-keepers, the French and American forces, and countless other expert agencies have had to expend in order to learn anything at all about the setting in which many of them have been deliberating over consequential interventions. One of the most consequential of these interventions still centres on the issue of the repatriation of the refugees from Zaire to Rwanda, a question that has been heatedly discussed ever since 1994.

But before considering the specific question of repatriation, it is worthwhile to try to identify the discursive forms and modes of knowledge that displaced local knowledge and understandings during the genocide and in the months after. At least three discursive registers were readily evident from that early media coverage. The first register of coverage (dating from the period when massive population displacements had already occurred) emphasized the bodily, physical evidence of violence and atrocity in Rwanda. A colleague has commented, cynically but accurately, that this was the period of "blood and gore." Photographic evidence of almost unimaginable violence flooded print media and television. Rivers swelling with bodies distended and bleached by death; crying, disoriented toddlers clinging to the bodies of their dying parents; people with limbs cut off or an infected panga slash over their nose: this flood of terrifying images will not be soon forgotten.[21]

One particularly clear illustration of the place of photographic images in this crisis is to be found in a *Life* magazine special feature called "Eyewitness Rwanda" (September 1994: 74–80). A short opening paragraph introduces six pages of full-colour photographs, six pages that seem almost like a religious gesture of mourning. The paragraph ends:

> What persists are images – a handful of pictures from among the thousands that have raced before our eyes on videotape or stared out from our daily newspapers. *They require no elaboration. In their silence, they tell the story of Rwanda, 1994.*
>
> (*Life* September 1994: 74; emphasis added)

The heavily visual documentation of violence was subsequently joined by accounts of human tragedy, or what are perhaps most accurately called human interest stories. There were especially many accounts of children in terrible circumstances. Again, the relevant historical and political contexts were missing.

The third register consisted of technical/heroic narratives. Here, the international aid effort had got underway among the Hutu refugees, and the papers were suddenly filled with detailed technical profiles of cholera, of the working principles of the water purification plants being flown in, of oral rehydration techniques, of the construction of airfields, and of the makes and capacities of the military transport planes and other heavy equipment involved in the relief operation centred in Goma. All three of these discursive registers share the feature that they do not require any sustained narrative inputs, any testimonial evidence, from the refugees on whose behalf all the activity was, and still is, being carried out. The refugees were relevant principally as the tragic mass of humanity that needed to be helped first and foremost not to die of cholera, dysentery, or other diseases, and to be treated and fed. Epidemics had to be contained, clean drinking water had to be provided, orphans needed to be taken care of, the dead had to be buried (McGreal 1994). The relief workers, medical and other, have understandably been overwhelmed by the enormity of the tragedy in Rwanda and of their mandate in the refugee camps. The genocide left over half a million people dead and untold others wounded, orphaned, widowed, or alone; and the cholera epidemic in the camps in Zaire killed 40,000–50,000 people in little more than a month.[22]

In the face of these terrible epidemics and the sheer mass of the refugee presence, most of the international organizations assisting them, the national governments sending in relief supplies, and even the journalists on site who were mostly echoing all of their policy statements, concluded early on that the only solution was to get people to go back into Rwanda. (It is difficult to determine how much agreement there really was among the relief workers, but the dominant stance being reported was – and is – one favoring quick repatriation.[23])The refugees have been in many cases told they would be safer there than in Zaire. Yet they have consistently expressed grave misgivings about returning. "Expert knowledge" has been terribly at odds with the principals' – the refugees' – knowledge of the situation, and it is clear that the latter has been almost automatically disqualified. For what reasons has this disqualification been considered rational or practically necessary? A vital part of the answer to this riddle is bound up with contemporary forms of humanitarianism. The speechlessness of the newest emissaries of suffering – the refugees from Rwanda – becomes intelligible in this light.

This is where the question of voice – the ability to establish narrative authority over one's own circumstances and future, and, also, the ability to claim an audience[24] – begins to show its teeth, then. Evidence suggests that the overwhelming majority of the Hutu refugees have never considered repatriation wise. They continue to fear retaliation from the new RPF-led government and from ordinary people for crimes for which, they know, the Hutu as a categorical collectivity are thought by many to bear responsibility. And they probably fear the spectre of returning to the devastation that their surviving Tutsi neighbors have witnessed. The Rwandan Hutu in Zaire are being urged to go "home," but a question of great practical importance has not been seriously addressed: can the places from which these people fled still serve as their "*homes*?" (Warner 1994). The physical sites might be there, even intact, but as social environments they are likely to be alien and terrifying to many. In addition to other considerations, people know that many of their houses and fields are likely to have been occupied by Tutsi repatriating from Uganda after decades in exile there. As Raymond Bonner, one of the few well-informed, seriously engaged journalists covering the Great Lakes region now, reported already in November 1994:

> Since the war ended in July [1994], a dual repatriation problem has engulfed the tiny war-torn country. Tens of thousands of Tutsi have returned to Rwanda, as many as 300,000 by unofficial counts.

> They are not among the refugees who fled after the massacres erupted in April, but refugees from ethnic violence of 20 and 30 years ago. Their return is creating demographic and political changes that are potentially explosive.
>
> (Bonner 1994: A3)

While officials of the new RPF government have stated publicly that "squatters must get out of houses when former owners return" from Zaire, the government has not the means to enforce this; and "sometimes the new occupants have the real owner killed or picked up and taken away, often paying a soldier to do the dirty work" (ibid.). One need only accuse the returnee of complicity in the genocide.

Journalists have mostly echoed the position of the UN and several other relief agencies: it is necessary and desirable that the refugees should be repatriated. That the refugees have in general refused to return to Rwanda has been widely attributed, by the UN and several other humanitarian agencies and by the international press, to their vulnerability to rumour-mongering and manipulations by the exiled and defeated remnants of the Rwandan armed forces. There is good evidence that the refugee populations in Zaire are being intimidated by political leaders who wish to keep them in exile (cf. Newbury and Newbury 1995; Prunier 1995). But to assume that they are all passive puppets moving mindlessly to the manipulations of a handful of callous politicians of the exiled Rwandan government may be unwise. In the early 1994 coverage of the crisis, the refugees were rendered as superstitious and hysterical, while Rwanda was painted for them as a safe and secure horn of plenty. Of the many news reports along these lines, it is sufficient to quote one.

> Aid officials say the estimated 1.2 million Rwandan refugees now facing the agony of Zaire's border camps have about two weeks to go home and harvest *the bursting fields of corn, beans and other crops that carpet the lush country*. . . . Yet the hungry refugees are fed a steady diet of fear and propaganda by former Hutu government officials and their minions, who insist they will be tortured and killed if they return to Rwanda. They claim that the estimated 30,000 refugees who have crossed the border since Sunday are dead, although journalists and other witnesses have seen them walking home safely. . . . So rumors and threats circulate daily from members of the former regime's murderous militias and the Interahamwe, the armed youth wing of the government party. . . .

> Their *propaganda machine* is in full swing again. Many refugees insist, for example, that the Tutsi caused the cholera epidemic by poisoning the water. And nearly all are convinced they will be mutilated or killed by the new regime if they go home. "We've heard all the refugees [who went back] have no eyes anymore," 28-year-old Primitiv Mukandemzo warned . . . Frediana Mukamunana, 54, using her finger to slash in the air as she spoke, shouted: "They cut out the heart, the eyes, the intestines! And they put people in cars and burn them!" "They will put us in houses and burn us," whispered 18-year-old Faustin Ntanshuti. . . . Educated Rwandans are just as terrified. "They will kill all the intellectuals," said Alphonse Harerimana, a physician working at the Doctors Without Borders tent hospital for cholera cases.
>
> (Drogin 1994: A3, A11; emphases added)

Such reports paint the refugees' refusal to comply with the repatriation policy as a symptom of their hysterical, superstitious, over-dramatic frame of mind. What fails to be mentioned is that violence such as that described above has repeatedly occurred in the region; there are numerous historical precedents for all these forms of atrocity, as any student of the area knows (African Rights 1994; Prunier 1995; Malkki 1995a). That the refugees talk about such terrifying violence is not a psychological fact, but an historical one.

In the face of the refugees' resistance, many tactics and arguments have been used to persuade and cajole the refugees since 1994. United Nations officials on the scene have on several occasions issued statements emphasizing the safety of returnees in spite of the fact that the UN has had no adequate staff of mobile observers on site within Rwanda, and no good way of knowing what has become of those who actually returned. The following was reported on 27 July 1994:

> Wilkinson of the U.N. refugee agency said not a single returnee is known to have been injured or killed by soldiers of the new regime. "All the indications we've got is *things are very stable there and the people who have gone back have had absolutely no problems*," he said.
>
> (Drogin 1994: A11; emphasis added)

The same 27 July 1994 news report stated that "a reporter who explained to several old women that it was safe to return" was shouted down by angry young refugee men. "'You're telling lies!' they shouted angrily. 'It is not possible. Those who went back yesterday were all killed yesterday!'" (ibid.). On 31 July 1994, it was further reported that

> U.S. Special Forces psychological warfare teams would bring in radio equipment to help the new government encourage more than a million refugees in neighboring Zaire to return home. The Tutsi-led government has assured Hutu refugees that there will be no reprisals for the massacres of Tutsis.
>
> (*Los Angeles Times*, 31 July 1994: A7)

Along the same lines, a 6 August 1994 report in *The Economist* (1994: 35) states:

> The UN hopes to persuade more to return by setting up counter-propaganda. It is establishing a "Blue Beret" radio station and is giving technical help to Radio Rwanda, now under RPF control, so that it can broadcast to the refugee camps. It also hopes to coax refugees back by deploying more peacekeepers in Rwanda and offering refugees food, water, and medical care at way-stations along the route home.

But how were these early assurances of safety to be reconciled with other, contradictory reports documenting the growing incidence of reprisals against returnees, seizures of land, disappearances, and other disturbing practices? *Le Monde*'s Langellier reported already on 7 August 1994 that "more and more people have been 'disappearing'" in Kigali, that homes and lands abandoned by the people fleeing into Zaire have been reallocated by the RPF, and that "arbitrary seizures, accompanied in rural areas by the large-scale displacement of communities, amount to a de facto ban on their rightful occupants' return" (Langellier 1994: 16). Some days later, on 16 August 1994, the *Los Angeles Times* quoted a "veteran relief agency leader" who declined to be identified as saying that the RPF army in Rwanda "has never shown any interest in keeping this [Hutu] population. Rwanda was overpopulated. Now they have an abundance of fields" (Balzar 1994c: A4; cf. Bonner 1994).

If reports of reprisals against the few Hutu returnees have convinced the refugees of the danger of repatriation, so, too, has the incarceration in Rwandan prisons of some 58,000–60,000 people accused of participation in the genocide. The criminal lawyer Adam Stapleton reports for the *Human Rights Tribune*:

> The single most pressing concern was the arbitrary arrest and detention of hundreds of people each week. Suspects were detained on the say-so of anyone, particularly if the suspect was

> Hutu and the accuser Tutsi, and charged with genocide. . . . The army arrested and detained people unchecked (by March [1994] the average weekly rate was estimated to be 1,300) and the displaced persons and refugees refused to move out of their camps arguing . . . that it was not safe to return home. The appalling conditions and increasing daily death toll from dysentery and diseases associated with chronic overcrowding make the prisons a time-bomb.
>
> (Stapleton 1995: 15)

The refugees' fears were further exacerbated in April 1995 when hundreds (by some accounts thousands[25]) of Hutu were killed by the RPF-led Rwandan forces in the displaced persons camp of Kibeho in southwestern Rwanda. Before people fled the camp in panic, 70,000–100,000 were living there. The government forces stated that the camp and others like it were "filled with armed militias" and had to be disbanded (Lorch 1995b: A1, A4).

It is plain to see that the repatriation question is very complex. It is problematic for many reasons to have hundreds of thousands of people living in exile outside of Rwanda; it is no less problematic to push them back into Rwanda. This chapter does not presume to propose a solution to the crisis. So much said, it was a terrible responsibility that the international organizations assumed in urging the refugees to go back "home," for this has been the predominant argument throughout, despite the fact that the United Nations has more recently expressed concern over the dangers of repatriation – and has publicly objected to Zaire's recent announcements about closing the camps one by one.

How could anyone guarantee that no retaliatory violence will erupt, when anyone familiar with the region's history (and with the social struggles over history there) would be forced to recognize that such violence would be, at best, unsurprising? How could anyone think that *in the wake of a genocide*, the political situation in Rwanda is "stable?" What questions, what considerations, override these in importance?

There is every reason to suppose that the violence that has so shocked the world has similarly shocked those who were its Rwandan victims and witnesses. This is a scale and kind of violence that is not often seen in the world. It is, literally, extraordinary. And because of this, it must have forced people in the region to rethink the universe of what is possible and thinkable (just as genocidal violence in recent European history has reconfigured social universes there). In the wake of the past two years, anything would seem to be possible. Politically, intellectually, conceptually, affectively – in all these ways it would seem wise and realistic to acknowledge the horror of what has happened by not forcing, cajoling, or tricking people to return to the still very dangerous sites of their shame and tragedy.

Time has to be allowed to pass so that the refugees waiting and watching in Zaire can make a reasonable, well-founded assessment of their alternatives. Time is also required from the humanitarian agencies involved. Surely they would not wish to have to acknowledge that they have marched people to their deaths in their desire to do away with a refugee crisis?

Time has to be given to the tasks of witnessing and testimony, on both sides of the Rwanda–Zaire border, among Tutsi and Hutu. Beresford has rightly observed that:

> There is . . . a forgetfulness in the world's fixation with the relief disaster that is Goma. The story of Rwanda is not that of a cholera epidemic, terrible though it may be; cholera is the consequence of the central horror of the last few months – genocide. . . . Genocide invites a Nuremberg.
>
> (Beresford 1994: 6)

For any kind of accounting or public justice to become a real possibility, all the (national, regional, and international) parties concerned would have to consent to become an audience to the "involved" stories that the inhabitants of this terrorized region have to tell. The obstacles to such accounting at all levels have become very clear in the funding and other difficulties that the United Nations-organized war-crimes tribunal has faced.

The genocide in Rwanda has already happened; it is not possible to go back and change interventions or omissions of the past. But the dangerous effects of silencing are still all too salient in currently unfolding events in the region. The Hutu refugees from Rwanda are still in Zaire, Tanzania, and elsewhere, and, as of this writing (February 1996), refusing repatriation, still the objects of concerted efforts from the Zairean government, the United Nations, and various other agencies to push them back where they "belong." The effects of such silencing are detectable in neighboring Burundi, also. By ignoring the continual political persecution, intimidation, and killings occurring in that country, the "international community" risks coming face to face with another Rwanda-like period of terror there and finding that nothing that could have been done has been done (Balzar 1994a).

But preventive measures do not come easily in the conventional logic of the "humanitarian operation." For humanitarian help to be mobilized, the disaster usually has to have happened already. When refugees and orphans have been produced, then the site for intervention is visible. Otherwise, the matter is "political" (or a "domestic" issue in a sovereign state) and thus beyond the realm of humanitarian intervention (de Waal 1994: 10).

CONCLUSION

It is obviously neither logically nor practically necessary that humanitarian intervention should in and of itself dehistoricize or depoliticize. And I would like to make it perfectly clear that by studying certain of the transnationally shared aspects of humanitarian intervention in refugee issues, I am not thereby seeking to belittle the importance of the moral/ethical/political motivations that are clearly at the core of humanitarian interventions.[26] It *is* necessary to state that these forms and practices of humanitarianism do not represent the best of all possible worlds, and that it is politically and intellectually possible to try to come up with something better. Especially in the face of the political crisis in Rwanda, and the very real possibility that the political situation in Burundi will soon become much worse than it already is, it is necessary to do better. Perhaps a part (a crucial part) of the improvement is to be found in a radically *historicizing humanism* that insists on acknowledging not only human suffering, but also narrative authority, historical agency, and political memory. Barthes's call for a progressive humanism (1980: 101) addresses this very issue, as do Foucault's later writings; he suggested why it is more useful to seek to connect people through history and historicity than through a human essence (or "human nature"). This is not to make a simple, romantic argument about "giving the people a voice"; for one would find underneath the silence not a voice waiting to be liberated but ever deeper historical layers of silencing and bitter, complicated regional struggles over history and truth.

It is a historicizing (and politicizing) humanism that would require us, politically and analytically, to examine our cherished notions of mankind and the human community, humanitarianism and humanitarian "crises," human rights and international justice. For if humanism can only constitute itself on the bodies of dehistoricized, archetypal refugees and other similarly styled victims – if clinical and philanthropic modes of humanitarianism are the only options – then citizenship in this human community itself remains curiously, indecently, outside of history.

ACKNOWLEDGMENTS

I would like to thank particularly David Newbury, René Lemarchand, Daniel Segal, Olli Alho, Michael Burton, Sharon Stephens, Eric Worby, Villia Jefremovas, Karen Fog Olwig, and Orvar Löfgren, Mariane Ferme, Caren Kaplan, Donald Moore, Louise Fortmann, Sherry Ortner, and the anonymous readers for *Cultural Anthropology* (especially Referee 1) for their feedback on this chapter. I am also grateful for the comments by students and faculty in the fora where earlier versions of this chapter were presented: the international workshop, "Finding a Place and Space for Culture," Institute of Anthropology, University of Copenhagen, 1–3 December 1993; the Department of Anthropology colloquium at McGill University in 1995; the University of California conference on "Censorship and Silencing" in 1995; the Center for African Studies and the Townsend Center for the Humanities at the University of California, Berkeley, in 1996, and the Department of Anthropology colloquium at Princeton University in 1996. The original, full-length version of this article appeared in *Cultural Anthropology* 11(3), 1996, 377–404.

NOTES

1 The term "selective genocide" is from Lemarchand and Martin (1974) and was widely used.

2 Cf. Rée (1992); Malkki (1994, 1995b).

3 I would like to thank Daniel Segal for pointing out the presence of the universal family in this imagery. The universal figures of man, woman, and child are, of course, often (but not always) constitutive of that other abstraction, "the family," as Barthes's classic essay on "The Great Family of Man" showed (Barthes 1980: 100–2; Segal, personal communication, 8 March 1996).

4 Humanitarian interventions largely take place within an internationalist institutional and conceptual framework; they depend, that is, on the concept of an "international community" (cf. Malkki 1994). Thus, the concept of internationalism is an integral part of any discussion of international community and international responsibility. In a longer essay, it would be productive to combine the critical study of humanitarianism with long-standing debates about internationalism. For the present, this larger set of questions may be indicated by Craig Calhoun's particularly clear-sighted discussion of internationalism in the context of Rwanda and Bosnia in his foreword to Micheline Ishay's important *Internationalism and Its Betrayal*:

> In both cases [Bosnia and Rwanda], the problem of internationalism does not just arise with questions about universal human rights and possible humanitarian interventions, but is constitutive of the very crises themselves in ways not unrelated to the blind spots of liberal individualism.

The problem is not just that international diplomats and multilateral agencies mishandled the two specific situations [Bosnia, Rwanda]: the entire international framework for understanding nationalism and related conflicts is deeply flawed. Among other things, it systematically obscures such international influences on the production of domestic, putatively entirely ethnic, struggles. It also leaves well-intentioned international actors with no good way of grasping their connection to the genocides and nationalist wars that have marred – but systematically marked – the twentieth century. Not only do these appear often as premodern inheritances, and therefore disconnected from genuinely modern and even contemporary sources, but *they appear as fundamentally separate from the institutions and discourse of the respectable international community. Diplomats and analysts fail to see the connection between the structuring of the international community as a world system of putative nation-states, of making adaptation to the rhetoric of nationalism a condition for entrance into the United Nations, and the pernicious forms of nationalism they decry.* Not only they but many of the rest of us fail to reflect on the ironic nationalism reproduced in asking whether intervention in genocidal wars is or is not a part of the compelling national interest of the United States or any other country.

(Calhoun 1995: xiii; emphasis added)

5 The official designation of these camps by the Tanzanian Ministry for Home Affairs as well as TCRS and UNHCR was "refugee settlement"; however, the refugee residents of Mishamo always referred to it as a camp. Their reasons have been discussed in Malkki (1995a).

6 It is not known how many people returned from the Hutu refugee camps in Tanzania to Burundi when the first democratic elections in that country brought a Hutu president, Melchior Ndadaye, to power in 1993. Cf. Lemarchand (1994b).

7 This discussion also appears in Malkki (1995a).

8 I would like to thank one of the anonymous referees (Referee 1) for *Cultural Anthropology* for helping me to think further about this issue. Referee 1 remarks: "Antagonism against commercial classes is especially strong during periods of significant inflation as occurred with the economic policies of 'liberalization' followed by the Tanzanian [government] over these years. The idea that a 'fellow refugee' could raise prices and create hardship for those of their own group was a contradiction to the norm of refugee culture."

9 The officials of the Ministry of Home Affairs (MHA) of the United Republic of Tanzania were also very generous in their assistance, but their relationship to the refugees was quite different from that of the non-governmental organizations, as I have shown elsewhere (Malkki 1995a).

10 I would like to thank Referee 1 for suggestions on this section.

11 Individual persons in the UNHCR and TCRS have also engaged very seriously with my research in the Hutu refugee communities in Tanzania, and have given me valuable critical feedback.

12 Fanon, cited in McClintock (1992: 97).

13 Referee 1 commented here: "From my experience, for example, in the Rwandan camps, it was astounding how the aid communities have selected texts that correspond with their image; having no other access to

a wider range of discourse, and often dependent on their own interpreters for their impressions, they simply end up magnifying the very oppositions they claim to oppose – in a process that amount[s] to an excellent example of creating alterity."

14 Ortner's essay of 1991 has helped me to think through issues of narrativity and historical agency.

15 Lamb (1994: H5). Another news photograph of a tightly packed group of children with cups in their hands has the caption: "A drop in the ocean of misery . . . Rwandan children wait for water at Kibumba camp near Goma, Zaire" (Trequesser 1994: 4).

16 Cf. Debord: "The spectacle is not a collection of images, but a social relation among people, mediated by images" (1983: 2, paragraph 5).

17 Other pictures with short captions but without stories appeared in the *New York Times* (1 April 1995: A5; 2 April 1995: E2). Cf. also *Life* (September 1994: 74–80).

18 This should be seen in the more general context of the gross underreporting of the violence that started in Burundi in October 1993.

19 Lemarchand (1994a: 1); Newbury and Newbury (1995: 2); Prunier (1995).

20 Stephen Smith, "A Butare," *Libération*, 27 May 1994, cited in Lemarchand (1994a: 11).

21 In a theme issue on Africa, *Granta*, the literary magazine, published 22 pages of black-and-white photographs of the dead and wounded in the Rwanda genocide. The photographs were taken by Gilles Peress (Magnum).

22 Estimates vary. The figure of 50,000 cholera victims is cited in Lorch (1995a: A1). Cf. Balzar (1994b: A23).

23 And, of course, "voluntary repatriation" is inscribed in the operating code of the UNHCR as the primary, and ideal, "durable solution" to displacement. See Warner's reflections on the implications of this ideal and its relation to the social imagination of "home" by refugee organizations (1994: 1ff.).

24 Cf. Balibar on citizenship (1988: 724): he contrasts "citizenship understood in its strict sense as the full exercise of political rights and in its broad sense as cultural initiative or *effective presence in the public space (the capacity to be 'listened to' there)*" (emphasis added). It is in this broad sense that the international citizenship of the refugees from Burundi and Rwanda has been denied in the arena commonly named "the international community." (Cf. Foucault, as cited in Macey 1993: 437–8).

25 Estimates vary. See, e.g., Lorch (1995b: A1, A4).

26 I also do not wish to imply that all relief, aid, refugee, and humanitarian agencies espouse the same philosophy; I am only attempting to identify a dominant tendency. There are, happily, dissonant voices in the ranks of these agencies, as in the following case: "'If the U.N. doesn't learn from this, God help the next poor souls of the world who need help,' said John O'Shea of the Irish relief agency GOAL, which has been active here [in Rwanda] since the beginning of the crisis. Using bitter profanities, O'Shea said the United Nations has failed to meet the refugees' needs and has made no serious effort to make them feel safe going home" (cited in Balzar 1994d: A6).

REFERENCES

African Rights (1994) *Rwanda: Death, Despair and Defiance*. London: African Rights.

Amnesty International (1993) "Rwanda. Extrajudicial execution/fear of extrajudicial execution/fear of torture/incommunicado detention." UA 41/93. AI Index: AFR 47/03/93, 18 February 1993, 1. (2-page mimeo. marked for general distribution).

Balibar, Etienne (1988) "Propositions on Citizenship," *Ethics* 98: 723–30.

—— (1995) "Ambiguous Universality," *Differences: A Journal of Feminist Cultural Studies* 7(1): 48–74.

Balzar, John (1994a) "Burundi Battles Its Demons in Fight to Survive," *Los Angeles Times*, 15 August: A3, A10.

—— (1994b) "Plight of Sick and Dying Refugees Is Price Rwandans Pay for Hatred," *Los Angeles Times*, 20 August: A23.

—— (1994c) "Rwanda's New Leaders Accused of Harassing Refugees," *Los Angeles Times*, 16 August: A4.

—— (1994d) "U.N. Admits Its Efforts to Persuade Rwandans to Go Home Are Failing," *Los Angeles Times*, 13 August: A6.

Barthes, Roland (1980) *Mythologies*. New York: Hill & Wang.

—— (1994) "The Photographic Message," in S. Sontag (ed.), *A Barthes Reader*, New York: Hill & Wang.

Beresford, David (1994) "Who Bears The Guilt of Africa's Horror?" *Manchester Guardian Weekly*, 7 August: 6.

Bonner, Raymond (1994) "Rwandan Refugees In Zaire Still Fear to Return," *New York Times*, 10 November: A3.

Calhoun, Craig (1995) "Foreword," in M. Ishay, *Internationalism and Its Betrayal*, Minneapolis: University of Minnesota Press.

Clifford, James (1988) *The Predicament of Culture: Twentieth-Century Ethnography, Literature, and Art*. Cambridge, MA: Harvard University Press.

Debord, Guy (1983) *Society of the Spectacle*, Detroit: Black & Red.

Destexhe, Alain (1994) *Rwanda: Essai sur le génocide*. Brussels: Editions Complexe.

de Waal, Alex (1994) *A Lesson to Learn From Rwanda. Wider Angle*, Helsinki: United Nations University/World Institute for Development Economics Research 2/94 (28 December): 9–10.

Drakulic, Slavenka (1993) *Balkan Express: Fragments from the Other Side of the War*, London: Hutchinson.

Drogin, Bob (1994) "Refugees Get Steady Diet of Propaganda," *Los Angeles Times*, 27 July: A3, A11.

Feldman, Allen (1994) "On Cultural Anesthesia: From Desert Storm to Rodney King," *American Ethnologist* 21, 2: 404–18.

Ferguson, James (1994) *The Anti-Politics Machine: "Development," Depoliticization, and Bureaucratic Power in Lesotho*. Minneapolis: University of Minnesota Press.

—— (1995) "From African Socialism to Scientific Capitalism: Reflections on the Legitimation Crisis in IMF-Ruled Africa," in D. B. Moore and G. J. Schmitz (eds), *Debating Development Discourse: Institutional and Popular Perspectives*, New York: St. Martin's Press.

Forbes Martin, Susan (1992) *Refugee Women*, London: Zed.

Guichaoua, André (1995) *Les crises politiques au Burundi et au Rwanda (1993–1994)*, Paris: Karthala.

Ishay, Micheline (1995) *Internationalism and Its Betrayal*. Minneapolis: University of Minnesota Press.

Jefremovas, Villia (n.d.) "The Rwandan State and Local Level Response: Class and Region in the Rwandan Genocide, the Refugee Crisis, Repatriation and the 'New Rwanda'." Unpublished ms.

Kismaric, Carole (1989) *Forced Out: The Agony of the Refugee in Our Time*, New York: Human Rights Watch and the J. M. Kaplan Fund in association with William Morrow, W. W. Norton, Penguin Books, and Random House.

Lamb, David (1994) "Threading Through a Surreal World on the Way to Tragedy in Rwanda," *Los Angeles Times*, 14 June: H1, H5.

Langellier, Jean-Pierre (1994) "Breaking Through the Fear Barrier," *Manchester Guardian Weekly*, 7 August: 16.

Lemarchand, René (1994a) "The Apocalypse in Rwanda." Unpublished ms. (Later published in *Cultural Survival Quarterly*, summer/fall 1994: 29–39.)

—— (1994b) *Burundi: Ethnocide as Discourse and Practice*. New York: Woodrow Wilson Center Press and Cambridge University Press.

Lemarchand, René and David Martin (1974) *Selective Genocide in Burundi* (Report no. 20), London: The Minority Rights Group.

Loescher, Gilbert and L. Monahan (eds) (1989) *Refugees and International Relations*. Oxford: Oxford University Press.

Lorch, Donatella (1995a) "A Year Later, Rwandans Stay and Chaos Looms," *New York Times*, 15 July: A1, A5.

—— (1995b) "As Many As 2,000 Are Reported Dead In Rwanda," *New York Times*, 24 April: A1, A4.

McClintock, Anne (1992) "The Angel of Progress: Pitfalls of the Term 'Post-Colonialism,'" *Social Text* 10, 2–3: 84–98.

Macey, David (1993) *The Lives of Michel Foucault: A Biography*. New York: Pantheon.

McGreal, Chris (1994) "Chaos and Cholera Ravage Rwandans," *Manchester Guardian Weekly*, 31 July: 151, 5: 1.

Malkki, Liisa (1994) "Citizens of Humanity: Internationalism and the Imagined Community of Nations," *Diaspora* 3, 1: 41–68.

—— (1995a) *Purity and Exile: Violence, Memory, and National Cosmology among Hutu Refugees in Tanzania*. Chicago: University of Chicago Press.

—— (1995b) "Refugees and Exile: From 'Refugee Studies' to the National Order of Things," *Annual Review of Anthropology* 24: 495–523.

Mbonimpa, Melchior (1993) *Hutu, Tutsi, Twa: Pour une Société sans Castes au Burundi*, Paris: L'Harmattan.

Newbury, Catherine and David Newbury (1994) "Rwanda: The Politics of Turmoil," *African Studies Association Newsletter* 27, 3: 9–11.

—— (1995) "Identity, Genocide, and Reconstruction in Rwanda." Unpublished ms.

Ortner, Sherry (1991) *Narrativity in History, Culture, and Lives,* CSST (Comparative Study in Social Transformations) Working Paper no. 66, Ann Arbor: University of Michigan.

Pottier, Johan (1994) "Representations of Ethnicity in Post-Genocide Writings in Rwanda." Unpublished ms.

Prunier, Gérard (1995) *The Rwanda Crisis: History of a Genocide*. New York: Columbia University Press.
Rée, Jonathan (1992) "Internationality," *Radical Philosophy* 60: 3–11.
Reyntjens, Filip (1994) *L'Afrique des Grands Lacs en crise: Rwanda, Burundi: 1988–1994*, Paris: Karthala.
Rusciano, Frank and Roberta Fiske-Rusciano (1990) "Towards a Notion of 'World Opinion,'" *International Journal of Public Opinion Research* 2, 4: 305–22.
Stapleton, Adam (1995) "Amateurs Posing As Professionals: The United Nations Human Rights Field Operation in Rwanda," *Human Rights Tribune* 3, 2: 13–15.
Stein, Barry (1981) "The Refugee Experience: Defining the Parameters of a Field of Study," *International Migration Review* 15, 1: 320–30.
Tambiah, Stanley (1985) *Culture, Thought, and Social Action: An Anthropological Perspective*. Cambridge, MA: Harvard University Press.
Trequesser, Gilles (1994) "UN Ready For New Refugee Exodus," *Manchester Guardian Weekly*, 14 August: 4.
Warner, Daniel (1994) "Voluntary Repatriation and the Meaning of Return to Home: A Critique of Liberal Mathematics." Paper prepared for the Fourth International Research and Advisory Panel Conference, Somerville College, University of Oxford, 5–9 January.
Warrick, Pamela (1994) "Tipper Gore's Mission of Mercy," *Los Angeles Times*, 15 August: E1, E2.
Zolberg, Aristide, Astri Suhrke, and Sergio Aguayo (1989) *Escape From Violence: Conflict and the Refugee Crisis In the Developing World*, Oxford: Oxford University Press.

11 "Roots" and "Mosaic" in a Balkan Border Village

Locating cultural production

Jonathan Schwartz

INTRODUCTION

Migration research provides much of the experience for building the concepts of global and local culture, of deterritorialization and reterritorialization. One time-worn convention in earlier migration research was to divide the causal forces into "push–pull factors." Poverty and oppression pushed the emigrant out of the mountain village, wage labor pulled him to industrial cities across the oceans. The migrant was the near-perfect "homo economicus" (Thomas and Znaniecki 1923: I: 193; Piore 1979: 52–9).

Another and related duality was to describe "both ends of the migration chain," usually referring to the "sending village" and the "receiving metropole." In this image of the "chain," social organization supplemented individual enterprise. One can recognize in this image shades of Robert Redfield's "folk–urban continuum," perhaps even of Tönnies's *Gemeinschaft* and *Gesellschaft* (Redfield 1955: 132–48). The polarity of two different socio-cultural forms permits gradations in between, but development and modernization move unilinearly from the small community to the large society.

The recent emphasis on globality and locality appears at first glance to duplicate the dualism of previous migration theory, but if the newer terms represent an improvement, it is because they capture the processual and coeval life histories of migrants, returnees, and those who stay at home. Global culture and local culture take place at both ends of the proverbial migration chain. The chain becomes then more like a loop, more electronic than rectilineal.

The ethnographies of contemporary migration with a global and local perspective make increasing use of the term "diaspora" to express the cultural production, reproduction, and communities among informants (Bauman 1989; Hall 1990; Gilroy 1993; Appadurai

1990 and forthcoming). The term "Diaspora," of course, is a term from Jewish self-identification, but with a small "d" the term is being diffused among many groups which emigrate. A term from scholarship enters into everyman's identity; nearly every ethnic community is somehow in diaspora. Nationalist, irredentist organizations, moreover, thrive in multicultural metropoles as, for example, in Toronto. Animosity between ethnic groups thus grows in places which are supposed to be peaceable, spacious gardens. Cracks form in the multi-ethnic mosaic.

The contemporary Balkans with its many diasporic communities is an obvious, complex context for perceiving global and local cultural production. "Balkanization" is one of the few geographic terms that takes a region's name for identifying a process of continuous conflict and fragmentation. Balkan history is invoked as certain evidence for this geopolitical reality. Essentialism in ethnonationalist ideologies permeates the field. A strange mosaic to say the least. More often the powder-keg.

If "creolization" speaks to cultural blendings and productions (Hannerz 1987) in global and local contexts, "Balkanization" speaks in a much more strident voice to the experience of the 1990s. This chapter will focus on cultural production in a single village in ex-Yugoslavian Macedonia, where migration history continues to shape the present. Nestled high in the wooded mountains, with fresh streams running through it, the last stop for local buses, the home village of migrants in North America and Scandinavia, Brajcino qualifies as a "remote area" (Ardener 1987).

Brajcino is within hiking distance over mountain trails to the Greek border. Villagers have pointed out a maize silo, the meeting place for men who planned to cross the border, two at a time, by night, clandestinely into Greece. From Thessaloniki the ocean route was to either North America or Australia. The illicit border crossing also took place in the reverse direction, when Macedonian refugees from the Greek Civil War (1947–9) crossed into socialist Yugoslavia and thence to other countries of the Soviet bloc. The possibility of subsequently emigrating to Canada and Australia came in the 1950s.

Macedonians in Toronto had already a well-established diaspora community. The first groups of men arrived in Canada after the failed Macedonian ("Ilinden") revolt against Ottoman Turkish power in 1903 (Petroff 1985). The Macedonian "charter" group in Canada descended primarily from villagers on what was to become the Greek side of the international border which was drawn as part of the European peace treaty following World War I.

The Macedonian cultural and political organizations in Melbourne and Toronto have as their most active members the "Runaway Children" (*Begaltsi Detsa*) who came from now-abandoned villages in Northern Greece. Diasporic Macedonia includes, then, several generations of migrants (*pechalbari*) and refugees (*Begaltsi Deta*) whose villages are on both sides of the Greek/ex-Yugoslavian border. The conflict over the use of the name "Macedonia" and its Alexandrian icons is daily, global news, but that conflict is probably more aggravated in the metropoles than in the villages (Danforth 1993).

Crossing the border between Greece and the Macedonian Republic, if allowed, could take place along the eastern shore of Prespa Lake (750 m) or along a mountain trail on the southern slope of Mount Pelistir (2,400 m). Amateur hikers could manage both tours. It is, however, forbidden and dangerous to approach this border region. A third nation-state, Albania, also has a border on the southwestern shore of Prespa Lake, so this remote Balkan triangle is a volatile place. Since February 1993 the presence of a UN peace-keeping mission (under Danish leadership) has helped to cushion both international conflicts and inter-ethnic conflicts, especially those between Macedonian and Albanian communities. In such a troubled border zone, the concerns of ethnic and migration researchers must also shift towards a form of peace-keeping mission. That is, we need to apply our close-range and sustained experience in the field to the goal of co-existence. That is the intention of this chapter.

THE USE AND ABUSE OF METAPHORS: ROOTS AND MOSAICS

Brajcino is one of the villages in the Prespa Lake region where I have been studying labor migration (*pechalba*) and identity since my first visit in 1977 (Schwartz 1993). What incited this first visit was a conversation with a Prespa-born guestworker in Copenhagen in February 1977. He, his wife, and I were watching one of the programs in the TV series "Roots" which was being shown on Danish television. Their two small children were close by.

Muamer's apartment was in Vognmandsmarken, a dilapidated housing project in Copenhagen, which had become a guestworker ghetto in the early 1970s. It was scheduled for demolition, and the municipal government had not bothered to maintain minimal sanitary conditions. In 1971, two infants had died from acute intestinal infection, so some public attention was being directed at the ghetto. I had been involved in an action anthropology project since 1974 to assist community organization among the 1,300 tenants, most of whom came from Turkey, Yugoslavia (i.e. Macedonia), Pakistan, and Morocco (Schwartz 1978, 1985). The local Macedonian organization in the ghetto was called "Prespa," which I soon found out was the name of a mountain lake. Members of "Prespa Club" came from three ethnic groups in the Prespa region: Macedonian, Albanian, and Turkish. Muamer was among the active members of the campaign for improved housing.

We sat in Muamer's cold and damp apartment watching an episode from "Roots." I asked him about his home, and he answered: "I know, you want to know where my roots are." Since then, I have made ten trips to the Prespa Lake region in the period 1977–93, mostly during the summer and autumn months, and these have added up to an ethnographic field work in migration.

"Roots" are a key symbol for migrants and scholars, and one is led to believe that the force of the arboreal metaphor expresses the endurance of bonds at least to family, village, or region, and perhaps to nation (Malkki 1992). The art of deconstruction can be rigorously applied to this root metaphor, but those who live by the metaphor (Lakoff and Johnson 1980) will not give it up. Numerous anecdotes from field work in the villages and in the metropoles add up to substantial evidence for the putative power of roots. Without essentializing the concept, there is nevertheless a cognitive meaning of roots that may shed light on global and local productions of culture.

Trees are good to think with. They are especially good to remember with. The Prespa Lake region is noted for its apple production. Beginning in the 1960s the development of small family-owned orchards in the Prespa Lake villages coincided with emigration, wage labor, saving, and remittances. To symbolize the Prespa region's gratitude to fruit trees, the local government in Resen erected in 1991 a monumental copper sculpture of a red delicious apple in the town square. To complete the region's economic symbolism a huge sculptured suitcase adjoining the apple would have been appropriate. Emigration and the maintenance of roots made the orchards possible. Intensive savings abroad, which meant living in tiny, poorly heated flats, provided the resources for home-building and apple-farming in the village.

Pechalba is the south Slavic term for migration, and the word's etymology can be traced to the old Church-Russian word for sorrow and loss (Herman 1979). Redemption following loss is represented in the cyclical migration process of leaving, suffering, and returning.

Loring Danforth (1982) observed among the performance of death rituals in northern Greece (Macedonia) homologies to male migrants' work careers and women's nuptial rites. The category "xenitia" (strangeness) embodies death, marriage, and migration.

The folklore of *pechalba* and the practices of *pechalbari* elaborate the symbolic meaning. In her ethnography of Balkan "tribalism," which was based to a great extent on Macedonian and Albanian studies, M. Edith Durham (1928: 321–40) noted the frequency of villages being named after species of trees, particularly fruit trees. An example is Krushevo (literally "pear place" in Macedonian). Several Albanian villages are given the names of nut and fruit trees.

The "summary symbol" of roots (Ortner 1973) enters into the work of remembrance for migrants and for those who remain at home. A popular folk song (ca. 1960) from Pretor, a Prespa Lake village, is voiced by a woman who was married to a man who had been away "in *pechalba*" for nine years. To test his identity, she asks him: "What is there special that grows in my garden?" When he answers that "It is a tall maple tree," she recognizes him as her long-lost husband (Karovski and Bichevski 1979: 175–6). The tacit promise of the *pechalbar* is that he will come home, and the conventional time spans are multiples of three years. "*Tre Godine*" ("Three years") is the mournful refrain of many Macedonian folk songs.

The shift from folklore to practice is not abrupt. Several men have pointed out the trees they or their fathers planted when they left as *pechalbari*. Simo, who comes from a Prespa Lake village and works as a welder in Hälsingborg, Sweden, planted a chestnut tree in his father's yard. To ensure the memory-marker, Simo engraved a stainless-steel plate and placed it at the foot of the tree. Even if the chestnut tree dies, the Swedish stainless steel will endure. It was Simo too who showed me the mulberry tree in the old abandoned village, Strbovo, which, as children, he and his brothers and sisters climbed on. A limb took the name of the child who climbed on it most often. Simo has three brothers and three sisters, so the tree is literally a "family tree." *Pechalba* has split the siblings into two nearly equal halves. Three have remained in Macedonia; four have emigrated, two in Canada, two in Sweden (Schwartz 1989: 134–6). This division of siblings into two equal segments is a characteristic practice in the Prespa Lake district. The practice, moreover, allows for the reproduction of global and local roots.

The linear migration "chain," the one-way migration "wave," and even the "cyclical" movement, are all too partial in their grasp of the experience. "Roots" are, like many summary symbols, a reduction, better yet, a condensation of experience. In a bi-focal study of metropolitan diaspora and native village, it is possible to reveal the rooting process in both contexts.

Brajcino is a good choice for such a project, and indeed the villagers seem quite aware of their cosmopolitan and their local connections. Inhabiting a "remote" place is a form of cultural production. It is for this reason no doubt that the village was chosen in 1983 as the site for producing a dramatic film about *pechalba*, its sorrows and joys. The film's title is "*Glas*," which means "Voice." The film has been shown on TV in many cities with large Macedonian communities. I first saw the film on a video cassette at Simo's apartment in Sweden (at Eastertime 1988). It had Swedish subtitles and had been shown on Swedish TV. Not knowing about the film, I asked Simo and his wife, Pera, "How do you remember your village?" She went to the shelf and put "*Glas*" into the video.

The hero of the film is in real life Vasily, a dwarf in Brajcino, who every day – not just for the filming – wears traditional Macedonian peasant clothes and works his small farm with old hand implements. Vasily lives alone in the family house. In the film, the lonesome hero receives a cassette letter from his brother in Buffalo, New York. Sitting at his table Vasily listens to the letter on his tape-recorder. Weeping, he answers his brother's message. He complains of being left alone, though there is one small joyful scene where several older villagers, including a few of Vasily's own family members, get together and share a dinner. One of them is Vasily's sister who had lived in Detroit before she returned to Brajcino after her husband died. There is a documentary quality to the *pechalba* melodrama.

The brother in Buffalo asks if there is a girl in the village who might be a marriage partner for his son. The boy will come on a visit to the village the next summer. The year goes and we see the changing seasons and the work that goes with them. Finally, a jet plane lands in the night, and the nephew arrives at the door. There is weeping at the film's end.

The film dramatizes, and thereby exaggerates, the cultural situation of *pechalba*. It attempts to bring home the messages of identity to the Buffalos and the Brajcinos, to both globalize the local and localize the global. The film's title, "*Glas*," conveys the resonance that crosses the distance between metropole and village. Tape-recorders, video cameras, and jet travel have no doubt transformed the techniques of *pechalba*, but the institution's meaning for the participants is still marked by long absences punctuated by temporary reunions.

The activities in Brajcino reveal the concurrence of several domestic styles, some rooted in the mountain village, others rooted in the North American suburb. Vasily may be the only man who wears traditional clothes, but there are several households which perform farm labor with older techniques and tools. The small, rocky, and steep fields prohibit modern machinery, so hay and grains are harvested by hand and often hauled back to the village by animals. A wooden sled is used for hauling by one family. Others use horse power to thresh wheat in their yards. During summer harvest, the concrete area used as a bus terminus is swept clean for threshing wheat by wooden hand tools. A colleague described Brajcino as a "living open air museum."

This traditional aspect of Brajcino is visible, and it draws artists and film-makers from Skopje to record the local life. Coeval with the traditional domestic labor is the transplanting of suburban taste. By pointing to this concurrence or conjuncture of style I by no means intend to advocate the "authentic" and condemn the "spurious" (Sapir 1924; Handler and Linnekin 1984). The villagers and the returnees surely feel at home with the contrasts, so why should the ethnographer pass judgement?

The only conflicts between villagers which I have heard about had to do with the sharing of water from the mountain brooks. A returned *pechalbar*, who had worked as a machinist in Detroit, built himself a Hacienda-style home based on blueprints from 1970s American suburban architecture. Beside the house he wanted to raise trout and he built two small stone ponds on his property. These ponds, after ten years, have never been filled with water, because the neighbor woman who lives upstream has not allowed him to dig channels from her land to his. Taking the matter stoically, the ex-Detroiter now earns his living by gathering mushrooms on the mountain, drying them, and selling them to medicinal firms in Italy. He hopes someday though to have trout swimming in his ponds.

The distribution of water is a problem, though Brajcino with its resources is surely one of the most fortunate villages in the entire region. The conflict just mentioned was not between traditional and modern dwellers, but between upstream and downstream neighbors. To earn funds for home-construction in the village is one of the reasons why *pechalbari* go abroad. Variations in domestic style and living are apparently not a cause of conflict.

In July 1993 (my most recent visit to Brajcino) I got to know Boris, whose property is adjacent to the town square. This dusty square is, as noted, the end station for buses, a car park, and, whenever possible, for boys' soccer games. Boris was clearing an area on his land for a private parking place. He has no car himself in Macedonia, but he said that his friends would use it for their cars. It is impossible to reach most of the houses in the village by car. He lives most of the year in Toronto and works as janitor in a suburban highschool. Boris had hired three men from a Macedonian village across Prespa Lake in Albania to do the hard labor of moving stones and putting up a wall. This work took over a week, and they were paid (meagerly) in Canadian dollars. A large old plum tree was chopped down, and Boris told Pero, a permanent resident, that he could have the tree for firewood. I helped cut the stump from the roots and then dig out the roots.

The work of removing roots in Boris's case was also a way of deepening roots in the place. The anecdote from Boris's former plum tree might indicate the resilience, not the frailty, of the root metaphor in an understanding of migrants' and villagers' exchanges.

The obverse symbolism – cutting away the actual roots in order to make space for other roots – underlines the plurality and simultaneity of fields in the migration process. Our study continues to be that of territorialization, but instead of reifying or essentializing the "two ends of the migration chain," the village and metropole can be experienced "in the making." Rather than merely deconstructing "roots," we can also perceive how the horticultural metaphors are practiced and, thereby, how they shape meaning for our informants' identities.

The second metaphor to come under scrutiny is the "mosaic." In this survey, the Canadian and Balkan variants will prove to be less congruent and more fragile than "roots." In short, the method of deconstruction works rather easily on the mosaic. Ulf Hannerz (1992) has tested the metaphor in the analysis of subcultures:

> The mosaic as root metaphor – a notion with an internal complexity which would allow the analytical elaboration of our understanding of how subcultures connect with one another – suggests for one thing that the subcultures as "pieces," are all of one kind, all largely homogeneous in their internal characteristics, and all hard-edged. All this is questionable, and the mosaic turns out to be in large part a negative root metaphor, a tool for understanding what subcultures are often not (Hannerz 1992: 73).

Mosaics are more likely to be the inventions of scholars. They are outsiders' mapping devices to help visualize diversity and difference. Multiculturalism as policy depends upon mosaic as a key metaphor. In contemporary representations of the Balkans, the multi-ethnic mosaic is said to be disappearing. "Ethnic cleansing" is a powerful agent in the process.

When I scanned European ethnographies of the Balkans since the start of the twentieth century, I found no case of "mosaic." English writers, like Durham (1905) and Brailsford (1906), who came to the region as refugee relief workers in the wake of Turkish repression, were impressed by the diversity of languages and races, but they found no aesthetic image like mosaic to describe the chaos. Villages were burned, survivors were scattered and gathered in temporary refugee camps. The Serbian geographer, J. Cvijic (1918: 103–4) spoke of Macedonia – particularly in the Prespa Lake region! – as a "chessboard," not as a "mosaic." Both images, however, convey the perspective of the objectifying viewer. "Mosaic" is evidently not a metaphor from the "native's point of view."

My search for explicit references to mosaic as self-representations of cultural space was amply rewarded in Canada. One salient reason for the Canadian mosaic's primacy is that it offers a counter-concept to the United States' "melting pot" (Palmer 1976). The first complete rendition of the metaphor was by the Canadian folklorist, John Murray Gibbon, *The Canadian Mosaic: the Making of a Northern Nation* (1938). This work attempted to soften the impact of large-scale immigration to Canada by showing how the various nationalities each made a contribution to the whole.

There is, however, a hierarchy in Gibbon's Canadian mosaic, with the British at the top. Resemblance to the British "stock," as, for example, Scandinavians ensured a relatively high position. The Nordic immigrants, he wrote (Gibbon 1938: 211), were more like "cousins" than "aliens."

John Porter (1965) published a critical class analysis of Canada entitled *The Vertical Mosaic*. Legislation for multiculturalism appeared in the wake of Porter's study, so that the ethnic, horizontal mosaic was incorporated into Canadian national identity. Just as social scientists (e.g. Novak 1972) in the United States were rediscovering the ethnic "unmeltables," their Canadian counterparts were expanding their own ethnic mosaic. The mosaic is surely a metaphor that Canadians live by, though a recent best-seller (Bibby 1990) is entitled *Mosaic Madness*. The author of this work claims that multicultural policy and programs have eroded basic Canadian values and tastes. "Too much of a good thing" (Bibby 1990: 10) is the temperate way in which Bibby expresses his criticism of multiculturalism.

My own impression of Macedonian cultural practice and production in multicultural contexts like Toronto, is that the mosaic metaphor is best able to capture the experience within an ethnic community, not between ethnic groups. Principles of segmentation and refraction (Herzfeld 1987, 1992) can be brought to bear on the activities of a Balkan community's members, with segmentation being the process of social divisions, and refraction speaking to the interpretation of these local events. The celebration of a Saint's day or a national holiday can reveal the cleavages and the unities of a village or ethnic community.

Thus, in Toronto, village organizations continue to inspire and direct "Macedonian culture." Annual picnics are held by the village groups. Specialized activities like folk dance draw upon village affiliations, and clearly the uprooted villagers from the Greek side of the border want to claim the more authentic cultural roots. The name of the folk-dance group which descends from Greek villages is "Selyani" which means "villagers." Segmentations within an ethnic community can emerge as rainbow-like refractions in the production of culture.

In a recent auto-ethnography of Toronto Macedonians, Vasiliadis (1989) focuses on the maintenance of village affiliation. "Whose are you?" is the idiomatic question asked by one Macedonian to another. The answer is supposed to be the name of the village.

Brajcino, near the border between Greece and the Republic of Macedonia, has a village organization in Toronto. The editor of the monthly bi-lingual newspaper, *Makedonija*, comes from Brajcino. He emigrated to Canada in the late 1960s, and his knowledge of Macedonian is therefore better than some of the strong culturalists whose ancestors came two generations ago from the desolate Greek villages. His knowledge of English, however, is not as strong as that of native Torontonians.

Thus, in an unexpected way, the mosaic image does fit the clustering of Macedonian identities in Toronto. Likewise, the village Brajcino itself, a homogeneous Macedonian village, can be described as a mosaic of various domestic styles and strategies. Brajcino does not have Albanian or Turkish inhabitants, and there are several villages on the eastern shore of Prespa Lake that do. These villages are probably the prototypical "ethnic mosaics," and indeed the entire region should look like a mosaic to an ethnographer.

The only occasion in the villages that I heard the word "mosaic" spoken was on the night (2 August 1993) of the festival that celebrated the St. Elias (Ilinden) rebellion in 1903 against Turkish domination. "Mosaic" occurred in a speech by a municipal politician. The commemoration was held in Lubojno, the neighboring, downstream village to Brajcino. Lubojno is also a completely Macedonian village.

None of my Turkish and Albanian informants wanted to come to the celebration. It was, in their eyes, a strictly Macedonian national event, one that perhaps aimed at excluding the Muslim minorities. A Turkish man I have known since 1977 told me: "Why come there? They just tell how bad Turks are. They tell about then, not now."

In fact there was not so much nationalism and no hatred of Turks mentioned in the speeches. The term "ethnic mosaic" was used to refer to the many countries where Macedonians live and work as *pechalbari*. Australia, the United States, Canada, Sweden, Germany, Switzerland, and Denmark were all named in the speech, and these countries formed "the mosaic," as perceived from the village.

CONCLUSION

Turkish, Albanian, and Rom (Gypsy) communities in the Prespa Lake region of Macedonia all send their members abroad to labor, save, and return. *Pechalba* is part of the inhabitants' collective – but seldom collected – history and memory. The representation of ethnic groups (1) as insular and separate parts of a mosaic, and (2) as being at various stages between traditional and modern development exacerbates an already dangerous situation in the Balkan. Critical applied anthropology in our decade can discover potential roots and mosaics for a shared, peaceable future. We need not make the method of deconstruction one of destruction. There is enough of that around.

Our critiques of essentialism are assuming a sensitive political vocation. Out of friendship and respect for our informants, we have to train a voice as well as a discourse. A thoughtful look at metaphors of affiliation and diversity can result in a valuable recycling. We need to look at our familiar fields from different angles, pointing out common ground between contesting groups. I suspect that some of our informants and friends will appreciate this sort of ethnography.

REFERENCES

Appadurai, A. (1990) 'Disjuncture and Difference in the Global Cultural Economy,' in M. Featherstone (ed.) *Global Culture: Nationalism, Globalization, and Modernity*, London: Sage.

—— (forthcoming) 'Global Culture and the Production of Locality,' paper presented at Oxford University, July 1993.

Ardener, E. (1987) "'Remote Areas': Some Theoretical Considerations," in A. Jackson (ed). *Anthropology at Home*, London: Tavistock.

Bauman, Z. (1989) *Modernity and the Holocaust*, Cambridge: Polity Press.

Bibby, R. (1990) *Mosaic Madness: The Poverty and Potential of Life in Canada*, Toronto: Stoddart.
Brailsford, H. (1906) *Macedonia: Its Races and its Future*, London.
Cvijic, J. (1918) *La Péninsule balkanique: géographie humaine*, Paris: Colin.
Danforth, L. (1982) *The Death Rituals of Rural Greece*, Princeton: Princeton University Press.
—— (1993) 'Claims to Macedonian Identity: The Macedonian Question and the Breakup of Yugoslavia,' *Anthropology Today* 9 (4): 8–10.
Durham, M. E. (1905) *The Burden of the Balkans*, London: Edward Arnold.
—— (1928) *Some Tribal Laws, Origins, and Customs of the Balkans*, London: George Allen & Unwin.
Gibbon, J. M. (1938) *The Canadian Mosaic: The Making of a Northern Nation*, Toronto.
Gilroy, P. (1993) *The Black Atlantic: Modernity and Double Consciousness*, London: Verso.
Hall, S. (1990) 'Cultural Identity and Diaspora,' in J. Rutherford (ed.) *Identity, Culture, Difference*, London: Lawrence & Wishart.
Handler, R. and J. Linnekin (1984) 'Tradition: Genuine or Spurious?' *Journal of American Folklore* 97: 273–90.
Hannerz, U. (1987) 'The World in Creolization,' *Africa* 4: 546–59.
—— (1992) *Cultural Complexity: The Social Organization of Meaning*, New York: Columbia University Press.
Herman, H. (1979) 'Dishwashers and Proprietors: A Study of Macedonian Restaurants in Toronto,' in H. Wallman (ed.) *Ethnicity at Work*, London: ASA monographs.
Herzfeld, M. (1987) *Anthropology Through the Looking-Glass: Critical Ethnography in the Margins of Europe*, Cambridge: Cambridge University Press.
—— (1992) 'Segmentation and Politics in the European Nation-State: Making Sense of Political Events,' in K. Hastrup (ed.) *Other Histories*, London: Routledge.
Karovski, L. and Bichevski, T. (1979) *Macedonian Folk Songs of Pechalba*, Skopje: Institute of Folklore.
Lakoff, G. and M. Johnson (1980) *Metaphors We Live By*, Chicago: University of Chicago Press.
Malkki, L. (1992) 'National Geographic: The Rooting of Peoples and the Territorialization of National Identity among Scholars and Refugees,' *Cultural Anthropology* 7, 1: 24–44.
Novak, M. (1972) *The Rise of the Unmeltable Ethnics*, New York: Macmillan.
Ortner, S. (1973) 'On Key Symbols,' *American Anthropologist* 75: 5, 1338–46.
Palmer, H. (1976) 'Mosaic versus Melting Pot? Immigration and Ethnicity in Canada and the United States,' *International Journal* 31: 488–529.
Petroff, L. (1985) 'Sojourner and Settler: The Macedonian Presence in the City, 1903–1940,' in R. Harner (ed.) *Gathering Places: Peoples and Neighborhoods of Toronto, 1834–1945*, Toronto: Multicultural History Society.
Piore, M. (1979) *Birds of Passage: Migrant Labor and Industrial Societies*, Cambridge, Mass. Massachusetts Institute of Technology.
Porter, J. (1965) *The Vertical Mosaic*, Toronto: University of Toronto Press.

Redfield, R. (1955) *The Little Community: Viewpoints for the Study of the Human Whole*, Chicago: University of Chicago Press.

Sapir, E. (1924) 'Culture: Genuine and Spurious,' *American Journal of Sociology* 29: 401–29.

Schwartz, J. (1978) 'Vogmandsmarken: A Guestworker Ghetto in Copenhagen,' *Scandinavian Review* 1: 66–73.

—— (1985) *Reluctant Hosts: Denmark's Reception of Guestworkers*, Copenhagen: Akademisk.

—— (1989) *In Defense of Home-Sickness: Nine Essays on Identity and Locality*, Copenhagen: Akademisk.

—— (1993) "'Macedonia': a Country in Quotation Marks," *Anthropology of Eastern Europe Review* 11: 1–2.

Thomas, W. I. and Znaniecki (1923) *The Polish Peasant in Europe and America*, New York: Dover.

Vasiliadis, P. (1989) *Whose are You? Identity and Ethnicity among Toronto Macedonians*, New York: AMS.

12 Simplifying complexity

Assimilating the global in a small paradise

Jonathan Friedman

This chapter concerns the way in which the inhabitants of a small village of Hawaiians practice a localization of their world, generating a structure of existence and a "space of experience" (Mannheim 1982) that in their turn produce cultural forms of a specific nature. As there has been a great deal of discussion of "hybridization," "creolization" and the like in reference to so-called modern cultures, the latter being themselves products of complex global and national processes, I shall begin with a discussion of these phenomena, before arguing that, to paraphrase Boas and Kroeber, it doesn't matter where you get it from, it matters what you do with it.

The notion of complex society and now complex culture are glosses in academic anthropology for one side of a contrast that is in many respects similar to the modern, the Western, the global. The terms are only comprehensible as oppositional terms to simple, traditional, and local. In the well-known ASA monograph on *The Social Anthropology of Complex Societies* (Barnes 1966) the studies concern the urban, peasant societies, Western societies, and contemporary India. Nowhere is the notion of complexity defined or situated. Rather it is simply used in opposition to the terms stated above. Hannerz (1992), concerned essentially with the culture concept which he discusses in terms of dimensions of ideas and modes of thought, forms of externalization and social distribution, finds it difficult to establish the nature of complexity. The first dimension is by and large impossible to discuss since there are no adequate criteria for establishing the degree of complexity of meaning. Forms of expression become complex as alternative interpretations increase. Distribution becomes complex as access to and control of meaning becomes more differentiated. The problem here is that this very conventional view is contradicted by the general critique of culture as homogeneous and uniform. Barth (1989) argues that uniformity is the result of authority, in the displacement of one interpretation by another. Complexity is, in this view, and by extension, the result of the lack of hegemonic interpretations of the world. Numerous anthropologists have stressed the degree to which homogeneity is a mirage produced by ethnographic authority itself, so that even where homogeneity does not exist it may often be assumed in the anthropologist's representation of a culture.

From this point of view, complexity in the sense of heterogeneity is the common substrate of all ethnographic reality. The problem is to discover the conditions in which such heterogeneity is either maintained or expanded, or reduced to homogeneity. This is a problem of power and authority, as Barth also seems to suggest, and not something that can be understood from within culture itself in the sense of meaning, modes of thought or whatever. And the notion that there are simple as opposed to complex cultures is a misleading carryover from previous distinctions between primitive/civilized and traditional/modern that does not adequately formulate the nature of the problem, i.e. the mechanisms of heterogenization and homogenization.

This does not imply, of course, that complexity is an illusion, only that it is ubiquitous in the analysis of any social reality rather than a phenomenon that has emerged recently. We have argued for a number of years that global systems are nothing new, and that from the emergence of the earliest commercial civilizations there were complex regional processes in which power, the flow of goods, people, and information played significant roles. There have, of course, been quantitative variations over time, but there is nothing in the recent globalization arguments that enlightens us as to where the quantitative thresholds that make the contemporary period unique might be found. I would suggest that notions of globalization, hybridization, and creolization are socially positioned concepts that in their classificatory thrust say very much about the classifiers and much less about those classified. Objective cultural hybridization is about the way external observers classify their objects, and it contains a genealogical bias in so far as it is entirely based on the definition of origins. There is an interest involved in this classification, of course, as all attempts to define reality for others are attempts to legitimate the position of the classifiers and definers. Cosmopolitan self-identity is closely related to defining the world as creolized. Now in structural terms creolization is a universal process seen from the outside. Its import depends not on the processes of cultural mixture and assimilation, but on the way in which such processes are recognized and expressed. Cultural self-identification has never had any problem with the objective facts of hybridization. On the contrary, such "facts" have been issues of relations between self-identifiers and their superordinate classifiers.

The term "complexity" has often been associated with the phenomenon of globalization, and it has sometimes been asserted that global culture was in some sense a new object of anthropological investigation. This was a means, at least, to carve out a niche for cultural experts (anthropologists) in the more general trend toward the study of global systemic processes. If the economists and economic historians and sociologists could have their world system, anthropologists could have their cultural world system or world system of culture. Now complexity could fit very nicely into this scheme of things since it enabled a modern restatement of the diffusionist argument with a more systematic claim on the origin of cultural things in the present state in which everything seems to be moving around. Thus one might trace the origins of "mixed" cultures that, for the cosmopolitan anthropologist, constitute the world today. This essentially museological approach to the objects and peoples of the world consists in the identification of peoples and their cultures in terms of origins or "cultural flows." This is an interesting turn for anthropological research, since it returns to a pre-Boasian culture history that even Boas would have rejected. For the latter the origin of the elements of a culture was less interesting than the way they were integrated in a particular social setting.

There is another way of understanding the global, one that has been suggested in previous works (Friedman 1994), in which what is referred to as globalization can be understood as an aspect rather than a system in itself as implied in much of the literature on both globalization and cultural complexity. Globalization is not about the flow or movement of culture. Culture does not move. It is not a substance. Rather we must investigate the relation between global social processes and the practices of social reproduction, and identification/representation of the world, the processes by which meaning is attributed in specific social contexts distributed in the global arena. The study of a fishing village in Hawaii raises questions of global connections and positioning.

SMALL VILLAGE IN A WORLD ARENA

Miloli'i is located on the southwest coast of the island of Hawaii. Hawaii is the largest of the islands of the Hawaii chain, once a kingdom, earlier a collection of chiefdoms. The usual economic organization of Hawaiian chiefdoms was such that one could not really speak of fishing villages as such, since they were based on a vertical ecology stretching from mountain to sea, a unit called an *ahupua'a* which was in principle self-sufficient in products ranging from fish, often raised in remarkably efficient man-made ponds, to a variety of domestic and wild animals as well as a broad assortment of vegetables, root and tree crops which were neatly distributed in vertically determinate zones. Each island was divided in pie shapes, according to this radial ecology.

The Hawaiian islands were probably contacted by Spanish ships during the trans-Pacific trade linking New Spain and the Spanish colonies in the western Pacific. With the arrival of the Cook expedition they were definitively drawn into the expanding Western world system. A series of trades – sandalwood, whaling, and finally a plantation economy – led to a profound transformation of the islands; the decimation of the population, the emergence of a constitutional monarchy under American missionary sway, an increasingly decadent aristocracy and an increasingly powerful white, ex-missionary plantation elite. The islands were finally incorporated in the United States as a territory after a brief republican period. Throughout the latter part of the nineteenth century, there was a transformation of the vertical onto a horizontal ecology. With the introduction of private property, ordinary Hawaiians were marginalized as whites were able to take advantage of the situation. The whites established ranches and plantations on horizontal sections of the mountain slopes. Hawaiians lost their access to extensive portions of their subsistence base. The formation of more isolated communities was a product of these processes. The transformation of the west coast of Hawaii left a number of horizontal privately owned strips as well as a number of local communities both in the uplands and along the coast. The latter were the fishing communities that existed until World War II. The South Kona coast was dotted with such settlements of several hundred people among whom there was extensive intermarriage. The war and its aftermath led to the abandonment of a large proportion of the coastal population as well as a centralization of those that remained. By the 1950s there were a number of intermarried families in Miloli'i, the last fishing village on the island. The memory of the former *ahupua'a* system is inscribed in the stories told by villagers. Most villagers have relatives who live on kin-based land on the higher slopes, most tell stories about how upland properties were lost by hook or crook. The situation today is fragmented, with some family members having lots several miles, and a thousand feet or more, above the village. The economy that made use of this vast expanse of ecological zones is for the most part defunct, although several families practice modern forms of the *mauka–makai* or upland–coastal combined subsistence base that has today included cash crops such as coffee and macadamia nuts.

Miloli'i is located on the southwest coast of the island. To get there in global terms involves a 24-hour flight from Europe ending at Kailua, once a sleepy little village that debated the advantages of an airport at the end of the 1940s, progress versus the peaceful colonial lethargy of the island. The airport arrived and is today an international airport where jumbo jets land at the juncture of lava fields and the Pacific Ocean. Just south of the airport is the rapidly expanding and asphalting town of Kailua, the first capital of the islands under Kamehameha I and a center of moderately upscaled tourism advertising golf and tennis clubs and the world's best deep-sea sport fishing. But hotels are rarely above the 50 percent occupancy mark and the wealth of the town depends on the retirement communities and other wealthy condominium settlements. Moving down the coast road at 1,000 feet above the ocean one passes increasingly rural settlements where once upon a time hippies had settled, living off (other people's) fruit trees and who today have developed a string of communities studded by health food stores, espresso shops and the like, all in the midst of Japanese communities, mixed Chinese and Hawaiian settlements, and occasional McDonald-focused shopping centers. All of this thins out rapidly as one passes through the Kona coffee-planted slopes at Honaunau and enters what is called "Hawaiian Territory." After travelling across the slopes of Mauna Loa with its vast rivers of petrified lava seeming to flow into the Pacific, a thousand or more feet below, occasional small ranches and sparsely distributed houses, a sign appears along one of the dangerous curves, pointing to Miloli'i. A pot-holed road meanders down and out over the slopes, five miles down . . . if it is evening the sun sinks into the ocean right before your eyes and the ocean glares in its reflection. Black lava rivers sweep the mountainside, but in the distance at the end of the black desert is what appears as an oasis, palm trees and greenery and houses growing right out of the ocean front. The approach to the village has undergone rapid transformation. Ten years ago one got to a junction at sea level where to one side there was the "subdivision," several hundred acres of lava without any infrastructure, five or six houses, most of them on the cliffs overlooking the ocean, and an occasional tent set up on a concrete foundation of a house never completed. The road then meandered past this desolation toward the relative lush of

Miloli'i, over the 30 foot high lava flow and into a string of shacks in dark-brown sun-beaten and sometimes termite-eaten wood. The first houses we met belonged to Waikini and were the residences of descendants of former refugees from the lava flow that destroyed the neighboring village of Ho'opuloa.

Here the road drops suddenly down into the old village of Miloli'i itself. On the right, on a hill overlooking Miloli'i bay was Elvis's house, a shack where Paramount studios made "Girls, Girls, Girls" in the early 1960s. A large quite modern house on the left, belonging to the family of the former "mayor" of the village, was followed by a more dismal construction inhabited by one of his sons and then the village store, also a ramshackle little house featuring a sun-faded sign: "Miloli'i General Store." All of this belonged to the same family. There were several other houses, a small wooded area with palms and pines, the Protestant church and then a new section of the village called Omoka'a. On the right side there is the ocean front . . . we are facing practically due west, marvelous for sunsets. The road ends in front of the church, where there is a state park, i.e. several parking places and room to set up tents, and a *halau*, a thatch-roof open house used for public meetings, parties, and the like. I first lived in a house just past this park at the tip of Lae Loa, a small peninsula jutting into the ocean. Behind the village are archeological sites of previous settlements, overgrown with boney-gray kiawe trees and green brush that contrasts starkly with the surrounding black lava. The village looked largely like an impoverished rural area in the 1980s. There were not more than twenty houses, and no infrastructure of any kind, no water, nor electricity. The inhabitants of the village, in the midst of one of the richest states in the United States, depended upon gas generators and water haulers. In the 1990s this has all changed dramatically. Today there are almost sixty houses now stretched out along the entire length of coast up to and including the buried village of Ho'opuloa. The houses are newly built by the residents with all the modern features of the nearby subdivision, which has also expanded somewhat. But unlike the subdivision, Miloli'i boasts its own water system and an unfinished solar-powered desalination plant, the new houses have large solar-panel systems and are filled with electrical appliances.

To unpack this description both in spatial and temporal terms, we must take a look at the past. The pre-colonial Hawaiian political and economic structure was framed by the territorial unit called an *ahupua'a*. This originally vertical ecology was, as we have seen, transformed throughout the nineteenth-century colonization and the introduction of private property, into a horizontal ecology based on specialized production of plantation and ranch commodities that were distributed primarily among different altitudinal niches. This all occurred in an era of severe depopulation (in the vicinity of 90 percent) and displacement and was followed by a massive import of foreign plantation labor. The *complex* ecosystem of the Hawaiians was dismembered and grossly simplified by such changes, and Hawaiians that remained were forced into residual niches. Miloli'i as a fishing village gained renown near the end of the nineteenth century. As it was located in a relatively dry zone, its "aristocrats" were able to maintain sizeable sections of their land base, but only up to the zone where rainfall increased significantly, and with the extreme depopulation and lack of any political organization, Miloli'i became a specialist producer, primarily of sea mackerel (*opelu*), but also of twine (*olona*). Once a month a ship from Honolulu docked at the Miloli'i pier to exchange dried mackerel for rice and flour. While some residents used their uplands to raise taro and other vegetables, there was a steady trade for products of the land with upland settlements further along the coast and as far as the illustriously fertile Waipio valley at the very north end of the island. So there were still traces of the former economy during this century and, in modified form, even today. Until World War II there was a string of settlements along the coast that were also specialized in fishing and undergoing steady depopulation as the result of the increasing integration of the islands into the political and economic world of the United States. In 1926 a major lava flow destroyed and buried the neighboring village to the north, Ho'opuloa. Refugees from that village settled gradually in the area designated as Waikini or moved in with Miloli'i kin. But this time even more of the land above the villages had been acquired by whites using well-known methods (i.e. adverse possession). The state had designated the area of Waikini as a settlement area and "cultural park" for the refugees, but the latter were never treated like anything more than official squatters until the 1980s. It was also a mystery for some how the Territory was able to claim this land, which had previously been part of a large local Hawaiian estate. Miloli'i grew as a result and this continued during World War II when many villagers along the coast were forced to evacuate or were simply conscripted into the military. The Kona coast was never to be the same. The villages simply disappeared. Only Miloli'i remained and even grew as Filipinos and Chinese, some of them part Hawaiian, established themselves as fishermen and traders in the village. But Hawaiian kin also moved in from the former settlements. As the villages had been intermarried previously, this was essentially a change in residential structure, a small-scale demographic implosion, rather than the formation of a new population.

After the war there were rapid changes. The decline of the plantation economy and the rapid and stronger integration into the American economy, triggered to a large extent by Hawaii's military position and the demographic changes of World War II, led to an exodus of Hawaiians from the village and the islands as a whole into the lower ranks of the military, the merchant marines, tourism, construction, etc. Hawaii became a state of the union in 1959. The strongly Asian (Japanese) Democratic party replaced the plantation-based Republican party and Hawaiians were more completely marginalized than ever before, having no place in the new tourist economy other than as maids, janitors, and waiters. Many identified out, calling themselves Chinese, Filipino, Japanese (i.e. part something other than Hawaiian). The Hawaiian language which still was spoken at the end of the war, began to disappear. It had, of course, been forbidden in schools at the start of the territorial era, but it lingered on in rural areas along with pidgin and neo-pidgin. From the 1950s and early 1960s we witness another process, that emigration is not absolute. It is followed most often by a return to the village, sometimes after decades in the "fast world." This is not a simple cyclical process related to the life cycle. It has more to do with the position of Miloli'i in the larger context.

Miloli'i in recent times has had the reputation of being an isolated village, difficult to get to and turned in on itself. For villagers it has been and continues to be a place of refuge, of security and freedom from the demands of the fast world. Here Hawaiians can subsist on the sea and small plots of agricultural land. They can engage in their own lives without the harassment of the larger society where they are ranked at the bottom. It is far enough from the mainstream life of the island to be able to maintain its own separate existence. It has become in some ways a closed corporate community, although this is more a question of identity to be presented to the outside world than a material reality. The distinction "inside/outside" has been used to refer to the nature of closed corporateness in world systemic terms (Friedman and Ekholm 1980; Linnekin 1991). Applied to the village of Keanae on Maui it has been used as a kind of model, a representation of the relation between Hawaiian villagers in a non-monetary world and the larger capitalist society (Linnekin 1991). For Miloli'i residents being inside is not so much a way of interpreting experience but the experience itself, one that many non-Hawaiians may have also felt in descending the south Kona slopes to the tiny fishing village. Inside, as I shall argue later, is practiced and practical. The village is a place of refuge where Hawaiians can survive doing things that are by and large unacceptable in the larger society. In this sense, the metaphor is constructed on much less than a general understanding of the larger world, and more immediately on the experience of literally being inside a community that is a shelter from the outside world.

PRACTICING THE LOCAL IN THE GLOBAL

Self-isolation has the effect of packing experience into a small geographical space. Demographically, Miloli'i is quite complete, unlike many Third World villages which often contain only the very old and the very young. Miloli'i maintains a rather high rate of endogamy. Almost all of the twenty (today forty-five) or so households are closely related to one another, forming a half-dozen extended families that are and continue to be intermarried. This is a thick core. "We are all family down here"!

There are many children, many first birthdays, many marriages, many occasions for *luaus*. The villagers practice a kind of generalized reciprocity, a group fusion, rather than exchange. That is, they continually practice the non-existence of households as political units. Relatives, near and far, even friends, often move in for periods of several months, even longer without arousing the least opposition or surprise. Such phenomena are unmarked for the Hawaiian household. In this respect the household is entirely open to the larger network of relatives and close friends. Expectations of generosity are high. One is to give oneself to the group and not exchange things with others. Conflicts and broken relations arise on the basis of the difficulty of maintaining this kind of giving/taking. At the same time the household is a fortress of privacy – "*kuleana* rule," no butting into family business. The generosity is an expected behavior, an overlay upon the separateness of the household, that fuses the larger community into a family despite clear internal boundaries. Nobody demands, nobody asks. One can go to a *luau* and take home all that one can carry without offence – and one is expected to give what one has, in the sense of making one's wares available for others. It is not so much giving as balanced taking, i.e. "to each according to his need," in this case from others in the community. Balance in transactions is only visible in the negative, i.e. in the visibility of non-generosity. This may be a correlate of closed corporateness. It clearly marks off the village from the outside world. Non-generosity is a heavily marked feature of village discourse. It defines the essence of evil and causes immense psychic pain among those affected. It causes fear of interaction and self-isolation. This experience of personal relations clearly resonates with the notion of *aloha* as it is used, politically, to distinguish the Hawaiian lifestyle. Village relations combine what might seem paradoxical; proximity and distance, openness and closedness, or perhaps, more accurately, distance in proximity and closedness in openness. It is the fragile and unstable encompassment of the centrifugal by the centripetal. This is fundamental to the social structure of the village, characterized by hierarchical households in which women are dominant and where separate projects are formulated and executed, and an egalitarian depoliticized (historically) public arena where men meet to practice equality, consensus, and generosity. This cannot be further dealt with here.

THE REGIONAL ARENA

The representational context of Miloli'i encompasses the island, the state, and the nation. The physical context concerns the immediate environment of the village, but that environment is itself deeply enmeshed in global economic and political processes. And to the extent that the region is a marketable commodity, its image; the romantic, the tropical, the sea, but not the lava, are instrumental representations in the organization of that region.

Just to the north of the village, in the *ahupua'a* of Ho'opuloa covered by lava from the 1926 flow, was a developer's paradise. Here, more than a thousand feet below the main road, began, in the 1960s, one of the land scams that are so well known in Hawaii. A developer bought a lava field from a ranch, 423 acres, and subdivided it into 1,000 houselots, advertised as Miloli'i beach lots, right on the Pacific. General Robert Lee Scott, of *God is My Co-Pilot* fame, became head of a community association for the potential military retirees expected to buy the lots. The owner paid $137,000 for the area and sold the unimproved properties for a sum of $3.5 million. If houses had been put up on all the lots it would conceivably have destroyed the integrity of Miloli'i, but as there is no beach and there was no infrastructure, no water, no electricity, the lots did not begin to be developed until very recently, and only a few of them. Instead the lots have become a kind of suburb of Miloli'i, or what I call downtown Miloli'i. The owners of the houses there number some restaurant owners, builders, and mainlanders who have retired to the island.

Some relatives and even residents of Miloli'i have lots in this area and others rent houses there.

Miloli'i is surrounded by ranches, a macadamia-nut plantation, and, further to the south, a number of housing developments, all in the uplands, i.e. more than a thousand feet above the village. The scam subdivision to the north is the only settlement in close proximity. To the south there is nothing, but there have been several attempts to "develop" some of the *ahupua'a* that are owned by large corporate interests. The enclave nature of the village is partly geographical and very much social. But the (en)closure of the village in the midst of a constant flow of transients, the movement of local goods and people back and forth between the village and the larger society, is a crucial property of the way in which the village reproduces itself, a foundational strategy of local existence in the global arena.

THE REPRESENTATIONAL CONTEXT

Miloli'i is thoroughly represented in the larger world, by films, from Hollywood to private educational and public broadcasting, and in the news media, where the villagers' struggles for their land and against developers have usually been accorded a great deal of sympathy. Miloli'i is also represented in the Hawaiian image of its own lifestyle, as an ideal type. This context is part of a century or more old representational scheme for Hawaiians, who have represented the remote and romantic paradise of many an American dream, made ambivalent by the ambiguous relations entertained by white women and their menfolk to the potentially dangerous sexuality of the colonized brown people. The major shift in Western identity concomitant upon the decline of hegemony has been a globally orchestrated shift to respect for the native past and a longing for a past of one's own. The ambivalent primitive has become the symbol of that which we others have lost. This is the predominant neo-traditionalism of the period. Modernists, certain anthropologists for example, struggle against the Hawaiian self-image as a romantic falsification of its real past to which only anthropologists have unobstructed access due to their ideological neutrality. All of these public representations partake of the larger struggle for control over Hawaiian identification. This identity contest is clearly global.

Two very different kinds of films have been made in part or in whole in the village:

In the early 1960s Paramount Studios made the Elvis film, "Girls, Girls, Girls" partly in Miloli'i. They paved the 5-mile road down to the village which previously took a day to travel and which now takes less than 30 minutes. The film team was there for several months and a small shack overlooking the bay, belonging to one of the villagers, is called "Elvis's House." It is where he lived during the shooting.

In the 1980s Chevron Oil made a film of Miloli'i that was part of its educational series on Native American lifestyles. Here Hawaiian life-ways are celebrated as part of the American heritage. Villagers don't remember so much about this particular film except for the fact that they had to get hold of some real Hawaiian canoes, i.e. *koa* (Hawaiian mahogany) wood canoes, in order to fish in the traditional style.

A number of TV films have also been made about the village. Public television made a film in the 1980s, also celebrating the traditional lifestyle of the village, very much inspired by the explosive increase of interest in Hawaiians, itself a partial result of the Hawaiian movement. Another film was made by the movement's own film team, *Maka'ainana* films, as a celebration of Hawaiian life on the land.

Miloli'i is a very important place for the Hawaiian movement. It represents something that has been lost to most Hawaiians. For ordinary Hawaiians it is not so much a question of tradition, but a place to live as Hawaiians not as some anthropological image of the past. In Waianae, the largest Hawaiian settlement along the coast outside of Honolulu, there are a number of homestead lands as well as shopping center based communities where a large portion of the population works in the city and commutes or is more generally unemployed. In interviews conducted here, Miloli'i was often referred to as a kind of paradise – not so much in cultural terms, but as a true place of sanctuary from the life that had destroyed many Hawaiians, relegated them to poverty and a marginalized existence in the State. Miloli'i was known to both young and old: "Oh they got that *ono opelu* [mackerel] . . . can live off the ocean . . . no more worries." All this in opposition to the Waianae coast, riddled with social problems, broken families, feuding, murder, drugs, and organized crime, from local politicians down, and of course in a position of practiced marginalization from the state, racist schools, Japanese golf-course invaders (there are upwards of forty golf courses on Oahu today, most of them Japanese, built in the 1980s – some on agricultural land and all taking huge amounts of the scarce island water for their greens).

The Hawaiian movement began its take-off in the mid to late 1970s. This was not an entirely new phenomenon. Hawaiians have in varying degrees resisted the takeover of their islands, the establishment of an American republic, Territory and then State. But this was all resistance in a period of vast economic expansion in the Pacific, the development of a large-scale plantation economy, followed by the tourist industry, the era of US global hegemony in which it was difficult to resist not only force but economic and political success. Hawaiians were not only oppressed, they were also in significant ways, shamed out of existence, very much by the parallel sequences of their own decline and the rise of a dominant White society. Poverty and stigma led to identification with other ethnic groups in a part-X society that enabled a number of choices of ethnic identity. The great change occurred in the mid-1970s, a change that cannot, as far as I can determine, be understood as the cumulative result of a long Hawaiian struggle, but as an outcome of the breakdown of US hegemony and the quite sudden dissolution of American modernist ideology or identity. Hawaiian identity re-emerged in the scramble for roots, a scramble that was legitimized by the hegemonic groups themselves. The Hawaiian movement is not an urban elite type of movement as some have described it (Linnekin 1983). Elites have, of course, played a role, in both the early years of the century as well as in more recent developments, but its roots lie in the rural areas where Hawaiian resistance is quite old and where it is difficult to speak of a single organized movement. Rather there have been a series of local groups often calling themselves *ohana* that became increasingly interconnected over time. There is, of course, a strong link to the renaissance of Hawaiian tradition, seen in terms of extended family, *ohana*, and a specific love for the land, *aloha 'aina*, set off against the creative destruction of modernity, more specifically modern capitalist civilization, but this was not an invention of academic elites. The Hawaiian movement very early on became anti-civilizational in its content, a Fourth World movement, as much against socialism as against capitalism, i.e. against modernist notions of development. Hawaiian life had to be salvaged – not so much ancient Hawaiian society and culture as those values still thought to exist among the population. For the members of this movement, Miloli'i was and is an idyllic ideal type of what life could be about. For the leadership it is, surely, a question of culture, not so much of symbolic systems and ritual, but of values and lifestyle, the latter still part of Hawaiian existence. But for many, the Hawaiian today still bears and can develop his culture. In fact the temples (*heiaus*) are now being restored and used on an increasing scale. Hawaiian language schools have developed. The *ahupua'a* economy is being reinstated, or at least serious attempts exist. The Hawaiian movement has claimed the return of a land base equivalent to half of the lands of the islands, and there is a move in the direction of the establishment of Hawaiian self-sufficiency.

It should be noted here that the Hawaiian movement has had a powerful effect on the self-identity of the islands in general, including the other ethnic groups. In the election of 1986, a Hawaiian became governor for the first time in the history of the state, which had been dominated for more than two decades by Japanese-Americans and *haoles*. His vice-governor was and is a Filipino. The inauguration was an event very unlike the usual gubernatorial happening. Heads of state from the entire Pacific were invited guests. The inauguration, held on the grounds of the Hawaiian royalty's palace, was attended by a large number of Hawaiians, also unusual for such an occasion. And thousands of people held hands and sang the Hawaiian national anthem. The Hickam, Honolulu, based airforce flew its jets over the palace grounds, creating a din that might have been the order of the day in another state, but was here understood as a just military noise staged to annoy and perhaps scare the new state government. There was a general atmosphere of jubilation and premonitions of change. Hawaii was, perhaps, to become more Hawaiian. While the ensuing years showed that this Democratic government was very similar to the preceding Japanese-American dominated regimes, the context of identification was radically changed. Hawaiians now existed and the general goal of Hawaiian independence was introduced into the realm of real possibilities. The Office of Hawaiian Affairs (OHA), a state organ in charge of Hawaiian issues (challenged at one point as unconstitutional since based on special-group interests) began to jostle for power. The current result is that there are two models of Hawaiian sovereignty, one non-government based, best represented by Kalahui Hawaii, the "Nation of Hawaii," and OHA, the official road to a top-steered Hawaiian entity within the state. The difference between the two models of sovereignty is less significant here than the structure of the power relations. Miloli'i has been able to use the Hawaiian movement, OHA, and the state itself in order to make significant improvements in its conditions of existence. This was not possible in the period from the 1950s to the 1970s. When the renowned double canoe, the Hokulea, symbol of Hawaiian renaissance, returned to Hawaii from a voyage to the South Pacific, it stopped in Miloli'i for a number of days. This was, of course, a media event. But even as it placed Miloli'i on the cultural map of the islands, it was a veritable carnival of cultural identity for the villagers, whose status was greatly enhanced by the occasion.

For culture experts, for anthropologists interested in "things Hawaiian," for Hawaiian modernists, Hawaiian is about a no-longer-existing reality, destroyed by the modern capitalist system or perhaps succumbing to a superior civilization. One modernist view of Hawaiians is that they ought to join the lower classes in a more general struggle against the evils of capitalist domination. For others, Hawaiians can indeed attempt to recall their heritage and even to be proud of it (although one anthropologist expressed his disbelief that such a "mixed" population could maintain a Hawaiian identity at all), but the idea of reliving, or practicing this heritage is absurd. This is very much because Hawaiians no longer have any other cultural project that they can really call their own. That project is the property of the anthropologists. They have been reduced to a mere ethnic group among others and must leave their nostalgia for traditions behind. For others, including many ethnic Hawaiians, the American ethnic strategy is the most adaptive. The latter is one in which ethnicity is carried in the body and in a certain number of practices that are clearly external to social life processes, economic survival, etc. Hawaiians should strive for success in American society while keeping their separate identity in the form of values and knowledge of history, i.e. the basis for ethnic pride.

The representational context described above is part of the institutionalized field of representation and discourse available for all those engaged in the highly politicized process of identification, either of self or of others. The positioned voices detailed here are not produced in the same way as the representations of those who are positioned in the immediate vicinity of Miloli'i, and we have kept them separate. Of course, local retirees who think of villagers as dangerous and engaged in illegitimate activities, may make use of the more general representations, just as ecological activists who support the village on the grounds that they are closer to nature. The distinctions are not categorical, but there are clearly two spheres of discourse and cultural production, the one establishing the framework for the other.

LOCALIZING THE GLOBAL IN THE LOCAL: THE FLOW OF PEOPLE

The internal relations of the village are not accessible from the outside and are not part of their model of village life. Various views of "what goes on down there" are entertained by various categories of people. Resident whites, lower-middle and middle-class working people, would never dream of going there. For them Miloli'i is a frightening, mean place.

> Don't go down there . . . it's a mean place . . . people, *haoles*, have got killed down there

One person, a Canadian, was in fact murdered along the coast after having spent some time in the village. And his accused murderer, an in-married Hawaiian, was sent to prison for his offense following a long series of false accusations, insinuations, and painful investigations. The village is also associated with various criminal and dangerous activities by those who have never been there. For such people the fact that the village is on the tourist map and that there is a camping ground located in its center, is a total mystery.

In contrast to this view, Miloli'i is a kind and generous place for the campers looking for a non-tourist Hawaii, "the other Hawaii." There is a State park in the middle of the village, parking space for ten cars or more – quite an institution in a village of 200. In the mid-1980s, the State park department built running-water bathrooms for the use of visitors, while most of the villagers had only outhouses and no running water of any kind. The system was based on brackish water that was pumped into the toilets and sinks while the sewage went down into the coral formation that at high tide could conceivably wash out in the front of the village. This has never been tested but there have been rumors, and rumors are central to the life of the village. Quite a few cars descend to the village and into the park area, which used to be the Miloli'i elementary school until it was destroyed by high surf. A Miloli'i summer program used the building skills of the inhabitants, most of them teenagers, to build several *halaus* and an extended lava-stone sea wall. Many visitors get out of their cars for only a minute or two, to take photographs and then disappear, apparently rather afraid of the place, especially if there are no other visitors present at the time. Others come to camp; some families, some pairs, some singles. They wander around the village or at least around the park area. Some hike down the coastline, after asking villagers or the visiting anthropologist how to get to a well-known black sand beach, Honomalino, which is inaccessible except by foot. A more interesting category of visitors are those who return year after year to the camping place. Some of these are older people who have established tourist friendships with the local people, often via the Protestant church which is located just above the parking place. For many of these people, Miloli'i is truly a "haven in a heartless world," a congenial place where folks are generous and the pace is human. There are also many Alaskans, often from the salmon-fishing industry, who come to Hawaii in the off-season, often with boats that they launch from the village. Many Alaskans having also bought second houses in the development known as Ocean View (see below). Relatives of the Hawaiian families may come, on occasion, from Honolulu or the mainland to visit the village of their childhood. In recent years this has sometimes been a step toward resettlement in the village. Finally, there are locals who descend to swim, fish, or just camp out. They are known to the villagers and are part of the village support network. There are in this category quite a large number of Hawaiians, who have a tradition of coming to Miloli'i from Hilo, on the other side of the island, or from Ka'u in the south. Many are related to Miloli'i residents. The range of visitors spans the most superficial visual relation of cautious distance to the well-integrated Hawaiian from across the island or across the state.

Every year Miloli'i puts on two game-fish tournaments in which sportsmen from the entire coast, Honolulu, and even the mainland can participate. Miloli'i fishermen and women almost always win as they are so familiar with the waters, and there is plenty of money to be made both by the fishermen and by those who bet on the winners. It is true that the sportsmen are by and large people who return from year to year, and thus fall into the category of perennial tourists or campers. The event combines a tournament with the usual all-night party and the visitors, if they stay, are easily assimilated into the occasion without in any way affecting its character.

Just as Miloli'i takes on innumerable visitors of different types, the villagers are very often on the move themselves. To go *holoholo* as they say, to go traveling to visit others, is a generally known phenomenon that has sometimes been reduced to cultural instinct, as in "Hawaiians have a penchant for travel" (Linnekin 1985: 35). But Hawaiians travel in groups, in their own pickups, and stay in the homes of relatives in other localities, or at least in specially designated hotels, often Hawaiian-owned. They manage, brilliantly, to avoid all contact with the larger society, i.e. traveling with their backs to the world they traverse, as if in conduits of their own making. Home is thus extended to the larger region via a complex of insulated networks. On the road they practice the obverse of that which is practiced at home. But the larger strategy is identical.

Miloli'i entertains, literally, a great many different categories of people. On the surface there is no closure to the outside world. This is, in one powerful respect, the result of the politics and economics of the state of Hawaii. The existence of a public park and camping site in the middle of the village, the public access to its boat ramp, the neighboring communities, all impinge upon the day-to-day existence of the village in physical terms. At the same time, as I shall argue, villagers assimilate outsiders into their lives in ways that they choose, from complete obliviousness to incorporation into the activities of village life, festivities, fishing, coffee production, etc. Those who are so integrated have to make sacrifices, to submit themselves to the needs and interests of the villagers. This is the demonstration of their *aloha*, their eligibility for membership.

COMPLEXITY AS THE BIRDSEYE VIEW

What is complex about the village of Miloli'i? From the anthropologist's perspective, arriving with the view of a world dichotomized into the modern and the traditional, Hawaiian villages, *both of them*, are very much inside the modern sector. One anthropologist was very much taken with the fact that the village of Keanae in Maui, "the taro place," was not a subsistence settlement but produced taro for the *poi* market in Hawaii, that they were very much locked into the larger economy and could not really be understood as an internally integrated traditional society (Linnekin 1985: 34–6). Even the population was seen as hopelessly mixed up, an ethnic hodgepodge. Several families are even left out of her study on the grounds that they are not Hawaiians but hippies. One has, perhaps, to draw the line somewhere, in the search for the *real thing*. The search for real things has been a hallmark of classical anthropology's attempt to simplify the complexity of the world. Nowadays, complexity itself, in all its cultural confusion, has become a new *real thing*. However, it might be suggested that the transition from the ethnographically pure-and-simple to the messy-but-real, is about the transgression of preconceived categories which define both sides of the supposed transition.

Miloli'i is involved in several economies. There is a strong subsistence component, based on the use that can be made of the resources of the sea and the uplands, affording fish, vegetables and fruits, and game. There is a cash economy on top of this based on the sale of fish and, to a lesser extent, of coffee and fruit. Today, coffee is milled and dried in the village on a significant scale and then sold after being sent for roasting. Villagers also work part time in the macadamia-nut plantation and in hotels along the coast. Welfare payments are a very large part of the local cash flow. The village might, in one sense, be a place of residence like any other poor modern rural settlement, but at the same time it has a very special local organization, identity, and symbolic activities. The practice of the economic reproduction of the village penetrates into the island's modern sector, but the social practice of villagehood sets a clear boundary between the village unit and the outside world. Miloli'i is a political unit, a practiced and reproduced place defined against the rest of the world. This is so in spite of the apparent paradox that there is a constant flow of various categories of outsiders in and out of the village and a plethora of contacts, political, economic, and otherwise with County and State agencies, upland communities, coffee companies, and fish markets.

This identification is practiced both ways and in several overlapping situations. The village is ascribed certain characteristics by the outside world; dangerous, primitive, pristine, traditional. It is native Hawaii as against *haole* Hawaii.

The village was formed by a regional depopulation and geographical implosion from the north and the south. Fishing villages at the shore lines of their respective *ahupua'a* were transformed into a single village surrounded by a horizontalized organization of ecological exploitation in which fishing became an increasingly specialized activity, ending with commercial tuna fishing. After the war the village became relatively poor in relation to its surroundings and Hawaiians lost increasingly in the status hierarchy with the emergence of the tourist economy, the decline of island food production, and increasing dependence on tourist income and imported products. Hawaiians identified out and moved out. Today it is estimated that over 100,000 Hawaiians live on the mainland, i.e. almost a third of all Hawaiians. In the period 1960–70 it even appears as if the Hawaiian population decreased. Self-identified Hawaiians declined by 16 percent in the national census. Miloli'i children sent to high school, especially the Hawaiian Kamehameha School in Honolulu, did not return home, not at first. Many found jobs in the city, or in the military. Many ended up in Germany or in Vietnam. Many, that is, entered the lower echelons of the national society, and many were confronted with a kind of racism that they had not encountered in Hawaii. Miloli'i contracted during this period, which lasted until the mid to late 1970s. In the latter period, of declining American hegemony and numerous ethnic movements, the Hawaiian movement also began its long trajectory, from being part of a larger radical student-based movement to an increasingly national or at least cultural-based movement. By the 1980s it was good to be Hawaiian. The state demographer, in an interview, suggested that Hawaiians were beginning to re-identify, often changing their names. Both this decline and the subsequent renaissance of cultural identity was a larger phenomenon that cannot be understood from the village perspective alone.

Miloli'i had been known throughout the century as a community that resisted the encroachment of the landowners. The former "mayor" of the village struggled for years against attempts to buy out his land above the village. Large landowners were and are known to have taken advantage of the complex ownership patterns of former *ahupua'a* lands, where titles are often divided among large numbers of heirs without clear boundaries having been established. Often one of the owners who found him- or herself in debt would sell off property that belonged to a dozen other cousins and siblings, by simply having access to the ownership papers. Conflicts, often ending in court, over the division of land title is still one of the great Hawaiian pastimes, one that goes well back into the last century, at least as far as the establishment of freehold title. Miloli'i is interesting in so far as the three main landowning families and their heirs have maintained large tracts of land intact throughout this century, although most of it is below the rain line.

The complexity of Miloli'i might appear bewildering from an external point of view, replete with ambiguities, a myriad of relations with outsiders, from intermarriage to beer parties, from land struggles to Hollywood films. Miloli'i is terribly entangled with the larger world, up to its neck in the modern sector. But, from the inside, things are simpler.

ENDOSOCIALITY, THE REDUCTION OF COMPLEXITY AND SOCIAL SURVIVAL

Miloli'i practices a strong form of assimilation of external circumstances. Villagers maintain their genealogies cognatically. If outsiders marry in their properties may be included, but the main lines of genealogy related to the village lands themselves are maintained with a vengeance. This includes court cases concerning inheritance, land boundaries, etc. which are a major local activity. Foreigners must adapt to the village in order to survive there. One wealthy resident of the neighboring subdivision, who really loves Hawaiians because they are so different from his own life experiences, has bought an old coffee mill and gone "into business" with a local coffee landowner. He works hard for his association with the village. Another resident has fallen in love with a Miloli'i man who is married in Honolulu and is getting a socialization that cannot be discussed here. In-marrying men, as I said, get a clearly violent initiation into their village identity. Miloli'i is dangerous for those who would turn it into part of their own project. Miloli'i has maintained its integrity, through some very difficult times. It is today expanding, building new houses for its growing local population and influx of other, more distant, relatives. This is the result of the conjuncture of local politics and the changing larger context which has made Miloli'i into a symbolically loaded place for the state and the federal governments as well as other Hawaiians. All houses are now solar powered, and there is a desalinization plant that produce running water for the village, while the wealthy neighboring subdivision is beginning to complain that Hawaiians get special treatment while they have to truck down water and pay for their own generators or solar panels. If I were to summarize the nature of the village practice delineated here it might appear as follows:

1. The village economy is integrated in important ways into the larger region. Incomes are gained by both wage work and by the sale of fish. This implies movement of Hawaiians in and out of the village on a daily basis.
2. The social relations of the village span the island, other islands and Honolulu. When villagers go *holoholo* (traveling), they do so in clearly established conduits within which they meet only their own kind, either family or perhaps other local Hawaiians. They travel often in groups, in their pickups. They live in other people's houses or in one of several Hawaiian hotels. There is a concerted practice of endosociality in all of this which makes travelling with Hawaiians quite special. It is possible to move through the dense tourist areas of the islands without meeting any visitors or other non-Hawaiians.
3. Villagers may often move to other islands or to other places in the world during part of their lifetimes. This is often the result of working in the military, or in various construction trades. Many villagers return to the village in their later years. This is often the case among the young today who find it increasingly difficult to survive in a stagnating tourist economy. In this sense, the village acts as a kind of centripetal force against the centrifugal forces of the larger regional and global contexts.
4. This endosociality provides a high level of satisfaction for the villagers, even as it leads to high levels of conflict, due not least to the contradiction between external resources and forces and the structure of everyday existence in the village itself.
5. The above is clearly evidenced in cases of in-marriage. This is of two types. The first and most common consists of downwardly mobile whites who marry or live with local girls. If they are white they usually go through a period of aggressive socialization

including beating, where they learn how to get along with the local boys. This is followed by partial acceptance. The next generation fares better. In-marrying Hawaiian men are accepted but do not in general play a significant role in the village. In-marrying women are usually Hawaiians. They too are very much marginalized and need to wait for the next generation which can then establish itself. The village, thus, does not practice exclusion but an aggressive form of assimilation, that works through the second generation.

6. Endosociality entails a high level of intensity in social life. At any one time there are a number of activities concentrated in several different central places and several different networks. The cores of these networks are kinship-based, often part of an extended family and a network of less closely related relatives and friends. Disputes over inheritance, marriage infidelity, conflicts over external intrusions, *luaus* for children or for numerous special occasions, night-time drinking at the store or on someone's porch. The level of commerce with the outside world is very high, and the assimilation of the outside into the practice of village life creates an activity level that is closer to an urban than a rural situation.

The relative success of Miloli'i, which harbors its own problems, is a product of the play of global forces as they have materialized in Hawaii. But the practice of villagehood still remains a constant through all of this, creating Miloli'i people as opposed to just islanders: "work hard, play hard . . . go fish, get your welfare check, pick coffee, go to court, come home and play cards and then party." Conflicts abound, but Miloli'i encompasses.

CONCLUDING NOTE

The notion or non-notion of cultural complexity is a way of identifying the meeting, combination, or fusion of practices and objects whose sources can be identified as disparate. But the way in which differences are combined in the life projects of a population can only be understood in terms of the practice of the relevant actors. I have argued here that the people of Miloli'i, in practicing endosociality, reduce complexity in a radical way; by assimilation, often violent, of outsiders and by the active elimination or avoidance of ambiguity and complexity that might appear as extremely intricate to the observer. Cultural anthropological definitions of "complex" situations often consist in a concerted effort to establish genealogies of "cultural" elements, in order correctly to "identify" the observed reality. This practice of historical continuity is just as specific, culturally, as the practices of those we observe. But the practice of cultural observation is not the practice of ordinary existence. The apprehension of complexity depends very much on perspective, on the position of the observer. It might appear strange to some dichotomizers that a so-called "global anthropologist" can make a plea for "the natives' point of view," but this is, of course, the only way to resolve an apparently incommensurable opposition between observed complexity and practiced simplicity. The fact that Miloli'i has been involved in the world system, both as an historical product of the formation of modern Hawaii and in its everyday relations with hotels, plantations, the police, welfare agencies, film productions, and the Hawaiian movement, implies, of course, that all kinds of objects, images, and expressions from the larger world circulate in the village. But this circulation is not what the village is all about, although Hawaiian life is replete with Americana. Hawaiians, after all, are American citizens, and they are perfectly aware of this. Hawaiians, the great majority of them, do practice a specific kind of existence that is distinctive with respect and in opposition to the larger society in which they participate, whether or not they drink Coca-Cola and ride American-style surfboards (the latter, apparently a creolized product), go to Hawaiian language schools and engage in rituals on Hawaiian *heiaus* (temples). The genealogies of the elements that participate in the structures that they generate are only of secondary museological importance. Otherwise the English are a motley blend of Celtic, Saxon, Scandinavian, and Norman "cultures," each of which in its turn is a motley blend of . . . Hybridity is only socially significant if it is practiced, i.e. if people actively identify as such.

I have not denied that the village of Miloli'i is intricately involved in the larger world. On the contrary, the global perspective insists upon precisely such an involvement. Miloli'i is economically dependent and politically integrated into a state, a national political sphere and, as such, into the global system. But that integration is not determinant of local strategies of social survival even if it sets the limits of their viability. Second, the integration is not merely a question of economic dependency, since conditions of identity and the politics of identity are directly involved in establishing the village's conditions of existence. The decline of Western hegemony, the result of a decentralization of world accumulation, has led to conditions in which a hegemonic modernist identity (in its American variant) has declined. This in its turn has led to a broad change in identification including the renaissance of indigenous culture. In this off-shore state it has empowered Hawaiians and enabled them to make gains on a number of fronts that would have been unthinkable a decade ago. Miloli'i has had a tradition of self-isolation in the midst of outside contacts and this has combined with the recent upsurge of Hawaiian power in the islands to afford them advantages that were previously inaccessible.

REFERENCES

Barnes, Michael (ed.) (1966) *The Social Anthropology of Complex Societies*, London: Tavistock.

Barth, Fredrik (1989) 'The Analysis of Culture in Complex Societies,' *Ethnos* 54, 3–4: 120–42.

Friedman, Jonathan (1994) *Cultural Identity and Global Process*, London: Sage, Theory, Culture and Society Series.

Friedman, Jonathan and Kajsa Ekholm (1980) 'Towards a Global Anthropology,' in L. Blussé, H. Wesseling and C.D. Winius (eds) *History and Underdevelopment*, Leiden: Center for the History of European Expansion.

Hannerz, Ulf (1992) *Cultural Complexity*, New York: Columbia University Press.

Linnekin, J. (1983) 'Defining Tradition: Variations on the Hawaiian Identity,' *American Ethnologist* 10: 241–52.

—— (1985) *Children of the Land*, Brunswick: Rutgers University Press.

—— (1991) 'Cultural Invention and the Dilemma of Authenticity,' *American Anthropologist* 93: 446–8.

Mannheim, Karl (1982) *Structures of Thinking*, London: Routledge & Kegan Paul.

13 There are no Indians in the Dominican Republic

The cultural construction of Dominican identities

Ninna Nyberg Sørensen

Dominican identity (in the singular) is generally portrayed as "Hispanic," which effectively amounts to a lack of distinction. This identity is moreover portrayed as "problematic." Several observers have stressed that "blackness" and "African roots" are heritages that are totally ignored in the Dominican construction of national identity, while Spanish culture, Catholicism and "white" European descent are publicly celebrated (e.g. David 1992, Ságas 1993). A superficial understanding of the Dominican concept of *indio* and other local color constructions have further added to this image. On the whole, this has fostered an image of Dominican identity as fake and racially self-denying, if not downright racist.

In this chapter I want to question the very notion of *local* identity by focusing on the migrant culture of the Dominican. Simultaneously, I will offer an alternative interpretation of the Dominican "Indian" – those people who are said to consider themselves "black without Africa." In the process we may see how Dominican identity is actually very distinct. Perhaps we may rather speak of several overlapping *identities* since no unequivocal and collectively shared *national identity* exists. I suggest, then, that we leave identity in the singular here. My reflections are based on field work among Dominican migrants in the Dominican Republic and New York City.[1]

Local identities are not easily apprehended by way of traditional ethnic labels or skin-color categories. However, an experiential approach to Dominican worlds makes way for a renewed understanding of the integrity of identity spaces. In a world characterized by transnational flows of people and meaning, the correspondence between physical worlds and social realities among people differently situated are far from simple, nor are they understandable in terms of bounded concepts (Ardener 1993; Barth 1993; Moore 1994). Though anthropologists have long acknowledged that individuals possess several identities, i.e. that gender, class, race, ethnicity, and age generate specific overlapping identities, the analyses of national identity have to a large extent confounded geographic maps with social and cultural maps. Accordingly, different interpretations of nationality and how particular national identities are constructed and contested have remained unexamined.

THE DOMINICAN INDIAN

> An ideology of nationalism and positive cultural identity has emerged – the Dominican is white, he is descended from the Spanish and he is Catholic. His skin may be somewhat on the black side, but that comes from the crossbreeding with the island's first occupants, Taino Indians. Some young historians say that the mix of Spanish and Indians at the time of Columbus has made it the most racially integrated country, claiming that the Indian race merged into the Dominican melting pot without getting lost. . . . However, all Dominicans who were not really black were registered as white in the 1960 census. Even today, skin colour is never described as "black" on passports or identity cards and the term "dark indian" (*indio oscuro*, my note) has to be used instead.
>
> (David 1992: 14)

Indio has by outsiders to Dominican culture been misinterpreted to mean belonging to the Indian race, though any Dominican knows that the concept refers to a color, a color of brown skin.[2] David's translation is, therefore, not only wrong but totally misses the (Dominican) point. There are no Indians in the Dominican Republic, but a great many people of mixed racial background who name their skin color brown (*indio*), and at times further subdivide it into light brown (*indio* claro) or dark brown (*indio* oscuro), and several other shades of brown not included here. Dominicans never refer to the extinct indigenous population as *indios*. When they speak of the island's first occupants, they almost always name them *Taínas*.[3]

Then again, since some Dominicans (e.g. parts of the light-skinned elite) may actually agree with David's statement, the problem is not his interpretation of the Dominican construction of *indio* but rather the overarching categorization of *the* Dominican as a fixed subject bearing a fixed identity, which is certainly not the case. Black African, White Catholic and indigenous Taína heritage provide the background for present-day images of local identities, which suggests that

Dominican identities are possibly constructed within a space in which multiple cultural, social, and racial orders co-exist. In order to grasp this complexity we need to deconstruct the category of space into different overlapping universes, distinguish between different forms of space, i.e. physical, historical, social, and cultural space, and observe to what extent such universes overlap and how they are manipulated through interpretations and practice. Contemporary perceptions of identity are *both* a reflection of historical developments in the Dominican Republic *and* ongoing reinterpretations of this past through time.

Though this chapter focuses on the making of Dominican identities and as such is delimited to people who call themselves Dominican, whether living in the Dominican Republic or abroad, Dominican encounters with their Haitian neighbors cannot be totally excluded. However, since I have elsewhere analyzed the complex relationship between migrating neighbors (see Sørensen 1993, 1994), I shall focus my attention on Dominican interpretations of Dominican-ness and only include Haiti and Haitians to the extent Dominicans themselves do when defining who they are.

Identities are expressed in many ways. In the following we shall listen to various Dominican voices and – along the way – explicate contexts and concepts.

THE COST OF LIVING

Somos un agujero
en medio del mar y el cielo
500 años después
una raza encendida
negra, blanca y taína
pero quien descubrió a quien?
um - es verdad

We are an aperture in
the middle of the ocean and the sky
500 years afterwards
a race was born
black, white, and taína
but who discovered whom?
huh – indeed

. . . a nadie le importa
pues, no hablamos inglés

ni a la mitsubishi
ni a la chevrolet.

. . . no one cares
since we don't speak English
neither at mitsubishi
nor at chevrolet.

In a popular merengue[4] of recent times, Dominican singer and songwriter Juan Luis Guerra describes Dominican identity as black, white, *and* Taína, as a new race born from conquest in which no skin color or continental origin is given precedence. If we view the lyrics as a symbolic statement of identity or as "works of moral imagination" (Coplan 1987), Guerra's message seems quite different from David's.

Very interestingly, Dominican identity is contextualized as bound to *both* the local national territory *and* the global space. The local is emphasized through the Taínas – the "indigenous" population of Hispaniola ("indigenous" because they themselves had Ciboney, Arawak, and Carib origins which locally developed into Taína culture) of whom none remained, apart from the offsprings of sexual conquest, as little as thirty years after the arrival of the Spaniards. In this sense, Taína claims are a way of localizing Dominican identity on Dominican territory. We shall return to this. Reference to a global space is made through an image of Dominicans' ability to penetrate the ocean and the sky. Given the fact that on a yearly basis approximately 200,000 to 300,000 Dominicans travel back and forth between the Dominican Republic and migrant destinations abroad, and that one million to one and a half million Dominicans are believed to be involved in international migration, Guerra's metaphors are certainly appropriate. The politics of time and space are indicated both by the question of who actually discovered whom and by reference to Dominican marginalization: no one cares about this Spanish-speaking population. Neither transnational corporations (such as Mitsubishi and Chevrolet) nor the local government which allows international capital to exploit Dominican workers in the more than twenty-five export-processing zones established since 1969 in the Dominican Republic.

Guerra and his band "4.40" are world-famous. While the international popularity of merengue probably is due to the music's cheerful and danceable rhythms, Guerra's local popularity derives from the outspoken role he has taken on contemporary Dominican discourses of identity. Several of his songs aim at retrieving and recreating suppressed notions of Dominican-ness and highlight existing social inequalities. First and foremost, he portrays Dominican identity as an identity to be proud of, an identity in its own right, a creole identity. Guerra's songs of resistance prove that more than one interpretation of Dominican-ness exists. Actually, several interpretations are current.[5]

While Dominican racism towards Haitian immigrants has been seen as an integral part of Dominican identity, the Dominican indisposition towards Spanish culture and colonial heritage has been ignored. The Spanish culture referred to by David (1992) and Ságas (1993) and by large segments of the Dominican political elite is not a proud national symbol to all Dominicans. Rather it is seen, by others, as the reason for backwardness, illiteracy, and underdevelopment.[6] Several older Dominicans express rather pessimistic views of their Spanish heritage. Listen to señor Victor, a retired garment worker, who left the Dominican Republic in 1946 but, nowadays, spends most of his time in a hammock in his home in the Dominican Republic, while his wife still travels back and forth between New York and Villa Esparanza:

> Back in those days – in the 1940s and 1950s – *Los Latinos* met in Riverside Park. On hot summer nights we sometimes stayed in the park all night long. Well, that's not possible any longer. Because of the crime it has become too dangerous. *Los Latinos* brought crime to New York. Today, the Dominicans who go to New York are *mal preparada*, they don't have any *educacíon cívica*. They conceive democracy and freedom as lawlessness; that they're free to do whatever they please. You see, the people who left [the Dominican Republic] before 1965 were people of a certain standard. After 1965 came *las malas*. This is part of our Spanish heritage: Theft, defilement, and lack of charity. I believe the French culture of the Haitians to be more civilized. In New York Haitians are not as bad as Dominicans. They live more decently, more civilized. They're not involved in drugs and crime to the extent Dominicans are.

The past, the present, as well as several border crossings are contextualized and synthesised in señor Victor's interpretation of migration, crime, and culture. When he moved to New York City he experienced that he not only was a Dominican but also a Latino sharing a language and a colonial past with other immigrants from the Latin American continent. In other words, his movement in physical space made him reinterpret his notions of social and cultural space. It is evident from this that several layers of colonial history, national independence, inter-regional and international migration, and cultural constructions of national identity co-exist.

The seemingly simultaneous presence of local and global images in Dominican identity may in fact be interpreted as an outcome of a *traveling culture* (Clifford 1992), capable of including a wide variety of differing cultural elements and, by inclusion, making them Dominican. Thus, Dominican identity construction cannot be understood as a linear process towards one common national identity. On the contrary, several identities – several ways of being Dominican and several ways of interpreting what that identity means – co-exist. I shall further illustrate this point by presenting a popular Dominican commercial, and Dominican responses to it, in which are communicated various Dominican interpretations of past and present, of migratory experiences, of discontent and affection, of knowing and not knowing how to behave in accordance with the Dominican creole continuum. However, in order to be able to peel off the multiple layers of time, space and place-making in the cultural construction of creolized identities, I shall give a short (and highly selective) summary of the Dominican past.

PEOPLE, PLACE, AND IDENTITY

Hispaniola is with its 76,000 km^2 the second largest island in the Caribbean and the only island in the archipelago divided into two nation-states: The eastern 48,442 km^2 comprise the Dominican Republic (the former Spanish colony of Santo Domingo) with a population of approximately 7.1 million; the western 28,018 km^2 comprise Haiti (the former French colony of Saint Domingue) with a population of approximately 6.4 million. Inhabitants on both sides of the border are descendants of one of the largest human migrations in the world. However, variations with respect to colonial history, establishment of plantations, reliance on import of African slaves, and struggles for national independence are considerable. All of which are matters of great – though not exclusive – importance for contemporary cultural and racial identities.

The Dominican past contains several conflicting and contradictory struggles. The Dominican Republic (and by implication Haiti) differs from other Caribbean islands by having been subjected to an internal division, first between two different colonial powers, later into two distinct nation-states. As the first colonized Caribbean island, Hispaniola served as a Spanish springboard for further expansion in the area. This means that although sugar plantations were established as early as 1515, and although approximately 30,000 African slaves had been shipped to the island by 1540, the discovery of the Latin American mainland caused the Spaniards to lose their economic interest in Hispaniola (Hoetink 1985; Benitez-Rojo 1992). Even though the Spanish colonization of the Americas was guided by an essentially urban ideology, colonial power was not able to prevent people from populating the interior and northern valleys. The contrast between the city (Santo Domingo) and the countryside permitted two separate economic systems to develop: An early established, but rapidly declining plantation economy, and a counter-economy based on subsistence agriculture, including cattle raising and tobacco cultivation, which were commercialized illegally (Baud 1988, 1991; Benitez Rojo 1992). In an attempt to regain colonial control (and control over the busy contraband trade), the Spanish crown ordered all towns and settlements on the northwestern coast burned down and "depopulated" in 1605–6, a process in which inhabitants were forcibly removed to the central part of the island. The Spanish crown did never succeed in controlling the illegal cattle and tobacco commerce. Rather, this displacement of people made it possible for "enemies" to land their ships on the coast, now nearly deserted. In 1697 Spain was forced, by the treaty of Ryswick, to give up the western part of Hispaniola, and the French colony of Saint Domingue was subsequently declared (Knight 1990).

In contrast to the Spanish, the French colony quickly developed into a prosperous sugar (plantation) economy, based on slave labor. Less than a hundred years later, French Saint Domingue had a population of about 500,000, of which more than 90 per cent were African slaves (Hoetink 1985; Klein 1991). Inhabitants of the Spanish part of the island continued to provide cattle and tobacco for the slave economy on the French side. At the same time, the meager population and large uninhabited areas on the Spanish side gave plenty of room for runaway slaves from the French side, who managed to establish maroon societies across the border (Hoetink 1985), and sometimes even to be absorbed in the counter-economy.

The counter-economy provided a material basis for developing a *creole culture*. Now, the concepts of creole culture or creolization easily end up as a grab bag of pluralisms if we do not carefully explore what is meant by creole and just how creolization comes about. I suggest that we begin with analyzing creolization as the outcome of colonialism and colonial attempts to control land and people in the Americas. In line with Benitez-Rojo, I further suggest that we – in the Dominican case – reserve the concept of creole culture for the "marginalized," and insist on an analytical distinction between a "creole culture," characterized by local customs, and a "national culture," in which "a group makes its desires transcend its minuscule place to encompass a greater national homeland" (Benitez-Rojo 1992: 274). In the Dominican Republic "creolization" was never about developing a multicultural nation, but was rather about ways in which marginalized individuals managed to withstand attempts at manipulation of their identity.

Relations between the two neighboring colonies became tense when social and political unrest began around 1790 in the slave communities of French Saint Domingue. The small Santo Domingo-based planter class feared that slave rebellions would spread to the entire island, and many left (for Cuba, Puerto Rico, Louisiana, and the northern parts of South America). In accordance with the treaty of Basel, Spain surrendered its part of the island to France (Hoetink 1970). While Haiti was declared independent in 1804, the Dominican Republic was in fact declared independent three times. The first time was in November 1821, when independent Spanish Haiti was declared. It endured but a few weeks and was then occupied by Haiti 1822–44. Independence was declared for a second time in 1844, but fear of Haitian aggression made the remaining planter class seek reannexation to Spain. Finally in 1865 Dominican independence was declared.

Though very brief, my description of Spanish (and French) colonialism, of plantations and counter-economies, and of Dominican (and Haitian) independence, should have outlined some sharply contrasting circumstances affecting the way the symbols of nationalism have evolved in the Dominican Republic. "Haiti developed from a colony that was the center of French Empire, with a predominant black population (albeit slaves) and a vibrant economy (albeit plantation-based)" (Knight 1990: 221). In the building of a national identity, Haiti promoted its African heritage – in particular following the US invasion in 1915 – as the proud symbol of the new state. "The colony of Santo Domingo, on the other hand, constituted a peripheral part of Spanish empire that was falling apart in the early nineteenth century. Its small population was about equally divided between Spanish and creoles, mestizos and blacks" (ibid.). With a heterogeneous population (in terms of racial, social, and cultural background) and a political scene played by political actors with very different ideas about national independence, the Dominican elite was unable to promote any cultural heritage into a strong national symbol. On the one hand, this gave the Dominican Republic considerable difficulties in creating a homogeneous state with a homogeneous national identity. On the other hand, it was perhaps the very absence of any strong overarching national symbol that allowed the population a space for creating their creole identities.

Sidney Mintz (1974) finds it probable that the planters of Spanish colonies were outstanding in the degree to which they developed creole identities – as opposed to metropolitan Spanish ones. The irregular development of the plantation system in the Spanish colonies (as compared to French, Dutch, and British colonies), the early growth of peasant or yeomen sectors, and the attenuated influence of the metropolis in the rural areas during the seventeenth and eighteenth centuries, most probably account for this creolization (Mintz 1974: 310–14). As I read Mintz, he places creolization and insularity on an equal footing whereby identity becomes somehow bound to the inhabited territory. However, in Santo Domingo/ The Dominican Republic marginalized peasants, more than fleeing planters, were creolizing their existence.

The history of the Dominican counter-economy is very much a history of people who had no legal rights to the land or the products they cultivated. Colonial attempts to control this group of people included displacement and deterritorialization. Fields were burned down and people were more than once forcibly removed from their settlements. It may well be that Dominican identity became "rooted" in people, not in place. What is mentioned as a curiosity regarding the first short-lived Dominican independence is precisely that there was no reference to territory or nation state in Núñez de Cáceres' constitution of 1821, but instead a reference to *dominicanos*, the people inhabiting the place. Dominican territory was not mentioned until Juan Pablo Duarte, a young creole who had spent his early years in Europe, started what is today perceived as *the* movement for independence under the device, *Dios, Patria y Libertad, República Dominicana* (God, Fatherland and Freedom, the Dominican Republic) (Pequero and de los Santos 1983; Nelson 1990).

The project of localizing Dominican identity to Dominican territory was intensified during various dictatorships up to 1916 and reached its peak during the Trujillo dictatorship (1930–61). Identity politics was a highly integral part of Trujillo's regime, and it was during his office that Dominicans were told that no matter the color of their skin, they were all a largely white, Catholic, and culturally Spanish people, and that Trujillo himself was the one to save the people and the Republic from a growing "Africanization" brought about by the Haitian presence in the country's rural areas. In this process, whiteness and European descent were invented by the ruling elite, but it remains questionable whether an imagined community (as a deep, horizontal comradeship [Anderson 1983]) ever was established. Trujillo powdered his skin and closed the borders for emigration, while immigration schemes to attract Europeans were set up. The Trujillo era therefore marks the ultimate border-drawing nationalization process in terms of attempting to root a specific Dominican identity in Dominican soil.

Today Dominicans (and Haitians) are strongly involved in international migration, very often of a transnational[7] character. Dominican migrants are a very diverse group of people including poets and peasants, doctors and home attendants, students and blue-collar workers – and the Dominican share of drug dealers (probably no more than any other nationalities') – who all move back and forth between the island and (primarily) New York City. The globalization of production, which in the Dominican Republic, among other things, has been characterized by foreign investments in export-oriented agriculture and the establishment of export processing zones, has produced new forms of internationalized labor demands. Through this process, local work structures have been disrupted; people living in the periphery have once again been uprooted and deterritorialized. The development of commercial, export-oriented agriculture has displaced farmers who are now left without means of subsistence; the widespread practice of firing the new (mostly female) workers in the export processing zones after a short (lower paid) period of "introduction" further adds to the pool of potential displacement. A common human response to the restructuring of the global economy has been to transnationalize one's economic and social existence (Sassen 1988). In this process, Dominican trans-migrants do not necessarily make a permanent shift from one locality to another, but rather seek to establish transnational networks that transcend borders. Therefore, transnational migration is not only a distinctive new form of migration where more than one nation-state is the basis for the trans-migrants' economic and social survival, but also a process in which the drawing of national borders (by the state) is accompanied by popular border-disintegrating movements. We may ask, then, what happens to identity when people transnationalize their existence?

LOCALIZING AND GLOBALIZING DOMINICAN IDENTITY

Field work among Dominicans invariably involves watching television, which is not so bad after all since both national-identity politics and migrant identity are highly communicated in this medium. Networks and channels transcend national boundaries while local and transnational audiences comment on and interpret whatever is on. It is perhaps by being exposed to television that contemporary anthropologists can enter into a dialogue on identity.

> The scene: A Dominican merengue band gives an open-air concert on a sunny Manhattan plaza. Inside a parked yellow cab, a male Dominican cab driver listens to the music. His face has a dreamy look. For a moment he is back on his island. A female (very blonde) North American customer climbs into the back seat. Since the cab driver makes no move to drive, she asks, slightly annoyed, if the cab is actually free? The driver explains that the music is merengue from his home country. In the back seat the woman makes some clumsy dancing moves and says: "Oh merengue, mucho buena" ("Oh merengue, very nice" [but grammatically incorrect]). As the driver starts driving he shakes his head and says: "Ay americana, no sabe nada" ("Hey American, you don't know anything").

A few months later this commercial is substituted with a new one, like the continuation of a serial. This time the setting is in the Dominican Republic. The same North American woman (now dressed as a tourist) enters a Dominican cab, and the same cab driver (now in his native environment) sits in his worn-out cab, listening to a merengue band playing outside the airport. The same conversation – with exactly the same words spoken – goes on.

These two short film strips – produced by Brugal, one of the larger Dominican rum companies – were probably the most popular commercials in the Dominican Republic during 1992. Based on the form of the popular *telenovelas*, both strips portrayed a stereotyped image of American culture as wealthy and ignorant, and of Dominican culture as proud tradition, despite poverty. Moreover, they depicted two very well-known forms of travel in Dominican society: that of New-York-bound migration and that of tourism. The transnational character of Dominican migration was highly emphasized by having the same driver installed in two cabs in two different locations. The globalization of Dominican culture was symbolized by merengue – first and foremost by merengue's World Music character, but also by the fact that it was played in New York, whereby a "Caribbeanization of New York City" (Sutton 1987) was indicated.

Dominican TV viewers loved this commercial and always responded with laughter. Everyone asked each other if they had seen *la Brugal*. Moreover, the words of the cab driver: "Ay americana, no sabe nada," almost totally substituted the frequent greeting, "Hola gringo/gringa," addressed to American or European tourists in the streets of Santo Domingo. Those of us who were able to respond with a "Merengue, mucho buena," were given a great deal of credit. Having gotten the joke, we were granted the status of *casi dominicana*, of almost-Dominican. "Ay, ella sabes" ("Oh, she knows (!)"), both friends and strangers commented whenever I used the phrase. Except in one particular case.

I was walking on a path in a rural mountain community on the outskirts of Jarabacoa when a young man, plastered with gold chains and very well-dressed (brand-new jeans and sneakers), suddenly approached me from his motorbike, saying in English: "Hey you American, you don't know nothing." Despite his aggressive tone I tried my "Merengue mucho buena," which he took as an insult. He threatened me fiercely, demanding I leave the village. I later learned that this aggressive young man had been deported from New York City and was charged with illegal drug and weapon possession. Since he had been denied his transnational transactions in what he thought to be my country, I was by no means supposed "to know" anything! In his (vulnerable) position he felt a need to draw a border between his territory (the village) and me (the intruding stranger).

Brugal produced this commercial in 1992, the year in which the celebration of the quincentenary of Columbus's discovery of Hispaniola reached hysterical heights. While the majority of Dominican commercials included this event in one way or the other, Brugal commercialized a critical counter-view. At least Dominican viewers interpreted the commercial as a Dominican reconquest of the First World, of New York City: "*Mira!* All New York cab drivers are Dominican."

At the same time, Balaguer, the Dominican president, had a prestigious lighthouse (the *Faro a Colon*) constructed in Santo Domingo (cost: more than US$ 250 million) as part of the quincentennial celebration. Thousands of slum dwellers had their homes bulldozed away and were rendered homeless in Balaguer's attempts to beautify the capital before the arrival of the Pope. Balaguer's behavior (spending enormous amounts of pesos on a good-for-nothing monument) caused a public scandal. Widespread indignation caused some to plan a mourning ceremony in honor of the Taínas. "How can we celebrate the genocide of the native population?" they asked. Genocide, not cross-breeding with the Taínas, became the symbol of resistance.

The global image of Dominican-ness expressed in Juan Luis Guerra's songs and Brugal's commercials appealed much more to the majority of Dominicans than did Balaguer's attempt to connect solely the Spanish part of the colonial heritage to Dominican identity – while ignoring the African and Taína contribution to Dominican culture. President Balaguer has more than once maintained that the natives were extinct, and that the population of the Dominican Republic was formed entirely by European (mainly Spanish but also French) families (See, e.g., Balaguer 1990: 59). Seen in this light the Dominican insistence on including Taína "roots" contains a cultural construction of a counter-identity. Taína becomes a way of localizing an oppositional Dominican identity in Dominican places, whether in New York City or the Dominican Republic.

Sidney Mintz has argued that color ideologies "do not travel well if they fail to become adapted to different cultural values, different codes of social assortment, and different economic settings" (Mintz 1974: 317). Dominicans know that. During my field work in New York I was told a migratory legend several times in which a Dominican was asked to respond to a census interviewer about her race. After responding *indio*, the interviewer asked: Which tribe? And the story-teller was always dying with laughter. Playing with the different interpretations of race, color, and origin, the Dominicans who related these legends never meant to be understood. Their secret ("indio is not a race but a color although you American census-takers think that race and color are the same thing") was intentionally used to trick the interviewers. The Dominican gift for playing with differing meanings of color and race denotes a well-developed sense of identity, not a fake identity or false consciousness.

NATIONAL FRONTIERS AND BORDERLAND IDENTITY

> The body of water that separates the Antilles from the United States serves as a frontier no less than Rio Grande, across which Mexicans and North Americans look at one another's faces, or sometimes only their backs. One might even ask if that strip of sea is not the real frontier, and our islands only borderlands.
>
> (Mañach 1975: 5)

Notions of locality, place, positionality, and space are central to the ongoing debate on identity and identity politics. Space and the spatial are increasingly integrated in analyses concerning the making of history, just as time and temporality are increasingly integrated in geography (Gupta and Ferguson 1992; Massey 1992). Through analyses concerned with intersections of time and space it has become clear that the world can no longer, if ever, be understood as international in the sense of being made up of independent, separate nations with solid boundaries. Instead it has become a transnational, interdependent system where national boundaries are increasingly permeable.[8] Whereas the common notions of culture have been "biased toward rooting rather than travel" (Clifford 1992), and culture has moreover been defined via boundaries, it has been regarded as normal or as an unmarked phenomenon to stay put within these boundaries (Carnegie 1987). The concept of culture has been sedentarist (Malkki 1992) and of little help in explaining Caribbean life and travelling creole cultures (as, for example, Dominican trans-migrants).

Several observers of transnational migratory movements have described the emerging world (dis)order as a process creating so-called *Borderlands* (Anzaldua 1987, 1993; Rosaldo 1989; Nathan 1991; Kearney 1991; Gupta and Ferguson 1992). Borderlands have mainly been thought of as terrestrial zones between nations: frontiers. But beyond signifying merely physical and political realities, borderlands consist of and create social and cultural meaning as well. Borderlands are places where national identity is contested and new identities are constructed.

> The border is a historical and metaphorical state, *un sitio ocupado*, an occupied borderland where individual artists and collaborating groups transform space, and the two home territories, Mexico and the United States, become one . . . to be disoriented in space is the "normal" way of being for us mestizas living in the borderlands. It is the sane way of coping with the accelerated pace of this complex, interdependent, and multicultural planet. To be disoriented in space is to be *en nepantla*, to experience bouts of disassociation of identity, identity breakdown and build-ups. The border is in a constant *nepantla state*, and it is an analog of the planet.
>
> (Anzaldua 1993: 39–40)

Caribbean borderlands are occupied spaces as well. But occupied in specific ways. Caribbean communities have almost always been frontier communities (defined as contact communities) in which populations of differing ethnicity and race have confronted each other (Mintz 1974: 53). In the Dominican Republic, however, one important category became vacant. After the extirpation of the Taínas, people were free to use this category for their own strategic purposes. Taína became the symbol of resistance and a way of localizing creole identity as opposed to national identity on the island. Today the symbol of

Taína has gained importance as a counter-identity to state-promoted "quintennial" views of a nation-wide common Spanish heritage. But that does not mean that Dominicans, by and large, think they are Indians, nor that they maintain that their blackness stems from cross-breeding with the island's first occupants. And Taína is not the sole Dominican identity discourse.

Social movements concerned with *negritude* and racial identity are beginning to voice themselves in Dominican society. Race, these voices maintain, is a more radical symbol than the counterinvention of Taína identity. Race is a social location, since blackness marks the bottom and most marginalized position in Dominican society.

> When you ask me if my skin color is not a mixture of black and white, my answer is no. *Mulattas* are not a race. *Mulattas* are black, and racism is what makes us black. As long as racism exists we'll have to acknowledge our *negritude Dominicana*.
>
> (Female Dominican community organizer from La Romana. We talked in Brooklyn)

My focus on *color indio* and *Taína* symbols (which are not the same!) is in no way intended to minimize the importance of *negritude* in Dominican identity. However, since the "indio" self-categorization has been subjected to several misinterpretations I have aimed at unraveling some of the layers in this particular Dominican way of constructing (and manipulating) a cultural belonging to specific physical, social, and cultural spaces embraced by Dominican-ness. The only way to deal with these spaces in the singular is to think in terms of a creole space.

Carrington has defined creole space as multidimensional. He attaches importance to the individuals who inhabit these spaces (not the inhabited places) and stresses that these individuals have multi-systemic repertoires. The density of networks of communication will determine the stability (and consequently the identifiability) of systems within such spaces. Moreover, he states, the spaces cohere because networks of communication overlap. Cross-network communication is possible because of the shared parts of repertoires, but the nature of the overlap may well be neither constant nor systematic (Carrington 1992: 98).

With Carrington – and the various examples given throughout this chapter – I conclude that Dominican identity is constructed within a space in which multiple cultural, social, and racial orders co-exist. Even though the national ideology promotes Spanish and Roman Catholic values, Dominicans respond in multiple ways to being

Dominican, elaborating on various aspects of Dominican-ness. These practices are further elaborated through transnational migration where Dominicans are forced to reconsider what it means to be Dominican in response to Latin and African diaspora identity constructs. Originating from a borderland (if 500 years is enough to "originate") nevertheless makes them confront the border and the twentieth-century borderlands with valuable luggage: experiences with a constant discourse on identity capable of transgressing and transcending territorial borders. Portable culture, one could say, as long as we acknowledge that people carry their culture *with* them (for strategic purposes) and not *within* them.

There are no Indians in the Dominican Republic but more and more Dominicans in New York City. To some of these Dominicans, migration is a sort of emergency exit, a way of escaping both poverty and "traditional" control. To them New York City represents liberation, emancipation, and an opportunity to "quit" culture. These migrants cross geographic, cultural, and often gendered borders (excellently depicted in, for example, Brugal's commercials) but do not necessarily maintain identities based on several locations. An attachment to local places a long time back, a long way south, is seen as an obstacle to future citizenship. Other migrants – the majority according to my findings – become transnational migrants, who "live a complex existence that forces them to confront, draw upon, and rework different identity constructs" (Glick Schiller *et al.* 1992: 5). Even when they are more or less permanently displaced, identity constructs that are experienced and practiced in the sending community – including intimate knowledge of place-making in creole spaces and a capacity for creative self-categorization – continue to shape their existence. Dominican identities are above all problematic for national power structures (be it in the Dominican Republic or the United States) that seek to keep people in place.

NOTES

1. My thoughts on Dominican identities build on field work in several locations. In the Dominican Republic: rural villages in the Cibao region, "nouveau riche" and not quite so rich migrant communities in and around Santiago, Santo Domingo, Puerto Plata and La Romana, and finally in the border areas close to Haiti. In the United States: primarily in Washington Heights (Upper West Manhattan), but also in the Bronx, Queens, Brooklyn, and Yonkers. Finally, I have joined migrants on several airtrips between Kennedy Airport and Santo Domingo as well as between Newark and Puerto Plata. Research was made possible by several grants. The University of Copenhagen supported a pilot study in

New York City in 1989. The Danish Council for Research on Developing Countries and the Danish Social Science Research Council have provided funds for research in 1990–3.

2. The adjective *indio* is always used in the masculine form whereby determination of gender is linked to color (masculine) not raza (feminine).
3. For several other views on Dominican "identity problems," see Sørensen 1993.
4. Merengue is the most popular Dominican music form. It was once played with instruments "originating" in different continents: A *tambora* (African bass drum), a *güira* (a dried gourd scraped with a stick, an indigenous instrument), and an accordion (Europe). Over time the instrumentalization has changed. If we apply the creole metaphor to merengue as, e.g., Benitez-Rojo (1992) does, it is clear that the music is not a mixture, if by mixture is meant to convey a kind of unity. On the contrary, merengue constitutes a polyrhythmic space that is Caribbean, African, and European *at once*. Emphasis on either Amer-Indian, African, or European rhythms has varied over time. The musical composition of the quoted merengue is actually a contemporary African hit from Zaire.
5. Speaking of identity politics: One picture on Guerra's album shows Guerra blindfolded with white gauze bandages (it looks white, still the gauze is transparent). Another shows his hands tied up in these bandages as he is about to get rid of his bonds. A third picture shows the blindfolded Guerra with his ears and mouth still free. The bondage of the state's identity politics cannot prevent people's construction of counter-identities.
6. See Dominican historian Moya Pons (1981) for further interpretations of identification with Spanish-ness.
7. Transnationalism is defined as either a "spatial extension of the local community . . . corresponding to the political, economic, and social ordering of late capitalism" (Kearney 1991: 53–7), or as a "social process in which migrants establish social fields that cross geographic, cultural, and political borders" (Glick Schiller *et al.* 1992: ix).
8. The extent to which national boundaries are permeable to different classes of people varies. So does the classification of people. Though almost exclusively described as a traditional labor migrant population, Dominicans in New York City also consist of a notable group of political exiles. These people mainly left the island in the turbulent years following the murder of Trujillo in 1961, but some managed to escape during the dictatorship. These exiles, however, did not achieve refugee status, which shows the importance of drawing attention to the context in which displaced persons are categorized as either immigrants or refugees. Both terms reflect the view of those who receive about those who come. Wong points to an important distinction in the semantics of migration: the rhetoric of the immigrant/refugee is focused on the intention of the newcomer, in contrast to the rhetoric of exile, which highlights the condition in which the migrants find themselves (Wong 1989: 61).

REFERENCES

Anderson, Benedict (1983) *Imagined Communities*, London: Verso.

Anzaldua, Gloria (1987) *Borderlands/La Frontera*, San Francisco: Spinsters/Aunt Lute.

—— (1993) 'Chicana Artists: Exploring nepantla, el lugar de la frontera,' *NACLA: Report on the Americas* 27, 1: 37–45.

Ardener, Shirley (1993) 'Ground Rules and Social Maps for Women: An Introduction,' in S. Ardener (ed.) *Women and Space: Ground Rules and Social Maps*, Oxford/Providence: Berg Publishers.

Balaguer, Joaquin [1983] (1990) *La Isla al Reves: Haiti y el Destino Dominicano*. Santo Domingo: Editora Corripio

Barth, Fredrik (1993) *Balinese Worlds*, Chicago and London: University of Chicago Press.

Baud, Michiel (1988) 'The Struggle for Autonomy: Peasant Resistance to Capitalism in the Dominican Republic 1870–1924,' in Malcolm Cross and Gad Heuman (eds) *Labour in the Caribbean*, London: Warwick University Caribbean Studies and Macmillan.

—— (1991) 'A Colonial Counter Economy: Tobacco Production on Hispaniola 1500–1870,' *New West Indian Guide* 65, 1 & 2: 27–49.

Benitez-Rojo, Antonio (1992) *The Repeating Island – The Caribbean and the Postmodern Perspective*, Durham and London: Duke University Press.

Carnegie, Charles V. (1987) 'A Social Psychology of Caribbean Migrations: Strategic Flexibility in the West Indies,' in Barry B. Levine (ed.) *The Caribbean Exodus*, New York: Praeger.

Carrington, Lawrence D. (1992) 'Images of Creole Space,' *Journal of Pidgin and Creole Languages*, 7, 1: 93–9.

Clifford, James (1992) 'Traveling Cultures,' in Lawrence Grossberg, Cary Nelson and Paula Treichler (eds) *Cultural Studies*, New York: Routledge.

Coplan, David B. (1987) 'Eloquent Knowledge: Lesotho Migrants' Songs and the Anthropology of Experience,' *American Ethnologist* 14, 3: 413–33.

David, Dominique (1992) 'Country Report: Dominican Republic – Land of Contrast,' *The Courier* 131 (January–February): 10–46.

Glick Schiller, Nina, Linda Basch and Christina Blanc-Szanton (1992) *Towards a Transnational Perspective on Migration: Race, Class, Ethnicity, and Nationalism Reconsidered*, New York: The New York Academy of Sciences.

Gupta, Akhil and James Ferguson (1992) "Beyond 'Culture': Space, Identity and the Politics of Difference," *Cultural Anthropology* 7, 1: 6–23.

Hoetink, Harry (1970) 'The Dominican Republic in the 19th Century: Some Notes on Stratification, Immigration and Race,' in Magnus Mörner (ed.) *Race and Class in Latin America*, New York: Columbia University Press.

—— (1985) 'Race and Color in the Caribbean,' in Sidney Mintz and Sally Price (eds) *Caribbean Contours*, Baltimore: Johns Hopkins University Press.

Kearney, Michael (1991) 'Borders and Boundaries of State and Self at the End of Empire,' *Journal of Historical Sociology* 4, 2: 52–74.

Klein, Alan M. (1991) *Sugarball: The American Game, the Dominican Dream*, New Haven: Yale University Press.

Knight, Franklin W. (1990) *The Caribbean – The Genesis of a Fragmented Nationalism*, New York: Oxford University Press.

Malkki, Liisa (1992) 'National Geographic: The Rooting of Peoples and the Territorialization of National Identity among Scholars and Refugees,' *Cultural Anthropology* 7, 1: 24–44.

Mañach, Jorge (1975) *Frontiers in the Americas: A Global Perspective*, New York: Teachers College Press.

Massey, Doreen (1992) 'Politics and Space/Time,' *New Left Review* 196: 65–84.

Mintz, Sidney W. (1974) *Caribbean Transformations*, Baltimore and London: Johns Hopkins University Press.

Moore, Henrietta L. (1994) *A Passion for Difference: Essays in Anthropology and Gender*, Oxford: Polity Press.

Moya Pons, Frank (1981) 'Dominican National Identity and Return Migration in the Dominican Republic: Implications for Development Planning,' Selected papers from the conference on Celebrating the 50th Anniversary of the Center. Caribbean Migration Program, Occasional papers no. 1.

Nathan, Debbie (1991) *Women and Other Aliens: Essays from the US–Mexican Border*, El Paso, Texas: Cinco Puntos Press.

Nelson, William Javier (1990) *Almost a Territory: America's Attempt to Annex the Dominican Republic*, USA: Associated Press.

Peguero, Valentina and Danilo de los Santos (1983) *Vision General de la Historia Dominicana*, Santo Domingo: Universidad Catolica Madre y Maestra.

Rosaldo, Renato (1989) *Culture and Truth: The Remaking of Social Analysis*, Boston: Beacon Press.

Ságas, Ernesto (1993) 'A Case of Mistaken Identity: Antihaitianismo in Dominican Culture,' *Latinamericanist*, Gainesville: University of Florida, 29, 1: 1–5.

Sassen, Saskia (1988) *The Mobility of Labor and Capital: A Study in International Investment and Labor Flow*, New York: Cambridge University Press.

Sutton, Constance R. (1987) "The Caribbeanization of New York City and the Emergence of a Transnational Socio-cultural System," in Constance R. Sutton and Elsa M. Chaney (eds) *Caribbean Life in New York City: Sociocultural Dimensions*, New York: Center for Migration Studies.

Sørensen, Ninna Nyberg (1993) 'Creole Culture, Dominican Identity,' *Folk* 35: 17–34.

—— (1994) *Telling Migrants Apart: The Experience of Migrancy Among Dominican Locals and Transnationals*, Ph.D. dissertation, Institute of Anthropology, University of Copenhagen.

Wong, Diana (1989) 'The Semantics of Migration,' *Sojourn*, Singapore, 4, 2: 59–64.

Subject index

Names index

40°

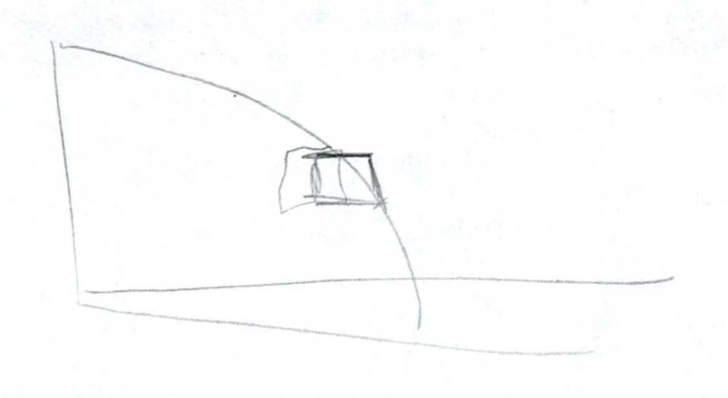